THE SECOND OR 1807 LAND LOTTERY OF GEORGIA

Compiled
by
The Rev. Silas Emmett Lucas, Jr.

**Southern Historical Press, Inc.
Greenville, South Carolina**

Copyright 1986
By: Southern Historical Press, Inc.

All rights reserved. No part of this publication may be reproduced, stored in a retrieval system, transmitted in any form, posted on to the web in any form or by any means without the prior written permission of the publisher.

Please direct all correspondence and orders to:

www.southernhistoricalpress.com
or
**SOUTHERN HISTORICAL PRESS, Inc.
PO BOX 1267
375 West Broad Street
Greenville, SC 29601
southernhistoricalpress@gmail.com**

ISBN #0-89308-020-9

Printed in the United States of America

With Deep Appreciation

this book

is

Dedicated

to

Carroll Hart, Ruth Corry,

Pat Bryant, Beatrice Lang

and

Marion R. Hemperley

of the

Department of Archives and

History, Atlanta

THE 1807 LAND LOTTERY

While the first, or 1805 Land Lottery settled original Wayne County in the southeast corner of the state, and the first five land districts of original Baldwin and Wilkinson Counties, Georgia, the 1807 Land Lottery completed the surveying and distribution of the land lots in Baldwin and Wilkinson; namely, land districts six through twenty in Baldwin, and six through twenty-eight in Wilkinson. The area was ceded by the Creek Nation of Indians to the United States for the use of Georgia, by a treaty held in Washington, D. C. on November 14, 1805.

This Lottery, then, together with the first one in 1805, opened up for white settlers a vast oval area between the Oconee and Ocmulgee Rivers and the Indian frontier was moved farther west from the Oconee to the Ocmulgee.

This land between the two rivers was good fertile ground for crops and Georgia citizens were anxious to avail themselves of it. By this time, also, they were acquainted with the Lottery method of allocating land and were willing to participate. Georgia now had twenty-six counties with a greater population than ever, and all those who had drawn a blank ticket in the first Lottery had another chance in this one.

In 1807 also, the Georgia Legislature met for the first time in their new capital at Milledgeville in Baldwin County. A great migration of state officials and business men made this entire area an important part of the state.

SECOND LAND LOTTERY - ALSO KNOWN AS THE 1807 LOTTERY

AUTHORITY	Act of June 26 1806		
YEAR OF DRAWING	1807		
COUNTIES	Baldwin	15 Districts (6 thru 20)	
	Wilkinson	23 Districts (6 thru 28)	
SIZE OF LAND LOTS	Baldwin	202½ acres	2970 feet square
	Wilkinson	202½ acres	2970 feet square
GRANT FEE	$12.15 per 202½ acre Lot		

PERSONS ENTITLED
TO DRAW

Bachelor, 21 years or over, three-year residence in Georgia, citizen of United States — 1 draw

Married man, with wife and/or minor child three-year residence in Georgia, citizen of United States — 2 draws

Widow, three-year residence in Georgia
Spinster, 21 years or over, three-year residence in Georgia — 1 draw

Minor orphan, father and mother dead, three-year residence in Georgia — 1 draw

Family of minor orphans, father and mother dead, three-year residence in Georgia — 2 draws

Minor orphan, father dead, mother living, three-year residence in Georgia — 1 draw

Family of minor orphans, father dead, mother living, three-year residence in Georgia — 1 draw

PERSONS EXCLUDED A fortunate drawer in the previous Land Lottery

NOTE The <u>oral</u> oath to be made by a married man, bachelor, widow, spinster or guardian of orphans did not require a detailed statement as to kinship, ancestry or descent. If, by chance, any such oath may have been written or transcribed, it could be found only in the Minutes of the Inferior Court of the County where made.

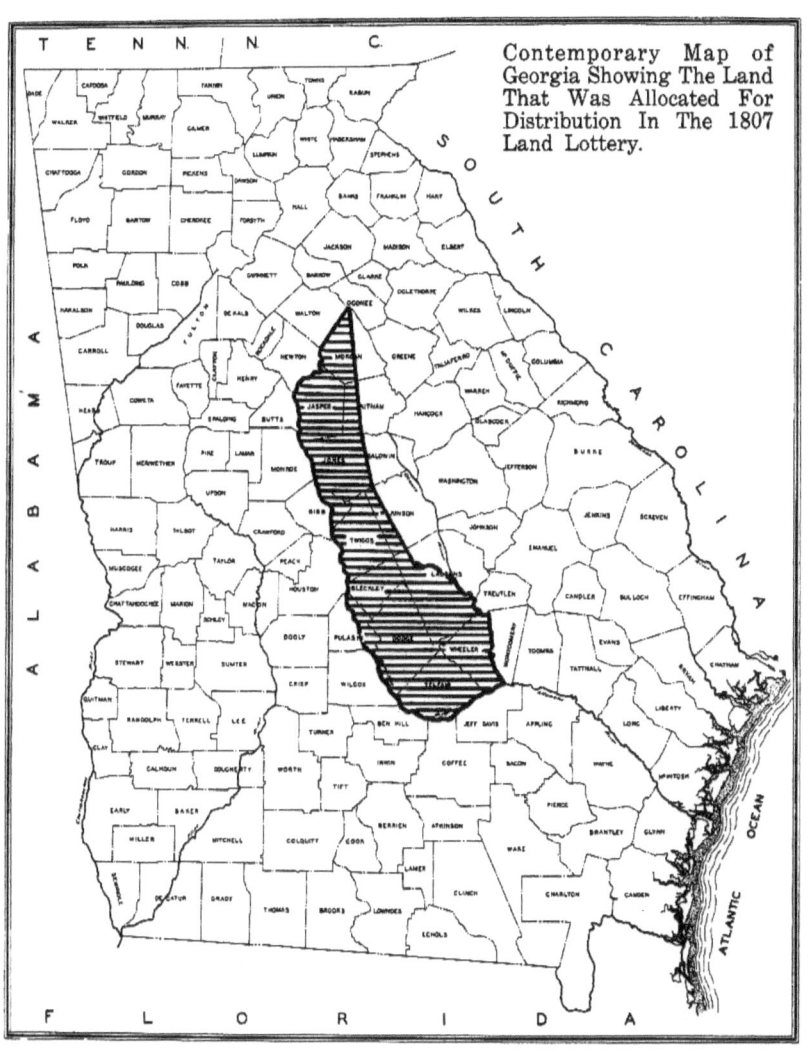

NAME	COUNTY	MIL.DIST.	LOT/DIST	DREW LAND
Aaron, Daniel	Franklin	Cornelius	3/20	Wilkinson
Aaron, George	Bulloch	Hendleys	16/13	Wilkinson
Aaron, William	Franklin	Griffiths	177/26	Wilkinson
Abbett, Elizabeth	Warren	Neals	261/13	Wilkinson
Abbett, James	Liberty		51/8	Wilkinson
Abbett, Joseph	Warren	Neals	155/9	Baldwin
Abbett, Joseph	Warren	Neals	266/12	Wilkinson
Abbett, Jourdan	Warren	Newsoms	174/13	Wilkinson
Abercrombie, Leonard	Baldwin	2	61/25	Wilkinson
Abercrombie, Robert	Warren	Flournoys	81/12	Baldwin
Achkers, Amelia L.C.(Wid.)	Chatham	Pembertons	34/14	Baldwin
Acree, John	Greene	Moores	263/15	Wilkinson
Acree, Sterling	Greene	Moores	271/15	Wilkinson
Acrey, William	Warren	Carters	100/19	Wilkinson
Adam, George	Richmond		218/21	Wilkinson
Adams, Absley	Burke	Blounts	141/19	Baldwin
Adams, Ann(Wid.)	Clarke	Martins	316/21	Wilkinson
Adams, Benjamin	Warren	Neals	99/11	Wilkinson
Adams, Deborah	Elbert	Moons	3/9	Wilkinson
Adams, Edmond	Liberty		340/12	Wilkinson
Adams, Godfrey	Clarke	Robinsons	210/12	Baldwin
Adams, James	Elbert	Morrisons	222/20	Baldwin
Adams, James	Hancock	Huffs	261/21	Wilkinson
Adams, Joseph	Wilkes	Milners	9/7	Baldwin
Adams, Margaret(Orph.)	Chatham	Neyles	108/16	Baldwin
Adams, Moore S.(Orph.)	Chatham	Neyles	108/16	Baldwin
Adams, Nathl.	Chatham	Neyles	16/19	Wilkinson
Adams, Thomas	Tattnall	Halls	223/12	Wilkinson
Adams, William	Clarke	Hitchcocks	278/20	Baldwin
Adams, William	Hancock	Huffs	242/14	Wilkinson
Adare, Susannah(Orph.)	Jackson	Johnsons	306/10	Wilkinson
Adcock, Joseph	Lincoln	Mays	118/24	Wilkinson
Addington, Nancy	Chatham	Neyles	39/17	Baldwin
Adley, Ambrose	Warren	Jones	232/12	Wilkinson
Aikins, James	Greene	Owsleys	81/17	Wilkinson
Aikins, Thomas	Franklin	Cornelius	16/17	Wilkinson
Akin, Diana S.W.	Clarke	Mitchells	351/10	Wilkinson
Akin, Frances B.(S.W.)	Clarke	Mitchells	297/14	Wilkinson
Akin, James Sr.	Clarke	Mitchells	34/11	Baldwin
Akin, James	Baldwin	4	162/13	Wilkinson
Akin, Martha(Wid.)	Wilkinson		64/16	Wilkinson
Akin, Thomas	Elbert	Thompsons	115/12	Wilkinson
Akin, Winney(Wid.)	Camden	Smiths	338/22	Wilkinson
Akridge, Eliz.(Wid.)	Jefferson	Bosticks	78/6	Wilkinson
Albert, Joseph	Greene	Baxters	99/8	Baldwin
Albritton, George	Wilkinson		72/11	Wilkinson
Albritton, Isaac D.	Wilkes	Stovalls	27/7	Baldwin
Albritton, Mathew	Bulloch	Denmarks	161/19	Wilkinson
Aldridge, Aaron	Columbia	6	60/8	Baldwin
Aldridge, Aaron	Warren	Neals	127/24	Wilkinson
Aldridge, Reubin	Baldwin	1	282/20	Wilkinson
Alexander, Adam	Liberty		120/12	Baldwin
Alexander, Allen(Orph.)	Elbert	Clarks	139/9	Baldwin
Alexander, Ezzy(Orph.)	Elbert	Clarks	109/8	Wilkinson
Alexander, Franky(Orph.)	Elbert	Clarks	109/8	Wilkinson
Alexander, Hugh	Jefferson	Tarvers	273/14	Baldwin
Alexander, John	Oglethorpe	Smiths	53/13	Wilkinson
Alexander, Milly(Orph.)	Elbert	Clarks	109/8	Wilkinson
Alexander, Mortikey(Orph.)	Elbert	Clarks	139/9	Baldwin
Alexander, Moses	Warren	Bakers	69/27	Wilkinson
Alexander, Nancy(Orph.)	Elbert	Clarks	139/9	Baldwin
Alexander, Sally(Orph.)	Elbert	Clarks	139/9	Baldwin
Alexander, Smith	Oglethorpe	Smiths	293/20	Baldwin
Alexander, William	Greene	Stewarts	32/18	Baldwin
Alexander, Willis(Orph.)	Elbert	Clarks	139/9	Baldwin
Alexander, Wm.(Orph.)	Elbert	Clarks	139/9	Baldwin
Alexander, Wm.	Jackson	Cockrans	113/27	Wilkinson

NAME	COUNTY	MIL.DIST.	LOT/DIST	DREW LAND
Alford, Jacob	Hancock	Coopers	98/11	Wilkinson
Alford, Jacob	Montgomery	51	50/17	Wilkinson
Alford, Kinchin	Hancock	Coffees	1/20	Baldwin
Alford, Owen	Hancock	Coopers	44/20	Baldwin
Alfred, John	Greene	Alfords	49/12	Wilkinson
Alger, James	Chatham	Pettybones	93/7	Baldwin
Allard, Ls.N.	Chatham	Abrahams	102/9	Baldwin
Allday, Elizabeth	Burke	Sandifords	60/21	Wilkinson
Allen's, John(Orphs.)	Oglethorpe	Hartsfields	28/9	Baldwin
Allen's, Robert(Orphs.)	Columbia	7	137/13	Baldwin
Allen's, Wm.(Orphs.)	Franklin	Everetts	206/20	Wilkinson
Allen, Alexander	Richmond		182/15	Wilkinson
Allen, Alice(Wid./Jos.)	Columbia	5	150/8	Baldwin
Allen, Betsy(Single)	Clarke	Martindales	72/20	Baldwin
Allen, Betsy	Baldwin	5	366/22	Wilkinson
Allen, Drury	Baldwin	4	214/12	Wilkinson
Allen, Elisha	Warren	Carters	278/7	Wilkinson
Allen, George	Chatham	McLeans	221/14	Wilkinson
Allen, George	Oglethorpe	Moores	114/6	Wilkinson
Allen, George	Oglethorpe	Moores	4/20	Wilkinson
Allen, Henry	Burke	Sharps	153/9	Baldwin
Allen, Henry	Clarke	Martindales	152/20	Wilkinson
Allen, Hezie	Hancock	Pinkstons	189/13	Wilkinson
Allen, James	Oglethorpe	Moores	34/10	Wilkinson
Allen, James	Washington	Kendricks	180/22	Wilkinson
Allen, James	Washington	Kindricks	238/19	Wilkinson
Allen, John Sr.	Greene	Davenports	157/28	Wilkinson
Allen, John Sr.	Greene	Davenports	230/19	Baldwin
Allen, John T.(Capt.)	Columbia	5	178/6	Baldwin
Allen, John	Jackson	Wrights	10/27	Wilkinson
Allen, John	Jackson	Wrights	258/16	Wilkinson
Allen, John	Oglethorpe	Moores	155/19	Wilkinson
Allen, John	Warren	Devereaux	203/25	Wilkinson
Allen, Joseph	Jefferson	Hardwicks	220/19	Wilkinson
Allen, Mark I.	Clarke	Martindales	159/18	Baldwin
Allen, Nancy	Hancock	Birdsongs	106/18	Baldwin
Allen, Nathl.Jr.	Lincoln	Kings	275/14	Wilkinson
Allen, Richard(Son/John)	Franklin	Cornelius	203/21	Wilkinson
Allen, Samuel Jr.	Richmond		306/8	Wilkinson
Allen, Sarah	Burke	Ballards	252/22	Wilkinson
Allen, Scarlett	Warren	Carters	207/26	Wilkinson
Allen, Susannah S.	Hancock	Pinkstons	315/17	Wilkinson
Allen, Thomas	Elbert	Blackwells	216/21	Wilkinson
Allen, William	Burke	Hilliards	321/9	Wilkinson
Allen, William	Burke	Hilliards	99/16	Baldwin
Allen, William	Elbert	Clarks	114/15	Wilkinson
Allen, William	Oglethorpe	Moores	61/22	Wilkinson
Allen, Woolson	Clarke	Cooks	41/17	Wilkinson
Allen, Woolson	Clarke	Cooks	9/11	Baldwin
Allen, Young	Jefferson	Bosticks	25/16	Wilkinson
Allen, Young	Jefferson	Bosticks	280/20	Baldwin
Alley, John	Chatham	Abrahams	333/24	Wilkinson
Allgood, John	Elbert	Olivers	16/9	Wilkinson
Allgood, Spencer	Elbert	Morrisons	290/17	Wilkinson
Alligood, Samuel	Burke	Mulkeys	103/20	Wilkinson
Allison's, Wm.(Orphs.)	Greene	Dawsons	152/13	Wilkinson
Allison, Alexander	Greene	Carletons	58/16	Baldwin
Allison, James	Baldwin	3	3/6	Baldwin
Allison, James	Chatham	Whites	290/7	Wilkinson
Allison, Robert	Jackson	Cockrans	74/12	Wilkinson
Allison, Watson	Jackson	Cockrans	10/24	Wilkinson
Allter, Mary	Chatham	Neyles	40/20	Wilkinson
Allums', John(Orphs.)	Washington	Delks	41/9	Wilkinson
Allums, Edmond	Washington	Delks	10/27	Wilkinson
Allums, Eliz.(Wid.)	Washington	Delks	276/21	Wilkinson
Almond, James	Baldwin	5	266/19	Wilkinson
Alor, George	Lincoln	Jones	211/28	Wilkinson

NAME	COUNTY	MIL.DIST.	LOT/DIST	DREW LAND
Alsobrook, Amos	Washington	Holts	61/19	Wilkinson
Alston, John	Effingham		259/19	Baldwin
Alston, John	Effingham		345/24	Wilkinson
Alston, Joshua	Effingham		345/24	Wilkinson
Alston, William Sr.	Elbert	Clarks	44/18	Wilkinson
Amerson, Britton	Hancock	Wallers	415/7	Wilkinson
Amerson, James	Hancock	Wallers	17/10	Baldwin
Ammonso, Jacob	Lincoln	Jones	101/24	Wilkinson
Amosson, Jesse	Washington	Garretts	65/8	Baldwin
Amosson, Uriah	Washington	Garretts	110/26	Wilkinson
Amus, Maulden	Columbia	10	205/24	Wilkinson
Amus, Maulden	Columbia	10	305/22	Wilkinson
Anderson's, Boazor(Orphs.)	Greene	Greers	172/13	Baldwin
Anderson, Charles	Wilkes	Parks	66/7	Baldwin
Anderson, Elijah(Orph.)	Jefferson	Bosticks	4/8	Baldwin
Anderson, Elisha	Burke	Martins	181/13	Wilkinson
Anderson, Elisha	Jefferson	Bosticks	90/18	Wilkinson
Anderson, Elizabeth(Orph.)	Jefferson	Bosticks	4/8	Baldwin
Anderson, Elva(Orph.)	Burke	Blounts	333/15	Baldwin
Anderson, Frederick	Baldwin	1	25/9	Wilkinson
Anderson, George	Chatham	Abrahams	73/9	Wilkinson
Anderson, John	Elbert	Morrisons	92/12	Wilkinson
Anderson, Lavina(Orph.)	Jefferson	Bosticks	4/8	Baldwin
Anderson, Levina(Wid.)	Jefferson	Bosticks	146/19	Wilkinson
Anderson, Martin	Wilkes	Parks	4/16	Wilkinson
Anderson, Mathew	Oglethorpe	Hudsons	217/20	Wilkinson
Anderson, Mathew	Oglethorpe	Hudsons	412/7	Wilkinson
Anderson, Nancy(Orph.)	Jefferson	Bosticks	4/8	Baldwin
Anderson, Rachel(Orph.)	Jefferson	Bosticks	4/8	Baldwin
Anderson, Rachel	Richmond		167/11	Wilkinson
Anderson, Rebecca(Orph.)	Jefferson	Bosticks	4/8	Baldwin
Anderson, Sally(Orph.)	Jefferson	Bosticks	4/8	Baldwin
Anderson, Sally	Jackson	Johnsons	68/21	Wilkinson
Anderson, Simeon(Orph.)	Richmond		359/13	Wilkinson
Anderson, Sterling	Washington	Blackshears	325/22	Wilkinson
Anderson, Thomas	Elbert	McGuires	209/7	Wilkinson
Anderson, Thomas	Elbert	McGuires	77/9	Wilkinson
Anderson, Uriah	Montgomery	58	212/15	Wilkinson
Anderson, William	Burke	Spains	264/24	Wilkinson
Anderson, William	Greene	Carletons	231/10	Wilkinson
Anderson, William	Greene	Reas	165/17	Wilkinson
Anderson, William	Liberty		276/7	Wilkinson
Anderson, Willis	Wilkinson		170/28	Wilkinson
Andrew's, Benj.(Orphs.)	Columbia	8	19/8	Baldwin
Andrew, John	Elbert	Mobleys	162/15	Baldwin
Andrew, Rachel(Wid.)	Screven	Hutchersons	68/6	Wilkinson
Andrew, Sanders	Liberty		35/6	Wilkinson
Andrews, Gray	Hancock	Birdsongs	120/15	Wilkinson
Andrews, Green	Hancock	Birdsongs	249/14	Wilkinson
Andrews, Green	Hancock	Birdsongs	293/6	Wilkinson
Andrews, Igantius	Screven		251/13	Wilkinson
Andrews, James	Franklin	Griffiths	64/18	Wilkinson
Andrews, John(Heirs)	Richmond		268/13	Wilkinson
Andrews, John	Wilkes	Stovalls	218/6	Wilkinson
Andrews, Michael	Wilkes	Sheets	110/22	Wilkinson
Andrews, Milly	Burke	Sandifords	69/10	Baldwin
Andrews, Robbins	Elbert	Morrisons	127/8	Wilkinson
Andrews, William	Burke	Burks	163/14	Wilkinson
Andrews, William	Hancock	Birdsongs	131/25	Wilkinson
Andrews, William	Hancock	Birdsongs	73/9	Baldwin
Angeilly, Alexander	Jefferson		101/25	Wilkinson
Angle, Charles	Franklin	Hollingsworth	46/9	Baldwin
Angle, John Jr.	Oglethorpe	Smiths	356/10	Wilkinson
Angle, John	Oglethorpe	Smiths	275/7	Wilkinson
Angle, Thomas	Oglethorpe	Smiths	158/24	Wilkinson
Anglin, Elijah	Baldwin	3	133/12	Baldwin
Anglin, Elijah	Baldwin	3	134/7	Wilkinson

NAME	COUNTY	MIL.DIST.	LOT/DIST	DREW LAND
Anglin, John Jr.	Baldwin	1	170/11	Wilkinson
Anglin, John Sr.	Baldwin	3	281/20	Wilkinson
Anglin, Joseph	Jackson	Wrights	180/6	Baldwin
Ansley, Benjamin	Chatham	Abrahams	304/24	Wilkinson
Ansley, William	Warren	Willsons	137/20	Baldwin
Anthony, Anselm	Wilkes	Heards	286/9	Wilkinson
Anthony, Anselm	Wilkes	Heards	56/27	Wilkinson
Anthony, James Sr.	Wilkes	Heards	4/9	Wilkinson
Anthony, James	Wilkes	Normans	82/13	Baldwin
Anthony, Nancy	Wilkes	Heards	394/21	Wilkinson
Appleby, Wm.Sr.	Jackson	Hendersons	161/8	Baldwin
Appling's, Wm.(Orphs.)	Columbia	5	236/7	Wilkinson
Appling, Joel	Wilkes	M.Hendersons	266/9	Wilkinson
Appling, Thos.(Son/David)	Columbia	11	276/17	Wilkinson
Archer, James	Screven		80/8	Wilkinson
Ard, Neill	Washington	Andersons	289/20	Baldwin
Ard, Thomas	Liberty		12/14	Wilkinson
Armor, James	Greene	Armors	250/19	Wilkinson
Armor, Jas.(School M.)	Chatham	Pettybones	333/9	Wilkinson
Armor, Mary	Greene	Carletons	235/23	Wilkinson
Armstrong, James	Franklin	Dixons	267/17	Wilkinson
Armstrong, James	Franklin	Dixons	68/14	Baldwin
Armstrong, James	Jackson	Cockrans	78/8	Wilkinson
Armstrong, Jesse	Clarke	Hitchcocks	240/16	Wilkinson
Armstrong, John C.	Hancock	Shivers	130/12	Baldwin
Armstrong, John Sr.	Clarke	Trammells	106/10	Wilkinson
Armstrong, John Sr.	Clarke	Trammells	51/18	Wilkinson
Armstrong, John	Franklin	Allens	324/17	Wilkinson
Armstrong, Joseph	Columbia	9	65/17	Baldwin
Armstrong, Kissy	Warren	Neals	63/11	Baldwin
Armstrong, Ludwell	Clarke	Martins	153/23	Wilkinson
Armstrong, Nancy	Franklin	Dixons	214/10	Wilkinson
Armstrong, Robert	Camden	Browns	45/21	Wilkinson
Armstrong, Thomas	Glynn		110/8	Wilkinson
Armstrong, Wm.	Glynn		310/14	Wilkinson
Arnall, Edmund	Wilkes	Malones	319/12	Wilkinson
Arnall, Sally(Wid.)	Wilkes	Malones	100/20	Baldwin
Arnett, William	Screven		170/10	Baldwin
Arnold, Allen	Oglethorpe	Bells	14/25	Wilkinson
Arnold, James Jr.	Elbert	Blackwells	29/13	Wilkinson
Arnold, John	Franklin	Allens	345/13	Wilkinson
Arnold, John	Oglethorpe	Hatchetts	168/19	Baldwin
Arnold, Nancy(Single)	Clarke	Butlers	403/8	Wilkinson
Arnold, Stephen	Baldwin	3	69/6	Baldwin
Arnold, Thomas	Oglethorpe	Watkins	50/18	Wilkinson
Arnold, William	Baldwin	5	57/21	Wilkinson
Arnold, William	Elbert	Clarks	139/28	Wilkinson
Arnold, Zachariah	Oglethorpe	Watkins	178/23	Wilkinson
Arrandel, Levine(Wid.)	Tattnall	Halls	278/12	Wilkinson
Arrant, Elizabeth	Lincoln	Mays	286/21	Wilkinson
Arrant, Nimrod	Lincoln	Mays	203/13	Wilkinson
Arrington, Eliz.H.(Orph.)	Richmond		215/17	Wilkinson
Arrington, Polly(Orph.)	Richmond		215/17	Wilkinson
Arrington, William	Baldwin	4	142/15	Wilkinson
Arthur, James	Baldwin	3	400/7	Wilkinson
Arthur, Talbert	Jackson	Cockrans	222/15	Baldwin
Arthur, William	Wilkes	M.Hendersons	115/9	Baldwin
Ash, John & Geo.(Orphs.)	Chatham	Abrahams	130/17	Baldwin
Ash, William	Franklin	Allens	89/12	Wilkinson
Ashbury, Nathan	Hancock	Wallers	280/9	Wilkinson
Ashford, Mary(Wid.)	Wilkes	Sidwells	212/20	Wilkinson
Ashley's, James(Orphs.)	Hancock	Coopers	257/6	Wilkinson
Ashley, John	Camden	Ashleys	118/23	Wilkinson
Ashley, Stephen	Lincoln	Kennons	147/14	Wilkinson
Ashmore, John	Wilkes	Wellborns	75/18	Baldwin
Ashton, Hannah(Wid.)	Chatham	Abrahams	128/17	Baldwin
Ashurst, John	Hancock	Smiths	66/25	Wilkinson

NAME	COUNTY	MIL.DIST.	LOT/DIST	DREW LAND
Ashworth, Joab	Elbert	McGuires	274/6	Wilkinson
Askew's, Thomas(Orphs.)	Washington	Andersons	209/16	Wilkinson
Askew, Molly(Wid.)	Franklin	Thompsons	117/9	Baldwin
Aston, Robert	Greene	Loves	80/16	Wilkinson
Atcherson, Nathaniel	Elbert	Groves	111/21	Wilkinson
Atchinson, Barton	Warren	Carters	161/20	Baldwin
Atchinson, Barton	Warren	Carters	344/14	Wilkinson
Atchinson, Heny	Warren	Carters	19/12	Wilkinson
Atha, Zepheniah	Columbia	1	268/10	Wilkinson
Atkerson, Lemuel	Oglethorpe	Hudsons	338/10	Wilkinson
Atkins, Arnold	Jackson	Johnsons	225/19	Baldwin
Atkins, Asa	Wilkes	I.Hendersons	73/17	Baldwin
Atkins, Joseph	Wilkinson		101/13	Wilkinson
Atkins, Ransom	Jackson	Johnsons	48/8	Wilkinson
Atkins, Robert	Jackson	Cockrans	348/10	Wilkinson
Atkinson, Abigail(Wid)	Jackson	Wrights	203/27	Wilkinson
Atkinson, Abner	Hancock	Shivers	184/13	Wilkinson
Atkinson, Armstead	Greene	Baxters	133/20	Wilkinson
Atkinson, Burwell	Camden	Hardys	317/10	Wilkinson
Atkinson, George	Chatham	Whites	30/10	Baldwin
Atkinson, John	Burke	Martins	57/9	Wilkinson
Atkinson, John	Greene	Butlers	68/8	Baldwin
Atkinson, Thomas	Wilkes	Wellborns	312/24	Wilkinson
Attaway, Ezekiel	Burke	Forths	290/13	Wilkinson
Attoway's, Benj.(Orphs.)	Washington	Howards	79/10	Baldwin
Austin, Harris	Burke	Bynes	113/16	Wilkinson
Austin, John	Jackson	Cockrans	343/9	Wilkinson
Austin, Joseph	Liberty		284/14	Wilkinson
Autry, Absalom	Greene	Greers	86/28	Wilkinson
Autry, Jacob Jr.	Greene	Davenports	5/7	Wilkinson
Autry, Jacob Sr.	Greene	Davenports	210/22	Wilkinson
Avary, Harbert	Columbia	3	138/13	Baldwin
Aven, Hicksey	Warren	Newsoms	39/13	Baldwin
Averett, Archelus	Hancock	Thomas	220/10	Wilkinson
Averett, John	Hancock	Thomas	226/14	Baldwin
Avery, Alexander	Lincoln	Gartrells	242/20	Wilkinson
Avery, Arthur	Lincoln	Busseys	195/18	Wilkinson
Avery, Needham	Lincoln	Busseys	284/15	Wilkinson
Awbrey, Philip	Jackson	Wrights	275/20	Baldwin
Awbrey, Samuel	Jackson	Wrights	333/21	Wilkinson
Awtry, Nancy(Single)	Clarke	Silmans	232/19	Baldwin
Awtry, Nancy(Single)	Clarke	Silmans	67/6	Wilkinson
Aycock, Benjamin	Washington	Burneys	281/12	Wilkinson
Aycock, Henry	Wilkes	Sheets	8/22	Wilkinson
Aycock, Jesse	Bulloch	Hendleys	113/22	Wilkinson
Aycock, Jesse	Bulloch	Hendleys	328/13	Wilkinson
Aycock, Jonathan	Oglethorpe	Popes	19/16	Wilkinson
Aycock, Richard	Lincoln	Kings	194/6	Wilkinson
Aycock, Richard	Wilkes	Sheets	178/18	Wilkinson
Aylor's, John(Orps/Alt.1811)	Oglethorpe	Hartsfields	28/9	Baldwin
Ayres, Moses Jr.	Franklin	Thompsons	199/26	Wilkinson
Ayres, Moses Sr.	Franklin	Thompsons	81/11	Wilkinson
Ayres, Thomas	Columbia	4	186/9	Baldwin
Ayres, Thomas	Washington	Holts	352/10	Wilkinson
Ayres, William	Columbia	7	130/21	Wilkinson
Baber, Ambrose	Oglethorpe	Jno.Smith	368/8	Wilkinson
Baber, Richard	Washington	Kendricks	194/19	Baldwin
Back, Mary(Wid.)	Oglethorpe	Jno.Smiths	231/25	Wilkinson
Backelow, James	Warren	Newsoms	297/8	Wilkinson
Backley, Elizabeth	Effingham		21/15	Baldwin
Bacon's, Samuel(Orphs.)	Liberty		145/12	Wilkinson
Bacon, Agnes	Richmond		193/13	Wilkinson
Bacon, Edmund	Richmond		172/9	Baldwin
Bacon, Edmund	Richmond		22/9	Baldwin
Bacon, Jonathan	Liberty		202/14	Baldwin

NAME	COUNTY	MIL.DIST.	LOT/DIST	DREW LAND
Bacon, Josiah	Liberty		5/19	Wilkinson
Bacon, Thomas Jr.	Liberty		26/23	Wilkinson
Bacon, Thomas (3rd)	Liberty		10/20	Wilkinson
Baduly's, Wm. (Orphs.)	Burke	Sandifords	134/25	Wilkinson
Baggett, John	Washington	Delks	125/21	Wilkinson
Baggett, Nancy	Clarke	Robinsons	160/11	Wilkinson
Baggett, Nichols	Jefferson		104/24	Wilkinson
Bailey's, Michael (Orphs.)	Wilkes	Sheets	116/26	Wilkinson
Bailey, David	Washington	Chivers	187/25	Wilkinson
Bailey, Edmund (S/Jas.)	Wilkes	Stovalls	104/20	Wilkinson
Bailey, Elias	Burke	Thompsons	220/24	Wilkinson
Bailey, Henry	Oglethorpe	Hatchetts	42/17	Baldwin
Bailey, James	Wilkes	Harris	180/9	Wilkinson
Bailey, John (S/James)	Wilkes	Stovalls	290/11	Wilkinson
Bailey, John	Hancock	Barnes	141/19	Wilkinson
Bailey, John	Hancock	Barnes	83/18	Wilkinson
Bailey, John	Jackson	Wright	123/16	Wilkinson
Bailey, Joseph	Oglethorpe	Bells	51/28	Wilkinson
Bailey, Joseph	Wilkes	Normans	64/6	Wilkinson
Bailey, Philip	Greene	Loves	180/11	Wilkinson
Bailey, Ralph	Jackson	Wright	304/9	Wilkinson
Bailey, Rose (Wid.)	Wilkes	Sheets	161/8	Wilkinson
Bailey, Samuel	Elbert	Blackwells	217/23	Wilkinson
Bailey, Simon	Greene	Loves	25/7	Wilkinson
Bailey, Stephen	Oglethorpe	Bells	185/16	Baldwin
Bailey, William	Oglethorpe	John Smith	156/16	Baldwin
Baillie, Abner	McIntosh		44/9	Baldwin
Baillie, John	McIntosh		201/10	Wilkinson
Baillie, Sarah	McIntosh		247/9	Wilkinson
Baily, Thomas S.	Oglethorpe	Beasleys	78/10	Wilkinson
Baird, Jonathan	Greene	Greers	133/16	Wilkinson
Baird, Thomas	Jackson	Wright	265/22	Wilkinson
Bairfield's, John (Orphs.)	Burke	Martins	175/17	Baldwin
Bairfield, Jerusha	Burke	Martins	59/25	Wilkinson
Bairfield, Jesse	Wilkinson		187/23	Wilkinson
Bairfield, Wm.	Burke	Thompsons	151/19	Baldwin
Baisden, Mary (Wid.)	Glynn		258/19	Baldwin
Baker's, Artema (Orph.)	Liberty		232/9	Baldwin
Baker's, Chas. (Orphs.)	Warren	Flournoys	250/17	Wilkinson
Baker's, John T. (Orph.)	Liberty		201/28	Wilkinson
Baker's, Wm. (Orphs.)	Burke	Fields	89/13	Wilkinson
Baker's, Wm.R. (Orphs.)	Liberty		240/8	Wilkinson
Baker's, Wm.Sr. (Orphs.)	Liberty		322/4	Wilkinson
Baker, Austin	Warren	Baker	144/17	Baldwin
Baker, Benjamin Jr.	Liberty		192/22	Wilkinson
Baker, Benjamin Jr.	McIntosh		2/20	Baldwin
Baker, Bright	McIntosh		128/13	Wilkinson
Baker, Ebenezer	Liberty		132/20	Baldwin
Baker, Elisha	Burke	Sharps	172/16	Baldwin
Baker, Elisha	Greene	Loves	135/13	Wilkinson
Baker, Eliz. (Orph.)	Baldwin	3	133/28	Wilkinson
Baker, Gabriel	Columbia	10	38/19	Wilkinson
Baker, James	Greene	Dawsons	258/9	Wilkinson
Baker, Jesse	Hancock	Barksdales	112/24	Wilkinson
Baker, John	Clarke	Martins	29/26	Wilkinson
Baker, John	Warren	Bakers	161/15	Wilkinson
Baker, Joseph	Bulloch	Parish	239/18	Wilkinson
Baker, Joshua Sr.	Clarke	Harpers	89/26	Wilkinson
Baker, Mary W. (Wid.)	Liberty		314/22	Wilkinson
Baker, Nancy	Columbia	1	42/10	Baldwin
Baker, Nicholas	Clarke	Martins	238/6	Wilkinson
Baker, Polly	Greene	Loves	194/26	Wilkinson
Baker, Rebecca (Orph.)	Jefferson	Thomas	209/25	Wilkinson
Baker, Stephen	Columbia	9	36/19	Baldwin
Baker, Thomas Sr.	Liberty		55/17	Wilkinson
Baker, William	Greene	Armors	199/14	Wilkinson
Baker, Wm.Jr.	Liberty		135/27	Wilkinson

NAME	COUNTY	MIL.DIST.	LOT/DIST	DREW LAND
Baldwin's, Thomas(Orphs.)	Greene	Dawsons	180/9	Baldwin
Baldwin, Augustus	Richmond		34/20	Baldwin
Baldwin, Benjamin	Oglethorpe	Bells	46/21	Wilkinson
Baldwin, David	Greene	Owsleys	141/11	Baldwin
Baldwin, George	Montgomery	56	213/10	Baldwin
Baldwin, Nancy	Greene	Dawsons	142/9	Wilkinson
Baldwin, Owen	Columbia	10	221/8	Wilkinson
Baldwin, Owen	Columbia	10	87/27	Wilkinson
Baldwin, Samuel	Greene	Greers	198/13	Baldwin
Baldwin, Thomas	Franklin	Hoopers	244/12	Wilkinson
Baldwin, William	Franklin	Hoopers	243/11	Wilkinson
Balflower, Robert	Burke	Mulkeys	26/17	Baldwin
Ball, Anson	Wilkinson		161/16	Wilkinson
Ball, Henrietta(Miss)	Warren	Jones	19/15	Wilkinson
Ball, John	Jackson	Wright	94/24	Wilkinson
Ball, Joseph	Chatham	Whites	309/20	Baldwin
Ball, Sally	Lincoln	Jones	145/20	Wilkinson
Ball, William	Richmond		144/6	Baldwin
Ballard's, Dred(Orphs.)	Jackson	Wright	328/10	Wilkinson
Ballard's, James(Orphs.)	Wilkes	Sidwells	356/21	Wilkinson
Ballard's, Wm.(Orphs.)	Greene	Dawsons	123/27	Wilkinson
Ballard, Bathsheba	Burke	Blounts	32/19	Wilkinson
Ballard, Benjamin	Wilkes	Wellborns	124/12	Wilkinson
Ballard, Edward	Burke	Blounts	251/16	Wilkinson
Ballard, Frederick	Richmond		69/12	Wilkinson
Ballard, Joshua	Wilkes	Wellborns	177/23	Wilkinson
Ballard, Leven Hill	Burke	Ballards	89/8	Wilkinson
Ballard, Reddick	Burke	Sandifords	110/6	Baldwin
Ballard, Sarah(Wid.)	Wilkinson		369/9	Wilkinson
Ballard, William	Burke	Blounts	49/18	Wilkinson
Ballinger, Wm.	Elbert	Keelings	270/21	Wilkinson
Banckson, Thomas	Baldwin	5	179/19	Wilkinson
Bandy, Lewis	Hancock	Wallers	118/14	Wilkinson
Banks, Dunstan	Oglethorpe	Smith	100/18	Wilkinson
Banks, Eaton	Oglethorpe	Stewarts	94/15	Wilkinson
Banks, John	Elbert	McGuires	11/18	Baldwin
Banks, Jourdan	Warren	Hills	144/7	Wilkinson
Bankston, Abner	Clarke	Harpers	145/9	Baldwin
Bankston, Daniel	Clarke	Silmans	18/11	Wilkinson
Bankston, Jacob	Clarke	Robinsons	240/12	Wilkinson
Bankston, Jacob	Clarke	Robinsons	475/7	Wilkinson
Bankston, John Sr.	Clarke	Robinsons	71/12	Wilkinson
Bankston, Laurence	Wilkes	I.Hendersons	289/13	Wilkinson
Barber's, Joseph(Orphs.)	Jefferson		126/6	Baldwin
Barber, Aaron	Montgomery	55	38/22	Wilkinson
Barber, George Jr.	Oglethorpe	Popes	35/18	Wilkinson
Barber, George Sr.	Oglethorpe	Pope	115/8	Baldwin
Barber, Priscilla(Wid.)	Jefferson		32/18	Wilkinson
Barber, William	Jefferson	Tarver	47/7	Wilkinson
Barber, William	Liberty		193/14	Wilkinson
Barber, William	Wayne	2	158/15	Baldwin
Barber, William	Wayne	2	30/6	Baldwin
Barden, Nancy	Richmond		297/22	Wilkinson
Barden, Simon	Jefferson	Hardwick	276/24	Wilkinson
Barden, William	Columbia	7	42/14	Baldwin
Bardsdale, William	Warren	Heaths	39/10	Baldwin
Barfield, Asa	Washington	Willis	322/11	Wilkinson
Barfield, Asa	Washington	Willis	9/18	Wilkinson
Barham, Timothy S.	Columbia	1	3/26	Wilkinson
Barker's, John(Orphs.)	Wilkes	Malones	142/26	Wilkinson
Barker, George	Columbia	2	170/15	Wilkinson
Barker, John	Columbia	2	15/8	Wilkinson
Barker, William	Wilkes	Milners	218/24	Wilkinson
Barksdale, Abner	Hancock	Cooper	329/9	Wilkinson
Barksdale, Collier	Hancock	Coopers	189/24	Wilkinson
Barksdale, William	Warren	Heaths	6/23	Wilkinson
Barlow, Henry	Washington	Kendricks	236/16	Wilkinson

NAME	COUNTY	MIL.DIST.	LOT/DIST	DREW LAND
Barlow, John	Washington	Kendricks	257/21	Wilkinson
Barlow, Wilie	Washington	Kendricks	36/6	Wilkinson
Barlow, William	Washington	Kendricks	104/15	Wilkinson
Barnaby's, Wm.(Orphs.)	Liberty		240/20	Baldwin
Barnard, John Sr.	Chatham	Herbs	145/13	Baldwin
Barnard, Mary E.	Chatham	Herbs	41/18	Baldwin
Barnard, Robert	Chatham	Herbs	44/17	Baldwin
Barnard, Timothy Jr.	Chatham	Herbs	121/8	Baldwin
Barnard, Timothy Jr.	Chatham	Herbs	443/7	Wilkinson
Barnard, William	Chatham	Herbs	277/21	Wilkinson
Barnard, William	Chatham	Herbs	69/6	Wilkinson
Barnes', Benj.(Orphs.)	Baldwin	1	76/18	Wilkinson
Barnes', Wm.(Orphs.)	Franklin	Christians	289/14	Wilkinson
Barnes, Catharine(Orph.)	Richmond		167/6	Baldwin
Barnes, Dempsey	Burke	Blounts	160/19	Wilkinson
Barnes, John B.	Richmond		44/15	Wilkinson
Barnes, John(Orph.)	Richmond		167/6	Baldwin
Barnes, John	Lincoln	Kennon	84/6	Baldwin
Barnes, Seleia	Hancock	Waller	252/10	Wilkinson
Barnes, William	Glynn		82/25	Wilkinson
Barnes, Wm.Edw.	Jefferson	Wright	75/15	Baldwin
Barnett, Douglass	Hancock	Pinkstons	72/6	Wilkinson
Barnett, George	Oglethorpe	Hatchetts	41/24	Wilkinson
Barnett, Jno.(Orp.of N.)	Greene	Butlers	259/14	Baldwin
Barnett, John	Oglethorpe	Hudson	112/25	Wilkinson
Barnett, John	Oglethorpe	Hudsons	321/14	Wilkinson
Barnett, Meal I.	Greene	Davenports	141/10	Baldwin
Barnett, Nathan	Greene	Davenports	242/15	Wilkinson
Barnett, Nathan	Greene	Jenkins	97/13	Wilkinson
Barnett, Nathaniel	Elbert	Mobleys	209/28	Wilkinson
Barnett, Nathaniel	Elbert	Mobleys	290/15	Baldwin
Barnett, Peggy	Greene	Carltons	201/20	Wilkinson
Barnett, Robert Sr.	Washington	Willis	16/14	Baldwin
Barnett, Samuel	Jackson	Henderson	260/23	Wilkinson
Barnett, Susannah	Oglethorpe	Hatchetts	92/21	Wilkinson
Barnett, Uriah	Franklin	Griffiths	57/13	Baldwin
Barnett, William	Greene	Carltons	93/17	Wilkinson
Barnett, Wm.C.	Greene	Butlers	194/9	Baldwin
Barnett, Wm.C.	Greene	Butlers	220/14	Baldwin
Barney, Job S.	Richmond		91/12	Wilkinson
Barnhart, George	Greene	Stewarts	121/21	Wilkinson
Barnwell, Robert	Franklin	Everetts	98/15	Wilkinson
Barr, James	Jackson	Johnson	181/16	Wilkinson
Barr, James	Jackson	Johnson	273/15	Wilkinson
Barr, Nathan	Burke	Carswells	18/6	Baldwin
Barrett, Isaac I.	Elbert	Barretts	32/23	Wilkinson
Barrett, Thomas	Richmond		94/17	Baldwin
Barrett, Winion Sr.	Franklin	Thompsons	223/8	Wilkinson
Barron, Barnabas	Washington	Collins	317/17	Wilkinson
Barron, James	Jackson	Johnson	113/9	Baldwin
Barron, John	Elbert	Thompsons	248/19	Wilkinson
Barron, John	Jackson	Wright	88/27	Wilkinson
Barron, Milly(Wid.)	Wilkinson		129/7	Baldwin
Barron, Polly	Baldwin	4	22/7	Baldwin
Barron, Robert	Baldwin	5	42/10	Wilkinson
Barron, Samuel	Hancock	Shiver	144/8	Baldwin
Barron, William	Washington	Collins	347/7	Wilkinson
Barrow, Abraham	Montgomery	50	73/28	Wilkinson
Barrow, Absalom	Montgomery	51	113/25	Wilkinson
Barrow, James	Burke	Gordons	245/14	Wilkinson
Barrow, Reubin	Warren	Devereux	324/24	Wilkinson
Bartee, Robert	Columbia	11	275/14	Wilkinson
Bartell, John	Columbia	11	279/10	Wilkinson
Bartley, Anne C.	Franklin	McDowells	43/14	Baldwin
Barton, Ann	Richmond		123/15	Baldwin
Barton, Benjamin	Franklin	Hoopers	257/20	Wilkinson
Barton, James	Warren	Newsoms	63/17	Wilkinson

NAME	COUNTY	MIL.DIST.	LOT/DIST	DREW LAND
Barton, Presley	Franklin	Yowells	185/7	Wilkinson
Barton, Thomas	Franklin	Hoopers	10/6	Baldwin
Barton, William	Baldwin	5	239/16	Wilkinson
Barton, William	Baldwin	5	311/22	Wilkinson
Barton, Willoughby	Richmond		154/17	Wilkinson
Barton, Wm.	Franklin	Hollingsworths	357/13	Wilkinson
Bartow, Theodorus	Glynn		115/11	Wilkinson
Basinger, Peter	Chatham	Abrahams	244/10	Baldwin
Basinger, Peter	Chatham	Abrahams	391/22	Wilkinson
Bass, Abraham	Burke	Fields	89/10	Wilkinson
Bass, Abraham	Burke	Fields	96/18	Wilkinson
Bass, Allen	Hancock	Holts	157/19	Wilkinson
Bass, Allen	Hancock	Holts	194/19	Wilkinson
Bass, Drury	Warren	Neals	74/7	Baldwin
Bass, Thomas	Hancock	Smiths	5/15	Baldwin
Bassett, John	McIntosh		197/24	Wilkinson
Batchellor, Alexr.	Jackson	Wright	195/20	Baldwin
Bateman's, Wm.(Orphs.)	Washington	Delks	159/6	Baldwin
Bateman, David	Washington	Howards	17/16	Baldwin
Bateman, Martha W.	Washington	Chivers	135/10	Wilkinson
Bates, David	Wilkes	Milners	97/20	Wilkinson
Bates, Thomas	Jackson	Johnson	205/13	Wilkinson
Batson, Thomas Sr.	Montgomery	54	92/7	Baldwin
Battle's, John(Orphs.)	Warren	Carters	181/18	Wilkinson
Battle, Wm.S.	Hancock	Shiver	133/21	Wilkinson
Batty, Nancy(Orph.)	Jackson	Johnson	40/23	Wilkinson
Baxter, Elizabeth	Bulloch	Godfreys	272/11	Wilkinson
Baxter, Stephen	Bryan	Birds	168/14	Baldwin
Bayler, Mathew	Chatham	Neyles	256/20	Baldwin
Bayless, Isham	Columbia	2	171/11	Wilkinson
Bayley, Elizabeth	Chatham	Hardens	78/15	Wilkinson
Bayley, Julian	Elbert	Blackwells	3/25	Wilkinson
Bayn, John	Warren	Willsons	308/8	Wilkinson
Bayn, John	Warren	Willsons	65/11	Baldwin
Bayne, Abraham	Wilkes	Edges	202/11	Wilkinson
Bays, Zachariah	Greene	Moores	153/17	Wilkinson
Baysmore, Thomas	Warren	Newsoms	145/13	Wilkinson
Bazemore, David	Baldwin	2	208/23	Wilkinson
Bazemore, David	Baldwin	2	48/16	Wilkinson
Bazer, Caleb	Baldwin	3	162/25	Wilkinson
Beagles, Joseph	Oglethorpe	Moores	26/10	Baldwin
Beal, Levi	Jefferson	Fulton	204/20	Wilkinson
Beall, Josiah	Warren	Neals	360/13	Wilkinson
Beall, Robert	Warren	Flournoys	163/9	Wilkinson
Beall, Ruth	Franklin	Allens	335/13	Wilkinson
Beall, Samuel	Hancock	Hudson	55/15	Baldwin
Beall, Samuel	Hancock	Hudsons	326/10	Wilkinson
Beall, Thaddeus	Columbia	10	133/11	Baldwin
Beall, William	Effingham		262/8	Wilkinson
Bealle, Francis S.	Columbia	1	187/15	Wilkinson
Bealle, Jane(Wid.)	Columbia	1	147/21	Wilkinson
Bealle, Lender(Dau/Thos.)	Columbia	1	198/12	Wilkinson
Bealle, Reason D.(Son/Thos.)	Columbia	1	96/22	Wilkinson
Beard, Alexander	Jackson	Johnson	13/21	Wilkinson
Beard, John	Chatham	Pettybones	51/25	Wilkinson
Beard, Keziah	Baldwin	1	82/13	Wilkinson
Beard, Rachel(Wid.)	Chatham	Whites	135/19	Wilkinson
Beard, Robert	Liberty		181/12	Wilkinson
Beard, William	Jackson	Johnson	114/24	Wilkinson
Beard, William	Jackson	Johnson	73/21	Wilkinson
Bearden, Ansel	Jackson	Wright	418/7	Wilkinson
Bearden, Arthur	Franklin	Allens	167/15	Baldwin
Bearden, John	Greene	Armors	13/16	Baldwin
Bearden, Richard	Jackson	Henderson	5/6	Baldwin
Beasley, Ann(Wid.)	Warren	Neals	262/12	Wilkinson
Beasley, Elizabeth	Greene	Watsons	385/22	Wilkinson
Beasley, Jarrell	Greene	Watsons	161/28	Wilkinson

NAME	COUNTY	MIL.DIST.	LOT/DIST	DREW LAND
Beasley, John	Liberty		308/17	Wilkinson
Beasley, Lydia(S.W.)	Clarke	Dukes	77/17	Baldwin
Beasley, Richard	Wilkes	Normans	82/27	Wilkinson
Beasley, Robert C.	Greene	Greers	96/21	Wilkinson
Beatheen, Angus	McIntosh		128/17	Wilkinson
Beaty, David	Oglethorpe	Moore	108/23	Wilkinson
Beaty, David	Oglethorpe	Moores	111/25	Wilkinson
Beaty, Francis	Oglethorpe	Moore	357/22	Wilkinson
Beaty, James Sr.	Jefferson	Bostick	33/16	Baldwin
Beaty, Sarah	Montgomery	59	62/24	Wilkinson
Beavers, Thomas	Wilkes	Wellborns	117/16	Baldwin
Beazley, John	Bulloch	Williams	37/16	Baldwin
Bebe, Adaline(Orph.)	Richmond		61/12	Baldwin
Bebe, Harriet(Orph.)	Richmond		61/12	Baldwin
Beck, Jesse	Columbia	4	90/19	Baldwin
Beck, William	Columbia	4	22/22	Wilkinson
Beckcom, Solomon	Washington	Garretts	217/14	Wilkinson
Beckham, Reubin	Jefferson	Thomas	399/8	Wilkinson
Beckham, Samuel	Wilkinson		163/11	Baldwin
Beckham, Young	Chatham	McLeans	302/14	Wilkinson
Beckton, Micajah	Screven		20/8	Baldwin
Becu, Abraham	Chatham	Pembertons	9/21	Wilkinson
Bedgood, John Sr.	Washington	Burneys	147/6	Wilkinson
Bedgood, Martha	Washington	Burneys	188/6	Baldwin
Bedgood, Richard	Washington	Burneys	25/10	Baldwin
Bedingfield, Charles	Wilkes	Stovalls	213/22	Wilkinson
Bedingfield, James	Burke	Bynes	102/20	Wilkinson
Bedingfield, Jno.	Burke	Bynes	92/18	Baldwin
Bedingfield, John	Burke	Bynes	128/19	Wilkinson
Beland, John	Oglethorpe	Stewarts	111/27	Wilkinson
Beland, John	Oglethorpe	Stewarts	148/20	Wilkinson
Belcher, Abraham Sr.	Burke	Martins	260/6	Wilkinson
Belcher, Allen	Montgomery	50	355/22	Wilkinson
Belcher, Eliz.(Wid.)	Burke	Forths	189/25	Wilkinson
Belcher, Mathew	Oglethorpe	Stewart	162/14	Wilkinson
Belcher, Mathew	Oglethorpe	Stewarts	163/21	Wilkinson
Belcher, Tabitha	Burke	Spains	316/20	Wilkinson
Belger, Eliz.(Wid.)	Warren	Devereux	261/23	Wilkinson
Bell's, Thos.(Orphs.)	Hancock	Barnes	96/26	Wilkinson
Bell, David	Greene	Baxters	8/9	Baldwin
Bell, Elizabeth	Elbert	Thompsons	102/18	Wilkinson
Bell, Ellenor(S.W.)	Screven		134/12	Baldwin
Bell, Esther(S.W.)	Jackson		171/16	Wilkinson
Bell, Harrison	Richmond		14/7	Baldwin
Bell, Hiram(Orph.)	Burke	Sandifords	54/19	Baldwin
Bell, Hugh	Washington	Paces	160/20	Wilkinson
Bell, James	Jackson	Henderson	9/14	Baldwin
Bell, Jane(Wid.)	Jackson	Cockran	32/21	Wilkinson
Bell, Jered	Hancock	Crowders	101/11	Wilkinson
Bell, John	Burke	Thompsons	338/13	Wilkinson
Bell, John	Jefferson		164/10	Wilkinson
Bell, Joseph	Camden	Crews	162/11	Baldwin
Bell, Martha(Orp.of Danl.)	Screven		155/9	Wilkinson
Bell, Mathew	Burke	Sandifords	37/6	Wilkinson
Bell, Mayfield	Elbert	Thompsons	15/11	Baldwin
Bell, Nancy	Burke	Burks	6/28	Wilkinson
Bell, Nathan	Burke	Burkes	265/12	Wilkinson
Bell, Samuel	Jackson	Johnson	89/15	Baldwin
Bell, Samuel	Oglethorpe	Hewell	135/12	Wilkinson
Bell, Samuel	Oglethorpe	Hewell	7/11	Wilkinson
Bell, Thomas	Clarke	Robinsons	103/15	Baldwin
Bell, Walter(Esq.)	Jackson	Wright	145/8	Baldwin
Bell, William	Jackson	Cockran	349/8	Wilkinson
Bellah, Moses(Heirs/1810)	Oglethorpe	Pope	31/11	Baldwin
Bellamy, Alexander	Hancock	Smith	169/20	Wilkinson
Bellamy, Richard	Oglethorpe	Jno.Smith	25/15	Wilkinson
Benefield, James	Tattnall	Halls	52/8	Wilkinson

NAME	COUNTY	MIL.DIST.	LOT/DIST	DREW LAND
Beningfield, Robert	Lincoln	King	360/9	Wilkinson
Benley's, James(Orphs.)	Burke	Martins	139/25	Wilkinson
Benley's, James(Orphs.)	Burke	Martins	90/7	Baldwin
Bennett, Benjamin	Franklin	Thompsons	82/15	Wilkinson
Bennett, Benjamin	Oglethorpe	Popes	100/13	Baldwin
Bennett, Henry	Bryan	Birds	258/14	Baldwin
Bennett, Hugh	Liberty		177/7	Wilkinson
Bennett, Hugh	Liberty		84/12	Wilkinson
Bennett, Jacob	Lincoln	Kennon	213/17	Wilkinson
Bennett, Jacob	Richmond		228/12	Wilkinson
Bennett, James	Burke	Montgomerys	102/26	Wilkinson
Bennett, Jesse	Jackson	Johnson	35/11	Baldwin
Bennett, Jesse	Jackson	Johnson	80/9	Baldwin
Bennett, Joel	Elbert	Barretts	279/21	Wilkinson
Bennett, John B.	Tattnall	Armstrongs	25/15	Baldwin
Bennett, John B.	Tattnall	Armstrongs	263/11	Wilkinson
Bennett, John Jr.	Franklin	Thompsons	224/20	Baldwin
Bennett, Moses	Elbert	Barretts	153/13	Baldwin
Bennett, Nancy	Lincoln	Kennon	11/20	Baldwin
Bennett, Rebecca(Wid.)	Washington	Kendricks	269/6	Wilkinson
Bennett, Richard	Columbia	3	177/18	Wilkinson
Bennett, Stephen	Jackson	Cockran	263/7	Wilkinson
Bennett, Thomas T.	Jackson	Wright	257/14	Wilkinson
Bennett, William	Bryan	Birds	246/19	Wilkinson
Benningfield, Lewis	Washington	Willis	192/17	Wilkinson
Benningfield, Lewis	Washington	Willis	70/16	Wilkinson
Benson, Isaac	Hancock	Wallers	281/19	Baldwin
Benson, Joseph	Lincoln	Kennon	65/24	Wilkinson
Benson, Richard	Lincoln	Fleming	161/6	Wilkinson
Bentley, Catharine(Orp/Wm.)	Wilkes	Wellborns	122/16	Wilkinson
Bentley, John	Wilkes	Sheets	170/20	Baldwin
Bentley, John	Wilkes	Wellborns	76/9	Wilkinson
Bentley, Lewis	Wilkes	Wellborns	133/14	Baldwin
Bentley, Sally	Elbert	Groves	220/25	Wilkinson
Bentley, Samuel Jr.	Elbert	Keelings	54/17	Baldwin
Benton, Nathan	Columbia	5	113/15	Wilkinson
Benton, Rhoda	Jefferson	Hardwick	38/14	Wilkinson
Bentow's, Thos.(Orphs.)	Jackson	Johnson	213/13	Wilkinson
Berch, Wm.S.	Elbert	Dyes	217/6	Baldwin
Bergman, John Ernst.	Effingham		33/19	Wilkinson
Berrien, John M.	Chatham	Whites	280/8	Wilkinson
Berry, Betsy(S.W.)	Oglethorpe	Hartsfields	150/22	Wilkinson
Berry, Elizabeth	Warren	Flournoys	64/7	Wilkinson
Berry, Gibson(Gilson)	Warren	Flournoys	284/21	Wilkinson
Berry, Isham	Oglethorpe	Hartsfield	54/8	Baldwin
Berry, John	Burke	Fields	69/22	Wilkinson
Berry, John	Effingham		43/12	Baldwin
Berry, Mary Ann Davies	Burke	Fields	257/15	Wilkinson
Berry, William	Warren	Flournoys	220/9	Wilkinson
Berryhill's, Andrw.(Orphs.)	Jefferson	Tarver	73/12	Baldwin
Berryhill, Andrew	Jefferson	Tarver	91/9	Baldwin
Berryhill, John	Montgomery	59	51/16	Baldwin
Berryhill, Thomas	Montgomery	59	143/12	Wilkinson
Berryhill, William	Jefferson	Thomas	118/13	Baldwin
Berryman, Charles	Elbert	Keelings	198/7	Wilkinson
Berson's, Enoch(Orphs.)	Washington	Wiggins	335/8	Wilkinson
Berson, Mary	Washington	Wiggins	224/13	Baldwin
Bethune, Lachlan	Greene	Jenkins	114/21	Wilkinson
Betsil, Elijah(Orp/Isaac)	Wilkes	Coopers	289/24	Wilkinson
Betsill, Godfrey	Jefferson		4/20	Baldwin
Betsill, Joseph	Washington	Willis	300/22	Wilkinson
Betteson, David	Chatham	Hardens	149/26	Wilkinson
Bettis, Wiott	Washington	Willis	92/22	Wilkinson
Betts, Joshua	Jackson	Wright	201/27	Wilkinson
Betts, Samuel Sr.	Hancock	Shiver	178/17	Baldwin
Betts, Samuel	Jackson	Wright	183/18	Wilkinson
Bevers, William	Elbert	McGuires	51/8	Baldwin

NAME	COUNTY	MIL.DIST.	LOT/DIST	DREW LAND
Bevill's, Robert(Orphs.)	Screven		216/6	Wilkinson
Bevill, John Jr.	Elbert	Thompsons	3/8	Wilkinson
Bevin, Benjamin	Columbia	11	126/26	Wilkinson
Bevin, Solomon	Hancock	Candlers	71/9	Baldwin
Bevin, William	Hancock	Candlers	215/12	Wilkinson
Bevins, John W.	Hancock	Candlers	176/20	Wilkinson
Bevins, Jonathan	Hancock	Holts	274/13	Wilkinson
Bevins, Jonathan	Hancock	Holts	87/15	Wilkinson
Bexley, John	Chatham	Abrahams	171/9	Wilkinson
Bexley, Sidda	Hancock	Barksdale	243/15	Wilkinson
Bexley, Simon	Chatham	Herbs	251/25	Wilkinson
Bezer, Polly(S)	Hancock	Winsletts	155/11	Wilkinson
Bibb, Isaac	Bulloch	Denmarks	284/12	Wilkinson
Bibb, Peyton	Elbert	Clarks	114/9	Baldwin
Bibb, Polly	Lincoln	Kennon	172/15	Baldwin
Bibb, Thomas	Elbert	Barretts	282/20	Baldwin
Bibb, Thomas	Elbert	Barretts	300/12	Wilkinson
Bickers, Lewis	Greene	Carltons	85/23	Wilkinson
Bickerstaff, Robert	Jackson	Henderson	12/17	Baldwin
Bickerstaff, Robert	Jackson	Henderson	13/10	Wilkinson
Biers, Susannah(S.W.)	Oglethorpe	Moores	85/19	Baldwin
Biers, Wm.Jr.	Oglethorpe	Moores	181/11	Wilkinson
Biers, Wm.Sr.	Oglethorpe	Moores	75/12	Wilkinson
Biggers, John	Wilkes	Sidwells	221/26	Wilkinson
Biggs, Aaron	Clarke	Tramells	25/18	Wilkinson
Biggs, Joseph(Orph.)	Clarke	Reads	247/13	Wilkinson
Bigham, Francis	Hancock	Barnes	214/23	Wilkinson
Bigham, John	Jefferson	Fulton	1/27	Wilkinson
Bigham, Joseph	Hancock	Barnes	40/16	Baldwin
Bigham, Samuel(Son/Jas.)	Jefferson	Hardwick	48/19	Baldwin
Bignon, Bernard	Richmond		52/24	Wilkinson
Bilbo, James	Chatham	Whites	149/20	Baldwin
Billingslea, Clement	Wilkes	Sidwells	292/16	Wilkinson
Billingslea, Cyrus	Wilkes	I.Hendersons	41/15	Baldwin
Billingslea, John	Wilkes	I.Hendersons	3/21	Wilkinson
Binion, William	Columbia	4	84/27	Wilkinson
Binns, Burrell	Wilkes.	Normans	192/18	Wilkinson
Bird's, Peter(Orphs.)	Hancock	Crowder	35/17	Baldwin
Bird, Henry(Orp./Thos.)	Jefferson	Hardwick	140/19	Baldwin
Bird, Henry	Washington	Willis	68/16	Wilkinson
Bird, James	Bryan	Birds	269/19	Wilkinson
Bird, James	Effingham		79/6	Wilkinson
Bird, James	Hancock	Crowders	58/19	Baldwin
Bird, James	Lincoln	King	29/27	Wilkinson
Bird, Jesse Jr.	Tattnall	McDonalds	218/11	Wilkinson
Bird, Job	Wilkes	Hendricks	178/26	Wilkinson
Bird, Joel	Bulloch	Hendleys	264/14	Wilkinson
Bird, Philemon	Wilkes	Wellborns	17/12	Wilkinson
Bird, Robert	Wilkes	Henricks	147/26	Wilkinson
Birdsong, Isaac	Hancock	Birdsongs	196/10	Wilkinson
Bishop, Charles	Montgomery	54	187/15	Baldwin
Bishop, Fanny	Greene	Butlers	340/22	Wilkinson
Bishop, Mary A.	McIntosh		189/28	Wilkinson
Bishop, Stephen	Greene	Butlers	171/28	Wilkinson
Bishop, Stephen	Hancock	Wallers	481/7	Wilkinson
Bishop, William	Clarke	Silmans	126/18	Wilkinson
Bishop, William	Montgomery	54	104/22	Wilkinson
Blache, Anthony	Chatham	Whites	129/16	Baldwin
Black, Margaret(Wid.)	Montgomery	51	127/18	Baldwin
Black, Robert	Screven		231/15	Wilkinson
Black, Skipp R.	Baldwin	3	437/7	Wilkinson
Black, William	Screven		167/21	Wilkinson
Blackbourn, John A.	Jackson	Wright	162/20	Wilkinson
Blackburn's, Augustin(Orps.)	Franklin	Thompsons	179/12	Baldwin
Blackburn, John	Screven		142/11	Baldwin
Blackman, Wm.Sr.	Screven		246/6	Wilkinson
Blacksell, Lee	Bryan	Austins	186/14	Baldwin

NAME	COUNTY	MIL.DIST.	LOT/DIST	DREW LAND
Blackshear, Abraham	Washington	Andersons	220/15	Baldwin
Blackshear, Edward	Montgomery	51	94/6	Baldwin
Blackshear, Elijah	Washington	Blackshears	148/19	Baldwin
Blackshear, Isaac	Hancock	Barksdale	230/13	Wilkinson
Blackshear, Joseph	Washington	Blackshears	100/16	Wilkinson
Blackshear, Moses	Washington	Collins	2/28	Wilkinson
Blackstone, Argile	Richmond		241/17	Wilkinson
Blackstone, James	Columbia	6	238/24	Wilkinson
Blackwell's, Geo.S.(Orphs.)	Columbia	1	146/17	Wilkinson
Blackwell, Dunstan	Elbert	Blackwells	87/9	Wilkinson
Blackwell, Jesse	Franklin	Everetts	29/15	Wilkinson
Blackwell, Jesse	Franklin	Everetts	37/13	Baldwin
Blackwell, John	Franklin	Allens	66/8	Wilkinson
Blackwell, Joseph	Franklin	Allens	27/11	Wilkinson
Blackwell, Lucy S.	Columbia	1	20/17	Baldwin
Blackwell, Wm.Sr.	Franklin	Allens	81/26	Wilkinson
Blair, Hugh Sr.	Columbia	11	70/26	Wilkinson
Blair, Thomas	Clarke	Tramells	83/19	Baldwin
Blakeley, Bland	Washington	Howards	367/9	Wilkinson
Blakeley, Blano	Washington	Howards	115/10	Baldwin
Blakely, James	Clarke	Hitchcocks	107/19	Baldwin
Blakey, John	Warren	Heaths	21/22	Wilkinson
Blakey, William	Hancock	Barnes	136/8	Baldwin
Blalock, John	Lincoln	May	42/20	Wilkinson
Blanchard, Jas.(Son/Reubin)	Columbia	3	222/25	Wilkinson
Blanchard, Uriah(Son/Reubin)	Columbia	3	173/22	Wilkinson
Bland's, Wm.(Orphs.)	Burke	Mulkeys	208/24	Wilkinson
Bland, Lucinda(Wid.)	Chatham	Whites	210/16	Baldwin
Blandford, Clark	Warren	Neals	293/8	Wilkinson
Blankinship, Hezekiah	Hancock	Crowders	24/14	Baldwin
Blankinship, Hezekiah	Hancock	Crowders	3/24	Wilkinson
Blankinship, Reubin	Baldwin	2	286/10	Wilkinson
Blanks, James	Greene	Loves	165/13	Wilkinson
Blanton's, Chas.(Orphs.)	Lincoln	Bussey	155/13	Wilkinson
Blassingame, Benj.	Greene	Davenports	17/10	Wilkinson
Blassingame, James	Jackson	Cockran	52/21	Wilkinson
Bledsoe's, Pitchy(Orphs.)	Warren	Bakers	299/20	Baldwin
Bledsoe, James	Oglethorpe	Hatchetts	32/20	Wilkinson
Bledsoe, Jno.	Oglethorpe	Hatchetts	104/23	Wilkinson
Bledsoe, John	Oglethorpe	Hatchett	76/17	Baldwin
Bledsoe, Moses	Oglethorpe	Beasley	221/9	Baldwin
Bledsoe, Wm.	Oglethorpe	Hatchetts	166/11	Wilkinson
Blitch, Benjamin	Effingham		110/12	Baldwin
Blitch, Benjamin	Effingham		9/26	Wilkinson
Blitch, Spear	Effingham		41/23	Wilkinson
Bloodworth, Henry	Jefferson	Bosticks	40/19	Baldwin
Bloodworth, Thomas	Wilkinson		335/12	Wilkinson
Blount, Abner	Hancock	Thomas	1/11	Baldwin
Blount, Benjamin	Warren	Heaths	228/14	Wilkinson
Blount, Elizabeth(Orph.)	Chatham	McLeans	39/22	Wilkinson
Blount, Jane(Orph.)	Chatham	McLeans	39/22	Wilkinson
Blount, Richard A.	Hancock	Barksdale	231/20	Baldwin
Blount, Wilie	Washington	Burneys	138/23	Wilkinson
Blount, William	Warren	Heaths	131/19	Wilkinson
Boatright, Wm.Sr.	Elbert	Roebucks	87/6	Wilkinson
Bobbet, Jacob	Lincoln	Jones	175/10	Baldwin
Bobo, Sampson	Franklin	Thompsons	192/16	Wilkinson
Bogan, Patrick	Richmond		111/20	Wilkinson
Boggess, Jeremiah	Oglethorpe	Watkins	105/14	Wilkinson
Boggs, Aaron	Clarke	Stewarts	48/14	Wilkinson
Boggs, Ezekiel	Wilkinson		40/18	Baldwin
Boggs, James Sr.	Jackson	Wright	320/9	Wilkinson
Boggs, Joseph	Wilkinson		4/15	Wilkinson
Boggs, Samuel	Wilkes	Hendricks	262/24	Wilkinson
Bohannon, Alexander	Lincoln	May	242/14	Baldwin
Bohannon, Isiah	Lincoln	King	88/7	Wilkinson
Bohannon, James	Franklin	Henrys	318/13	Wilkinson

NAME	COUNTY	MIL.DIST.	LOT/DIST	DREW LAND
Bohannon, John Jr.	Liberty		48/13	Baldwin
Bohannon, John Sr.	Liberty		12/10	Baldwin
Bohannon, Kinchin	Oglethorpe	Smith	329/10	Wilkinson
Bohannon, William	Franklin	Henrys	268/19	Wilkinson
Bohannon, Wm.	Elbert	Morrisons	242/10	Wilkinson
Boid, John	Warren	Newsoms	109/15	Wilkinson
Boid, John	Warren	Newsoms	35/14	Baldwin
Boling's, Samuel(Orphs.)	Clarke	Hopkins	118/12	Wilkinson
Boling, Henry	Clarke	Hopkins	84/9	Baldwin
Boling, Samuel	Franklin	Cornelius	173/6	Wilkinson
Boling, Samuel	Franklin	Cornelius	49/8	Baldwin
Boling, Thornberry	Oglethorpe	Popes	233/21	Wilkinson
Boling, Thornberry	Oglethorpe	Popes	59/11	Baldwin
Boling, Wm.	Burke	Bynes	11/19	Wilkinson
Bolle, Henry H.(Orp.of H.V.)	Greene	Butlers	238/14	Baldwin
Bolton, Christian(Wid.)	Wilkes	Coopers	271/21	Wilkinson
Bolton, Curtis	Chatham	Whites	115/6	Baldwin
Bolton, James	Burke	Mulkeys	24/27	Wilkinson
Bolton, Reubin	Screven		190/11	Baldwin
Bolton, Samuel	Washington	Howards	253/15	Baldwin
Boman, Ezekiel	Jackson	Johnson	33/23	Wilkinson
Boman, Robert	Oglethorpe	Moores	91/22	Wilkinson
Bond, Edward	Clarke	Browns	95/12	Baldwin
Bond, Henry	Hancock	Weeks	7/18	Baldwin
Bond, John Sr.	Baldwin	2	16/6	Baldwin
Bond, Judy(Wid.)	Lincoln	Jones	97/9	Wilkinson
Bond, Sally	Elbert	Keelings	17/8	Wilkinson
Bond, Thomas	Lincoln	Jones	259/7	Wilkinson
Bond, Venable(Dr.)	Bryan	Austins	141/12	Wilkinson
Bonds, Nathan Jr.	Elbert	Blackwells	114/27	Wilkinson
Bonds, Nathan Jr.	Elbert	Blackwells	74/16	Wilkinson
Boner, Wm.H.	Greene	Davenports	102/10	Wilkinson
Bonnell, John Sr.	Screven		284/24	Wilkinson
Bonner, James	Hancock	Barksdales	11610	Baldwin
Bonner, James	Hancock	Barksdales	271/19	Baldwin
Bonner, Jeremiah	Hancock	Holt	313/13	Wilkinson
Bonner, Jourdan	Clarke	Hopkins	195/9	Wilkinson
Bonner, Thomas	Clarke	Hopkins	57/10	Wilkinson
Bonner, Zadock	Clarke	Hopkins	223/15	Wilkinson
Bonner, Zadock	Clarke	Hopkins	27/20	Baldwin
Booker, Ann(Wid.)	Elbert	Clarks	40/13	Baldwin
Booker, Wm.Sr.	Wilkes	Coopers	91/6	Baldwin
Booles, John Jr.	Greene	Greers	106/15	Wilkinson
Booles, Wm.Sr.	Greene	Greers	28/24	Wilkinson
Boon's, Wm.(Orphs.)	Jefferson		99/7	Wilkinson
Boon, Jacob	Greene	Greers	258/20	Wilkinson
Boon, Jesse	Greene	Flournoys	197/16	Baldwin
Boothe, Gabriel	Elbert	Faulkners	25/11	Wilkinson
Boothe, George	Elbert	Dyes	1/14	Wilkinson
Boothe, Gilbert	Screven	Hutchinsons	251/22	Wilkinson
Boothe, Gilbert	Screven	Hutchinsons	35/10	Wilkinson
Boothe, Nathaniel	Elbert	Faulkners	272/16	Wilkinson
Boothe, Reubin	Baldwin	5	163/8	Baldwin
Boothe, Robert	Elbert	Faulkners	200/9	Wilkinson
Booty, Nichols	Warren	Heaths	360/10	Wilkinson
Boran's, Jesse(Orphs.)	Hancock	Huffs	11/24	Wilkinson
Boran, Benjamin	Wilkes	Sidwells	66/12	Baldwin
Borders, Isaac	Jackson	Johnson	202/15	Wilkinson
Borders, Isaac	Jackson	Johnson	248/7	Wilkinson
Borders, Michael	Jackson	Johnson	64/14	Baldwin
Boren, James Sr.	Wilkes	Roreys	281/10	Wilkinson
Boren, John(S/James)	Wilkes	Roreys	15/20	Baldwin
Boren, John	Wilkinson		117/13	Baldwin
Boren, John	Wilkinson		77/9	Baldwin
Boren, Thomas	Burke	Gordons	4/14	Baldwin
Borland, Abraham	Hancock	Gumm	228/10	Baldwin
Born, Jacob	Oglethorpe	Moores	104/10	Baldwin

NAME	COUNTY	MIL.DIST.	LOT/DIST	DREW LAND
Born, John	Oglethorpe	Moores	4/6	Wilkinson
Borum, George	Oglethorpe	Smith	139/18	Wilkinson
Bostick, Chesley Jr.	Richmond		46/7	Baldwin
Bostick, David	Lincoln	May	39/20	Wilkinson
Bostick, David	Lincoln	May	43/22	Wilkinson
Bostick, Hillery	Burke	Carswells	196/14	Baldwin
Bostick, Holmes G.	Burke	Ballards	48/11	Wilkinson
Bostick, John	Wilkes	Harris	215/15	Baldwin
Bostick, Nathan	Burke	Bynes	144/19	Baldwin
Bostick, Nathan	Jefferson	Bostick	127/26	Wilkinson
Bostick, Rhesa	Burke	Sharps	302/15	Wilkinson
Bostick, William	Wilkes	Harris	284/19	Baldwin
Bostick, William	Wilkes	Harris	318/20	Baldwin
Boston, James	Effingham		75/13	Wilkinson
Boston, John Jr.	Effingham		117/26	Wilkinson
Boswell, Jesse	Wilkes	Malones	14/24	Wilkinson
Boswell, Jesse	Wilkes	Malones	87/18	Wilkinson
Boswell, Josias	Columbia	2	116/16	Wilkinson
Boswell, Josias	Columbia	2	58/28	Wilkinson
Bouitte, Peter	Richmond		294/20	Wilkinson
Bourke, Jeane	Chatham	Herbs	134/23	Wilkinson
Bourke, Thomas	Chatham	Whites	337/9	Wilkinson
Bouty, William	Warren	Devereux	129/6	Wilkinson
Bowan, Ezekiel	Hancock	Barksdales	30/8	Wilkinson
Bowdre, Samuel	Columbia	5	113/20	Baldwin
Bowdris, Robert	Columbia	6	137/17	Wilkinson
Bowen's, Jonathan(Orphs.)	Washington	Howards	46/20	Wilkinson
Bowen, Charles B.	Washington	Kendricks	117/11	Wilkinson
Bowen, Christopher(Orph.)	Elbert	Mobleys	237/26	Wilkinson
Bowen, Elijah	Tattnall	Halls	184/10	Baldwin
Bowen, Elijah	Tattnall	Halls	280/21	Wilkinson
Bowen, Eliza(Orph.)	Chatham	Whites	90/16	Baldwin
Bowen, Herod	Washington	Howards	166/26	Wilkinson
Bowen, Horatio(Orph.)	Elbert	Mobleys	237/26	Wilkinson
Bowen, Jas.(Orph.)	Chatham	Whites	90/16	Baldwin
Bowen, Mary	Chatham	Pettybones	5/27	Wilkinson
Bowen, Patsey	Washington	Howards	112/18	Baldwin
Bowen, Stephen	Tattnall	Armstrongs	447/7	Wilkinson
Bowen, William(Orph.)	Elbert	Mobleys	237/26	Wilkinson
Bowen, William	Tattnall	McDonalds	137/22	Wilkinson
Bowen, Wm.Henry	Chatham	Pettybones	5/27	Wilkinson
Bowen, Wm.Parker(Orph.)	Chatham	Whites	90/16	Baldwin
Bower, Isaac	Jefferson	Wright	220/6	Baldwin
Bowers, Arthur	Burke	Forths	227/11	Wilkinson
Bowles, Amelia(Wid.)	Oglethorpe	Bells	196/18	Wilkinson
Bowling, Asenath(Orph.)	Burke	Blounts	139/26	Wilkinson
Bowling, Mary(Wid.)	Burke	Blounts	166/18	Wilkinson
Box, Elizabeth	Chatham	Whites	86/27	Wilkinson
Box, James	Chatham	Neyles	305/11	Wilkinson
Box, John	Wayne	1	17/16	Wilkinson
Box, Michael	Franklin	Everetts	267/22	Wilkinson
Box, Thomas R.	Chatham	Neyles	128/16	Wilkinson
Boyakin, Eliza	Washington	Wiggins	123/19	Wilkinson
Boyakin, Francis	Greene	Reas	265/21	Wilkinson
Boyakin, Francis	Washington	Wiggins	106/22	Wilkinson
Boyakin, Jesse	Burke	Martins	241/19	Wilkinson
Boyakin, John Jr.	Screven		23/15	Baldwin
Boyakin, Sarah(Wid.)	Washington	Kendricks	158/8	Wilkinson
Boyakin, William	Washington	Chivers	407/8	Wilkinson
Boyce, Cyrus	Greene	Owsleys	150/9	Baldwin
Boyce, Elsey	Hancock	Wallers	215/9	Baldwin
Boyd, Archibald	Burke	Montgomerys	483/7	Wilkinson
Boyd, Charles Jr.	Chatham	Abrahams	45/16	Wilkinson
Boyd, James	Columbia	3	23/15	Baldwin
Boyd, James	Jefferson	Tarver	43/9	Wilkinson
Boyd, Richard	Clarke	Martindales	151/26	Wilkinson
Boyd, Richard	Clarke	Martindales	210/11	Wilkinson

NAME	COUNTY	MIL.DIST.	LOT/DIST	DREW LAND
Boyd, Robert	Chatham	McLeans	7/9	Wilkinson
Boyd, Robert	Jefferson	Tarver	29/13	Baldwin
Boyd, Seth	Burke	Thompsons	232/19	Wilkinson
Boyd, Seth	Burke	Thompsons	91/8	Wilkinson
Boyd, William Sr.	Jackson	Henderson	385/8	Wilkinson
Boyd, Wm.Jr.	Jackson	Henderson	86/18	Baldwin
Boyd, Wm.Sr.	Jackson	Henderson	97/6	Baldwin
Boyde, John	Washington	Willis	452/7	Wilkinson
Boyle, Peter	Jackson	Henderson	129/9	Baldwin
Boyle, Peter	Jackson	Henderson	192/17	Baldwin
Boynton's, Amos(Orphs.)	Wilkes	Edges	266/13	Wilkinson
Boynton, Amos	Wilkes	Edges	219/21	Wilkinson
Boys, George	Jefferson	Tarver	240/7	Wilkinson
Boyt, Benjamin	Burke	Martins	339/13	Wilkinson
Boyt, James	Burke	Gordons	259/25	Wilkinson
Boyt, John	Burke	Gordons	165/14	Baldwin
Boyt, John	Burke	Gordons	238/15	Wilkinson
Bozeman, Luke	Montgomery	56	77/13	Baldwin
Bozeman, Luke	Montgomery	56	93/24	Wilkinson
Bozeman, Samuel	Wilkinson		268/9	Wilkinson
Brack, Elizabeth	Burke	Spains	258/14	Wilkinson
Brack, William	Burke	Burks	142/18	Wilkinson
Brackenridge, Jas.(Orph.)	Jefferson	Tarver	53/21	Wilkinson
Bradberry, James	Oglethorpe	Hewell	27/12	Baldwin
Braddy, Lewis	Warren	Devereux	131/24	Wilkinson
Braddy, Mary	Warren	Devereux	175/18	Wilkinson
Braden, Isaac	Washington	Chivers	182/19	Wilkinson
Braden, Isaac	Washington	Chivers	236/11	Wilkinson
Bradford, Jane	McIntosh		7/15	Baldwin
Bradford, John Sr.	Wilkes	Sheets	42/27	Wilkinson
Bradford, Richd.Sr.	Oglethorpe	Hitchcocks	213/9	Baldwin
Bradley's, John(Orphs.)	Baldwin	5	117/10	Wilkinson
Bradley, Hesther	Glynn		27/12	Wilkinson
Bradley, John A.	Oglethorpe	Hewells	108/14	Baldwin
Bradley, John	Clarke	Cooks	49/13	Baldwin
Bradshaw's, James(Orphs.)	Oglethorpe	Popes	218/22	Wilkinson
Bradshaw, Peter	Oglethorpe	Hatchetts	133/27	Wilkinson
Bradwell, Thomas	Liberty		259/20	Wilkinson
Brady, Enoch	Franklin	Dixons	178/13	Baldwin
Brady, John	Columbia		236/12	Wilkinson
Brady, Thomas	Wilkinson		22/17	Baldwin
Bragg, Elijah	Bulloch	Denmarks	71/20	Baldwin
Bragg, Wm.S.	Jackson	Henderson	205/14	Baldwin
Bramblet, John	Elbert	Blackwells	222/13	Wilkinson
Bramblett's, Ambrose(Orphs.)	Wilkes	M.Hendersons	67/9	Baldwin
Bramblett, William	Wilkes	M.Hendersons	195/28	Wilkinson
Bramlett, Jesse H.	Wilkes	M.Hendersons	289/17	Wilkinson
Branam's, Robert(Orphs.)	Clarke	Mitchells	164/14	Wilkinson
Brandon, James	Richmond		158/16	Baldwin
Brandon, Judy	Richmond		45/17	Wilkinson
Brannen, Harris	Franklin	Bryants	86/13	Baldwin
Brannen, John	Screven	Williamsons	110/23	Wilkinson
Brannen, Thomas	Screven	Williamsons	92/17	Baldwin
Brannon, John	Screven	Williamsons	222/9	Baldwin
Brannon, William	Screven		124/8	Baldwin
Bransford, James	Clarke	Dukes	105/18	Wilkinson
Bransford, James	Clarke	Dukes	94/13	Wilkinson
Brantley, Benj.Jr.	Hancock	Holts	133/26	Wilkinson
Brantley, Godwin	Hancock	Shivers	158/27	Wilkinson
Brantley, Harris	Hancock	Barnes	112/6	Baldwin
Brantley, James	Bulloch	Hendleys	90/14	Baldwin
Brantley, Malachi	Hancock	Barnes	264/11	Wilkinson
Brantley, Theophilus	Baldwin	1	208/12	Baldwin
Brantley, Thomas	Washington	Kendricks	394/8	Wilkinson
Brantly, Mary	Wayne	1	315/12	Wilkinson
Brasel, Wm.(Orph.)	Elbert	Mobleys	89/18	Wilkinson
Brassel, Nathan	Jefferson	Coleman	78/27	Wilkinson

NAME	COUNTY	MIL.DIST.	LOT/DIST	DREW LAND
Brassel, Sarah(Wid.)	Baldwin	5	168/13	Wilkinson
Braswell, Eliz.(Wid.)	Screven		202/19	Wilkinson
Braswell, Jacob	Clarke	Butlers	46/6	Baldwin
Braswell, Jno.(Orp/Jas.)	Screven		254/10	Wilkinson
Braswell, Kendred Jr.	Montgomery	57	262/20	Baldwin
Braswell, Robt.(S./Kindred)	Montgomery	57	83/20	Baldwin
Braswell, Robt.(S/Kind.Sr.)	Montgomery	57	130/12	Wilkinson
Braswell, Samuel Sr.	Clarke	Butlers	110/19	Baldwin
Braswell, Samuel	Clarke	Silmans	247/6	Wilkinson
Braswell, Samuel	Montgomery	57	262/9	Wilkinson
Braswell, Valentine	Baldwin	1	35/14	Wilkinson
Bray, Peter	Washington	Andersons	30/14	Wilkinson
Bray, Peter	Washington	Andersons	79/22	Wilkinson
Brazeal, Willis	Burke	Spains	330/22	Wilkinson
Brazzel, Benjamin	Franklin	Cornelius	143/13	Baldwin
Brazzel, Frederick	Franklin	McDowells	374/8	Wilkinson
Breed, John	Warren	Hills	291/21	Wilkinson
Breed, William	Warren	Hills	229/19	Baldwin
Breeden's, Richard(Orph.)	Elbert	Roebucks	26/14	Wilkinson
Breedlove, John	Baldwin	2	211/9	Baldwin
Brett, Jesse	Washington	Burneys	19/10	Wilkinson
Brett, John Jr.	Washington	Burneys	281/22	Wilkinson
Brett, John Jr.	Washington	Burneys	287/7	Wilkinson
Brett, John Sr.	Washington	Burneys	88/24	Wilkinson
Brett, Mary	Washington	Burneys	63/6	Wilkinson
Brewer's, Burl(Orphs.)	Oglethorpe	Pope	16/22	Wilkinson
Brewer, Benjamin	Franklin	Cornelius	38/8	Baldwin
Brewer, David	Greene	Jenkins	76/11	Baldwin
Brewer, Elizabeth	Clarke	Harpers	365/21	Wilkinson
Brewer, George Jr.	Hancock	Weeks	159/12	Baldwin
Brewer, Henry	Franklin	Cornelius	198/19	Wilkinson
Brewer, James	Greene	Jenkins	138/13	Wilkinson
Brewer, John	Glynn		108/16	Wilkinson
Brewer, John	Glynn		11/17	Baldwin
Brewer, Joseph	Effingham		240/14	Baldwin
Brewer, Joseph	Effingham		367/21	Wilkinson
Brewer, Nathan	Warren	Heaths	157/12	Wilkinson
Brewer, Polly(S)	Hancock	Weeks	249/8	Wilkinson
Brewer, Simon	Hancock	Weeks	67/24	Wilkinson
Brewer, William	Baldwin	1	102/20	Baldwin
Bridger, Joseph L.	Chatham	Hardens	103/16	Wilkinson
Bridgers, Edney	Washington	Kendricks	209/16	Wilkinson
Bridgers, Silas	Washington	Kendricks	107/19	Wilkinson
Bridges', John(Orphs.)	Hancock	Weeks	22/19	Baldwin
Bridges, Allen I.	Oglethorpe	Hatchetts	55/23	Wilkinson
Bridges, Durrel D.	Oglethorpe	Hitchcocks	28/18	Baldwin
Bridges, John	Jackson	Johnson	335/14	Wilkinson
Bridges, Joseph Jr.	Baldwin	1	89/19	Baldwin
Bridges, Joseph	Baldwin	5	54/9	Wilkinson
Bridges, Nathan Sr.	Baldwin	1	17/18	Baldwin
Bridges, Nathan	Baldwin	1	148/25	Wilkinson
Bridges, Nathaniel	Oglethorpe	Hitchcock	202/16	Baldwin
Bridges, Nathl.	Oglethorpe	Hitchcock	32/10	Baldwin
Bridges, Solomon	Oglethorpe	Jno.Smith	16/18	Baldwin
Bridges, Thomas	Oglethorpe	Hitchcocks	31/18	Baldwin
Briggs, James	Montgomery	57	127/28	Wilkinson
Brinkley, John	Baldwin	3	265/24	Wilkinson
Brinson's, Isaac(Orphs.)	Burke	Martins	319/9	Wilkinson
Brinson, Daniel	Tattnall	Halls	209/10	Baldwin
Brinson, Isaac	Screven		80/18	Wilkinson
Brinson, Moses	Jefferson	Bostick	153/13	Wilkinson
Brinson, Stephen	Burke	Martins	299/15	Wilkinson
Briscoe's, Trueman(Orphs.)	Columbia	11	58/13	Wilkinson
Briscoe, John	Richmond		204/18	Wilkinson
Brison, Sipean	Burke	Martins	278/22	Wilkinson
Britton, Berry	Oglethorpe	Hatchetts	39/19	Wilkinson
Britton, Burwell	Oglethorpe	Pope	172/6	Baldwin

NAME	COUNTY	MIL.DIST.	LOT/DIST	DREW LAND
Britton, George Sr.	Oglethorpe	Hatchetts	2/18	Wilkinson
Britton, John	Chatham	Neyles	70/6	Baldwin
Britton, Stephen	Effingham		301/10	Wilkinson
Brixey, Thomas	Clarke	Martins	226/7	Wilkinson
Broach, George	Greene	Butlers	235/19	Baldwin
Broadnax, John T.	Hancock	Hudsons	157/17	Wilkinson
Broadnax, William	Hancock	Huffs	56/12	Wilkinson
Brock, James Sr.	Franklin	Henrys	175/12	Wilkinson
Brock, John Jr.	Montgomery	52	246/15	Wilkinson
Brockington, Danl.Sr.	Camden	Johnsons	229/14	Baldwin
Brockington, Danl.Sr.	Camden	Johnsons	266/20	Wilkinson
Brockman, Bledsoe	Oglethorpe	Pope	170/13	Baldwin
Brook, Henry	Greene	Watsons	197/27	Wilkinson
Brooker, John	Glynn		181/26	Wilkinson
Brooker, John	Glynn		191/10	Baldwin
Brooker, William	Glynn		265/8	Wilkinson
Brookins, Theophilus	Tattnall	Halls	217/7	Wilkinson
Brookins, Theophilus	Tattnall	Halls	262/13	Wilkinson
Brookins, Thomas	Washington	Kendricks	203/26	Wilkinson
Brookins, Treasa	Burke	Martins	21/18	Baldwin
Brooks, Ann	Franklin	Christians	270/15	Wilkinson
Brooks, Bailey C.	Franklin	Christians	223/13	Baldwin
Brooks, Bailey C.	Franklin	Christians	265/13	Wilkinson
Brooks, Balaam	Warren	Newsoms	222/14	Wilkinson
Brooks, Charles	Warren	Flournoys	163/24	Wilkinson
Brooks, Charles	Warren	Flournoys	55/13	Wilkinson
Brooks, James	Oglethorpe	Pope	180/20	Wilkinson
Brooks, James	Oglethorpe	Popes	175/6	Baldwin
Brooks, James	Warren	Newsoms	167/16	Wilkinson
Brooks, Joab	Warren	Neals	293/12	Wilkinson
Brooks, John Jr.	Warren	Newsoms	47/13	Wilkinson
Brooks, John	Baldwin	5	11/19	Baldwin
Brooks, John	Jackson	Wright	159/25	Wilkinson
Brooks, Littleberry	Jackson	Johnson	215/22	Wilkinson
Brooks, Peter Sr.	Jackson	Johnson	297/11	Wilkinson
Brooks, Peter Sr.	Jackson	Johnson	44/26	Wilkinson
Brooks, Thomas	Franklin	Christians	104/9	Wilkinson
Brooks, William	Greene	Jenkins	19/6	Wilkinson
Brooks, Wm.(S/Peter)	Wilkes	Milners	189/23	Wilkinson
Broom, Martha(Wid.)	Warren	Jones	252/12	Wilkinson
Brothers', John(Orphs.)	Warren	Heaths	111/11	Wilkinson
Brothers', John(Orphs.)	Warren	Heaths	359/12	Wilkinson
Broughton, Belitha Sr.	Hancock	Wallers	105/11	Wilkinson
Broughton, Charles	Hancock	Wallers	84/13	Wilkinson
Broughton, Jno.H.	Liberty		111/9	Baldwin
Broughton, John H.	Liberty		67/18	Baldwin
Broughton, John	Wilkinson		78/20	Baldwin
Broughton, Ruth	Hancock	Wallers	33/18	Wilkinson
Brown's, Isaac(Orphs.)	Wilkinson		279/22	Wilkinson
Brown's, Jeremiah(Orphs.)	Greene	Watsons	256/15	Wilkinson
Brown's, John(Orphs.)	Elbert	Keelings	71/16	Wilkinson
Brown's, Robert(Orphs.)	Elbert	Keelings	117/20	Wilkinson
Brown, Alice	Burke	Gordons	192/26	Wilkinson
Brown, Andrew	Elbert	McGuires	169/16	Baldwin
Brown, Andrew	McIntosh		329/20	Baldwin
Brown, Augustin Sr.	Franklin	Hollingsworths	85/19	Wilkinson
Brown, Benjamin	Elbert	Blackwells	132/23	Wilkinson
Brown, Benjamin	Montgomery	51	150/13	Baldwin
Brown, Burrell	Greene	Armors	205/10	Wilkinson
Brown, Daniel	Elbert	Barretts	100/10	Baldwin
Brown, Daniel	Elbert	Dyes	150/24	Wilkinson
Brown, Daniel	Hancock	Thomas	386/21	Wilkinson
Brown, Delila	Wayne	1	47/11	Wilkinson
Brown, Dempsey	Washington	Chivers	62/12	Baldwin
Brown, Elisha	Columbia	10	401/7	Wilkinson
Brown, Elisha	Hancock	Winsletts	163/7	Wilkinson
Brown, Elizabeth(S)	Hancock	Smith	51/10	Wilkinson

NAME	COUNTY	MIL.DIST.	LOT/DIST	DREW LAND
Brown, Elizabeth	Columbia	4	276/15	Wilkinson
Brown, Elizabeth	Lincoln	Kennon	201/11	Wilkinson
Brown, Epps	Hancock	Barnes	218/25	Wilkinson
Brown, Ezekiel	Greene	Owsleys	224/22	Wilkinson
Brown, Frederick	Columbia	9	91/7	Baldwin
Brown, Geo.R.	Jefferson	Coleman	124/9	Wilkinson
Brown, James B.	Burke	Carswells	214/6	Wilkinson
Brown, James N.	Elbert	Blackwells	169/12	Baldwin
Brown, James Sr.	Elbert	McGuires	24/16	Wilkinson
Brown, James	Clarke	Silmans	308/9	Wilkinson
Brown, Jesse	Jefferson	Thomas	5/26	Wilkinson
Brown, John Sr.	Franklin	Bryants	47/10	Baldwin
Brown, John Turner	Screven		26/28	Wilkinson
Brown, John(Son/Moses)	Hancock	Pinkston	50/12	Baldwin
Brown, John	Jackson	Cockran	50/15	Wilkinson
Brown, John	Washington	Garretts	165/20	Wilkinson
Brown, Lewis	Hancock	Smiths	119/10	Wilkinson
Brown, Meredeth	Franklin	Bryants	161/6	Baldwin
Brown, Meredith	Wilkes	Normans	162/15	Wilkinson
Brown, Morgan	Elbert	Keelings	109/15	Baldwin
Brown, Moses	Hancock	Pinkston	128/23	Wilkinson
Brown, Nancy(Dau/Wm.)	Jefferson	Hardwick	139/6	Baldwin
Brown, Nancy	Columbia	4	246/16	Wilkinson
Brown, Nathaniel	Franklin	Griffiths	58/15	Wilkinson
Brown, Polly(S)	Hancock	Candlers	124/28	Wilkinson
Brown, Polly	Oglethorpe	Beasleys	130/18	Wilkinson
Brown, Richard G.	Washington	Holts	109/9	Baldwin
Brown, Samuel	Columbia	10	81/14	Wilkinson
Brown, Samuel	Columbia	10	87/19	Baldwin
Brown, Sarah	Bulloch	Godfreys	313/21	Wilkinson
Brown, Sarah	Wayne	1	33/7	Baldwin
Brown, Stephen	Franklin	Wims	24/14	Wilkinson
Brown, Thomas Sr.	Wilkes	Stovalls	48/11	Baldwin
Brown, Thomas	Chatham	Pembertons	201/15	Wilkinson
Brown, Thos.R.	Oglethorpe	Beasleys	283/20	Baldwin
Brown, William	Baldwin	4	285/15	Baldwin
Brown, William	Bulloch	Denmarks	161/17	Wilkinson
Brown, William	Franklin	Dixons	115/8	Wilkinson
Brown, William	Hancock	Barnes	50/25	Wilkinson
Brown, William	Hancock	Candlers	38/18	Wilkinson
Brown, William	Hancock	Crowders	323/12	Wilkinson
Brown, William	Oglethorpe	Hatchetts	75/8	Wilkinson
Brown, Wilson	Hancock	Candlers	202/8	Wilkinson
Brown,..(Orphs.)	Jackson	Cockran	222/23	Wilkinson
Browning, Andrew	Wilkes	Heards	286/14	Wilkinson
Browning, George Jr.	Tattnall	Halls	215/13	Wilkinson
Browning, Joshua Sr.	Clarke	Robinsons	124/14	Baldwin
Browning, William	Baldwin	5	137/18	Wilkinson
Browning, Wm(Esq.)	Greene	Watts	92/10	Baldwin
Brownjohn, Samuel	Chatham	Herbs	205/13	Baldwin
Bruce's, Daniel(Orphs.)	Wilkes	I.Hendersons	240/22	Wilkinson
Bruce, George	Jackson	Johnson	124/10	Wilkinson
Brumbley, Wm.	Washington	Burneys	49/25	Wilkinson
Brumfield, James	Baldwin	1	330/9	Wilkinson
Brux, William	Richmond		54/10	Wilkinson
Bryan, Elizabeth	Chatham	Pettybones	232/17	Wilkinson
Bryan, Elizabeth	Liberty		119/16	Wilkinson
Bryan, Isaac	Hancock	Wallers	104/18	Wilkinson
Bryan, James	Chatham	Hardens	116/18	Wilkinson
Bryan, James	Chatham	Hardens	459/7	Wilkinson
Bryan, John H.	Tattnall	Sherrards	31/17	Baldwin
Bryan, John Jr.	Jefferson	Fulton	300/20	Baldwin
Bryan, John Jr.	Screven	Williamsons	295/10	Wilkinson
Bryan, John	Hancock	Crowder	134/15	Wilkinson
Bryan, Joseph	Chatham	Herbs	176/18	Wilkinson
Bryan, Joseph	Hancock	Wallers	17/8	Baldwin
Bryan, Temperance	Wayne	1	195/19	Baldwin

NAME	COUNTY	MIL.DIST.	LOT/DIST	DREW LAND
Bryan, Thomas	Franklin	Bryants	174/20	Wilkinson
Bryan, Zachariah	Franklin	Bryants	234/12	Wilkinson
Bryant, Benjamin	Jefferson	Hardwick	386/22	Wilkinson
Bryant, Daniel	Screven		159/15	Wilkinson
Bryant, Edward	Franklin	Griffiths	238/21	Wilkinson
Bryant, James	Greene	Butlers	16/7	Wilkinson
Bryant, James	Oglethorpe	Popes	36/12	Wilkinson
Bryant, James	Screven	Hutchinsons	358/13	Wilkinson
Bryant, Jane	Columbia	7	131/15	Wilkinson
Bryant, Jesse	Wilkes	Youngs	350/22	Wilkinson
Bryant, John	Hancock	Thomas	114/19	Wilkinson
Bryant, John	Oglethorpe	Stewarts	77/12	Wilkinson
Bryant, Langley	Camden	Crews	217/10	Wilkinson
Bryant, Mary(Wid.)	Glynn		197/19	Baldwin
Bryant, Moses	Burke	Fields	95/13	Wilkinson
Bryant, Pleasant	Jackson	Henderson	67/23	Wilkinson
Bryant, Rebecca	Oglethorpe	Popes	278/13	Wilkinson
Bryant, Samuel(Orph.)	Jackson	Johnson	294/9	Wilkinson
Bryant, Thomas	Richmond		23/17	Baldwin
Bryant, Thomas	Richmond		254/14	Wilkinson
Bryant, William	Baldwin	1	9/12	Baldwin
Bryant, William	Columbia	1	242/9	Baldwin
Buckhannon, John D.	Greene	Jenkins	303/10	Wilkinson
Buckhannon, Robert	Baldwin	1	210/9	Wilkinson
Buckhanon, James	Washington	Andersons	313/17	Wilkinson
Buckley, Butler	Burke	Burks	99/8	Wilkinson
Buckner, Charles	Hancock	Shiver	125/25	Wilkinson
Buckner, David	Franklin	Cornelius	233/10	Wilkinson
Buckner, David	Franklin	Cornelius	32/20	Baldwin
Bugg's, Shar'd(Orphs.)	Screven	Hutchinsons	274/15	Baldwin
Bugg, Dorcas	Columbia	1	156/9	Wilkinson
Bugg, Edmund	Columbia	8	2/6	Baldwin
Bugg, Edward(Orph.)	Richmond		354/24	Wilkinson
Bugg, Obedience(Heirs)	Richmond		7/26	Wilkinson
Bugg, Peter(Orph.)	Richmond		354/24	Wilkinson
Bugg, Samuel(Orph.)	Richmond		354/24	Wilkinson
Bugg, Susannah(Orph.)	Richmond		354/24	Wilkinson
Bugg, Thos.Jeff.(Orph.)	Richmond		354/24	Wilkinson
Buie, Jno.H.	Tattnall	Halls	271/12	Wilkinson
Buis, John	Hancock	Gumm	56/23	Wilkinson
Bullard, Allen	Elbert	Morrisons	191/24	Wilkinson
Bullard, Thomas	Elbert	Morrisons	232/9	Wilkinson
Bullard, William	Greene	Moores	152/11	Wilkinson
Bulloch, Batson	Hancock	Barnes	164/16	Baldwin
Bulloch, Charles	Hancock	Barnes	30/7	Baldwin
Bulloch, Dinah(Wid.)	Bryan	Birds	51/10	Baldwin
Bulloch, Ephraim	Jefferson		39/27	Wilkinson
Bulloch, Hawkins	Oglethorpe	Moores	130/20	Wilkinson
Bulloch, Mary(Wid.)	Chatham	Pembertons	99/17	Wilkinson
Bulloch, Polly(Dau/Richd.)	Columbia	6	254/22	Wilkinson
Bulloch, Wyatt	Oglethorpe	Moore	61/9	Baldwin
Bulman, Thomas	Columbia	2	113/19	Wilkinson
Bunch, Hill	Richmond		10/10	Wilkinson
Bunkley, Britton	Camden	Hardys	170/8	Baldwin
Bunkley, Britton	Camden	Hardys	334/21	Wilkinson
Bunkley, Wm.D.	Warren	Neals	73/11	Wilkinson
Buntz, Semon(Orph.)	Effingham		37/11	Baldwin
Bunyard, Ephraim	Clarke	Martins	197/7	Wilkinson
Bunyer, John(Heirs)	Chatham	Abrahams	43/9	Baldwin
Bunyer, John	Chatham	Abrahams	43/9	Baldwin
Burch, Charles Jr.	Richmond		373/8	Wilkinson
Burch, Charles	Montgomery	51	248/10	Wilkinson
Burch, John Jr.	Hancock	Crowder	346/9	Wilkinson
Burch, John	Richmond		234/13	Wilkinson
Burch, Joseph	Montgomery	51	69/11	Baldwin
Burden, Archibald	Elbert	Olivers	200/7	Wilkinson
Burden, Hannah(Wid.)	Elbert	Olivers	264/21	Wilkinson

NAME	COUNTY	MIL.DIST.	LOT/DIST	DREW LAND
Burden, Henry	Jackson	Henderson	97/8	Baldwin
Burden, James	Elbert	Olivers	37/12	Baldwin
Burditt, James	Wilkes	Coopers	248/24	Wilkinson
Burdwell, Moses	Franklin	Bryants	147/10	Baldwin
Burford, Daniel	Greene	Carltons	83/11	Baldwin
Burford, Leonard	Clarke	Martindales	68/14	Wilkinson
Burford, William	Greene	Reas	223/24	Wilkinson
Burgan, Martha C.(Orph.)	Burke	Sharps	419/8	Wilkinson
Burge, Frances(Wid.)	Warren	Carters	141/25	Wilkinson
Burge, Willie	Hancock	Weeks	231/19	Wilkinson
Burgeron, Abi	Burke	Mulkeys	78/28	Wilkinson
Burgess', Bry't(Orphs.)	Screven	Hutchinsons	39/16	Wilkinson
Burgess, James	Franklin	Hoopers	159/15	Baldwin
Burgess, James	Franklin	Hoopers	5/14	Baldwin
Burgess, John	Franklin	Hoopers	74/8	Baldwin
Burgess, Joseph	Hancock	Cooper	16/9	Baldwin
Burgess, Richard	Greene	Butlers	205/20	Wilkinson
Burgsteiner, Samuel	Effingham		153/16	Wilkinson
Burk, Charles Sr.	Greene	Flournoys	32/11	Baldwin
Burk, John	Burke	Martins	48/26	Wilkinson
Burk, Nimrod	Washington	Willis	141/6	Baldwin
Burk, Thomas Sr.	Burke	Burks	78/7	Baldwin
Burke, Edward	Richmond		262/23	Wilkinson
Burke, Edward	Richmond		275/25	Wilkinson
Burke, Nancy	Greene	Flournoys	112/14	Wilkinson
Burkhalter, Jno.Jr.	Warren	Neals	198/22	Wilkinson
Burkhalter, John Sr.	Warren	Neals	27/20	Wilkinson
Burkhalter, John Sr.	Warren	Neals	359/24	Wilkinson
Burkhalter, Joshua	Chatham	Neyles	117/9	Wilkinson
Burkhalter, Michael	Warren	Neals	108/22	Wilkinson
Burks, Elisha	Oglethorpe	Smiths	10/13	Wilkinson
Burks, Elisha	Oglethorpe	Smiths	464/7	Wilkinson
Burks, John H.	Lincoln	Kennon	125/17	Wilkinson
Burks, Joseph	Wilkes	Normans	68/20	Baldwin
Burks, Nancy	Clarke	Mitchells	305/17	Wilkinson
Burks, Wm.Sr.	Oglethorpe	Smiths	71/16	Baldwin
Burlison, Aaron	Baldwin	4	190/16	Baldwin
Burlison, Aaron	Screven	Hutchinsons	41/7	Wilkinson
Burlison, Jesse	Screven	Williamsons	38/12	Baldwin
Burlong, Henry	Wilkes	Roreys	46/20	Baldwin
Burnell, Anthony Jr.	Burke	Thompsons	4/17	Baldwin
Burnes, Isaac	Greene	Alfords	87/8	Wilkinson
Burnes, James	Clarke	Mitchells	1/19	Wilkinson
Burnes, Joseph	Washington	Blackshears	209/14	Baldwin
Burnes, Joseph	Washington	Blackshears	330/20	Baldwin
Burnett, John	Bulloch	Williams	164/15	Baldwin
Burnett, John	Glynn		152/15	Wilkinson
Burnett, Mary	Bulloch	Williams	201/24	Wilkinson
Burnett, Robert	Camden	Ashleys	45/13	Wilkinson
Burney's, John(Orphs.)	Bryan	Birds	190/18	Baldwin
Burney's, Richard(Orphs.)	Baldwin	2	117/17	Baldwin
Burney, Arthur	Wilkinson		61/9	Wilkinson
Burney, Betsy(Wid.)	Washington	Burneys	12/19	Baldwin
Burney, Willis	Washington	Burneys	10/6	Wilkinson
Burnsides, Thomas	Baldwin	2	219/13	Wilkinson
Burrougs, Bennett	Columbia	1	40/21	Wilkinson
Burson, Jesse	Baldwin	1	139/23	Wilkinson
Burson, Joseph	Jackson	Wright	119/14	Baldwin
Burt, Christopher	Tattnall	McDonalds	206/28	Wilkinson
Burt, John Jr.	Franklin	Bryants	141/21	Wilkinson
Burt, John	Baldwin	2	333/13	Wilkinson
Burt, John	Tattnall	McDonalds	368/22	Wilkinson
Burt, John	Tattnall	McDonalds	99/14	Baldwin
Burt, William	Franklin	Bryants	182/7	Wilkinson
Burt, William	Franklin	Bryants	21/25	Wilkinson
Burton, Abraham Jr.	Elbert	Morrisons	45/14	Baldwin
Burton, Abraham Sr.	Elbert	Thompsons	245/11	Wilkinson

NAME	COUNTY	MIL.DIST.	LOT/DIST	DREW LAND
Burton, Archer	Elbert	Morrisons	118/15	Wilkinson
Burton, Elizabeth	Lincoln	Kennon	82/16	Baldwin
Burton, Jacob	Franklin	Cleghorns	56/6	Baldwin
Burton, John	Burke	Gordons	18/23	Wilkinson
Burton, John	Burke	Gordons	38/6	Wilkinson
Burton, Patsy W.	Franklin	Christians	14/14	Baldwin
Burton, Robert	Effingham		216/10	Baldwin
Burton, Thomas Sr.	Elbert	Thompsons	190/21	Wilkinson
Buse, John	Clarke	Hopkins	214/16	Wilkinson
Buse, John	Clarke	Hopkins	356/9	Wilkinson
Bush's, John(Orphs.)	Wilkes	Youngs	202/17	Wilkinson
Bush, Abram(Old Man)	Jefferson	Hardwick	182/9	Baldwin
Bush, James Jr.	Wilkinson		236/19	Wilkinson
Bush, James Jr.	Wilkinson		284/13	Wilkinson
Bush, John Sr.	Montgomery	50	253/22	Wilkinson
Bush, John	Greene	Alfords	8/16	Wilkinson
Bush, Sanders(Son/Abram)	Jefferson	Hardwick	138/21	Wilkinson
Bush, Thomas	Warren	Bakers	26/21	Wilkinson
Bussy's, Hezekiah(Orphs.)	Lincoln	Bussey	87/24	Wilkinson
Bussy, Benjamin	Lincoln	Bussey	121/18	Wilkinson
Butler's, Edmund(Orphs.)	Hancock	Coopers	41/14	Baldwin
Butler's, John(Orphs.)	Hancock	Wallers	197/18	Wilkinson
Butler, Aaron	Clarke	Butlers	87/20	Baldwin
Butler, Daniel	Warren	Newsoms	14	Baldwin
Butler, James Sr.	Jackson	Cockran	62/26	Wilkinson
Butler, James	Baldwin	2	142/14	Baldwin
Butler, James	Franklin	Henrys	45/18	Baldwin
Butler, Joel	Elbert	Dyes	81/8	Baldwin
Butler, Robert	Baldwin	1	108/11	Baldwin
Butler, Shem	Liberty		129/8	Baldwin
Butler, William	Hancock	Waller	196/10	Baldwin
Butler, William	Hancock	Wallers	141/17	Baldwin
Butler, William	Richmond		29/12	Baldwin
Butler, Zachariah Jr.	Elbert	Morrisons	113/20	Wilkinson
Butler, Zachariah Jr.	Elbert	Morrisons	230/15	Wilkinson
Butt, Henry	Greene	Butlers	74/19	Baldwin
Butt, Jeremiah	Warren	Neals	76/20	Wilkinson
Butt, John	Warren	Neals	199/15	Baldwin
Butt, Noah	Warren	Hills	142/16	Baldwin
Butt, Noah	Warren	Hills	17/12	Baldwin
Butts, Clement	Hancock	Weeks	69/19	Wilkinson
Butts, James Sr.	Hancock	Weeks	115/20	Wilkinson
Butts, Karen(W)	Hancock	Smiths	209/9	Wilkinson
Byne's, Edmd.(Orphs.)	Burke	Bynes	136/25	Wilkinson
Byne's, Edmd.(Orphs.)	Burke	Bynes	180/10	Baldwin
Byne, Thomas	Burke	Carswells	180/17	Wilkinson
Byne, Thomas	Burke	Carswells	31/24	Wilkinson
Bynum's, Arthur(Orphs.)	Hancock	Shivers	15/7	Wilkinson
Bynum, Reubin	Hancock	Shiver	12/20	Baldwin
Byrom, Wm.Sr.(Esq.)	Warren	Carters	139/11	Baldwin
Byrom, Wm.Sr.(Esq.)	Warren	Carters	169/13	Baldwin
Cabiness, Geo.Sr.	Greene	Watsons	88/8	Wilkinson
Cabiness, George Jr.	Greene	Watsons	77/18	Wilkinson
Cabiness, Henry B.	Greene	Watsons	11/14	Wilkinson
Cabiness, Henry B.	Greene	Watsons	308/15	Baldwin
Cade, James	Wilkes	Sheets	267/6	Wilkinson
Cadenhead, James Jr.	Hancock	Smiths	167/12	Wilkinson
Caen, John	Franklin	Hoopers	110/17	Wilkinson
Caen, Polly Tucker	Franklin	Hoopers	131/13	Wilkinson
Cagle, George	Clarke	Robinsons	88/23	Wilkinson
Cahill, William	Chatham	Neyles	49/27	Wilkinson
Cain, Mauris	Wilkes	Parks	94/27	Wilkinson
Cain, Nathaniel	Washington	Wiggins	1/7	Wilkinson
Cain, Patrick	Jackson	Wrights	359/10	Wilkinson
Cain, Wm.T.	Baldwin	1	303/14	Wilkinson
Calder, Christian	McIntosh		172/12	Wilkinson
Caldwell, Eliz.(Dau/Jno.)	Columbia	2	222/10	Wilkinson

NAME	COUNTY	MIL.DIST.	LOT/DIST	DREW LAND
Caldwell, John	Columbia	2	233/23	Wilkinson
Caldwell, John	Columbia	2	34/19	Baldwin
Caldwell, John	Greene	Loves	182/12	Baldwin
Caldwell, William	Screven		30/13	Baldwin
Caldwell, Wm.Sr.	Greene	Carletons	107/11	Baldwin
Calhoon, Eliz.(Single)	Jefferson	Colemans	346/7	Wilkinson
Calhoon, Ephraim	Greene	Alfords	50/13	Baldwin
Calhoon, Irwin	Washington	Renfroes	168/16	Wilkinson
Calhoon, John	Screven		15/8	Baldwin
Calhoon, Mary	Screven		306/12	Wilkinson
Calhoon, Micah	Jefferson		115/6	Wilkinson
Calhoon, Micah	Jefferson		79/26	Wilkinson
Calhoon, Patience	Hancock	Birdsongs	58/11	Baldwin
Calhoon, Rachel	Richmond		99/20	Baldwin
Calhoon, Samuel	Jefferson	Colemans	12/28	Wilkinson
Calhoon, Samuel	Jefferson	Colemans	95/9	Baldwin
Calk, Elijah	Wayne	2	61/17	Baldwin
Callahan, Joshua	Jackson	Johnsons	168/13	Baldwin
Callaway, Ebenezer	Hancock	Barnes	9/18	Baldwin
Callaway, Edw'd.(Son/Joshua)	Wilkes	M.Hendersons	108/19	Wilkinson
Callaway, Jos.(Son/Job)	Wilkes	Heards	162/21	Wilkinson
Callaway, Jos.(Son/Job)	Wilkes	Heards	3/15	Baldwin
Callaway, Joshua(Son/Job)	Wilkes	Heards	195/16	Baldwin
Callaway, Joshua	Jackson	Wrights	122/17	Baldwin
Callaway, Peter	Clarke	Cooks	159/21	Wilkinson
Callaway, Thomas	Hancock	Candlers	264/20	Baldwin
Callaway, Wm.W.	Hancock	Shivers	178/8	Wilkinson
Calliway, William	Franklin	Hoopers	299/12	Wilkinson
Calwell, James	Clarke	Silmans	93/20	Wilkinson
Cammeran, Dicey	Wayne	2	61/15	Wilkinson
Camp, Abner	Jackson	Cockrans	37/13	Wilkinson
Camp, Benj.Jr.	Jackson	Cockrans	151/12	Wilkinson
Camp, Cecelius	Clarke	Browns	352/24	Wilkinson
Camp, Cloudiusly	Warren	Flournoys	279/20	Baldwin
Camp, Hosea Sr.	Jackson	Cockrans	74/11	Baldwin
Camp, John Jr.	Jackson	Cockrans	89/8	Baldwin
Camp, Nathan	Jackson	Wrights	166/24	Wilkinson
Camp, Nathan	Jackson	Wrights	4/12	Baldwin
Camp, Sherwood	Jackson	Cockrans	154/15	Wilkinson
Campbell, Alexander	Columbia	3	326/24	Wilkinson
Campbell, Archibald	McIntosh		93/14	Baldwin
Campbell, Charles	Jackson	Johnsons	390/7	Wilkinson
Campbell, Duncan	Jackson	Cockrans	170/19	Baldwin
Campbell, Jacob	Camden	Hardys	117/15	Wilkinson
Campbell, Jarrett	Jackson	Hendersons	11/14	Baldwin
Campbell, Joseph	Columbia	3	83/14	Baldwin
Campbell, Martin	Warren	Flournoys	234/14	Baldwin
Campbell, Moses	Greene	Stewarts	158/19	Wilkinson
Campbell, Thomas	Baldwin	4	283/19	Baldwin
Canafax, Benjamin	Greene	Owsleys	272/22	Wilkinson
Canafax, Benjamin	Greene	Owsleys	75/28	Wilkinson
Candler, Henry	Warren	Flournoys	251/14	Baldwin
Cannon, Burrell	Wilkes	I.Hendersons	45/25	Wilkinson
Cannon, Elizabeth	Richmond		348/7	Wilkinson
Cannon, Henry	McIntosh		218/14	Wilkinson
Cannon, Rachel(Wid.)	Burke	Hilliards	252/7	Wilkinson
Cannon, Samuel	Washington	Holts	258/12	Wilkinson
Cannon, Samuel	Washington	Holts	266/11	Wilkinson
Cannon, William	Jefferson		25/17	Wilkinson
Cannon, Wylie	Washington	Howards	79/6	Baldwin
Cantelow, Lewis Sr.	Richmond		28/17	Baldwin
Canter, Richard	Washington	Garretts	83/12	Wilkinson
Canterberry, Jeremiah	Oglethorpe	Hewells	249/15	Baldwin
Capp, Reuhmy	Oglethorpe	Stewarts	30/9	Wilkinson
Cardell's, Cornelius(Orphs.)	Warren	Willsons	47/19	Baldwin
Carden, John	Clarke	Tramells	103/19	Wilkinson
Carden, Robert	Clarke	Tramells	208/22	Wilkinson

NAME	COUNTY	MIL.DIST.	LOT/DIST	DREW LAND
Carey, John	Tattnall	Armstrongs	243/19	Wilkinson
Cargile, Charles	Greene	Flournoys	35/11	Wilkinson
Carleton, Stephen	Wilkes	Sheets	138/22	Wilkinson
Carlisle's, John(Orphs.)	Baldwin	5	88/10	Wilkinson
Carlisle, Edmund	Baldwin	4	27/19	Baldwin
Carlisle, Edmund	Baldwin	4	89/28	Wilkinson
Carlisle, Edward	Lincoln	Flemings	106/17	Wilkinson
Carlisle, Hosea	Jackson	Wrights	56/28	Wilkinson
Carlisle, Mason	Washington	Paces	30/7	Wilkinson
Carlisle, Micajah	Washington	Paces	321/8	Wilkinson
Carlton, Martha	Greene	Carletons	118/16	Baldwin
Carlton, Theodore	Chatham	Pettybones	9/28	Wilkinson
Carlton, Thomas Sr.	Greene	Carletons	251/21	Wilkinson
Carmon, William	Clarke	Stewarts	99/19	Baldwin
Carnals, William	Wayne	1	167/12	Baldwin
Carnes, Patrick(Orph.)	Richmond		19/7	Baldwin
Carnes, Richard	Franklin	Conners	278/10	Wilkinson
Carney, Elijah	Camden	Hardys	77/27	Wilkinson
Carothers, Wm.Jr.	Franklin	Dixons	130/22	Wilkinson
Carpenter, Bailey	Burke	Burks	405/7	Wilkinson
Carpenter, Harriett(Orph.)	Chatham	Pettybones	169/25	Wilkinson
Carpenter, Thomas	Warren	Jones	59/10	Baldwin
Carr, Archibald	Bulloch	Williams	307/14	Wilkinson
Carr, Henry	Baldwin	2	187/17	Wilkinson
Carr, Joseph Sr.	Hancock	Smiths	7/19	Baldwin
Carr, Robert	Wilkes	I.Hendersons	92/6	Baldwin
Carr, William	Bulloch	Williams	34/27	Wilkinson
Carragan, John	Jackson	Hendersons	121/10	Wilkinson
Carrell's, John(Orphs.)	Columbia	6	46/16	Baldwin
Carrell, Benjamin	Greene	Armors	177/16	Wilkinson
Carrell, Edward	Franklin	Cornelius	137/27	Wilkinson
Carrell, James	Columbia	6	173/21	Wilkinson
Carrell, Jesse	Oglethorpe	Bells	84/10	Baldwin
Carrell, John	Baldwin	4	329/24	Wilkinson
Carrell, John	Elbert	Clarks	152/8	Baldwin
Carrell, Margarett	Franklin	McDowells	344/9	Wilkinson
Carrell, Nancy	Bulloch	Williams	115/27	Wilkinson
Carrington, Henson	Elbert	Groves	249/9	Wilkinson
Carroll, David	Greene	Loves	134/14	Baldwin
Carroll, David	Greene	Loves	215/13	Baldwin
Carroll, Sterling	Greene	Loves	21/12	Wilkinson
Carroll, Thomas	Jackson	Cockrans	383/9	Wilkinson
Carswell, Alexander	Burke	Carswells	243/15	Baldwin
Carter's, Kindred(Orphs.)	Warren	Neals	286/12	Wilkinson
Carter's, Kindred(Orphs.)	Warren	Neals	86/19	Wilkinson
Carter, Allen	Warren	Willsons	59/7	Wilkinson
Carter, Cader	Greene	Alfords	57/28	Wilkinson
Carter, Charles	Burke	Ballards	132/19	Wilkinson
Carter, Charles	Elbert	Olivers	282/21	Wilkinson
Carter, Edward	Oglethorpe	Hartsfields	232/26	Wilkinson
Carter, Farish	Baldwin	1	274/23	Wilkinson
Carter, Giles Sr.	Montgomery	56	100/18	Baldwin
Carter, James	Baldwin	1	2/14	Baldwin
Carter, James	Baldwin	1	285/24	Wilkinson
Carter, James	Elbert	Blackwells	300/15	Wilkinson
Carter, James	Warren	Willsons	103/24	Wilkinson
Carter, Jesse	Oglethorpe	Hartsfields	190/11	Wilkinson
Carter, Joel	Lincoln	Kennons	200/14	Wilkinson
Carter, Joel	Lincoln	Kennons	8/10	Wilkinson
Carter, John	Wilkes	Normans	97/13	Baldwin
Carter, Joseph	Greene	Carletons	204/19	Wilkinson
Carter, Joseph	Warren	Carters	194/24	Wilkinson
Carter, Josiah	Warren	Carters	293/7	Wilkinson
Carter, Kilpatrick	Wilkes	Renders	52/9	Wilkinson
Carter, Littleton	Hancock	Wallers	1/13	Baldwin
Carter, Mary(Wid.)	Hancock	Pinkstons	73/22	Wilkinson
Carter, Mathew Jr.	Bulloch	Denmarks	168/25	Wilkinson

NAME	COUNTY	MIL.DIST.	LOT/DIST	DREW LAND
Carter, Mathew	Montgomery	54	27/10	Baldwin
Carter, Moses	Montgomery	59	159/8	Wilkinson
Carter, Rachel (Miss)	Warren	Carters	51/13	Baldwin
Carter, Rachel	Franklin	Thompsons	101/16	Baldwin
Carter, Robert	Montgomery	56	168/10	Baldwin
Carter, Ruth	Baldwin	2	89/10	Baldwin
Carter, Samuel	Montgomery		49/12	Baldwin
Carter, Samuel	Wilkinson		45/15	Wilkinson
Carter, Samuel	Wilkinson		97/18	Wilkinson
Carter, Sarah	Elbert	Barretts	31/9	Baldwin
Carter, Secutary	Oglethorpe	Hartsfields	123/7	Baldwin
Carter, Thomas	Baldwin	2	186/25	Wilkinson
Carter, Thomas	Elbert	Olivers	38/11	Baldwin
Carter, Thomas	Franklin	Cornelius	94/9	Wilkinson
Carter, Thomas	Franklin	Thompsons	188/11	Wilkinson
Carter, Thomas	Oglethorpe	Hartsfields	72/13	Baldwin
Carter, Thomas	Warren	Carters	183/16	Baldwin
Carter, William	Baldwin	1	115/18	Baldwin
Carter, William	Bulloch	Denmarks	300/17	Wilkinson
Carter, William	Jackson	Cockrans	151/11	Baldwin
Cartledge's, John (Orphs.)	Columbia	3	58/26	Wilkinson
Cartledge's, Jos. (Orphs.)	Columbia	4	348/9	Wilkinson
Cartledge, Ayres	Columbia	4	133/25	Wilkinson
Cartright, Hezekiah	Greene	Greers	140/26	Wilkinson
Cartright, Hezekiah	Greene	Greers	219/20	Baldwin
Cartright, Peter	Greene	Dawsons	26/15	Baldwin
Cartright, Thomas	Greene	Carletons	110/8	Baldwin
Cartwright, Jonas	Greene	Dawsons	52/12	Wilkinson
Caruthers, Robert	Oglethorpe	Hitchcocks	4/14	Wilkinson
Carver, Jesse	Tattnall	Sherrards	322/21	Wilkinson
Cary, Jesse	Jefferson	Tarvers	191/17	Wilkinson
Casey, Elenor	Lincoln	Kings	128/22	Wilkinson
Casey, Elizabeth	Franklin	Yowells	154/19	Wilkinson
Casey, James	Franklin	Yowells	53/14	Baldwin
Casey, John	Jackson	Hendersons	123/25	Wilkinson
Casey, John	Jackson	Johnsons	273/20	Wilkinson
Casey, Sally	Lincoln	Kings	64/8	Baldwin
Casey, William	Baldwin	5	147/23	Wilkinson
Cash, Dawson	Columbia	11	12/11	Baldwin
Cash, James	Elbert	Roebucks	182/20	Baldwin
Cash, James	Elbert	Roebucks	208/14	Wilkinson
Cash, James	Franklin	Conners	98/18	Baldwin
Cash, Jesse	Elbert	Roebucks	262/15	Baldwin
Cash, Jesse	Elbert	Roebucks	264/22	Wilkinson
Cash, John	Jackson	Johnsons	441/7	Wilkinson
Cash, John	Washington	Collins	71/12	Baldwin
Cashin, John	Richmond		47/8	Baldwin
Cason, Hillery Sr.	Screven		100/8	Wilkinson
Cason, John	Burke	Fields	20/7	Baldwin
Cason, John	Elbert	McGuires	292/17	Wilkinson
Cason, William	Warren	Newsoms	210/15	Wilkinson
Cason, Willis	Montgomery	50	214/19	Baldwin
Cassels, Elias	Liberty		232/8	Wilkinson
Castle, John	Columbia	9	131/19	Baldwin
Castleberry, Peter	Warren	Flournoys	39/18	Baldwin
Castleberry, Rachel	Clarke	Robinsons	13/11	Baldwin
Castleberry, Solomon	Warren	Flournoys	106/19	Wilkinson
Castleberry, Solomon	Warren	Flournoys	164/18	Baldwin
Castleberry, Susannah (S)	Warren	Jones	199/9	Wilkinson
Castleberry, Thomas	Jackson	Wrights	137/15	Wilkinson
Caswell, Alexander	Jefferson	Fultons	292/8	Wilkinson
Cates, John	Burke	Forths	296/15	Baldwin
Cates, Thomas	Baldwin	3	184/7	Wilkinson
Cates, William	Jackson	Cockrans	148/9	Wilkinson
Cates, William	Jackson	Cockrans	230/15	Baldwin
Catlett, John	Burke	Gordons	97/21	Wilkinson
Cato, Francis	Washington	Garretts	313/20	Baldwin

NAME	COUNTY	MIL.DIST.	LOT/DIST	DREW LAND
Cato, Green	Hancock	Huffs	51/27	Wilkinson
Cato, Wyche	Greene	Rea	103/8	Baldwin
Causbey, Thomas	Columbia	7	152/12	Baldwin
Causby, Thomas	Columbia	7	145/6	Baldwin
Cauthorn, William	Wilkinson		184/28	Wilkinson
Cavenah's, Chas.(Orphs.)	Burke	Burks	186/20	Wilkinson
Cavenah, Thomas	Hancock	Candlers	232/7	Wilkinson
Cavenah, William	Montgomery	50	64/20	Wilkinson
Cawley, George	Montgomery	54	152/24	Wilkinson
Cawley, George	Montgomery	54	228/9	Wilkinson
Cawthon, Elizabeth	Franklin	Conners	342/7	Wilkinson
Cawthon, John	Franklin	Thompsons	74/28	Wilkinson
Cawthorn, Polly(Wid.)	Montgomery	56	159/12	Wilkinson
Ceasar, Peter	Chatham	Herbs	204/12	Wilkinson
Ceely, Ezekiel	Jackson	Wrights	267/21	Wilkinson
Chaffin, John(Son/Isham)	Wilkes	Malones	311/11	Wilkinson
Chaffin, Joshua	Wilkes	Malones	9/16	Wilkinson
Chaffin, Nathan	Wilkes	Malones	181/24	Wilkinson
Chaffin, William	Wilkes	Malones	8/17	Wilkinson
Chamberlin, Charity(Wid.)	Lincoln	Flemings	117/7	Wilkinson
Chambers', Henry(Orphs.)	Baldwin	3	233/20	Wilkinson
Chambers, David	Hancock	Huffs	197/9	Wilkinson
Chambers, Jonas	Screven	Olivers	197/15	Wilkinson
Chambers, Joseph B.	Hancock	Wallers	18/18	Wilkinson
Chambers, Nancy	Jefferson	Thomas	189/27	Wilkinson
Chambless, Christopher	Warren	Flournoys	24/16	Baldwin
Chambless, Henry	Warren	Flournoys	72/6	Baldwin
Chambless, Mary(Wid/Henry)	Columbia	2	262/22	Wilkinson
Chambless, Samuel	Hancock	Birdsongs	192/9	Baldwin
Champ, Wm.	Wilkes	Normans	199/16	Wilkinson
Champion, John	Warren	Newsoms	138/10	Baldwin
Chandler's, Francis(Orps.)	Warren	Newsoms	195/22	Wilkinson
Chandler, Bailey	Jackson	Wrights	146/15	Wilkinson
Chandler, Elizabeth	Franklin	Christians	30/15	Baldwin
Chandler, James	Franklin	Bryants	80/15	Baldwin
Chandler, Joseph	Franklin	Bryants	49/10	Wilkinson
Chandler, Robert	Franklin	Bryants	74/19	Wilkinson
Channell, Thomas	Greene	Alfords	123/18	Wilkinson
Chapell, John	Washington	Renfroes	189/12	Wilkinson
Chapman, Abner Jr.	Warren	Bakers	94/8	Wilkinson
Chapman, Abner Sr.	Warren	Bakers	14/12	Wilkinson
Chapman, Ambrose	Warren	Bakers	123/20	Wilkinson
Chapman, Ambrose	Warren	Bakers	215/14	Wilkinson
Chapman, Benjamin	Baldwin	2	67/20	Baldwin
Chapman, David	Warren	Bakers	102/14	Wilkinson
Chapman, David	Warren	Bakers	201/21	Wilkinson
Chapman, Debera	Hancock	Candlers	231/21	Wilkinson
Chapman, Henry	Hancock	Holts	7/13	Wilkinson
Chapman, John	Wilkes	Wellborns	112/23	Wilkinson
Chapman, Mary(Wid.)	Liberty		285/16	Wilkinson
Chapman, Nancy(Wid.)	Hancock	Candlers	122/6	Wilkinson
Chapman, William	Chatham	Pettybones	84/24	Wilkinson
Chapman, William	Hancock	Birdsongs	27/23	Wilkinson
Chapman, William	Jackson	Johnsons	254/7	Wilkinson
Chapman, Wm.(Orp/Wm.)	Wilkes	Wellborns	69/21	Wilkinson
Chappell, Abraham	Lincoln	Normans	115/15	Baldwin
Chappell, Jno.Jr.	Hancock	Huffs	201/9	Wilkinson
Chappell, John Jr.	Hancock	Huffs	14/28	Wilkinson
Chappell, Nancy(Miss)	Warren	Bakers	115/18	Wilkinson
Chappellier, Henry	Franklin	Conners	183/14	Baldwin
Chapton, William	Columbia	7	63/23	Wilkinson
Charham, Epps	Franklin	McDowells	145/27	Wilkinson
Charlton, Arthur M.	Wilkes	I.Hendersons	203/9	Wilkinson
Charlton, Tho's U.P.	Chatham	Pettybones	382/7	Wilkinson
Chastain, Peter	Washington	Kendricks	207/14	Wilkinson
Chatfield, Hiel	Richmond		25/17	Baldwin
Chatfield, Hiel	Richmond		34/11	Wilkinson

NAME	COUNTY	MIL.DIST.	LOT/DIST	DREW LAND
Chatham's, Geo.H.(Orphs.)	Hancock	Wallers	219/20	Wilkinson
Chatham, Epps	Franklin	McDowells	268/7	Wilkinson
Chatham, Stephen	Franklin	McDowells	152/9	Wilkinson
Chavalier, John	Camden	Smiths	56/10	Wilkinson
Cheatham, Arthur	Jefferson	Thomas	7/6	Wilkinson
Cheatham, William	Elbert	Groves	209/14	Wilkinson
Chenault, John	Columbia	2	12/22	Wilkinson
Chesnut, Mary(Wid.)	Jefferson	Tarvers	98/6	Baldwin
Chewning, David	Greene	Stewarts	143/19	Wilkinson
Chewning, Samuel	Greene	Stewarts	114/6	Baldwin
Childers, James	Elbert	Thompsons	196/22	Wilkinson
Childers, James	Elbert	Thompsons	53/28	Wilkinson
Childers, John	Oglethorpe	Jno.Smiths	76/25	Wilkinson
Childers, Joshua	Warren	Carters	37/21	Wilkinson
Childers, Wylie	Elbert	Thompsons	198/26	Wilkinson
Childes, Wm.	Clarke	Silmans	162/12	Wilkinson
Childree, Sarah	Bulloch	Denmarks	63/12	Wilkinson
Childree, Thomas	Bulloch	Denmarks	9/17	Wilkinson
Childs, James	Hancock	Weeks	230/23	Wilkinson
Childs, John(Son/Nathan)	Elbert	Clarks	62/14	Baldwin
Chisolm, Angus	Hancock	Pinkston	82/10	Wilkinson
Chisolm, John	Elbert	Dyes	103/14	Wilkinson
Chisolm, John	Elbert	Dyes	220/11	Wilkinson
Chitwood, Daniel	Franklin	Griffiths	182/25	Wilkinson
Chivers, Jacob	Washington	Renfroes	82/26	Wilkinson
Choice, Tully	Hancock	Weeks	192/12	Wilkinson
Chrestler, Absalom	Jackson	Johnsons	45/26	Wilkinson
Christian, Elizabeth	Franklin	Christians	131/14	Wilkinson
Christian, Jesse	Elbert	Olivers	54/18	Baldwin
Christian, Reubin	Elbert	Faulkners	91/14	Baldwin
Christler, Joseph	Elbert	Clarks	173/25	Wilkinson
Christmas, Wm.	Richmond		232/11	Wilkinson
Christopher's, Benj.(Orphs.)	Greene	Moores	10/28	Wilkinson
Christopher, David	Greene	Watts	145/16	Wilkinson
Churchwell, James	Richmond		153/26	Wilkinson
Churchwell, Jonathan	Jefferson	Thomas	188/12	Baldwin
Clark's, Johnson(Orphs.)	Jackson	Hendersons	220/14	Wilkinson
Clark's, Thos.(Orphs.)	Warren	Devereux	209/20	Wilkinson
Clark, Absalom	Clarke	Dukes	19/10	Baldwin
Clark, Archibald	Camden	Johnsons	246/11	Wilkinson
Clark, Christopher	Elbert	Morrisons	206/6	Baldwin
Clark, Daniel M.	Washington	Paces	289/9	Wilkinson
Clark, Dicey	Jefferson	Bosticks	147/14	Baldwin
Clark, Drury	Hancock	Gumms	72/16	Wilkinson
Clark, Edward	Lincoln	Jones	212/10	Baldwin
Clark, Edward	Lincoln	Jones	97/20	Baldwin
Clark, Gabriel	Richmond		43/15	Wilkinson
Clark, Gibson	Lincoln		216/23	Wilkinson
Clark, Larkin	Elbert	Clarks	223/11	Wilkinson
Clark, Larkin	Elbert	Clarks	36/23	Wilkinson
Clark, Micajah	Jackson	Hendersons	158/16	Wilkinson
Clark, Nathan	Baldwin	1	16/18	Wilkinson
Clark, Nathaniel	Greene	Watsons	171/12	Wilkinson
Clark, Richard	Baldwin	2	187/18	Baldwin
Clark, Thomas	Franklin	Cornelius	14/9	Baldwin
Clark, Warren	Burke	Ballards	52/16	Wilkinson
Clark, William	Hancock	Huffs	340/10	Wilkinson
Clark, William	Jefferson	Hardwicks	157/9	Wilkinson
Clark, Wm.I.	Baldwin	2	347/10	Wilkinson
Clark, Wm.W.	Richmond		7/12	Baldwin
Clarke, Eliz.(Wid.)	Baldwin	4	353/22	Wilkinson
Clay's, Chas.(Orphs.)	Washington	Collins	215/6	Baldwin
Clay, Jesse	Greene	Watsons	105/13	Baldwin
Clay, Jesse	Greene	Watsons	91/21	Wilkinson
Clay, Samuel	Greene	Watsons	157/14	Wilkinson
Clay, Samuel	Greene	Watsons	161/13	Wilkinson
Clayton, Geo.Rootes	Jefferson	Wrights	4/18	Wilkinson

NAME	COUNTY	MIL.DIST.	LOT/DIST	DREW LAND
Clayton, James	Jackson	Johnsons	323/24	Wilkinson
Clayton, William	Franklin	Wems'	57/18	Wilkinson
Cleark, Amy & Anna(Orphs.)	Burke	Burks	277/6	Wilkinson
Cleark, Eli	Burke	Martins	107/12	Wilkinson
Cleark, James	Burke	Burks	55/12	Baldwin
Cleark, John	Burke	Martins	221/28	Wilkinson
Clefton, George	Clarke	Cooks	151/25	Wilkinson
Cleghorn, Rebecca	Franklin	Cleghorns	343/24	Wilkinson
Cleghorn, William	Franklin	Cleghorns	85/10	Wilkinson
Cleland, James	Chatham	Pembertons	96/9	Baldwin
Clem, Mary	Jefferson	Bosticks	266/6	Wilkinson
Clements', David(Orphs.)	Hancock	Barnes	198/6	Baldwin
Clements, Benjamin	Clarke	Stewarts	88/20	Wilkinson
Clements, Henry	Wilkes	Edges	205/18	Wilkinson
Clements, James	Jackson	Cockrans	248/20	Baldwin
Clements, Jesse	Baldwin	2	86/11	Baldwin
Clements, John	Hancock	Barnes	343/21	Wilkinson
Clements, John	Wilkes	Harris	133/19	Wilkinson
Clements, John	Wilkes	Harris	152/7	Wilkinson
Clements, Phillip	Baldwin	5	269/8	Wilkinson
Clements, William	Jefferson	Tarvers	187/19	Wilkinson
Clements, Wm.	Jefferson	Tarvers	109/20	Wilkinson
Clemmons, James	Wilkes	Edges	141/28	Wilkinson
Clemmons, John	Wilkes	Edges	27/17	Wilkinson
Clerk's, Young(Orphs.)	Columbia	9	172/28	Wilkinson
Cleveland, Benjamin	Franklin	Conners	66/10	Wilkinson
Cleveland, Jacob	Elbert	Clarks	178/12	Baldwin
Cleveland, John(Little)	Franklin	Hoopers	311/7	Wilkinson
Cleveland, Larkin	Franklin	Conners	288/12	Wilkinson
Cleveland, Reubin	Elbert	Clarks	120/13	Wilkinson
Cleveland, Reubin	Elbert	Clarks	31/14	Wilkinson
Cleveland, William	Franklin	Conners	74/6.	Baldwin
Cleveland, Wyatt	Franklin	Wems'	23/19	Wilkinson
Clift, Henry	Clarke	Stewarts	150/16	Wilkinson
Clifton's, John(Orph.)	Liberty		119/11	Baldwin
Clifton, Curtis	Greene	Armors	35/21	Wilkinson
Clifton, Ezekiel	Tattnall	Halls	45/9	Baldwin
Cloud, Adam	Richmond		193/16	Baldwin
Cloud, Jeremiah Sr.	Washington	Wm.Renfroes	76/6	Baldwin
Clowd, Hannah(Miss)	Warren	Hills	307/12	Wilkinson
Clowd, Joel	Warren	Hills	20/19	Wilkinson
Clower, John	Hancock	Smiths	60/17	Baldwin
Clower, Morgan	Hancock	Barnes	31/15	Wilkinson
Clowers, Jacob	Baldwin	2	126/15	Baldwin
Cloyne, Pheneas	Chatham	Pembertons	62/12	Wilkinson
Clubb, George Sr.	Camden	Crews	191/20	Wilkinson
Clubb, John	Glynn		163/19	Baldwin
Clubb, Wm.Sr.	Glynn		258/8	Wilkinson
Clyne, Jonathan	Chatham	Pettybones	7/17	Wilkinson
Coates', Chas.(Orphs.)	Jefferson	Colemans	68/9	Baldwin
Coates', Wm.(Orphs.)	Wilkes	Milners	200/19	Wilkinson
Coates, Nathaniel Jr.	Wilkes	Sidwells	131/12	Wilkinson
Coates, Nathaniel Sr.	Wilkes	Roreys	255/24	Wilkinson
Coates, William	Jefferson	Colemans	314/16	Wilkinson
Cobb's, Lewis(Orphs.)	Montgomery	58	110/16	Baldwin
Cobb, Abraham	Columbia	6	151/28	Wilkinson
Cobb, Benjamin	Baldwin	1	374/22	Wilkinson
Cobb, Daniel Sr.	Columbia	6	160/6	Baldwin
Cobb, Howell(Orph.)	Chatham	Whites	190/17	Wilkinson
Cobb, James	Wilkinson		81/10	Baldwin
Cobb, Jas.(Son/Ezekiel)	Columbia	6	23/22	Wilkinson
Cobb, John	Greene	Flournoys	75/17	Wilkinson
Cobb, Joseph	Baldwin	1	108/9	Wilkinson
Cobb, Nathaniel	Columbia	6	203/11	Wilkinson
Cobbs, John A.	Jefferson	Colemans	154/20	Wilkinson
Cobourn, Mary(Wid.)	Burke	Bynes	111/28	Wilkinson
Cobourn, Susannah(Orph.)	Burke	Bynes	30/17	Wilkinson

NAME	COUNTY	MIL.DIST.	LOT/DIST	DREW LAND
Cock, Needham	Montgomery	57	337/20	Baldwin
Cockburn, Ezekiel	Wayne	1	176/13	Wilkinson
Cockburn, George	Jackson	Hendersons	76/21	Wilkinson
Cockram, Prudence	Jackson	Hendersons	137/9	Wilkinson
Cockran's, Rickens(Orphs.)	Jackson	Johnsons	81/16	Baldwin
Cockran, James(Maj.)	Jackson	Cockrans	134/14	Wilkinson
Cockran, John M.	Greene	Jenkins	343/11	Wilkinson
Cockran, Mary	Elbert	Groves	89/27	Wilkinson
Cockran, Thomas	Jackson	Cockrans	307/17	Wilkinson
Cockran, William	Oglethorpe	Bells	184/11	Wilkinson
Cody, Edmund	Warren	Neals	157/24	Wilkinson
Cody, Jesse	Baldwin	2	1/17	Wilkinson
Cody, John	Jackson	Wrights	122/12	Baldwin
Cody, John	Jackson	Wrights	38/24	Wilkinson
Cody, Michael	Warren	Neals	58/14	Wilkinson
Cofield, John	Burke	Martins	336/13	Wilkinson
Cohoon, John	Clarke	Cooks	95/11	Baldwin
Cohran, John	Wilkes	Edges	49/10	Baldwin
Cohran, Joseph	Wilkes	Edges	127/9	Wilkinson
Coil, John	Elbert	Willifords	14/16	Baldwin
Coker's, John(Orphs.)	Jackson	Cockrans	172/19	Wilkinson
Coker, Malachi	Elbert	Olivers	77/22	Wilkinson
Coker, Robert Sr.	Jackson	Wrights	121/16	Wilkinson
Coker, Solomon	Jackson	Cockrans	147/8	Baldwin
Coker, William	Washington	Howards	292/12	Wilkinson
Colah, Turner	Jefferson	Hardwicks	101/17	Baldwin
Colbert, James	Elbert	Morrisons	28/12	Baldwin
Colbert, John	Hancock	Crowders	178/17	Wilkinson
Colbert, John	Hancock	Crowders	80/6	Wilkinson
Colbert, Jonathan	Hancock	Candlers	265/7	Wilkinson
Colbert, Philip P.	Oglethorpe	Hitchcocks	108/28	Wilkinson
Colbert, Thomas	Clarke	Cooks	273/22	Wilkinson
Colbert, William	Greene	Dawsons	175/11	Wilkinson
Colbert, William	Greene	Dawsons	55/8	Baldwin
Cole's, Wm.(Orphs.)	Wilkes	Heards	148/14	Baldwin
Cole, Jacob	Jackson	Cockrans	304/10	Wilkinson
Cole, Martha	Wilkes	Hendricks	51/19	Wilkinson
Cole, Thomas	Greene	Carletons	105/16	Baldwin
Cole, Thomas	Greene	Carltons	260/7	Baldwin
Cole, Wm.B.	Clarke	Harpers	370/7	Wilkinson
Coleman, Benjamin	Jefferson	Hardwicks	251/15	Wilkinson
Coleman, Charles	Burke	Montgomerys	193/20	Wilkinson
Coleman, Isaac	Jefferson	Tarvers	40/15	Baldwin
Coleman, Jesse	Burke	Hilliards	142/13	Wilkinson
Coleman, Jesse	Greene	Alfords	217/19	Wilkinson
Coleman, Jesse	Greene	Alfords	67/6	Baldwin
Coleman, Jonathan	Montgomery	57	275/21	Wilkinson
Coleman, Josiah	Greene	Loves	214/19	Wilkinson
Coleman, Menan	Wilkinson		200/8	Wilkinson
Coleman, Obedience	Tattnall	Armstrongs	190/13	Baldwin
Coleman, Samuel(Orph.)	Richmond		91/20	Baldwin
Coleman, Thomas H.	Screven	Williamsons	51/6	Baldwin
Coleman, Thomas	Burke	Carswells	263/6	Wilkinson
Coleman, William	Burke	Hilliards	96/10	Wilkinson
Coleman, Wm.	Tattnall	Armstrongs	144/14	Wilkinson
Collet, John	Elbert	Faulkners	167/17	Wilkinson
Colley's, Zachariah(Orphs.)	Elbert	Moons	227/15	Wilkinson
Colley, Anderson	Oglethorpe	Watkins	18/17	Wilkinson
Colley, James	Oglethorpe	Watkins	229/24	Wilkinson
Colliday, William	Elbert	Moons	161/14	Baldwin
Collier, Barnett(Orph.)	Franklin	Hollingsworths	257/12	Wilkinson
Collier, Isaac	Oglethorpe	Beasleys	265/25	Wilkinson
Collier, John	Oglethorpe	Beasleys	124/15	Wilkinson
Collier, Williamson	Oglethorpe	Beasleys	54/14	Wilkinson
Collins, Caty	Richmond		61/10	Wilkinson
Collins, Henderson	Hancock	Winslets	155/16	Baldwin
Collins, Henry	Montgomery	58	51/17	Wilkinson

NAME	COUNTY	MIL.DIST.	LOT/DIST	DREW LAND
Collins, Jeremiah	Greene	Greers	148/9	Baldwin
Collins, John	Columbia	4	31/7	Wilkinson
Collins, John	Franklin	Henrys	270/17	Wilkinson
Collins, John	McIntosh		82/9	Wilkinson
Collins, Joseph	Baldwin	1	382/8	Wilkinson
Collins, Major	Jefferson	Thomas	107/20	Baldwin
Collins, Major	Jefferson	Thomas	79/8	Baldwin
Collins, Moses Sr.	Richmond		27/19	Wilkinson
Collins, Samuel	Jackson	Wrights	113/23	Wilkinson
Collins, Washington	Wilkes	Normans	112/6	Wilkinson
Collins, William	Wayne	1	210/8	Wilkinson
Collum's, Will(Orphs.)	Baldwin	1	243/21	Wilkinson
Colly, Gabriel	Baldwin	1	44/20	Wilkinson
Colquett, Eliz.(Wid.)	Oglethorpe	Hartsfields	188/7	Wilkinson
Colquett, Henry	Hancock	Coopers	313/11	Wilkinson
Colquett, Robert	Oglethorpe	Hartsfields	76/16	Wilkinson
Colquett, Samuel	Oglethorpe	Hartsfields	289/8	Wilkinson
Colson, Sally(Wid.)	Oglethorpe	Smiths	221/13	Baldwin
Colson, Siney(Wid.)	Oglethorpe	Smiths	221/13	Baldwin
Colson, Thomas	Oglethorpe	Smiths	285/10	Wilkinson
Colston, Jacob	Lincoln	Flemings	194/7	Wilkinson
Colvert, Joseph	Elbert	Groves	145/17	Baldwin
Combs, Enock	Wilkes	Parks	87/12	Wilkinson
Combs, John	Baldwin	1	132/18	Wilkinson
Combs, Jonathan	Oglethorpe	Hudsons	117/19	Wilkinson
Comer, Anderson	Hancock	Weeks	222/19	Wilkinson
Comer, Hugh M.	Hancock	Gumms	88/14	Wilkinson
Comer, James	Hancock	Weeks	93/6	Wilkinson
Compton, Pleasant	Oglethorpe	Smiths	191/14	Wilkinson
Cone's, Richard(Orphs.)	Greene	Dawsons	179/11	Wilkinson
Cone, John	Greene	Greers	148/9	Baldwin
Cone, John	Jackson		172/14	Wilkinson
Cone, John	Washington	Garretts	168/24	Wilkinson
Cone, William	Columbia	1	44/14	Baldwin
Coney, Aquilla	Montgomery	50	224/20	Wilkinson
Coney, Jeremiah	Montgomery	50	29/20	Baldwin
Coney, May A.	Chatham		197/21	Wilkinson
Conn's, John(Orphs.)	Franklin	Dixons	230/21	Wilkinson
Conn, George	Richmond		82/11	Wilkinson
Conn, John	Franklin	Dixons	232/22	Wilkinson
Conn, Thomas	Franklin	Dixons	250/15	Baldwin
Connell, Daniel	Greene	Loves	23/9	Baldwin
Connell, Jeremiah	Greene	Loves	16/25	Wilkinson
Connell, William	Hancock	Coopers	44/18	Baldwin
Connelly's, Patrick(Orphs.)	Burke	Bynes	219/18	Wilkinson
Connelly, Keziah	Franklin	Allens	128/8	Wilkinson
Connelly, Polly	Franklin	Christians	148/16	Baldwin
Connelly, Price	Clarke	Browns	165/27	Wilkinson
Connelly, Thomas	Franklin	Allens	86/6	Baldwin
Conner's, Cornelius(Orph.)	Tattnall	Sherrards	291/10	Wilkinson
Conner, Boley	Franklin	Conners	72/15	Baldwin
Conner, Eoley	Franklin	Conners	201/8	Wilkinson
Conner, Henry	Lincoln	Jones	306/13	Wilkinson
Conner, Henry	Lincoln	Jones	426/7	Wilkinson
Conner, James	Hancock	Holts	183/10	Wilkinson
Conner, John	Hancock	Candlers	125/20	Baldwin
Conner, Joseph	Burke	Forths	97/15	Wilkinson
Conyers, John Jr.	Screven	Williamsons	16/28	Wilkinson
Coobs, Jesse	Clarke	Stewarts	167/26	Wilkinson
Coody, Edward	Lincoln	Mays	269/22	Wilkinson
Cook's, Nicholas(Orphs.)	Burke	Gordons	64/15	Baldwin
Cook's, Reubin(Orph.)	Clarke	Robinsons	27/8	Wilkinson
Cook's, Sion(Orphs.)	Columbia	4	176/7	Wilkinson
Cook's, Wm.(Orphs.)	Greene	Loves	61/11	Baldwin
Cook, Abraham	Washington	Garretts	155/15	Baldwin
Cook, Benjamin	Elbert	Keelings	283/13	Wilkinson
Cook, Benjamin	Elbert	Keelings	46/17	Baldwin

NAME	COUNTY	MIL.DIST.	LOT/DIST	DREW LAND
Cook, Benjamin	Washington	Collins	300/16	Wilkinson
Cook, Drury	Clarke	Cooks	147/12	Baldwin
Cook, Francis	Elbert	Dyes	208/6	Baldwin
Cook, Francis	Elbert	Dyes	286/24	Wilkinson
Cook, Green	Hancock	Birdsongs	10/15	Wilkinson
Cook, Greenberry	Baldwin	4	200/13	Wilkinson
Cook, Greenberry	Baldwin	4	69/12	Baldwin
Cook, Henry	Effingham		183/19	Baldwin
Cook, Israel	Burke	Ballards	108/13	Baldwin
Cook, James Jr.	Effingham		173/11	Wilkinson
Cook, Jas. Watson	Franklin	Dixons	26/12	Wilkinson
Cook, Joanna	Washington	Garretts	185/12	Wilkinson
Cook, John F.	Elbert	Morrisons	148/13	Wilkinson
Cook, John Sr.	Bulloch	Godfreys	137/9	Baldwin
Cook, John	Baldwin	4	209/13	Baldwin
Cook, John	Elbert	Morrisons	202/7	Wilkinson
Cook, John	Washington	Kendricks	216/20	Baldwin
Cook, Lewis	Bulloch	Godfreys	322/9	Wilkinson
Cook, Marian	Washington	Garretts	50/14	Baldwin
Cook, Merryman	Columbia	4	21/12	Baldwin
Cook, Nancy	Elbert	Morrisons	238/10	Wilkinson
Cook, Polly	Wilkes	Heards	145/11	Wilkinson
Cook, Smith	Elbert	Morrisons	229/12	Wilkinson
Cook, William B.	Clarke	Robinsons	336/12	Wilkinson
Cook, William	Chatham	Pettybones	12/17	Wilkinson
Cook, William	Chatham	Pettybones	218/16	Wilkinson
Cook, William	Elbert	Barretts	34/21	Wilkinson
Cook, William	Glynn		87/11	Wilkinson
Cook, William	Jackson	Hendersons	229/16	Wilkinson
Coon, Henry	Jackson	Johnsons	132/28	Wilkinson
Cooper's, Geo. (Orph.)	Warren	Heaths	220/9	Baldwin
Cooper's, Thomas (Orphs.)	Columbia	10	294/20	Baldwin
Cooper, Ananias	Richmond		355/8	Wilkinson
Cooper, Ephraim	Chatham	Pettybones	29/14	Wilkinson
Cooper, Ephraim	Chatham	Pettybones	328/20	Baldwin
Cooper, George	Wilkinson		52/19	Baldwin
Cooper, James	Wilkes	M. Hendersons	33/12	Wilkinson
Cooper, John (Esq.)	Wilkes	Coopers	288/15	Baldwin
Cooper, John	Chatham	Pettybones	125/27	Wilkinson
Cooper, John	Greene	Owsleys	74/17	Baldwin
Cooper, Jos. (Esq.)	Hancock	Weeks	4/19	Baldwin
Cooper, Nancy (S)	Hancock	Gumms	244/22	Wilkinson
Cooper, Ransom	Baldwin	2	24/23	Wilkinson
Cooper, Richard	Tattnall	Armstrongs	53/22	Wilkinson
Cooper, Rosanna	Columbia	11	198/19	Baldwin
Cooper, Susan	McIntosh		115/17	Wilkinson
Cooper, Vining	Oglethorpe	Hitchcocks	7/19	Wilkinson
Cooper, W. John	Wilkes	Coopers	275/6	Wilkinson
Cope, Adam	Chatham	Pettybones	123/24	Wilkinson
Cope, Adam	Chatham	Pettybones	148/24	Wilkinson
Cope, Charles	Chatham	Pettybones	283/22	Wilkinson
Cope, Charles	Chatham	Pettybones	96/19	Wilkinson
Cope, Christian	Effingham		230/9	Baldwin
Cope, Rosanna (Wid.)	Chatham	Pettybones	117/19	Baldwin
Cope, William	Jackson	Cockrans	146/25	Wilkinson
Copeland, James	Jackson	Hendersons	24/21	Wilkinson
Copeland, John R.	Greene	Butlers	142/16	Wilkinson
Copeland, Sally	Oglethorpe	Bells	82/23	Wilkinson
Copeland, Unity	Oglethorpe	Bells	77/18	Baldwin
Copland, Oney	Oglethorpe	Bells	262/25	Wilkinson
Coppedge, Lewis	Wilkes	Heards	73/10	Baldwin
Coppedge, William	Wilkes	Heards	265/20	Wilkinson
Coquillon, F's Bj.	Chatham		160/18	Wilkinson
Corain, William	Columbia	9	83/24	Wilkinson
Corbitt, Isham	Bulloch	Hendleys	182/21	Wilkinson
Corbitt, James	Wilkes	Roreys	199/30	Wilkinson
Corbitt, James	Wilkes	Roreys	54/15	Wilkinson

NAME	COUNTY	MIL.DIST.	LOT/DIST	DREW LAND
Cordrey, Nancy(Orph.)	Washington	Chivers	92/10	Wilkinson
Corker, Jesse	Liberty		177/10	Baldwin
Cornelison, Andrew	Franklin	Griffiths	280/17	Wilkinson
Cornelison, Andrew	Franklin	Griffiths	344/7	Wilkinson
Cornelison, John	Chatham	Pettybones	32/15	Baldwin
Cornelius, Elizabeth	Chatham	Hardens	94/26	Wilkinson
Cornett's, Jones(Orphs.)	Burke	Sharps	91/11	Wilkinson
Cornett, Josiah	Burke	Sharps	253/9	Wilkinson
Cornett, Randall	Burke	Montgomerys	363/24	Wilkinson
Corpinger, Penelope	Richmond		305/21	Wilkinson
Corvan, Mary(Wid/Thos.)	Columbia	5	40/13	Wilkinson
Cosby, Garland	Wilkes	Coopers	130/7	Baldwin
Cosby, Wid.(Jas.O's Mother)	Elbert	Thompsons	84/23	Wilkinson
Cosley, Pierce	Warren	Hills	109/19	Baldwin
Costly, Michael	Columbia	6	94/17	Wilkinson
Cotter, John	Screven		119/7	Baldwin
Cotter, Sarah	Screven		268/17	Wilkinson
Cottle, Delilah	Montgomery	51	43/21	Wilkinson
Cottle, John	Jefferson		305/12	Wilkinson
Cotton, Abner	Baldwin	1	83/17	Baldwin
Cotton, John	Baldwin	1	220/21	Wilkinson
Cotton, Smith	Hancock	Barksdales	330/21	Wilkinson
Couch, John	Elbert	Barretts	106/12	Wilkinson
Coughron, Joseph	Screven		268/6	Wilkinson
Coughron, Robert	Screven		139/27	Wilkinson
Coulter's, Jesse(Orphs.)	Hancock	Gumms	166/21	Wilkinson
Course, Caroline(Orph.)	Richmond		51/11	Wilkinson
Course, John	Richmond		33/27	Wilkinson
Coursey, Zachariah	Chatham	Hardens	5/8	Baldwin
Courson's, James(Orphs.)	Columbia	1	241/11	Wilkinson
Courter, Harmon	Camden	Smiths	156/15	Wilkinson
Cousins, Adam	Clarke	Dukes	69/13	Wilkinson
Cousins, Fanny(S.W.)	Clarke	Dukes	176/20	Baldwin
Coventon, Wm.(Orph.)	Jefferson	Bosticks	108/17	Baldwin
Covington, Thomas	Franklin	Allens	135/17	Wilkinson
Cowan, Joseph	Baldwin	1	183/24	Wilkinson
Coward, Abraham	Bulloch	Hendleys	99/18	Baldwin
Coward, Doreas	Bulloch	Hendleys	406/7	Wilkinson
Coward, James R.	Bulloch	Hendleys	246/17	Wilkinson
Coward, Stephen(Orph.)	Bulloch	Hendleys	12/21	Wilkinson
Cowart, Hannah	Burke	Blounts	75/20	Baldwin
Cowart, John	Jefferson		134/26	Wilkinson
Cowart, Zachariah	Burke	Hilliards	135/6	Baldwin
Cowden, David	Clarke	Robinsons	179/19	Baldwin
Cowden, Robert	Jackson	Hendersons	21/17	Wilkinson
Cowen's, Wm.(Orphs.)	Jackson	Wrights	187/11	Baldwin
Cowen, George(Esq.)	Jackson	Wrights	130/8	Baldwin
Cowen, Isaac(B.S.)	Jackson	Wrights	127/13	Baldwin
Cowen, Isaac(B.S.)	Jackson	Wrights	38/8	Wilkinson
Cowen, Joseph	Jackson	Wrights	290/21	Wilkinson
Cowles, Wm.M.	Richmond		210/16	Wilkinson
Cox's, Asa(Orphs.)	Baldwin	4	152/27	Wilkinson
Cox's, Daniel(Orphs.)	Washington	Paces	11/21	Wilkinson
Cox, Aris	Franklin	Everetts	104/12	Wilkinson
Cox, Aris	Franklin	Everetts	16/23	Wilkinson
Cox, Cordy Jr.	Warren	Bakers	246/9	Wilkinson
Cox, David	Warren	Jones	45/28	Wilkinson
Cox, Delia(Orph.)	Richmond		26/9	Baldwin
Cox, Edmund	Baldwin	3	266/24	Wilkinson
Cox, George	Jefferson	Thomas	12/11	Wilkinson
Cox, George	Jefferson	Thomas	190/15	Wilkinson
Cox, Henry	Jefferson	Wrights	237/22	Wilkinson
Cox, Henry	Warren	Hills	205/20	Baldwin
Cox, Henry	Warren	Hills	52/16	Baldwin
Cox, Ichabud	Warren	Bakers	133/6	Baldwin
Cox, Isaac	Baldwin	2	70/8	Baldwin
Cox, Isaac	Baldwin	2	94/8	Baldwin

NAME	COUNTY	MIL.DIST.	LOT/DIST	DREW LAND
Cox, Jesse	Wilkes	Stovalls	57/14	Wilkinson
Cox, John	Franklin	Griffiths	171/13	Baldwin
Cox, Keziah(Orph.)	Richmond		26/9	Baldwin
Cox, Martha(Orph.)	Richmond		26/9	Baldwin
Cox, Mastin	Warren	Devereux	188/15	Wilkinson
Cox, Robert	Wilkes	Heards	103/11	Baldwin
Cox, Samuel	Baldwin	2	474/7	Wilkinson
Cox, Sarah(Wid.)	Burke	Bynes	287/14	Wilkinson
Cox, Thomas	Franklin	Hoopers	87/17	Baldwin
Cox, William	Washington	Delks	165/9	Wilkinson
Cozart, Jenny(S)	Hancock	Barnes	65/28	Wilkinson
Crabb, Asa	Columbia	4	14/20	Baldwin
Crabb, Asa	Columbia	4	202/25	Wilkinson
Crabb, Daniel Sr.	Wilkinson		144/17	Wilkinson
Crabb, Enoch	Columbia	4	224/9	Wilkinson
Crabb, Enoch	Columbia	4	3/17	Wilkinson
Craddock, Roberts	Screven		227/15	Baldwin
Craddock, Roberts	Screven		295/15	Baldwin
Crafford, Henry	Screven		59/15	Wilkinson
Craft, Charles	Wilkinson		125/15	Baldwin
Craft, Charles	Wilkinson		165/17	Baldwin
Craig, Robert	Montgomery	57	275/24	Wilkinson
Crain, Anna	Burke	Gordons	85/26	Wilkinson
Crain, Joel	Franklin	Yowells	122/11	Baldwin
Crain, John	Burke	Ballards	259/22	Wilkinson
Crain, Rachel	Burke	Ballards	310/9	Wilkinson
Crain, Stephen	Franklin	Yowells	241/10	Baldwin
Crain, Thomas Sr.	Clarke	Martins	292/7	Wilkinson
Crain, William	Baldwin	2	323/20	Wilkinson
Crane, Jeremiah	Jackson	Wrights	71/18	Baldwin
Crane, Spencer Sr.	Wilkes	Stovalls	137/11	Baldwin
Cranford, Philip	Wilkes	Milners	54/11	Baldwin
Cravy's, Owen(Orphs.)	Burke	Spains	268/16	Wilkinson
Cravy, Hugh Jr.	Burke	Spains	21/23	Wilkinson
Crawford, Alexander	Jackson	Hendersons	54/13	Baldwin
Crawford, James	Effingham		350/9	Wilkinson
Crawford, John(Son/Chas.)	Columbia	6	100/11	Baldwin
Crawford, John	Camden	Ashleys	115/17	Baldwin
Crawford, John	Greene	Butlers	268/15	Wilkinson
Crawford, Peter	Columbia	2	302/13	Wilkinson
Crawford, Sally	Greene	Butlers	149/16	Wilkinson
Crawford, William	Glynn		16/27	Wilkinson
Crawford, William	Greene	Jenkins	110/6	Wilkinson
Crawley, Charles	Wilkes	M.Hendersons	304/8	Wilkinson
Crawley, Charles	Wilkes	M.Hendersons	76/13	Baldwin
Cray, Scott	McIntosh		165/18	Wilkinson
Crayne, James	McIntosh		229/17	Wilkinson
Creamshaw, Patsy	Wilkes	Edges	50/9	Wilkinson
Creswell, David	Jackson	Wrights	97/18	Baldwin
Crews', Joseph(Orphs.)	Oglethorpe	Hatchetts	154/9	Wilkinson
Crews, David	Franklin	Cornelius	13/7	Baldwin
Crim, Ann & John	Chatham	Abrahams	45/11	Baldwin
Crim, Elizabeth	Chatham	Abrahams	45/11	Baldwin
Crim, George	Wilkes	Coopers	124/11	Wilkinson
Crittenden's, Thos.(Orphs.)	Hancock	Candlers	360/22	Wilkinson
Crittenden, John	Washington	Garretts	117/12	Wilkinson
Crittenden, John	Washington	Garretts	117/12	Wilkinson
Crittenden, John	Washington	Garretts	60/10	Wilkinson
Crittington, Prior	Elbert	Olivers	171/9	Baldwin
Crittington, Pryor	Elbert	Olivers	117/18	Wilkinson
Crocker, Arthur	Baldwin	2	151/9	Baldwin
Crocker, William	Greene	Watts	19/13	Wilkinson
Crockett, Floyd	Burke	Ballards	99/15	Baldwin
Crockett, John	Jackson	Wrights	239/8	Wilkinson
Crockett, Samuel	Jackson	Wrights	195/14	Wilkinson
Crockett, Samuel	Jackson	Wrights	84/19	Baldwin
Croll, James	Jackson	Wrights	224/14	Wilkinson

NAME	COUNTY	MIL.DIST.	LOT/DIST	DREW LAND
Cron, George	Wilkes	Wellborns	147/6	Baldwin
Cron, George	Wilkes	Wellborns	44/7	Wilkinson
Crook, Jonathan	Richmond		153/8	Baldwin
Crop, Sarah(Orph.)	Chatham	Pettybones	84/7	Baldwin
Crosbe, George	Baldwin	1	102/6	Wilkinson
Crosbe, George	Baldwin	1	114/16	Baldwin
Cross, George	Oglethorpe	Smiths	50/8	Baldwin
Crow's, Jacob(Orphs.)	Jackson	Hendersons	96/10	Baldwin
Crow, Stephen	Clarke	Browns	152/28	Wilkinson
Crow, Wm.	Baldwin	2	298/15	Wilkinson
Crowder, Thomas	Hancock	Crowders	46/15	Wilkinson
Crowell, Nancy(Wid/Zeanay)	Columbia	11	160/16	Baldwin
Crowley, Abraham	Oglethorpe	Hatchetts	4/25	Wilkinson
Crowley, Archibald	Clarke	Tramells	95/21	Wilkinson
Crowley, Benj.Sr.	Oglethorpe	Hatchetts	117/27	Wilkinson
Crowley, James	Oglethorpe	Hatchetts	11/12	Baldwin
Crowley, Samuel	Clarke	Tramells	225/14	Baldwin
Crowley, Samuel	Clarke	Tramells	242/15	Baldwin
Crozier, James	Burke	Burks	138/28	Wilkinson
Crozier, Thomas	Burke	Burks	291/13	Wilkinson
Crum, Herman	Effingham		73/26	Wilkinson
Crumbly, John	Wilkinson		194/17	Wilkinson
Crumbly, John	Wilkinson		6/24	Wilkinson
Crump, Reason	Burke	Spains	142/19	Baldwin
Cruse, James	Effingham		219/10	Wilkinson
Crutchfield, Lucy	Greene	Dawsons	196/14	Wilkinson
Crutchfield, Lydda	Burke	Ballards	160/6	Wilkinson
Crutchfield, Robert	Greene	Flournoys	24/10	Wilkinson
Cubbage, George(Son/Geo.)	Bryan	Austins	230/26	Wilkinson
Cuddy, Margaret(Wid.)	Jefferson	Wrights	213/12	Wilkinson
Culbertson's, David(Orps.)	Clarke	Butlers	20/20	Wilkinson
Culbreath's, Dan'l.(Orphs.)	Jefferson		83/7	Wilkinson
Culbreath, Daniel	Montgomery	53	297/15	Baldwin
Culbreath, Nevin	Montgomery	53	173/8	Wilkinson
Cullam, George	Columbia	4	323/7	Wilkinson
Cullers, George	Lincoln	Jones	20/10	Baldwin
Culpepper, Agnes	Washington	Andersons	178/15	Wilkinson
Culpepper, Daniel Jr.	Warren	Jones	126/19	Baldwin
Culpepper, Daniel Sr.	Warren	Jones	72/11	Baldwin
Culpepper, David	Washington	Blackshears	11/13	Baldwin
Culpepper, Dickerson	Warren	Jones	22/25	Wilkinson
Culpepper, Elender	Washington	Andersons	297/9	Wilkinson
Culpepper, Joel	Washington	Andersons	213/10	Wilkinson
Culpepper, Joseph	Jackson	Hendersons	154/7	Wilkinson
Culpepper, Joseph	Jackson	Hendersons	352/7	Wilkinson
Culpepper, Robert	Warren	Jones	71/14	Baldwin
Culver, Joshua	Hancock	Wallers	16/14	Wilkinson
Culver, Nathan	Hancock	Wallers	247/11	Wilkinson
Culver, Nathan	Hancock	Wallers	299/9	Wilkinson
Cummins, Eleazer Sr.	Washington	Collins	197/28	Wilkinson
Cunes, Jacob	Chatham	Whites	213/16	Baldwin
Cunningham, James	Baldwin	4	62/22	Wilkinson
Cunningham, John Sr.	Elbert	Roebucks	87/17	Wilkinson
Cunningham, John	Elbert	Thompsons	153/15	Wilkinson
Cunningham, Robert	Columbia	10	288/16	Wilkinson
Cunningham, Samuel	Clarke	Hitchcocks	98/14	Baldwin
Cunningham, Wm.	Elbert	Thompsons	203/12	Baldwin
Cureton, Boling	Hancock	Thomas	52/15	Baldwin
Cureton, Martha	Hancock	Thomas'	43/20	Baldwin
Curl, Amelia	Liberty		28/8	Baldwin
Curl, Mathew	Montgomery	56	311/20	Baldwin
Curlle, John	Lincoln	Mays	8/18	Baldwin
Curmeen, John	Hancock	Wallers	250/8	Wilkinson
Currie, Richard	Hancock	Birdsongs	186/20	Baldwin
Currooth, Robert	Oglethorpe	Moores	202/16	Wilkinson
Curry, David	Jackson	Johnsons	86/22	Wilkinson
Curry, James	Lincoln	Busseys	160/17	Wilkinson

NAME	COUNTY	MIL.DIST.	LOT/DIST	DREW LAND
Curry, John C.	Hancock	Winsletts	143/14	Baldwin
Curry, John	Greene	Greers	206/18	Wilkinson
Curry, John	Jackson	Johnsons	153/9	Wilkinson
Curry, Margarett(Wid.)	Jackson	Johnsons	98/12	Baldwin
Curry, Nathaniel	Lincoln	Busseys	92/11	Wilkinson
Curry, Nicholas	Washington	Kendricks	116/17	Wilkinson
Curry, Peggy(Wid.)	Lincoln		165/23	Wilkinson
Curry, Robert	Greene	Greers	37/8	Wilkinson
Curry, Thomas	Lincoln	Busseys	257/16	Wilkinson
Curry, Thompson	Washington	Chivers	45/23	Wilkinson
Curry, William	Greene	Carletons	303/24	Wilkinson
Curtis, Eliz.(Orph.)	Clarke	Mitchells	2/9	Wilkinson
Curtis, John	Greene	Dawsons	21/10	Baldwin
Cutliff, Nancy	Wilkes	Coopers	215/10	Baldwin
Cutts, Joseph	Washington	Delks	268/8	Wilkinson
Cuyler, Jeremiah	Chatham	Abrahams	196/16	Wilkinson
Dabardeaux, Eleanor E.(Orp.)	Chatham	Pemberton	86/10	Wilkinson
Dail, Simon	Bulloch	Hendleys	190/14	Baldwin
Dale, Martha	Greene	Jenkins	204/13	Baldwin
Dale, Robert	Greene	Carletons	15/18	Baldwin
Dallas, Sarah(Wid.)	Camden	Ashleys	222/20	Wilkinson
Dallas, Thomas	Lincoln	Jones	13/26	Wilkinson
Dalton, Henry	Richmond		37/20	Wilkinson
Dampier, Daniel	Effingham		30/18	Wilkinson
Dampier, William	Effingham		99/13	Baldwin
Daniel's, Chas.(Orphs.)	Greene	Carletons	81/19	Baldwin
Daniel, Aaron	Chatham	McClains	62/19	Wilkinson
Daniel, Abraham	Burke	Ballards	134/13	Baldwin
Daniel, Abraham	Hancock	Gumms	133/10	Wilkinson
Daniel, Amos	Hancock	Wallers	161/26	Wilkinson
Daniel, Amos	Washington	Kendricks	68/9	Wilkinson
Daniel, Appellus	Burke	Ballards	6/15	Wilkinson
Daniel, Benjamin	Montgomery	50	120/24	Wilkinson
Daniel, Charles	Washington	Delks	250/16	Wilkinson
Daniel, David	Burke	Ballards	277/23	Wilkinson
Daniel, David	Burke	Ballards	79/28	Wilkinson
Daniel, Eliz.(Wid.)	Montgomery	51	37/7	Baldwin
Daniel, Ezekiel	Greene	Watts	192/11	Wilkinson
Daniel, George	Clarke	Harpers	195/24	Wilkinson
Daniel, Henning	Greene	Moores	238/20	Baldwin
Daniel, Isaac	Columbia	10	176/13	Baldwin
Daniel, Isaac	Montgomery	52	11/6	Baldwin
Daniel, James	Greene	Watts	127/17	Wilkinson
Daniel, Jepthah	Burke	Carswells	71/10	Baldwin
Daniel, Jepthah	Burke	Carswells	96/6	Baldwin
Daniel, John O.	Hancock	Gumms	189/12	Baldwin
Daniel, Jonas	Washington	Kendricks	113/24	Wilkinson
Daniel, Joseph(Orph.)	Washington	Chivers	168/22	Wilkinson
Daniel, Mary	Franklin	Griffiths	264/7	Wilkinson
Daniel, Moses	Washington	Chivers	204/13	Wilkinson
Daniel, Richard	Clarke	Stewarts	142/19	Wilkinson
Daniel, Richard	Clarke	Stewarts	65/9	Wilkinson
Daniel, Stephen	Baldwin	3	344/24	Wilkinson
Daniel, Thomas	Oglethorpe	Bells	19/6	Baldwin
Daniel, Thos.(Orph/Berry)	Clarke	Robinsons	327/9	Wilkinson
Daniel, William	Greene	Baxters	501/7	Wilkinson
Daniel, Wm.Major	Greene	Watts	137/25	Wilkinson
Daniel, Wright	Baldwin	1	134/7	Baldwin
Danielly, Andrew	Warren	Flournoys	137/16	Wilkinson
Danielly, Arthur	Hancock	Candlers	24/17	Baldwin
Danielly, Jane(S)	Hancock	Weeks	86/14	Wilkinson
Danielly, Mehaly(Dau/Jno.)	Columbia	6	211/16	Wilkinson
Darbey, John	Jefferson	Colemans	176/28	Wilkinson
Darby, Jacob	Montgomery	54	394/7	Wilkinson
Darden, John	Elbert	Thompsons	204/27	Wilkinson
Darden, Zaecheus	Warren	Bakers	353/13	Wilkinson
Darnell's, Ward(Orphs.)	Baldwin	1	300/15	Baldwin

NAME	COUNTY	MIL.DIST.	LOT/DIST	DREW LAND
Darnell, James	Baldwin	2	269/16	Wilkinson
Darnell, John	Baldwin	1	121/10	Baldwin
Darnell, Joseph	Clarke	Silmans	372/8	Wilkinson
Darracott, John	Wilkes	Roreys	242/21	Wilkinson
Darsey, John	Franklin	McDowells	1/22	Wilkinson
Darsey, Joseph	Columbia	7	212/17	Baldwin
Dasher, Christian L.	Effingham		250/20	Wilkinson
Dasher, Christiana A.(Wid.)	Effingham		186/8	Baldwin
Dasher, Thomas(Orph.)	Effingham		167/20	Baldwin
Daughtre, William	Greene	Baxters	260/15	Wilkinson
Davenport, William	Hancock	Coopers	105/18	Baldwin
Davey, Polly	Columbia	4	21/11	Baldwin
David, Henry Sr.	Franklin	Christians	200/6	Wilkinson
David, Isaac	Elbert	Moons	264/19	Baldwin
David, Peter	Elbert	Dyes	223/21	Wilkinson
David, William	Elbert	Moons	337/11	Wilkinson
Davidson, Isaac	Warren	Willsons	150/15	Baldwin
Davidson, Isaac	Warren	Willsons	39/13	Wilkinson
Davidson, James	Warren	Bakers	129/10	Baldwin
Davidson, Jesse	Warren	Carters	191/25	Wilkinson
Davidson, Joseph	Clarke	Mitchells	231/14	Baldwin
Davidson, Joseph	Clarke	Mitchells	297/13	Wilkinson
Davidson, Joseph	Warren	Newsoms	12/8	Wilkinson
Davidson, William	Warren	Hills	32/9	Baldwin
Davidson, William	Warren	Neals	178/9	Baldwin
Davidson, Wm.	Clarke	Stewarts	193/19	Wilkinson
Davies, Isham	Burke	Gordans	206/15	Wilkinson
Davies, Isham	Burke	Gordons	266/14	Wilkinson
Davies, Wm.B.	Burke	Gordans	261/9	Wilkinson
Davinport's, John(Orphs.)	Burke	Fields	142/11	Wilkinson
Davinport, John(Capt.)	Greene	Davinports	246/13	Wilkinson
Davis', Brock(Orphs.)	Warren	Neals	130/8	Wilkinson
Davis', Wm.(Orphs.)	Greene	Davinports	89/20	Wilkinson
Davis's, James(Orphs.)	Clarke	Hitchcocks	309/22	Wilkinson
Davis's, Thos.(Orphs.)	Burke	Ballards	246/21	Wilkinson
Davis, Abraham	Columbia	9	31/20	Baldwin
Davis, Absalom Jr.	Elbert	Thompsons	69/20	Wilkinson
Davis, Absalom Sr.	Elbert	Thompsons	302/24	Wilkinson
Davis, Allen	Baldwin	4	83/19	Wilkinson
Davis, Ann	Elbert	Thompsons	191/16	Wilkinson
Davis, Arthur Jr.	Warren	Hills	220/16	Wilkinson
Davis, Benjamin	Jefferson	Tarvers	7/16	Wilkinson
Davis, Blanaford	Columbia	1	194/12	Wilkinson
Davis, Charles	Wilkes	I.Hendersons	207/12	Wilkinson
Davis, David(Son/Toliver)	Oglethorpe	Bells	177/22	Wilkinson
Davis, Dempsey	Burke	Thompsons	134/13	Wilkinson
Davis, Dolly(Orph.)	Screven		30/15	Wilkinson
Davis, Edward	Clarke	Browns	93/16	Baldwin
Davis, Elijah	Washington	Carretts	216/19	Baldwin
Davis, Evan	Columbia	9	42/11	Wilkinson
Davis, George	Screven		165/21	Wilkinson
Davis, George	Warren	Neals	207/6	Wilkinson
Davis, Hansom	Lincoln	Normans	120/17	Wilkinson
Davis, Hezekiah	Effingham		46/19	Baldwin
Davis, Hugh	Baldwin	2	153/20	Baldwin
Davis, James	Greene	Butlers	138/18	Wilkinson
Davis, James	Jefferson	Colemans	106/8	Wilkinson
Davis, Jeremiah	Warren	Jones	277/12	Wilkinson
Davis, John Jr.	Columbia	9	271/14	Baldwin
Davis, John Jr.	Jackson	Cockrans	98/6	Wilkinson
Davis, John Sr.(See Orig.)	Washington	Burneys	3/20	Baldwin
Davis, John	Baldwin	5	123/28	Wilkinson
Davis, John	Burke	Martins	34/23	Wilkinson
Davis, John	Columbia	6	38/14	Baldwin
Davis, John	Oglethorpe	Popes	84/16	Baldwin
Davis, John	Washington	Chivers	235/14	Wilkinson
Davis, John	Washington	Chivers	296/16	Wilkinson

NAME	COUNTY	MIL.DIST.	LOT/DIST	DREW LAND
Davis, John	Wilkes	Edges	116/13	Wilkinson
Davis, Jonathan	Wilkes	Stovalls	120/6	Baldwin
Davis, Jonathan	Wilkes	Stovalls	225/19	Wilkinson
Davis, Joseph(Son/Jas.)	Columbia	3	1/10	Baldwin
Davis, Joseph	Jackson	Cockrans	80/11	Wilkinson
Davis, Joshua	Wilkes	Wellborns	198/11	Wilkinson
Davis, Josiah	Burke	Forths	355/13	Wilkinson
Davis, Josiah	Wayne	2	18/9	Wilkinson
Davis, Lewis	Burke	Thompsons	216/10	Wilkinson
Davis, Lewis	Burke	Thompsons	240/11	Wilkinson
Davis, Lewis	Franklin	Griffiths	30/12	Wilkinson
Davis, Lucy	Burke	Forths	221/10	Wilkinson
Davis, Margaret	Warren	Neals	372/22	Wilkinson
Davis, Martha	Columbia	1	179/16	Baldwin
Davis, Mary	Elbert	Clarks	252/23	Wilkinson
Davis, Mary	Tattnall	Staffords	204/21	Wilkinson
Davis, Mathew	Jefferson	Wrights	97/19	Baldwin
Davis, Merideth	Elbert	Blackwells	73/18	Baldwin
Davis, Moses	Burke	Bynes	77/12	Wilkinson
Davis, Moses	Elbert	Willifords	15/9	Baldwin
Davis, Moses	Elbert	Willifords	284/6	Wilkinson
Davis, Nathan	Warren	Willsons	144/10	Baldwin
Davis, Nathaniel	Columbia	9	33/17	Wilkinson
Davis, Peter	Warren	Willsons	36/16	Wilkinson
Davis, Reubin	Wilkes	Heards	211/18	Wilkinson
Davis, Ruth	Burke	Sandifords	140/18	Baldwin
Davis, Sally(Miss)	Warren	Jones	5/22	Wilkinson
Davis, Samuel	Effingham		319/10	Wilkinson
Davis, Sarah	Greene	Davinports	219/17	Wilkinson
Davis, Sherwood	Oglethorpe	Moores	63/19	Wilkinson
Davis, Solomon	Bulloch	Denmarks	19/12	Baldwin
Davis, Thomas	Greene	Stewarts	90/6	Baldwin
Davis, Thos.(Red)	Baldwin	5	77/16	Baldwin
Davis, Vincent	Warren	Devereux	41/10	Wilkinson
Davis, William	Burke	Sandifords	145/14	Baldwin
Davis, William	Elbert	Faulkners	189/26	Wilkinson
Davis, William	Jefferson	Colemans	231/18	Wilkinson
Davis, William	Jefferson	Colemans	5/16	Wilkinson
Davis, Wm.P.	Baldwin	5	295/14	Baldwin
Davis, Wm.Sr.	Wilkes	Milners	22/13	Baldwin
Dawdy, Henry M.	Wilkes	Heards	181/23	Wilkinson
Daws, George W.	Wilkes	Heards	171/15	Wilkinson
Dawson's, James(Orphs.)	Washington	Howards	25/9	Baldwin
Dawson, William	Oglethorpe	Hewells	196/23	Wilkinson
Day, Ambrose	Jefferson	Wrights	14/19	Wilkinson
Day, Eliz.(Wid.)	Clarke	Browns	326/20	Baldwin
Day, Eliza(Orph.)	Jefferson	Wrights	156/20	Wilkinson
Day, Jonathan	Baldwin	1	110/14	Baldwin
Day, Jonathan	Baldwin	1	85/16	Wilkinson
DeShazo, Lewis	Putnam	Neyles	40/20	Wilkinson
Deadwiler, Christopher	Elbert	Faulkners	53/6	Wilkinson
Deadwiler, Christopher	Elbert	Faulkners	98/10	Baldwin
Deadwiler, Eve	Elbert	Faulkners	110/19	Wilkinson
Deadwiler, Martin	Elbert	Faulkners	114/23	Wilkinson
Deakle, Charles	Montgomery	59	130/6	Baldwin
Deakle, John	Montgomery	59	213/8	Wilkinson
Deal's, Wm.(Orphs.)	Jackson	Hendersons	131/7	Baldwin
Deal, Ephraim	Jackson	Hendersons	18/15	Baldwin
Deal, Ephraim	Jackson	Hendersons	267/16	Wilkinson
Deal, Jarvis	Jackson	Hendersons	216/11	Wilkinson
Dean, Charles	Columbia	10	52/7	Baldwin
Dean, Charles	Elbert	Keelings	123/12	Wilkinson
Dean, James	Burke	Burkes	294/14	Wilkinson
Dean, Milly(S.W.)	Clarke	Hitchcocks	6/25	Wilkinson
Dean, Moses	Washington	Paces	242/16	Wilkinson
Dean, Moses	Washington	Paces	93/19	Baldwin
Dean, Shadrack Sr.	Elbert	Willifords	196/17	Wilkinson

NAME	COUNTY	MIL.DIST.	LOT/DIST	DREW LAND
Dean, Thomas	Elbert	Willifords	113/28	Wilkinson
Deans', Jeremiah(Orphs.)	Jackson	Cockrans	74/24	Wilkinson
Deans, Jeremiah	Jackson	Cockrans	85/18	Wilkinson
Deans, Mary(Wid.)	Jackson	Cockrans	133/17	Baldwin
Deans, Mary(Wid.)	Washington	Burneys	217/24	Wilkinson
Dearman, Delila	Jefferson	Hardwicks	80/21	Wilkinson
Dearman, Eliz.(Wid.)	Jefferson	Hardwicks	29/14	Baldwin
Dearmond, Wm.P.(Orph.)	Richmond		111/23	Wilkinson
Deas, Nancy	Jefferson		171/17	Wilkinson
Decheneaux, Thos.	Chatham	Pembertons	115/23	Wilkinson
Deck, Samuel	Washington	Andersons	108/9	Baldwin
Decker, Allen R.	Elbert	Thompsons	116/19	Wilkinson
Decker, Allen R.	Elbert	Thompsons	311/20	Wilkinson
Deering, John B.	Wilkes	Heards	8/9	Wilkinson
Deering, Keziah	Wilkes	Heards	267/10	Wilkinson
Deering, Thomas	Wilkes	Heards	4/13	Baldwin
Dees, Duett	Jefferson		108/12	Wilkinson
Dees, John(Orph.)	Wayne	2	207/15	Baldwin
Dees, Martha	Tattnall	Armstrongs	15/28	Wilkinson
Delian, Abraham	Chatham	Pembertons	186/26	Wilkinson
Delk, Jacob	Washington	Delks	209/17	Wilkinson
Delk, Samuel	Liberty		436/7	Wilkinson
Delk, Thomas	Wilkinson		175/28	Wilkinson
Deloatch, William	Liberty		156/19	Wilkinson
Demere's, Raymond(Orphs.)	Bryan	Austins	68/15	Baldwin
Denmark, Readin	Bulloch	Denmarks	279/9	Wilkinson
Dennard, Abner	Washington	Wiggins	59/18	Wilkinson
Dennard, James	Wilkinson		127/22	Wilkinson
Dennard, William	Wilkinson		36/28	Wilkinson
Denney, Caty	Elbert	Groves	295/8	Wilkinson
Denney, Edward Sr.	Elbert	Groves	65/20	Baldwin
Dennis, Asa	Warren	Willsons	56/25	Wilkinson
Dennis, Isaac Jr.	Hancock	Pinkstons	178/16	Wilkinson
Dennis, Isaac Jr.	Hancock	Pinkstons	309/10	Wilkinson
Dennis, Isaac	Hancock	Barksdales	308/13	Wilkinson
Dennis, Isaac	Hancock	Barksdales	81/18	Wilkinson
Dennis, John	Greene	Armours	82/12	Baldwin
Dennis, Josiah	Hancock	Coopers	163/20	Baldwin
Dennison, William	Wayne	3	240/20	Wilkinson
Dennison, Wm.	Wayne	3	332/22	Wilkinson
Denslar, Philip	Chatham	Herbs	207/19	Baldwin
Densler, Barbary	Chatham	Abrahams	81/9	Wilkinson
Densler, Sophia	Chatham	Whites	17/25	Wilkinson
Denson, Joel	Wilkinson		116/25	Wilkinson
Denson, Joel	Wilkinson		187/13	Wilkinson
Denson, John	Jefferson		146/17	Baldwin
Denson, Joseph	Wilkinson		120/10	Wilkinson
Denson, Joseph	Wilkinson		139/14	Wilkinson
Dent, George	Columbia	1	248/20	Wilkinson
Dent, Sarah	Columbia	1	118/9	Baldwin
Denton, Edward	Hancock	Pinkstons	140/19	Wilkinson
Denton, James	Columbia	9	191/18	Wilkinson
Derden, John	Columbia	9	178/10	Baldwin
Deshield, George	Hancock	Coopers	28/14	Baldwin
Deubignon, Christopher	Glynn		151/8	Baldwin
Deveaux, John B.	Screven		22/11	Baldwin
Deveney, James	Franklin	Everetts	261/20	Wilkinson
Devereux, Archibald M.	Baldwin	1	128/8	Baldwin
Devine, James	Liberty		83/11	Wilkinson
Dews, John(Orph.)	Chatham	Pettybones	348/12	Wilkinson
Dews, Josiah(Orph.)	Chatham	Pettybones	348/13	Wilkinson
Dews, Susannah	Chatham	Neals	279/17	Wilkinson
Dial, Elizabeth	Franklin	Cleghorns	419/7	Wilkinson
Dial, John	Franklin	Cleghorns	204/26	Wilkinson
Dick's, John(Orphs.)	Hancock	Crowders	171/10	Baldwin
Dicken's, Joseph(Orphs.)	Wilkes		3/9	Baldwin
Dicken, John	Wilkes	M.Hendersons	235/13	Wilkinson

NAME	COUNTY	MIL.DIST.	LOT/DIST	DREW LAND
Dicken, Joseph	Baldwin	1	196/13	Baldwin
Dicken, Richard	Clarke	Browns	29/9	Baldwin
Dickens, John Jr.	Warren	Devereux	307/8	Wilkinson
Dickens, John Jr.	Warren	Devereux	71/9	Wilkinson
Dickens, John Sr.	Warren	Devereux	348/22	Wilkinson
Dickenson, Joel	Clarke	Robinsons	340/9	Wilkinson
Dickerson, Henry	Washington	Holts	261/10	Wilkinson
Dickerson, John	Hancock	Coopers	86/17	Wilkinson
Dicks', David(Orph.)	Liberty		107/17	Wilkinson
Dicks, Alexander	Bryan	Austins	90/16	Wilkinson
Dicky, Joseph	Screven		150/18	Baldwin
Dicky, Patrick	Screven		145/10	Baldwin
Diell, James	Jackson	Cockrans	243/25	Wilkinson
Dier, John	Baldwin	4	211/11	Wilkinson
Digby, William	Baldwin	1	360/7	Wilkinson
Digby, William	Wilkes	Edges	299/7	Wilkinson
Digby, Wm.	Baldwin	1	71/28	Wilkinson
Dill's, Michael(Orphs.)	Oglethorpe	Hudsons	154/20	Baldwin
Dill, Daniel	Richmond		203/28	Wilkinson
Dill, Philip	Lincoln	Gatrills	42/6	Wilkinson
Dillard, Jeriah(Wid/Geo.)	Columbia	6	368/7	Wilkinson
Dillard, Nathan	Washington	Paces	114/18	Baldwin
Dillard, Nicholas	Washington	Paces	349/13	Wilkinson
Dillard, Priscilla	Washington	Paces	42/26	Wilkinson
Dillard, Sampson	Montgomery	53	73/16	Wilkinson
Dillard, Thomas	Burke	Caswells	84/15	Baldwin
Dingler, William	Elbert	Thompsons	172/27	Wilkinson
Disablew, Lewis P.	Washington	Andersons	277/11	Wilkinson
Dismuke, Wm.	Hancock	Smiths	35/12	Baldwin
Dismukes, Fenny(C.W.)	Baldwin	1	267/20	Baldwin
Dismukes, John Jr.	Baldwin	1	20/23	Wilkinson
Dismukes, John Sr.	Baldwin	1	29/7	Wilkinson
Dismukes, Reubin	Columbia	1	322/10	Wilkinson
Dixon's, Wm.(Orphs.)	Washington	Paces	50/23	Wilkinson
Dixon, David	Franklin	Dixons	249/10	Baldwin
Dixon, George	Burke	Blounts	65/17	Wilkinson
Dixon, Joel	Hancock	Hudsons	48/12	Baldwin
Dixon, John	Hancock	Barksdales	148/22	Wilkinson
Dixon, John	Jefferson	Thomas	165/12	Wilkinson
Dixon, John	Jefferson	Thomas	173/10	Wilkinson
Dixon, Mary(Wid.)	Franklin	Dixons	182/17	Wilkinson
Dixon, Michael	Screven		49/26	Wilkinson
Dixon, Nicholas	Hancock	Hudsons	207/24	Wilkinson
Dixon, Phoebe	Washington	Willis	259/24	Wilkinson
Dixon, Robert	Elbert	Thompsons	131/22	Wilkinson
Dixon, Robert	Elbert	Thompsons	31/20	Wilkinson
Dixon, Robert	Montgomery	58	276/8	Wilkinson
Dixon, Robert	Screven		66/27	Wilkinson
Dixon, Solomon	Greene	Butlers	74/17	Wilkinson
Dixon, Thomas	Franklin	Dixons	8/19	Wilkinson
Dixon, Windsor	Screven		402/8	Wilkinson
Dixon, Wm.(Esq.)	Greene	Butlers	326/17	Wilkinson
Dobbins, James	Franklin	Everetts	142/6	Wilkinson
Dobbins, Jane(Wid.)	Clarke	Trammells	26/24	Wilkinson
Dobbins, Thomas	Franklin	Everetts	75/9	Wilkinson
Dobbins, Thomas	Franklin	Everretts	350/12	Wilkinson
Dobbs, John	Elbert	Barretts	93/17	Baldwin
Dobbs, Lott	Elbert	Barretts	209/12	Baldwin
Dobbs, Lucy(Wid.)	Elbert	Barretts	205/15	Wilkinson
Dobbs, Nathaniel	Clarke	Hopkins	338/7	Wilkinson
Dobbs, Peter	Elbert	Barretts	82/20	Baldwin
Dodd, William	Elbert	McGuires	187/10	Baldwin
Dodson, Anne	Chatham	Hardens	8/7	Baldwin
Dodson, Isaac	Clarke	Silmans	60/7	Baldwin
Dodson, William	Chatham	Hardens	89/11	Baldwin
Doggett, Asa(Son/John)	Columbia	3	128/9	Baldwin
Doggett, Chatten	Clarke	Robinsons	206/21	Wilkinson

NAME	COUNTY	MIL.DIST.	LOT/DIST	DREW LAND
Doggett, Thomas	Clarke	Robinsons	103/18	Wilkinson
Doggett, Thomas	Clarke	Robinsons	31/22	Wilkinson
Dollaghan, Thomas	Chatham	Pembertons	13/13	Wilkinson
Dolvin, John	Greene	Dawsons	170/12	Wilkinson
Dolvin, John	Greene	Dawsons	267/12	Wilkinson
Donaghey, Samuel	Clarke	Hitchcocks	34/8	Baldwin
Donago, John	Hancock	Weeks	103/12	Baldwin
Donaldson, Mary(S)	Jefferson	Hardwicks	284/13	Wilkinson
Donaldson, Robert	Bulloch	Williams	256/14	Baldwin
Donaldson, Wm.	Chatham	Pettybones	52/25	Wilkinson
Donalson, William	Burke	Montgomerys	136/10	Baldwin
Donstan, Charles	Oglethorpe	Smiths	96/15	Wilkinson
Dooly, William Jr.	Elbert	McGuires	67/12	Baldwin
Dooly, Wm.Sr.	Elbert	McGuires	184/8	Wilkinson
Dorman, Allen	Warren	Flournoys	208/14	Baldwin
Dorman, Allen	Warren	Flournoys	5/7	Baldwin
Dorman, John	Clarke	Cooks	26/6	Wilkinson
Dorsett, John	Columbia	5	216/19	Wilkinson
Dorsett, Nancy(Dau/Jno.)	Columbia	5	285/22	Wilkinson
Dorsey, Mathew	Greene	Alfords	98/9	Baldwin
Doss, Clayborn	Jackson	Johnsons	202/28	Wilkinson
Doss, Edward	Jackson	Hendersons	77/28	Wilkinson
Doss, John(Son/Wm.)	Columbia	11	13/22	Wilkinson
Doss, Urshla(Wid.)	Jackson	Johnsons	71/26	Wilkinson
Doster, James	Franklin	Everetts	232/21	Wilkinson
Doudle's, James(Orphs.)	Hancock	Weeks	35/19	Baldwin
Dougherty, Charles	Clarke	Hitchcocks	160/26	Wilkinson
Dougherty, Daniel	Tattnall	Halls	62/23	Wilkinson
Dougherty, Jacob	Tattnall	Armstrongs	52/10	Baldwin
Dougherty, Michael	Columbia	7	178/27	Wilkinson
Douglas, Benjamin	Chatham	McClains	306/11	Wilkinson
Douglass', James(Orphs.)	Wilkinson		291/20	Wilkinson
Douglass, Alexander	Screven		97/6	Wilkinson
Douglass, David Jr.	Jefferson		214/18	Wilkinson
Douglass, George	Columbia	11	244/19	Baldwin
Douglass, James	Franklin	Griffiths	57/12	Wilkinson
Douglass, John	Chatham	McLeans	422/7	Wilkinson
Douglass, John	Chatham	Pembertons	262/19	Wilkinson
Douglass, John	Jefferson	Thomas	174/10	Baldwin
Douglass, Mary Ann	Hancock	Thomas	57/10	Baldwin
Douglass, Samuel	Wilkes	Harris	2/13	Baldwin
Douglass, Samuel	Wilkes	Harris	384/8	Wilkinson
Douglass, Thomas	Wilkes	Harris	172/10	Wilkinson
Doussett, Auguste G.	Chatham	Abrahams	246/5	Baldwin
Dove, David	Wilkes	Hendricks	358/12	Wilkinson
Dove, Richard	Burke	Mulkeys	31/17	Wilkinson
Dover, Thomas	Glynn		28/7	Wilkinson
Dowdy, James	Franklin	Dixons	143/8	Baldwin
Dowdy, Richard	Montgomery	51	162/22	Wilkinson
Downer, Joseph	Elbert	Dyes	126/10	Baldwin
Downie, David	Richmond		231/22	Wilkinson
Downie, Margarett	Richmond		325/21	Wilkinson
Downing, Abednego	Franklin	Henrys	335/10	Wilkinson
Downing, Edward	Baldwin	1	181/15	Wilkinson
Downman, William	Hancock	Barnes	325/13	Wilkinson
Downs, Barnett	Clarke	Cooks	111/18	Wilkinson
Downs, David	Greene	Butlers	361/7	Wilkinson
Downs, Geo.Jr.	Columbia	7	42/15	Wilkinson
Downs, George	Columbia	1	265/6	Wilkinson
Downs, James Jr.	Baldwin	2	32/16	Baldwin
Downs, Joseph	Columbia	1	156/8	Wilkinson
Downs, Mary	Greene	Butlers	95/20	Wilkinson
Downs, William	Camden	Crews	156/14	Wilkinson
Downs, William	Effingham		190/23	Wilkinson
Dows, Parker	Wilkes	Heards	15/12	Baldwin
Dowsing, Wm.Jr.	Lincoln	Busseys	26/10	Wilkinson
Doyle, Francis	Chatham	Pembertons	116/12	Baldwin

NAME	COUNTY	MIL.DIST.	LOT/DIST	DREW LAND
Dozer, Thomas	Columbia	10	152/18	Wilkinson
Drake's, Shemy(Orphs.)	Hancock	Coffees	230/25	Wilkinson
Drake's, Thomas(Orphs.)	Jefferson	Wrights	301/9	Wilkinson
Drake, Ephroditus	Hancock	Hudsons	43/15	Baldwin
Drake, Turner	Elbert	Groves	212/15	Wilkinson
Drane, Walter	Columbia	7	209/19	Wilkinson
Drane, William	Columbia	7	20/25	Wilkinson
Draper, Joshua	Warren	Willsons	112/26	Wilkinson
Draper, Josiah	Warren	Willsons	266/22	Wilkinson
Drawdy's, James(Orphs.)	Montgomery	56	209/22	Wilkinson
Drawdy's, James(Orphs.)	Montgomery	56	351/12	Wilkinson
Dreaden, Jonathan	Jackson	Hendersons	89/14	Baldwin
Dredden, William	Wilkinson		221/24	Wilkinson
Dregors, Henry	Liberty		13/17	Baldwin
Drew, William	Montgomery	52	99/17	Baldwin
Drew, Willoby	Burke	Fields	300/21	Wilkinson
Driscal, Laurence C.	Chatham	Pettybones	67/7	Wilkinson
Driscol, Dennis	Richmond		242/7	Wilkinson
Driskell, John	Hancock	Wallers	74/20	Baldwin
Driver, Betsey(Wid.)	Elbert	Blackwells	10/19	Baldwin
Driver, William	Elbert	McGuires	194/17	Baldwin
Druillard, Andre	Chatham	Abrams	88/11	Wilkinson
Drury, Mills	Camden	Crews	161/12	Baldwin
Dryden's, John(Orphs.)	Liberty		128/9	Wilkinson
Dryer, Nathan	Liberty		63/20	Baldwin
Dubell, John H.	Chatham	Pettybones	285/11	Wilkinson
Duberry, Anna(Wid.)	Warren	Heaths	254/24	Wilkinson
Duck, Timothy	Baldwin	4	227/21	Wilkinson
Duckworth, Jeremiah	Warren	Willsons	12/6	Baldwin
Duckworth, Randall	Warren	Willsons	124/15	Baldwin
Duckworth, Randall	Warren	Willsons	144/9	Baldwin
Dudley's, Aaron(Orph.)	Liberty		71/23	Wilkinson
Dudley, James	Baldwin	5	302/17	Wilkinson
Dudley, James	Elbert	Keelings	280/14	Wilkinson
Dudley, John	Hancock	Hudsons	319/21	Wilkinson
Dudley, John	Jefferson	Wrights	156/17	Wilkinson
Duff, Moses	Jackson	Hendersons	342/9	Wilkinson
Duffill, Thomas	Washington	Wiggins	107/24	Wilkinson
Duffill, Thomas	Washington	Wiggins	160/20	Baldwin
Duggar, Sampson	Hancock	Crowders	196/7	Wilkinson
Duke, Chaney(Wid.)	Burke	Sharps	7/24	Wilkinson
Duke, Edmond	Clarke	Hopkins	310/7	Wilkinson
Duke, Edmund	Clarke	Hopkins	234/10	Wilkinson
Duke, Eliz.(Orph.)	Burke	Sharps	208/18	Wilkinson
Duke, Epps	Greene	Davinports	230/20	Baldwin
Duke, Greene R.	Chatham	Pembertons	144/14	Baldwin
Duke, Hardiman	Clarke	Hopkins	253/16	Wilkinson
Duke, Hardy	Greene	Baxters	280/19	Baldwin
Duke, Henry	Wilkes	Coopers	61/16	Wilkinson
Duke, John	Baldwin	1	133/9	Wilkinson
Duke, John	Baldwin	1	49/9	Baldwin
Duke, John	Franklin	Hoopers	145/21	Wilkinson
Duke, John	Franklin	Hoopers	233/20	Baldwin
Duke, John	Tattnall	Staffords	62/19	Baldwin
Duke, M.Jr.	Oglethorpe	Watkins	46/14	Baldwin
Duke, Willis	Burke	Forths	12/19	Wilkinson
Dukes, Abraham	Jackson	Wrights	301/8	Wilkinson
Dukes, John	Clarke	Dukes	184/25	Wilkinson
Dukes, John	Clarke	Dukes	229/23	Wilkinson
Dukes, Keziah	Hancock	Coffees	145/26	Wilkinson
Dukes, Starling	Clarke	Cooks	189/6	Baldwin
Dukes, Thomas Jr.	Oglethorpe	Smiths	50/24	Wilkinson
Dukes, Wm.Sr.	Clarke	Hopkins	3/28	Wilkinson
Dunagan, Abner	Franklin	Hollingsworths	132/12	Wilkinson
Dunahoo, Cornelius	Elbert	Barretts	388/21	Wilkinson
Dunaway, Timothy C.	Wilkes	Normans	167/24	Wilkinson
Dunaway, William	Warren	Neals	47/9	Baldwin

NAME	COUNTY	MIL.DIST.	LOT/DIST	DREW LAND
Duncan, Benjamin(Orph.)	Jackson	Johnsons	125/23	Wilkinson
Duncan, Eliz.(Wid.)	Screven	Williamsons	43/25	Wilkinson
Duncan, Elizabeth(Wid.)	Jefferson	Hardwicks	216/6	Baldwin
Duncan, Jane(Wid.)	Greene	Jenkins	281/14	Wilkinson
Duncan, Pearson	Elbert	Keelings	64/27	Wilkinson
Duncan, Sarah Ann	Liberty		261/15	Wilkinson
Duncan, William	Elbert	Keelings	8/25	Wilkinson
Dunford, Jesse	Burke	Spains	80/25	Wilkinson
Dunford, John	Burke	Spains	169/18	Baldwin
Dunford, John	Burke	Spains	83/16	Wilkinson
Dunham, Mathew	Hancock	Weeks	341/9	Wilkinson
Dunham, Samuel	Richmond		94/10	Baldwin
Dunlap, William	Elbert	Thompsons	36/13	Baldwin
Dunn's, John(Orphs.)	Jackson	Johnsons	120/10	Baldwin
Dunn, Alexander	Baldwin	3	332/21	Wilkinson
Dunn, Ephraim	Hancock	Crowders	236/9	Wilkinson
Dunn, Holden	Washington	Delks	47/17	Baldwin
Dunn, Jacob	Screven		85/9	Wilkinson
Dunn, John	Oglethorpe	Stewarts	267/9	Wilkinson
Dunn, John	Wilkes	Parks	191/13	Wilkinson
Dunn, John	Wilkes	Parks	98/17	Baldwin
Dunn, Joseph	Franklin	Hoopers	85/7	Wilkinson
Dunn, Joseph	Wilkes	Youngs	52/10	Wilkinson
Dunn, Mathew	Burke	Thompsons	75/7	Wilkinson
Dunn, Milly(Wid.)	Burke	Thompsons	50/27	Wilkinson
Dunn, Nancy(Wid.)	Burke	Thompsons	209/12	Wilkinson
Dunn, Polly	Oglethorpe	Beasleys	126/20	Baldwin
Dunn, William	Burke	Burkes	499/7	Wilkinson
Dunn, William	Jackson	Johnsons	76/9	Baldwin
Dunwody, James	Liberty		17/11	Baldwin
Dupree, Daniel	Oglethorpe	Moores	150/8	Wilkinson
Dupree, Rebecca	Jefferson		53/15	Wilkinson
Dupree, Thomas	Burke	Fields	34/7	Baldwin
Durbin's, Luke(Orphs.)	Jackson	Wrights	118/19	Baldwin
Durden, Jesse	Columbia	9	176/16	Baldwin
Durden, Jesse	Columbia	9	88/16	Baldwin
Durden, John	Montgomery	59	42/16	Wilkinson
Durden, Josiah	Baldwin	1	28/20	Wilkinson
Durden, Josiah	Baldwin	1	29/12	Wilkinson
Durden, Stephen	Hancock	Huffs	165/6	Wilkinson
Durden, Stephen	Hancock	Huffs	50/19	Baldwin
Durham's, Samuel(Orphs.)	Washington	Willis	154/8	Wilkinson
Durowzeux, Peter	Jefferson		245/25	Wilkinson
Durowzeux, Stephen	Jefferson		288/10	Wilkinson
Durrence, Francis	Tattnall	McDonalds	12/23	Wilkinson
Durrence, Francis	Tattnall	McDonalds	53/26	Wilkinson
Duskin, Hannah	Elbert	Willifords	159/22	Wilkinson
Dutton, Thomas	Elbert	Roebucks	30/19	Baldwin
Duvall, Alexander	Jackson	Hendersons	154/28	Wilkinson
Duyckinck, Benjamin T.	Richmond		104/28	Wilkinson
Dwight, John P.	Baldwin	1	4/27	Wilkinson
Dyall, Thomas	McIntosh		287/9	Wilkinson
Dyall, Thomas	McIntosh		9/17	Baldwin
Dyche, John	Franklin	Hoopers	178/19	Baldwin
Dye, Elizabeth	Warren	Neals	86/13	Wilkinson
Dye, Hopkins	Burke	Carswells	120/13	Baldwin
Dye, Hopkins	Burke	Carswells	210/13	Baldwin
Dye, Mary	Warren	Neals	362/24	Wilkinson
Dye, Thompson	Elbert	Mobleys	392/22	Wilkinson
Dyer, Abner	Wilkes	Wellborns	55/8	Wilkinson
Dyer, Elijah	Burke	Ballards	130/16	Baldwin
Dyer, John	Clarke	Silmans	107/18	Baldwin
Dyess, John	Liberty		195/26	Wilkinson
Dykes, George P.	Baldwin	2	8/6	Wilkinson
Dyson, John	Wilkes	Heards	101/12	Wilkinson
Eads, Danl.(Indian Dr.)	Warren	Neals	129/12	Baldwin
Eads, Randle	Oglethorpe	Jno.Smiths	100/8	Baldwin

NAME	COUNTY	MIL.DIST.	LOT/DIST	DREW LAND
Eads, Sally(Orph.)	Oglethorpe	Jno.Smiths	100/26	Wilkinson
Eady, Elizabeth(Wid.)	Lincoln	Flemings	86/15	Baldwin
Eakin, Absalom	Elbert	Keelings	129/25	Wilkinson
Eakin, Moses	Baldwin	2	12/12	Baldwin
Earhart, Fanny(at Hersmans)	Chatham	Pettybones	78/10	Baldwin
Early, Eleazer	Jefferson	Wrights	169/18	Wilkinson
Early, Jeffrey	Oglethorpe	Stewarts	217/11	Wilkinson
Early, Jesse	Washington	Andersons	294/7	Wilkinson
Early, Joel	Greene	Watts	233/24	Wilkinson
Early, Joel	Greene	Watts	278/15	Baldwin
Early, Peter	Greene	Butlers	309/21	Wilkinson
Earnest, George Jr.	Hancock	Pinkstons	27/15	Wilkinson
Earnest, George Sr.	Hancock	Pinkstons	124/24	Wilkinson
Earnest, George	Clarke	Silmans	289/11	Wilkinson
Earnest, James	Clarke	Silmans	16/19	Baldwin
Earnest, John J.	Hancock	Pinkstons	21/9	Baldwin
Earnest, William	Clarke	Silmans	244/21	Wilkinson
Earp, Joseph	Washington	Delks	157/6	Wilkinson
Easley, Roderick Jr.	Wilkes	Sheets	40/11	Baldwin
Easly, Daniel W.	Clarke	Martins	203/8	Wilkinson
Easly, Richard S.	Clarke	Cooks	153/11	Wilkinson
Eason, Assenah(Wid.)	Oglethorpe	Watkins	137/23	Wilkinson
Easter's, Augustus(Orps.)	Tattnall	Sherrards	43/6	Baldwin
Easter, George	Tattnall	Sherrards	54/27	Wilkinson
Eastin, Reubin	Elbert	Faulkners	15/13	Wilkinson
Eastis, Zachariah Jr.	Oglethorpe	Smiths	10/17	Baldwin
Eastwood, ELijah	Washington	Holts	72/7	Baldwin
Eavans, Wm.	Chatham	Neals	269/17	Wilkinson
Eberhart, John	Elbert	Moons	97/16	Wilkinson
Echols, Absalom	Clarke	Harpers	169/13	Wilkinson
Echols, Betsy	Franklin	Hoopers	192/21	Wilkinson
Echols, Caleb	Hancock	Pinkstons	83/6	Baldwin
Echols, Elijah	Columbia	4	469/7	Wilkinson
Echols, Iasal	Franklin	Bryants	72/22	Wilkinson
Echols, James Sr.	Clarke	Harpers	101/16	Wilkinson
Echols, James Sr.	Clarke	Harpers	367/8	Wilkinson
Echols, John	Baldwin	4	342/13	Wilkinson
Echols, Richard	Franklin	Yowells	75/15	Wilkinson
Echols, Robert E.	Clarke	Browns	247/20	Wilkinson
Eckels, Nathan	Wilkes	Milners	122/13	Wilkinson
Ector, Hugh	Oglethorpe	Hartsfields	101/23	Wilkinson
Ector, Hugh	Oglethorpe	Hartsfields	51/7	Wilkinson
Ector, John	Oglethorpe	Hartsfields	103/17	Wilkinson
Ector, Joseph	Oglethorpe	Hewells	122/9	Wilkinson
Ector, Joseph	Oglethorpe	Hewells	212/13	Baldwin
Edge, Obadiah	Wilkes	Edges	72/14	Wilkinson
Edmondson, John	Washington	Wiggins	187/14	Baldwin
Edmonds, James	Lincoln	Normans	44/13	Baldwin
Edmonds, Rachal	Wilkes	Heards(See Orig.)	6/16	Baldwin
Edmondson, Crafford	Oglethorpe	Stewarts	56/14	Wilkinson
Edmondson, Philip	Oglethorpe	Stewarts	2/8	Baldwin
Edmondson, Richard	Greene	Flournoys	360/12	Wilkinson
Edmondson, Samuel	Oglethorpe	Stewarts	136/9	Wilkinson
Edmondson, Thomas	Oglethorpe	Stewarts	133/16	Baldwin
Edmunds, David	Baldwin	2	102/12	Wilkinson
Edmunds, John Jr.	Lincoln	Normans	14/9	Wilkinson
Edmunds, Rachal	Wilkes	Harris	6/16	Baldwin
Edmundson, Isaac	Bulloch	Parish	182/24	Wilkinson
Edwards, Ambrose	Baldwin	2	115/9	Wilkinson
Edwards, Cullin	Montgomery	54	121/19	Wilkinson
Edwards, James	Wilkes	Roreys	129/27	Wilkinson
Edwards, Miles	Burke	Carswells	219/12	Wilkinson
Edwards, Phereby	Burke	Carswells	113/19	Wilkinson
Edwards, Sarah	Greene	Moores	44/23	Wilkinson
Edwards, Thomas L.	Washington	Howards	98/26	Wilkinson
Edwards, Thomas	Greene	Moores	95/25	Wilkinson
Edwards, William	Effingham		122/6	Baldwin

NAME	COUNTY	MIL.DIST.	LOT/DIST	DREW LAND
Edwards, William	Montgomery	54	294/16	Wilkinson
Edwards, Wm.	Baldwin	4	179/14	Wilkinson
Edwards, Wm.H.(Orp/Willis)	Bryan	Birds	27/17	Baldwin
Edy, John Sr.	Wilkinson		288/17	Wilkinson
Eidson, Thomas	Wilkes	Coopers	295/7	Wilkinson
Eikley, Mary	Burke	Sandifords	64/20	Baldwin
Eiland's, James(Orphs.)	Hancock	Pinkstons	131/6	Baldwin
Eiland, Absalom	Hancock	Pinkstons	56/9	Baldwin
Eiland, Asa	Hancock	Pinkstons	208/10	Wilkinson
Eiland, Asa	Hancock	Pinkstons	253/14	Wilkinson
Eiland, Isiah	Hancock	Candlers	309/13	Wilkinson
Eiland, Ruth(Wid.)	Hancock	Candlers	12/9	Wilkinson
Eilands, Abigail	Glynn		221/15	Baldwin
Eilands, James	McIntosh		32/11	Wilkinson
Eilands, William	Glynn		300/13	Wilkinson
Elder, Joshua	Clarke	Martindales	15/9	Wilkinson
Elders, James	Chatham	Herbs	158/14	Wilkinson
Elkins, John Jr.	Effingham		312/13	Wilkinson
Ellet, William	Washington	Wm.Renfroes	22/15	Baldwin
Ellington, Josiah Jr.	Wilkes	Edges	185/22	Wilkinson
Ellington, Josiah(2 draws)	Wilkes	Hendrix	51/26	Wilkinson
Ellington, Rice	Elbert	Morrisons	183/28	Wilkinson
Elliott's, Amos(Orphs.)	Burke	Gordons	274/20	Baldwin
Elliott, Alexr.	Oglethorpe	Hewells	249/22	Wilkinson
Elliott, Alexr.	Oglethorpe	Hewells	353/9	Wilkinson
Elliott, Cornelius	Oglethorpe	Beasleys	232/14	Baldwin
Elliott, George	Oglethorpe	Hewells	39/24	Wilkinson
Elliott, Jane(Wid.)	Lincoln	Gartrells	73/7	Baldwin
Elliott, John	Liberty		54/17	Wilkinson
Elliott, Thomas	Jackson	Wrights	129/15	Baldwin
Elliott, William	Franklin	Cornelius	207/9	Wilkinson
Ellis, Daniel	Columbia	4	252/19	Baldwin
Ellis, Edward	Greene	Loves	124/17	Baldwin
Ellis, Hicks	Columbia	1	260/22	Wilkinson
Ellis, Isaac	Hancock	Coopers	87/9	Baldwin
Ellis, James	Hancock	Weeks	70/18	Baldwin
Ellis, John	Greene	Reas	157/14	Baldwin
Ellis, Joshua	Hancock	Weeks	8/8	Baldwin
Ellis, Leven	Hancock	Wallers	9/19	Baldwin
Ellis, Levi	Hancock	Smiths	264/16	Wilkinson
Ellis, Levi	Hancock	Smiths	3/6	Wilkinson
Ellis, Mary	Tattnall	Staffords	145/20	Baldwin
Ellis, Walter	Jackson	Wrights	327/21	Wilkinson
Ellis, Wm.Jr.	Oglethorpe	Hudsons	121/17	Wilkinson
Ellis, Wm.Jr.	Oglethorpe	Hudsons	4/6	Baldwin
Ellis, Zillar	Elbert	Olivers	84/18	Wilkinson
Ellison, Nancy	Jackson	Cockrans	83/28	Wilkinson
Ellison, Polly	Franklin	Cornelius	197/26	Wilkinson
Ellison, Robt.Sr.	Jackson	Cockrans	26/27	Wilkinson
Ellison, Samuel	Franklin	Everetts	55/20	Wilkinson
Elon, Felix	Chatham	Pembertons	141/24	Wilkinson
Elon, Sally	Chatham	Pembertons	141/24	Wilkinson
Elon, Wm.	Chatham	Pembertons	141/24	Wilkinson
Elzey, Elizabeth(Wid.)	Camden	Browns	24/18	Wilkinson
Emanuel, Asa	Tattnall	McDonalds	9/12	Wilkinson
Emanuel, David	Burke	Blounts	18/9	Baldwin
Emberson's, Jas.(Orphs.)	Greene	Watts	84/18	Baldwin
Embrie, Enoch	Oglethorpe	Hartsfields	175/27	Wilkinson
Embrie, John	Jackson	Johnsons	334/9	Wilkinson
Embrie, Joseph	Oglethorpe	Hartsfields	132/12	Baldwin
Emerson, William	Hancock	Gumms	36/8	Baldwin
England's, John(Orphs.)	Jackson	Johnsons	154/9	Baldwin
England, William	Franklin	Hollingsworths	133/13	Wilkinson
English, Cornelius	Tattnall	Halls	366/7	Wilkinson
English, James	Baldwin	2	238/22	Wilkinson
English, John	Washington	Garretts	239/20	Wilkinson
English, Perminus	Oglethorpe	Stewarts	88/26	Wilkinson

NAME	COUNTY	MIL.DIST.	LOT/DIST	DREW LAND
Epperson, Thomas	Oglethorpe	Popes	155/22	Wilkinson
Ernaud, Ranald D.(Orph.)	Chatham	Whites	108/6	Baldwin
Erwin, James	Jackson	Hendersons	79/27	Wilkinson
Erwin, Josiah	Wilkes	Sidwells	29/25	Wilkinson
Esham, Mary(Orph.)	Washington	Chivers	89/17	Baldwin
Espey, James	Lincoln	Busseys	206/14	Wilkinson
Espey, James	Oglethorpe	Popes	298/12	Wilkinson
Espey, John	Columbia	4	195/21	Wilkinson
Espey, Joseph	Oglethorpe	Popes	264/8	Wilkinson
Espey, Martha(Wid.)	Oglethorpe	Popes	174/11	Baldwin
Espey, Mary	Oglethorpe	Popes	256/12	Wilkinson
Espey, Wiley	Columbia	4	169/26	Wilkinson
Espy, Thomas	Jackson	Johnsons	177/20	Wilkinson
Estis, George	Wilkes	Milners	31/10	Baldwin
Estis, Zachary	Elbert	Hylliers	120/17	Baldwin
Etheridge, Elizabeth	Baldwin	1	20/18	Wilkinson
Etherington, Daniel(Orph.)	Richmond		221/25	Wilkinson
Etherington, Daniel(Orph.)	Richmond		84/11	Wilkinson
Etherington, Eliz.(Orph.)	Richmond		221/25	Wilkinson
Etherington, Eliz.(Orph.)	Richmond		84/11	Wilkinson
Etherington, Fanny(Orph.)	Richmond		221/25	Wilkinson
Etherington, Fanny(Orph.)	Richmond		84/11	Wilkinson
Etherington, Frizzel(Orp.)	Richmond		84/11	Wilkinson
Etherington, Frizzell(Orp.)	Richmond		221/25	Wilkinson
Etherington, Wm.	Jackson	Wrights	281/19	Wilkinson
Eubank, Garner	Baldwin	1	51/9	Baldwin
Eubank, George	Jefferson	Wrights	99/21	Wilkinson
Eubank, John	Jefferson	Wrights	341/7	Wilkinson
Eubank, Richard	Columbia	3	229/7	Wilkinson
Evans', James(Orphs.)	Wilkes	J.Hendersons	186/18	Baldwin
Evans, Absalom	Greene	Moores	53/27	Wilkinson
Evans, Benjamin	Wilkinson		111/15	Wilkinson
Evans, Daniel	Baldwin	5	125/28	Wilkinson
Evans, David	Wilkes	J.Hendersons	165/10	Baldwin
Evans, David	Wilkes	J.Hendersons	290/10	Wilkinson
Evans, Elli	Jackson	Hendersons	174/19	Wilkinson
Evans, George	Burke	Blounts	45/16	Baldwin
Evans, Henry(Orph.)	Burke	Blounts	15/27	Wilkinson
Evans, Henry	Richmond		103/8	Wilkinson
Evans, Hezekiah	Montgomery	50	190/6	Baldwin
Evans, Jabin	Hancock	Huffs	5/19	Baldwin
Evans, James	Hancock	Shivers	315/20	Wilkinson
Evans, Jehu	Jackson	Cockrans	158/26	Wilkinson
Evans, Jesse	Baldwin	5	114/28	Wilkinson
Evans, Jesse	Baldwin	5	49/15	Baldwin
Evans, John	Franklin	Everetts	221/23	Wilkinson
Evans, John	Jackson	Cockrans	44/9	Wilkinson
Evans, John	Washington	Burneys	313/15	Baldwin
Evans, Nathan	Washington	Blackshears	178/22	Wilkinson
Evans, Obadiah	Montgomery	50	31/9	Wilkinson
Evans, Rachel	Hancock	Shivers	153/18	Wilkinson
Evans, Sarah(Wid.)	Chatham	Whites	32/14	Baldwin
Evans, Stephen Sr.	Hancock	Huffs	216/13	Wilkinson
Evans, Stephen Sr.	Hancock	Huffs	49/17	Baldwin
Evans, Stephen	Wilkes	Malones	91/19	Wilkinson
Evans, Stith	Hancock	Huffs	121/28	Wilkinson
Evans, Thos.Sr.	Wilkes	Heards	312/10	Wilkinson
Evans, Wiliam Jr.	Greene	Baxters	191/8	Wilkinson
Evans, Will Jr.	Wilkes	Malones	242/23	Wilkinson
Evans, William	Lincoln	Gartrells	236/14	Wilkinson
Evans, Wm.(Son/Thos.)	Wilkes	Heards	1/13	Wilkinson
Eve, Oswell	Richmond		111/17	Baldwin
Everett, Enoch	Bryan	Birds	159/11	Wilkinson
Everett, Henry	Bulloch	Williams	6/6	Baldwin
Everett, Henry	Washington	Kendricks	210/13	Wilkinson
Everett, Jeremiah	Hancock	Thomas	68/6	Baldwin
Everett, John F.	Chatham	Whites	2/12	Wilkinson

NAME	COUNTY	MIL.DIST.	LOT/DIST	DREW LAND
Everett, John	Bulloch	Denmarks	47/16	Baldwin
Everett, Joshua	Bulloch	Parish	71/6	Wilkinson
Everett, Travis	Oglethorpe	Bells	48/22	Wilkinson
Everett, Turner	Washington	Kendricks	166/9	Wilkinson
Evers, John	Jefferson		211/23	Wilkinson
Evers, Mary(Wid.)	Effingham		75/22	Wilkinson
Evinson, George	Elbert	Blackwells	139/13	Baldwin
Ewin, Thomas(Esq.)	Jackson	Hendersons	154/21	Wilkinson
Ewing's, James(Orphs.)	Elbert	Groves	207/6	Baldwin
Ewing, Samuel	Hancock	Barnes	11/11	Wilkinson
Ezzard, William	Jackson	Wrights	226/11	Wilkinson
Ezzell, Henry	Hancock	Birdsongs	227/24	Wilkinson
Fain, Thomas	Screven		187/20	Wilkinson
Fain, William	Lincoln	Jones	329/21	Wilkinson
Fairchild, Cader	Bryan	Austins	198/9	Baldwin
Fairchild, Robert	Wilkinson		48/28	Wilkinson
Faircloth, Benjamin	Wilkinson		291/14	Wilkinson
Faircloth, Elizabeth	Jefferson		116/14	Wilkinson
Faircloth, Thomas	Screven		395/7	Wilkinson
Fambrough, Anderson	Oglethorpe	Hudsons	15/18	Wilkinson
Fambrough, Elizabeth	Oglethorpe	Hudsons	202/6	Baldwin
Fambrough, Thomas	Oglethorpe	Hudsons	107/14	Baldwin
Fannen, Laughlin	Elbert	Blackwells	485/7	Wilkinson
Fannin, William	Greene	Greers	146/9	Baldwin
Fanning, Jeptha	Greene	Alfords	263/21	Wilkinson
Fanning, Wm.Y.	Hancock	Huffs	145/15	Baldwin
Far, Celath	Warren	Willsons	5/13	Baldwin
Far, Darcus	Warren	Willsons	47/15	Wilkinson
Faris, Betty	Wilkes	Sidwells	171/20	Baldwin
Faris, Josiah	Wilkes	Sidwells	182/18	Wilkinson
Faris, Julius	Wilkes	Sidwells	282/6	Wilkinson
Farley, Gatesfield	Greene	Jinkins	215/21	Wilkinson
Farley, Grace	Chatham	Herbs	113/14	Baldwin
Farmer, Asael	Chatham	Abrahams	100/10	Wilkinson
Farmer, David	Burke	Bynes	219/19	Wilkinson
Farmer, Elizabeth(Wid.)	Burke	Bynes	23/17	Wilkinson
Farmer, Enoch	Burke	Bynes	260/21	Wilkinson
Farmer, George	Oglethorpe	Moores	30/23	Wilkinson
Farmer, Isaac	Burke	Bynes	150/14	Wilkinson
Farmer, Verity	Burke	Bynes	122/24	Wilkinson
Farmer, Verity	Burke	Bynes	136/18	Wilkinson
Farmer, William	Columbia	4	214/10	Baldwin
Farmer, Wm.	Screven		108/15	Baldwin
Farnell, James	Burke	Martins	317/12	Wilkinson
Farrar, Abner	Franklin	Allens	4/10	Baldwin
Farrar, Thomas	Franklin	Allens	116/8	Wilkinson
Farrell, John	Wilkes	Roreys	378/7	Wilkinson
Farrell, John	Wilkes	Roreys	93/25	Wilkinson
Farrer, Absalom	Columbia	4	79/23	Wilkinson
Farrow's, Bartholomew(Orps.)	Liberty		104/17	Wilkinson
Farrow, Henry	Oglethorpe	Popes	35/28	Wilkinson
Farrow, John S.	Oglethorpe	Hatchetts	163/22	Wilkinson
Farrow, Perren	Jackson	Cockrans	104/25	Wilkinson
Faucett, George	Columbia	10	146/14	Baldwin
Faucett, George	Columbia	10	49/6	Wilkinson
Fauche, Jonas	Greene	Carletons	88/7	Baldwin
Faulk, Henry	Elbert	Dyes	66/11	Wilkinson
Faulk, Lucretia(Wid.)	Wilkinson		129/21	Wilkinson
Faulkner, James	Elbert	Mobleys	315/10	Wilkinson
Faulkner, Jno.Sr.	Elbert	Faulkners	184/14	Wilkinson
Faulkner, John	Elbert	Mobleys	262/7	Wilkinson
Faver, John Sr.	Wilkes	Milners	152/14	Wilkinson
Faver, Wm.Jr.	Baldwin	4	91/13	Wilkinson
Faver, Wm.Sr.	Baldwin	4	227/22	Wilkinson
Faver, Wm.Sr.	Baldwin	4	357/9	Wilkinson
Feagin, Thomas	Hancock	Bardsdales	50/28	Wilkinson
Fears, Absalom(Orph.)	Richmond		361/21	Wilkinson

NAME	COUNTY	MIL.DIST.	LOT/DIST	DREW LAND
Fears, Ezekiel	Greene	Davenports	223/10	Baldwin
Fears, James(Orph.)	Richmond		185/19	Baldwin
Fears, Jas.(Orph.)	Richmond		361/21	Wilkinson
Fears, Keziah(Orph.)	Richmond		361/21	Wilkinson
Fears, Kitty(Orph.)	Richmond		361/21	Wilkinson
Fears, Price(Orph.)	Richmond		361/21	Wilkinson
Fears, Richard(Orph.)	Richmond		185/19	Baldwin
Fears, William	Greene	Davenports	358/10	Wilkinson
Fears, Wm.(Orph.)	Richmond		361/21	Wilkinson
Fee, William	Richmond		26/20	Wilkinson
Fell, Isaac	Chatham	Neyles	83/23	Wilkinson
Felps, David D.	Hancock	Smiths	357/21	Wilkinson
Felps, David	Elbert	Morrisons	85/22	Wilkinson
Felts, James(B.C.)	Baldwin	2	289/16	Wilkinson
Fenn's, Zacharias(Orphs.)	Jefferson	Colemans	191/15	Wilkinson
Fenn, Nancy(Wid.)	Jefferson	Colemans	46/11	Wilkinson
Fenn, Williby	Clarke	Robinsons	132/25	Wilkinson
Fennell's, Ephraim(Orphs.)	Wilkinson		143/26	Wilkinson
Fennell, Famey(Wid.)	Wilkinson		53/23	Wilkinson
Fennell, Isham	Wilkinson		323/22	Wilkinson
Fequet, Alexis	Oglethorpe	Hewells	47/6	Baldwin
Fergesson, Neal	Hancock	Candlers	268/20	Baldwin
Ferrel, Benjamin	Screven	Williamsons	303/9	Wilkinson
Ferrel, Bryant	Screven	Williamsons	172/15	Wilkinson
Ferrell, Archelaus	Hancock	Holts	78/11	Wilkinson
Ferrell, Benjamin	Screven	Williamsons	27/18	Wilkinson
Ferrell, Nicholas	Columbia	10	149/19	Baldwin
Ferrell, Williamson	Hancock	Smiths	157/6	Baldwin
Ferrell, Williamson	Hancock	Smiths	75/20	Wilkinson
Few, Ignatius	Columbia	8	101/10	Wilkinson
Few, James	Baldwin	5	112/20	Wilkinson
Few, Joseph	Greene	Butlers	11/18	Wilkinson
Few, Wm.(Son/Benj.)	Columbia	8	68/13	Baldwin
Fielder, James Sr.	Greene	Butlers	240/15	Baldwin
Fielder, John	Baldwin	5	56/24	Wilkinson
Fielder, William	Clarke	Cooks	9/9	Wilkinson
Fields, Jeremiah	Elbert	Faulkners	336/21	Wilkinson
Figgs, Jesse(Orph.)	Elbert	Hillyers	153/28	Wilkinson
Figgs, Jinsey(Orph.)	Elbert	Hillyers	153/28	Wilkinson
Figgs, Wm.(Orph.)	Elbert	Hillyers	153/28	Wilkinson
Files, Stephen	Baldwin	1	210/7	Wilkinson
Fillingin's, John(Orphs.)	Greene	Dawsons	384/21	Wilkinson
Fillingin, Jarvis	Greene	Flournoys	89/7	Baldwin
Fillingin, Moses	Greene	Dawsons	107/25	Wilkinson
Finch, Charles	Oglethorpe	Popes	70/24	Wilkinson
Finch, Charles	Oglethorpe	Popes	84/17	Baldwin
Finch, James	Hancock	Hudsons	250/25	Wilkinson
Finch, William	Oglethorpe	Beasleys	109/17	Wilkinson
Findley, James	Wilkinson		200/18	Wilkinson
Findley, James	Wilkinson		347/20	Baldwin
Findley, Nicholas	Clarke	Browns	7/6	Baldwin
Findley, Thomas	Burke	Blounts	121/25	Wilkinson
Finley, Jacob	Greene	Dawsons	3/18	Baldwin
Finley, Jacob	Greene	Dawsons	99/18	Wilkinson
Finley, James	Greene	Carletons	56/12	Baldwin
Finley, James	Greene	Carletons	83/13	Baldwin
Finley, James	Wilkes	Malones	82/9	Baldwin
Finley, Jane(Wid.)	Greene	Greers	196/24	Wilkinson
Finley, Mathew	Oglethorpe	Popes	297/17	Wilkinson
Finley, Richard	Greene	Carletons	198/15	Baldwin
Finley, Robert	Greene	Greers	113/17	Baldwin
Finley, Thomas	Clarke	Martins	9/15	Baldwin
Finney, Murrell	Burke	Martins	167/9	Wilkinson
Finny, Benj.(Son/Benj.)	Columbia	6	280/24	Wilkinson
Fisher, David	Chatham	Pettybones	373/21	Wilkinson
Fisher, Henry	Chatham	Neyles	187/20	Baldwin
Fitts', Tandy(Orphs.)	Elbert	Faulkners	264/17	Wilkinson

NAME	COUNTY	MIL.DIST.	LOT/DIST	DREW LAND
Fitts, Mary(Wid.)	Elbert	Faulkners	110/9	Wilkinson
Fitzgerald's, John(Orphs.)	Columbia	1	160/14	Baldwin
Fitzgerald, David	McIntosh		149/12	Wilkinson
Fitzgerald, Geo.Sr.	Elbert	Barretts	49/20	Wilkinson
Fitzgerald, James	Montgomery	57	246/19	Baldwin
Fitzgerald, William	Richmond		35/16	Wilkinson
Fitzpatrick, Joseph	Greene	Jenkins	51/23	Wilkinson
Fitzpatrick, Wm.	Baldwin	1	180/16	Wilkinson
Fitzpatrick, Wm.	Baldwin	1	196/21	Wilkinson
Fitzpatrick, Wm.	Bulloch	Williams	119/17	Baldwin
Flake, William	Screven		126/16	Baldwin
Flake, William	Warren	Flournoys	38/20	Wilkinson
Flanagan's, John(Orphs.)	Lincoln	Mays	88/11	Baldwin
Flanders, Barnabas	Wilkinson		72/20	Wilkinson
Flanders, Elizabeth(S)	Wilkinson		108/14	Wilkinson
Flanegin, Lecrecy	Franklin	Hoopers	161/13	Baldwin
Flaningham, Rutha	Lincoln	Cartrells	80/7	Wilkinson
Flecher, John	Tattnall	McDonalds	156/11	Baldwin
Flecher, Joseph	Tattnall	McDonalds	114/12	Baldwin
Fleetwood, Gray	Camden	Smiths	62/9	Baldwin
Fleetwood, John	Screven		357/12	Wilkinson
Fleman, Henry	Oglethorpe	Hartsfields	174/28	Wilkinson
Fleman, Thomas Jr.	Oglethorpe	Hartsfields	67/14	Wilkinson
Fleming, John	Lincoln	Flemings	211/7	Wilkinson
Fleming, Moses	Elbert	Blackwells	349/12	Wilkinson
Fleming, Moses	Elbert	Blackwells	91/27	Wilkinson
Fleming, Robert	Lincoln	Flemings	66/16	Baldwin
Fleming, Samuel	Jefferson	Fultons	8/7	Wilkinson
Fleming, Samuel	Lincoln	Kennons	198/6	Wilkinson
Fleming, Samuel	Lincoln	Kennons	87/11	Baldwin
Flerl, Israel	Effingham		371/8	Wilkinson
Fletcher, Henry	Bulloch	Parishs	132/24	Wilkinson
Fletcher, Jeremiah	Oglethorpe	Hudsons	7/11	Baldwin
Fletcher, John	Warren	Jones	74/14	Wilkinson
Fletcher, Joseph	Washington	Howards	30/21	Wilkinson
Fletcher, Thomas	Oglethorpe	Hatchetts	309/15	Wilkinson
Fletcher, Wm.Sr.	Bulloch	Williams	22/18	Wilkinson
Flinn, Thomas	Warren	Bakers	91/8	Baldwin
Flint, John	Richmond		189/15	Wilkinson
Flint, John	Wilkes	Sidwells	129/18	Baldwin
Flint, Thomas	Columbia	4	174/19	Baldwin
Flippin, Jesse	Clarke	Dukes	153/14	Baldwin
Flood, James	Franklin	Bryants	154/15	Baldwin
Flourance's, John(Orphs.)	Lincoln	Jones	262/11	Wilkinson
Flourance, Obadiah	Lincoln	Mays	184/16	Wilkinson
Flourance, Polly(Wid.)	Lincoln	Jones	192/15	Baldwin
Flournoy's, Jacob(Orphs.)	Warren	Flournoys	39/25	Wilkinson
Flournoy, Francis	Baldwin	4	216/14	Baldwin
Flournoy, Francis	Wilkes	J.Hendersons	21/21	Wilkinson
Flournoy, John B.	Warren	Flournoys	150/9	Wilkinson
Flournoy, John F.	Warren	Heaths	100/13	Wilkinson
Flournoy, Robert	Jefferson	Fultons	353/8	Wilkinson
Flournoy, Robert	Jefferson	Fultons	58/24	Wilkinson
Flournoy, Thomas	Richmond		62/27	Wilkinson
Flournoy, William	Hancock	Smiths	144/24	Wilkinson
Floyd's, Anthony(Orphs.)	Burke	Fields	21/13	Wilkinson
Floyd, Eli	Elbert	Groves	54/20	Baldwin
Floyd, Jordin	Burke	Thompsons	276/19	Baldwin
Floyd, Prudence	Wilkes	Stovalls	183/10	Baldwin
Floyd, Richard	Chatham	Neyles	105/22	Wilkinson
Floyd, Shadrack	Elbert	Clarks	67/27	Wilkinson
Floyd, Thomas	Screven	Olivers	255/17	Wilkinson
Floyd, William	Elbert	Groves	198/13	Wilkinson
Fluellen, Alexander	Warren	Jones	206/14	Baldwin
Fluellen, Archelaus	Warren	Jones	28/26	Wilkinson
Fluellen, Shadrack	Warren	Jones	230/9	Wilkinson
Fluellen, Shadrack	Warren	Jones	302/22	Wilkinson

NAME	COUNTY	MIL.DIST.	LOT/DIST	DREW LAND
Fluker, Baldwin	Washington	Willis	106/26	Wilkinson
Fluker, Baldwin	Washington	Willis	23/24	Wilkinson
Fluker, John	Greene	Flournoys	310/8	Wilkinson
Fluker, Robert	Washington	Willis	57/6	Wilkinson
Flyming, Mary(Wid.)	Chatham	Abrahams	33/15	Wilkinson
Foard, Braxton	Chatham	Hardens	166/14	Wilkinson
Foil, Robert	Baldwin	4	136/20	Wilkinson
Folds, Conrod	Columbia	6	161/19	Baldwin
Folk, John	Jefferson	Colemans	103/21	Wilkinson
Folk, Mark	Wilkinson		86/18	Wilkinson
Folks, John	Jefferson		72/9	Wilkinson
Folly, Thomas	Oglethorpe	Smiths	212/8	Wilkinson
Folsum, John	Hancock	Birdsongs	124/22	Wilkinson
Fontain, Thomas	Warren	Jones	240/24	Wilkinson
Footman's, Rich.S.(Orphs.)	Bryan	Austins	143/25	Wilkinson
Ford, Charles	Franklin	Conners	158/14	Baldwin
Ford, James	Montgomery	53	157/8	Wilkinson
Ford, James	Montgomery	53	290/6	Wilkinson
Ford, John I.	Wilkinson		116/6	Wilkinson
Ford, John	Tattnall	Sherrards	112/16	Wilkinson
Ford, Thomas	Hancock	Barnes	286/19	Baldwin
Foreman, William	Jefferson	Colemans	125/12	Wilkinson
Foresythe, Serlester(Wid.)	Effingham		253/20	Wilkinson
Forrester, Alexander	Franklin	McDowells	306/7	Wilkinson
Forrester, Alexander	Liberty		53/10	Baldwin
Fort, Arthur Jr.	Warren	Devereuxs	240/23	Wilkinson
Fort, Arthur Sr.	Warren	Devereuxs	15/13	Baldwin
Fort, James	Glynn		318/17	Wilkinson
Fortenberry, Jacob	Richmond		466/7	Wilkinson
Fortson, Benjamin	Elbert	Blackwells	16/6	Wilkinson
Foster's, John H.(Orphs.)	Wilkes	Roreys	6/9	Wilkinson
Foster's, Samuel(Orphs.)	Hancock	Weeks	260/24	Wilkinson
Foster, Anderson	Lincoln	Mays	197/17	Wilkinson
Foster, Arthur	Greene	Jenkins	260/16	Wilkinson
Foster, Arthur	Greene	Jinkins	87/6	Baldwin
Foster, Ebenezer	Chatham	Pembertons	200/15	Wilkinson
Foster, John Jr.	Jackson	Cockrans	164/11	Wilkinson
Foster, John Sr.	Oglethorpe	Hudsons	260/19	Wilkinson
Foster, John	Warren	Bakers	228/16	Wilkinson
Foster, William	Greene	Owsleys	33/8	Wilkinson
Foster, William	Greene	Owsleys	64/11	Wilkinson
Foster, Wm.(Esq.)	Jackson	Cockrans	203/19	Baldwin
Foulk's, Richard(Orphs.)	Wilkinson		43/11	Baldwin
Fountain's, Jonathan(Orphs.)	Jefferson		65/14	Wilkinson
Fowler, Edward	Franklin	Cleghorns	106/9	Wilkinson
Fowler, John	Washington	Paces	183/15	Baldwin
Fowler, Mark	Elbert	Keelings	269/11	Wilkinson
Fowler, Minty	Jefferson	Fultons	203/6	Wilkinson
Fowler, Simmons	Jefferson	Fultons	42/20	Baldwin
Fox, Matthew	Richmond		203/20	Baldwin
Fox, Thomas	Columbia	5	315/7	Wilkinson
Francis, Nathaniel	Hancock	Candlers	92/13	Wilkinson
Franklin's, Phileman(Orps.)	Elbert	Roebucks	335/21	Wilkinson
Franklin, Abraham	Columbia	11	172/12	Baldwin
Franklin, Abraham	Columbia	11	175/8	Wilkinson
Franklin, David	Elbert	Roebucks	74/16	Baldwin
Franklin, Henry	Elbert	Roebucks	323/10	Wilkinson
Franklin, Mary(Wid.)	Jackson	Johnsons	68/11	Wilkinson
Franklin, Thomas	Wilkinson		283/24	Wilkinson
Franklin, Thomas	Wilkinson		405/8	Wilkinson
Franklin, Zepheniah	Warren	Hills	43/17	Wilkinson
Frantom, John	Burke	Sharps	73/14	Wilkinson
Fraser's, John(Orphs.)	Washington	Garretts	132/13	Wilkinson
Fraser, Robert	Chatham	Pembertons	166/15	Baldwin
Fraser, Simon	Liberty		18/24	Wilkinson
Fraser, Simon	Liberty		97/14	Baldwin
Frashure, Wm.	Washington	Willis	43/19	Wilkinson

NAME	COUNTY	MIL.DIST.	LOT/DIST	DREW LAND
Frasier, Eliz.(Wid.)	Wilkinson		144/9	Wilkinson
Frazer, John	Lincoln	Jones	216/24	Wilkinson
Frazer, Moses	Lincoln	Mays	194/15	Wilkinson
Frazer, Moses	Lincoln	Mays	59/7	Baldwin
Frederick, Henry	Washington	Chivers	104/16	Wilkinson
Freel, John Sr.	Columbia	4	33/14	Baldwin
Freeland, Bazil	Richmond		124/7	Wilkinson
Freeland, R.L.	McIntosh		6/14	Wilkinson
Freeman's, John(Orph.)	Tattnall	McDonalds	376/8	Wilkinson
Freeman, Bailey	Oglethorpe	Stewarts	135/15	Wilkinson
Freeman, Catherine(Wid.)	Wilkes	Stovalls	76/20	Baldwin
Freeman, Daniel	Oglethorpe	Smiths	179/9	Wilkinson
Freeman, Hartwell	Oglethorpe	Hitchcocks	184/12	Baldwin
Freeman, Hollman	Wilkes	Stovalls	216/13	Baldwin
Freeman, Jacob Sr.	Greene	Davenports	142/17	Wilkinson
Freeman, Jacob	Screven	Hutchersons	232/14	Wilkinson
Freeman, Jane	Wilkes	Stovalls	154/10	Baldwin
Freeman, John Jr.	Screven	Hutchersons	462/7	Wilkinson
Freeman, John	Hancock	Barnes	40/14	Baldwin
Freeman, Richard	Franklin	Christians	110/15	Wilkinson
Freeman, Robert	Clarke	Martins	281/6	Wilkinson
Freeman, Robert	Oglethorpe	Hatchetts	51/12	Wilkinson
Freeman, Sam'l.	Greene	Davenports	70/11	Baldwin
Freeman, Samuel	Lincoln	Jones	135/20	Wilkinson
Freeman, Samuel	Lincoln	Jones	30/8	Baldwin
Freeman, Sarah	Screven	Hutchersons	30/320	Wilkinson
Freeman, Thomas	Oglethorpe	Hudsons	191/11	Wilkinson
Freeman, Timothy	Oglethorpe	Hatchetts	53/14	Wilkinson
Freeman, William	Clarke	Mitchells	276/15	Baldwin
Freeman, William	Clarke	Mitchells	8/11	Wilkinson
Freeman, Wm.	Screven		193/26	Wilkinson
Freeney's, John(Orphs.)	Hancock	Winsletts	111/7	Baldwin
Freeze's, James(Orphs.)	Lincoln	Jones	191/23	Wilkinson
Fretwell, Richard	Baldwin	2	152/19	Baldwin
Fretwell, Richard	Baldwin	2	188/9	Wilkinson
Fretwell, William	Greene	Carletons	90/8	Baldwin
Freyermuth, John Sr.	Effingham		104/17	Baldwin
Freyermuth, John Sr.	Effingham		90/18	Baldwin
Freyermuth, Sarah(Wid.)	Effingham		156/18	Wilkinson
Friar, Darcus(Wid.)	Liberty		1/18	Wilkinson
Friend, Thomas	Warren	Flournoys	311/10	Wilkinson
Frizzil, Eliz.(Wid.)	Washington	Garretts	16/11	Wilkinson
Frizzil, Thomas	Washington	Garretts	68/23	Wilkinson
Frizzil, Thomas	Washington	Garretts	87/20	Wilkinson
Frost, Mary	Richmond		231/6	Wilkinson
Fry, Susannah	Oglethorpe	Watkins	242/25	Wilkinson
Fryar, John Sr.	Burke	Gordons	175/10	Wilkinson
Fryar, Zachariah L.Sr.	Burke	Gordons	256/24	Wilkinson
Fudge, Benjamin	Richmond		336/10	Wilkinson
Fulch, John	Liberty		19/17	Baldwin
Fulcher's, Wm.(Orphs.)	Jackson	Wrights	351/9	Wilkinson
Fulcher, James	Richmond		40/6	Wilkinson
Fulcher, James	Tattnall	McDonalds	134/24	Wilkinson
Fulgham, Jesse	Washington	Kendricks	185/15	Wilkinson
Fulgham, Thomas	Montgomery	52	22/16	Wilkinson
Fuller, Abner	Columbia	6	210/17	Wilkinson
Fuller, Isaac	Washington	Holts	164/23	Wilkinson
Fuller, Isaac	Washington	Holts	298/11	Wilkinson
Fuller, John Sr.	Columbia	8	236/9	Baldwin
Fuller, Samuel	Columbia	5	85/8	Baldwin
Fullerton, Adam	Jackson	Johnsons	218/7	Wilkinson
Fullilove, Ludwell	Wilkes	Stovalls	289/21	Wilkinson
Fullington's, Chas.(Orphs.)	Warren	Willsons	54/9	Baldwin
Fulton, John	Liberty		169/20	Baldwin
Fulton, John	Liberty		223/9	Wilkinson
Fuqua's, Thomas(Orphs.)	Burke	Montgomerys	15/19	Wilkinson
Furgerson, James	Oglethorpe	Moores	152/13	Baldwin

NAME	COUNTY	MIL.DIST.	LOT/DIST	DREW LAND
Furlow, David	Greene	Carletons	261/16	Wilkinson
Furlow, John T.	McIntosh		112/15	Wilkinson
Furlow, John	Greene	Carletons	216/17	Wilkinson
Furlow, John	Wilkes	Sheets	285/20	Wilkinson
Fuselnecker, Ann	Chatham	Abrahams	88/19	Wilkinson
Fuselnecker, Catharine	Chatham	Pembertons	304/16	Wilkinson
Fussell, William	Clarke	Hopkins	111/16	Wilkinson
Futch, Isaac	Bulloch	Denmarks	62/15	Wilkinson
Futch, Oneacimus	Bryan	Birds	288/11	Wilkinson
Gachett, Charles	Jefferson	Fultons	230/22	Wilkinson
Gaddy, Betsy	Wilkes	Coopers	119/15	Baldwin
Gaddy, David	Clarke	Hitchcocks	88/17	Wilkinson
Gaddy, James	Screven		293/15	Wilkinson
Gaddy, Nicholas	Screven		135/22	Wilkinson
Gaffney, James	Effingham		147/16	Wilkinson
Gafford, James	Columbia	10	6/14	Baldwin
Gage, Mathew	Oglethorpe	Hatchetts	106/6	Wilkinson
Gage, Mathew	Oglethorpe	Hatchetts	263/9	Wilkinson
Gailey, Joseph	Franklin	Cleghorns	2/19	Baldwin
Gainer, James	Washington	Burneys	269/12	Wilkinson
Gainer, Samuel	Washington	Burneys	227/14	Wilkinson
Gaines, Francis	Elbert	Roebucks	283/16	Wilkinson
Gaines, Theophilus	Burke	Blounts	80/19	Baldwin
Gaines, William	Burke	Blounts	275/23	Wilkinson
Galesby, Drury	Columbia	4	129/19	Baldwin
Galesby, Robert	Oglethorpe	Moores	248/22	Wilkinson
Gallaway, Mathew	Oglethorpe	Moores	140/17	Wilkinson
Gamble, Elizabeth	Jackson	Wrights	102/10	Baldwin
Gandy, Britton	Baldwin	2	144/15	Wilkinson
Gann's, William(Orphs.)	Baldwin	2	83/8	Baldwin
Gann, John	Clarke	Harpers	248/16	Wilkinson
Gantt, Lunsford	Lincoln	Mays	111/12	Wilkinson
Garbot, Elisha	Chatham	Neals	63/11	Wilkinson
Garbot, Mary	Chatham	Neals	63/11	Wilkinson
Garbot, Nancy	Chatham	Neals	63/11	Wilkinson
Gardner's, Lewis(Orphs.)	Columbia	5	95/17	Wilkinson
Gardner's, Stephen(Orphs.)	Jackson	Hendersons	154/13	Baldwin
Gardner, Aaron	Montgomery	56	173/23	Wilkinson
Gardner, Christ'r	Franklin	Allens	115/20	Baldwin
Gardner, Christ'r	Franklin	Allens	190/19	Baldwin
Gardner, John	Chatham	Abrahams	241/15	Wilkinson
Gardner, Lewis(Son/Lewis)	Columbia	5	12/13	Wilkinson
Gardner, Mary(Wid.)	Jackson	Hendersons	159/13	Wilkinson
Gardner, Nancy(Dau/Lewis)	Columbia	5	104/16	Baldwin
Gardner, Wm.	Warren	Newsoms	345/22	Wilkinson
Garmony, Robert	Oglethorpe	Bells	20/16	Wilkinson
Garmony, Robert	Oglethorpe	Bells	94/15	Baldwin
Garner, Charles	Clarke	Dukes	59/26	Wilkinson
Garner, George	Franklin	Cornelius	31/14	Baldwin
Garner, Harper	Camden	Ashleys	45/12	Baldwin
Garner, James	Franklin	Griffiths	95/6	Baldwin
Garner, Joseph	Clarke	Tramells	181/15	Baldwin
Garner, Martha(Wid.)	Jackson	Wrights	83/15	Wilkinson
Garner, Martin	Jackson	Wrights	302/10	Wilkinson
Garner, Presley	Clarke	Tramells	105/8	Baldwin
Garner, William	Jackson	Wrights	348/13	Wilkinson
Garnett, Anthony	Columbia	3	103/27	Wilkinson
Garnett, Reubin	Columbia	3	212/13	Wilkinson
Garnett, Reubin	Columbia	3	219/8	Wilkinson
Garnett, Zachariah	Columbia	1	278/6	Wilkinson
Garr's, Michael(Orph.)	Elbert	Blackwells	203/14	Baldwin
Garr, Joel	Elbert	Blackwells	121/19	Baldwin
Garr, Lewis	Elbert	Blackwells	68/18	Baldwin
Garr, William	Elbert	Clarkes	332/24	Wilkinson
Garrad, Nancy(Single)	Hancock	Winsletts	185/21	Wilkinson
Garrard, Robert	Wilkes	Sidwells	145/25	Wilkinson
Garrett's, Henry(Orphs.)	Hancock	Coffees	69/23	Wilkinson

NAME	COUNTY	MIL.DIST.	LOT/DIST	DREW LAND
Garrett's, James(Orphs.)	Hancock	Coopers	175/17	Wilkinson
Garrett's, Wm. (Orphs.)	Hancock	Coopers	187/10	Wilkinson
Garrett, Daniel	Baldwin	2	186/11	Wilkinson
Garrett, Elizabeth(Wid.)	Clarke	Browns	12/7	Baldwin
Garrett, Henry	Oglethorpe	Stewarts	6/11	Wilkinson
Garrett, James	Washington	Collins	179/21	Wilkinson
Garrison, Caleb	Franklin	Dixons	88/10	Baldwin
Garrison, Ellender(Wid.)	Franklin	Dixons	225/8	Wilkinson
Garrison, Zebulon	Franklin	Christians	62/18	Wilkinson
Gartrell, Francis	Wilkes	Wellborns	52/23	Wilkinson
Garvin, John	Richmond		139/13	Wilkinson
Gary, Richard	Hancock	Barksdales	13/13	Baldwin
Gass, Benjamin	Wilkes	Stovalls	156/19	Baldwin
Gass, Benjamin	Wilkes	Stovalls	174/12	Wilkinson
Gaston, Ann(Orph.)	Greene	Armors	310/21	Wilkinson
Gaston, John	Greene	Armors	149/28	Wilkinson
Gaston, Mathew(Orph.)	Greene	Armors	310/21	Wilkinson
Gater, Vachal	Lincoln	Flemings	23/26	Wilkinson
Gates, George	Camden	Crews	254/16	Wilkinson
Gates, Hezekiah Jr.	Jefferson	Wrights	219/26	Wilkinson
Gates, Horatio	Washington	Burneys	120/14	Baldwin
Gates, Josiah	Baldwin	1	122/8	Baldwin
Gates, Peter	Franklin	Thompsons	184/12	Wilkinson
Gates, Peter	Franklin	Thompsons	66/12	Wilkinson
Gatewood, Dosha	Franklin	McDowells	182/9	Wilkinson
Gatewood, Eliz.(Wid.)	Elbert	Blackwells	66/11	Baldwin
Gatewood, John	Franklin	McDowells	41/19	Wilkinson
Gatewood, Sally	Elbert	Faulkners	480/7	Wilkinson
Gawley, Thomas(Orphs.)	Jefferson	Tarvers	188/14	Wilkinson
Gay, Ann(Wid.)	Elbert	McGuires	89/19	Wilkinson
Gay, Gilbert	Clarke	Martindales	124/6	Baldwin
Gay, Gilbert	Clarke	Martindales	127/6	Wilkinson
Gay, Lewis	Montgomery	58	59/12	Baldwin
Gay, Mary(Wid.)	Burke	Bynes	117/22	Wilkinson
Gay, Rebecca	Burke	Hilliards	116/9	Wilkinson
Gay, Thomas	Burke	Bynes	94/19	Wilkinson
Gay, William	Hancock	Shivers	333/14	Wilkinson
Gaylord, Giles	Richmond		77/6	Wilkinson
Geasling, Benj.	Warren	Neals	252/20	Wilkinson
Geasling, Charles	Warren	Neals	45/10	Wilkinson
Geasling, Charles	Warren	Neals	79/13	Baldwin
Gelder, Jacob	Washington	Andersons	354/10	Wilkinson
Gellaspie, Lowry	Franklin	Griffiths	116/20	Baldwin
Gennuway, Ann(Wid.)	Jefferson	Hardwichs	66/13	Baldwin
Gent, Charles	Clarke	Dukes	109/13	Baldwin
Gentry, Elijah	Clarke	Stewarts	203/13	Baldwin
Gentry, William	Clarke	Martins	56/17	Baldwin
Geordan, John	Franklin	Cornelius	428/7	Wilkinson
George's, John(Orphs.)	Greene	Baxters	212/19	Baldwin
George, Bailey	Clarke	Robinsons	245/14	Baldwin
George, James	Wilkes	Sidwells	36/15	Wilkinson
George, Jesse	Warren	Willsons	164/7	Wilkinson
George, Jordan(Orp/Jno.)	Columbia	2	274/19	Wilkinson
George, Reubin	Greene	Baxters	207/16	Wilkinson
George, Richard	Warren	Hills	328/14	Wilkinson
George, Travis	McIntosh		51/13	Wilkinson
George, Wm.(Esq.)	Greene	Watts	184/9	Baldwin
Germany, Hannah(Wid/Jas.)	Columbia	1	308/21	Wilkinson
Germany, John Jr.	Columbia	3	72/24	Wilkinson
Germany, John Sr.	Columbia	3	207/25	Wilkinson
Germany, John(Son/Wm.)	Columbia	1	87/10	Wilkinson
Germany, Joseph(Son/Jno.)	Columbia	2	53/6	Baldwin
Gess, Moses Sr.	Franklin	Hollingsworths	10/18	Wilkinson
Gibbons', James(Orphs.)	Jackson	Hendersons	280/19	Wilkinson
Gibbons, Broadbelt J.	Chatham	McClains	201/20	Baldwin
Gibbons, John B.	Chatham	McLeans	88/21	Wilkinson
Gibbs', Philip(Orphs.)	Hancock	Candlers	76/8	Baldwin

NAME	COUNTY	MIL.DIST.	LOT/DIST	DREW LAND
Gibson's, Abraham(Orphs.)	Columbia	5	40/26	Wilkinson
Gibson's, John(Orphs.)	Franklin	Wems'	288/9	Wilkinson
Gibson's, Roger(Orphs.)	Baldwin	4	33/13	Wilkinson
Gibson, Ann(Wid.)	Jefferson	Tarvers	171/10	Wilkinson
Gibson, Elijah	Baldwin	3	175/21	Wilkinson
Gibson, Elijah	Columbia	4	301/12	Wilkinson
Gibson, Hugh	Oglethorpe	Hudsons	338/11	Wilkinson
Gibson, John	Warren	Heaths	182/14	Wilkinson
Gibson, John	Warren	Hills	155/18	Wilkinson
Gibson, Mary Ann	Jefferson	Tarvers	37/10	Baldwin
Gibson, Rachel(Wid.)	Warren	Hills	13/6	Baldwin
Gibson, Samuel	Jefferson	Tarvers	359/8	Wilkinson
Gibson, Samuel	Jefferson	Tarvers	81/12	Wilkinson
Gibson, William	Camden	Smiths	149/25	Wilkinson
Gibson, William	Jefferson	Tarvers	41/12	Wilkinson
Giddings, William	Jackson	Cockrans	224/15	Wilkinson
Gideon, Richard	Jackson	Hendersons	93/28	Wilkinson
Gideons, Francis	Wilkes	Coopers	48/19	Wilkinson
Gieger, Cornelius	Bulloch	Denmarks	132/8	Wilkinson
Gieger, John	Bulloch	Denmarks	177/11	Baldwin
Gignilliat, Henry	McIntosh		69/28	Wilkinson
Gilbert, Bird	Hancock	Hudsons	183/7	Wilkinson
Gilbert, Drury	Wilkinson		33/20	Baldwin
Gilbert, Jesse Sr.	Wilkinson		326/15	Baldwin
Gilbert, John(Orph.)	Chatham	Pettybones	148/27	Wilkinson
Gilbert, John	Washington	Andersons	6/17	Baldwin
Gilbert, Mary(Wid.)	Chatham	Pettybones	193/19	Baldwin
Gilbert, Polly	Franklin	Thompsons	141/14	Wilkinson
Gilbert, Sarah(Oprh.)	Chatham	Pettybones	148/27	Wilkinson
Gilbert, Wm.G.	Wilkes	Coopers	123/13	Baldwin
Gildersleeve, Cyrus	Liberty		127/23	Wilkinson
Giles', Nathaniel(Orp.)	Warren	Devereuxs	328/9	Wilkinson
Giles, John	Clarke	Harpers	7/12	Wilkinson
Giles, Samuel	Greene	Armors	240/19	Wilkinson
Giles, Thomas Jr.	Greene	Armors	159/7	Wilkinson
Gilford, Isaac	Tattnall	Halls	103/13	Wilkinson
Gilford, John	Tattnall	Halls	305/15	Baldwin
Gilham, John	Lincoln	Mays	185/11	Wilkinson
Gilham, Sarah(Wid.)	Oglethorpe	Beasleys	347/12	Wilkinson
Gilham, Thomas	Oglethorpe	Beasleys	143/24	Wilkinson
Gill's, John(Orphs.)	Bulloch	Denmarks	261/11	WIlkinson
Gill, James	Columbia	4	274/14	Baldwin
Gill, Jeremiah	Effingham		321/20	Baldwin
Gill, John	Bulloch	Denmarks	114/8	Wilkinson
Gill, Peter	Greene	Loves	180/15	Wilkinson
Gill, Robert	Columbia	3	157/11	Wilkinson
Gill, Thomas	Effingham		205/10	Baldwin
Gillaspie, William	Baldwin	1	249/11	Wilkinson
Gillet, William	Camden	Ashleys	242/12	Wilkinson
Gilley, Henry	Montgomery	51	117/23	Wilkinson
Gilliland, Wm.	Hancock	Barksdales	132/26	Wilkinson
Gillstrap, Jeremiah(Orph.)	Burke	Martins	72/27	Wilkinson
Gillum, Patsy	Greene	Flournoys	150/10	Wilkinson
Gilmore's, Chas.H.(Orphs.)	Baldwin	5	94/20	Wilkinson
Gilmore, Ann	Jackson	Johnsons	208/6	Wilkinson
Gilmore, George Sr.	Wilkinson		229/6	Wilkinson
Gilmore, George	Jefferson	Thomas	324/11	Wilkinson
Gilmore, Harrison B.(S.W.)	Oglethorpe	Smiths	177/14	Baldwin
Gilmore, Hugh	Clarke	Hopkins	234/17	Wilkinson
Gilmore, James	Lincoln	Flemings	92/19	Wilkinson
Gilmore, James	Washington	Garretts	339/9	Wilkinson
Gilmore, John	Wilkinson		97/11	Wilkinson
Gilmore, Nicholas M.	Oglethorpe	Jno.Smiths	186/18	Wilkinson
Gilmore, Robert	Hancock	Huffs	274/7	Wilkinson
Gilmore, Thomas M.	Oglethorpe	Jno.Smiths	256/7	Wilkinson
Gilmore, William	Greene	Carletons	124/12	Baldwin
Gilpin, John	Warren	Bakers	69/15	Baldwin

NAME	COUNTY	MIL.DIST.	LOT/DIST	DREW LAND
Gilstrap, John	Burke	Martins	175/13	Wilkinson
Ginn, Jordan	Jackson	Wrights	192/13	Wilkinson
Ginnings, Myles	Baldwin	5	327/14	Wilkinson
Girvin, Thomas	Jefferson	Tarvers	309/11	Wilkinson
Glass, Hubbard	Baldwin	4	94/28	Wilkinson
Glass, James	Baldwin	3	66/20	Wilkinson
Glass, Thomas	Montgomery	50	74/21	Wilkinson
Glass, William	Baldwin	3	146/19	Baldwin
Glass, William	Baldwin	3	336/9	Wilkinson
Glass, William	Baldwin	4	176/11	Baldwin
Glass, William	Baldwin	4	289/20	Wilkinson
Glass, William	Wilkes	Heards	188/23	Wilkinson
Glaze, David	Lincoln	Normans	203/10	Baldwin
Glaze, Jonathan	Richmond		72/23	Wilkinson
Glaze, Lewis	Lincoln	Jones	220/13	Wilkinson
Glaze, Samuel	Jackson	Wrights	276/19	Wilkinson
Glazier, Adam	Greene	Flournoys	67/16	Baldwin
Glenn, Andrew	Franklin	Cornelius	366/9	Wilkinson
Glenn, Betsy	Oglethorpe	Bells	231/13	Wilkinson
Glenn, Eliza(Orp/Thos.)	Columbia	2	115/12	Baldwin
Glenn, Ezra	Oglethorpe	Bells	328/21	Wilkinson
Glenn, John	Washington	Willis	35/17	Wilkinson
Glenn, Joseph Jr.	Elbert	Mobleys	167/8	Wilkinson
Glenn, Noble	Chatham	Neyles	89/18	Baldwin
Glenn, Robert Sr.	Washington	Andersons	215/6	Wilkinson
Glenn, Thomas	Washington	Willis	358/22	Wilkinson
Glenn, William	Elbert	Faulkners	504/7	Wilkinson
Glenn, Wm.(Dr.)	Oglethorpe	Bells	198/15	Wilkinson
Glisson, Brinkley	Bulloch	Godfreys	243/8	Wilkinson
Gliston, James	Burke	Mulkeys	118/18	Baldwin
Glosson, Hugh	Clarke	Harpers	159/17	Wilkinson
Glover, Darling	Jefferson		177/27	Wilkinson
Glover, Frederick	Warren	Flournoys	350/10	Wilkinson
Glover, Jesse Jr.	Jefferson	Hardwichs	71/15	Wilkinson
Gnann, Jacob	Effingham		50/22	Wilkinson
Gnann, John	Effingham		245/10	Wilkinson
Gnann, Solomon	Effingham		38/17	Wilkinson
Gnann, Solomon	Effingham		38/17	Wilkinson
Goar, John	Columbia	6	130/9	Wilkinson
Gober, George	Franklin	Allens	209/6	Wilkinson
Gober, John Jr.	Franklin	Allens	11/12	Wilkinson
Gober, Wm.Jr.	Franklin	Allens	121/12	Baldwin
Godbee, James	Burke	Mulkeys	105/12	Wilkinson
Godbee, Samuel	Burke	Mulkeys	162/10	Wilkinson
Godbey, William	Burke	Mulkeys	219/23	Wilkinson
Godfrey, William	Chatham	Pettybones	206/17	Wilkinson
Godley, John	Burke	Ballards	255/12	Wilkinson
Godwin's, Richard(Orps.)	Washington	Burneys	18/19	Baldwin
Goff's, Nathaniel(Orphs.)	Jefferson		59/20	Wilkinson
Goff, Cath.Jarvey(Orph.)	Jefferson	Wrights	34/26	Wilkinson
Golcher, Thos.Sr.	Wilkes	Heards	6/11	Baldwin
Golden, Henry	Warren	Hills	26/12	Baldwin
Golden, John Sr.	Lincoln	Mays	43/27	Wilkinson
Golding's, Peter(Orphs.)	Liberty		3/19	Wilkinson
Golding, James	Lincoln	Flemings	59/11	Wilkinson
Goldsmith, John	Baldwin	3	144/12	Baldwin
Goldsmith, John	Baldwin	3	73/11	Baldwin
Goldwire, James	Effingham		50/17	Baldwin
Gollcher, James	Wilkes	Heards	24/25	Wilkinson
Gooche, Nathan	Greene	Jenkins	55/10	Baldwin
Goocher, Wm.	Lincoln	Kings	171/20	Wilkinson
Good, Mackerness	Washington	Holts	272/21	Wilkinson
Good, Theophilus	Columbia	2	119/14	Wilkinson
Good, Theophilus	Columbia	2	216/15	Wilkinson
Good, Thomas	Oglethorpe	Hatchetts	169/15	Wilkinson
Goode, John	Greene	Stewarts	54/7	Wilkinson
Goode, Nicholas	Elbert	Morrisons	71/7	Wilkinson

NAME	COUNTY	MIL.DIST.	LOT/DIST	DREW LAND
Goodman, David	Bulloch	Williams	163/18	Wilkinson
Goodman, David	Bulloch	Williams	67/15	Wilkinson
Goodman, John	Oglethorpe	Moores	234/19	Baldwin
Goodson's, Demsey(Orphs.)	Hancock	Barksdales	214/13	Wilkinson
Goodwin's, Jonathan(Orps.)	Hancock	Gumms	446/7	Wilkinson
Goodwin, Harwood	Greene	Jenkins	206/6	Wilkinson
Goodwin, James A.	Greene	Carletons	145/15	Wilkinson
Goodwin, John	Hancock	Shivers	104/14	Wilkinson
Goodwin, Shadrack	Baldwin	1	66/10	Baldwin
Goodwin, Wm.W.(Orp/Jno.)	Columbia	1	133/11	Wilkinson
Goody, George	Elbert	Mobleys	145/7	Baldwin
Goolesby, Aaron	Oglethorpe	Smiths	144/25	Wilkinson
Goolesby, Charles M.	Effingham		81/23	Wilkinson
Goolesby, Eliz.(Wid.)	Ogelthorpe	Hewells	87/12	Baldwin
Goolesby, Fleming	Wilkes	Heards	338/12	Wilkinson
Goolesby, Isaac	Oglethorpe	Jno.Smiths	163/10	Wilkinson
Goolesby, Isaac	Oglethorpe	Jno.Smiths	61/10	Baldwin
Goolesby, Isiah	Oglethorpe	Jno.Smiths	105/9	Baldwin
Goolesby, James B.	Oglethorpe	Smiths	2/24	Wilkinson
Goolesby, John C.(Orph.)	Oglethorpe	Jno.Smiths	160/21	Wilkinson
Goolesby, John H.	Wilkes	Heards	36/11	Wilkinson
Goolesby, John Sr.	Oglethorpe	Jno.Smiths	12/10	Wilkinson
Goolesby, Peter Sr.	Oglethorpe	J.Smiths	179/13	Baldwin
Goolesby, Peter Sr.	Oglethorpe	Jno.Smiths	356/24	Wilkinson
Goolesby, Samuel	Elbert	Mobleys	149/12	Baldwin
Goolesby, Thomas	Elbert	Mobleys	80/8	Baldwin
Goolesby, Wm.Sr.	Oglethorpe	Smiths	32/12	Wilkinson
Gordie, Peter	Hancock	Winsletts	50/7	Wilkinson
Gordon, Alexander	Jefferson	Fultons	1/26	Wilkinson
Gordon, Alexander	Jefferson	Fultons	23/13	Baldwin
Gordon, Allen	Washington	Burneys	201/12	Baldwin
Gordon, Ephraim	Baldwin	4	236/20	Baldwin
Gordon, George	Oglethorpe	Moores	45/6	Baldwin
Gordon, John F.	Oglethorpe	Moores	257/14	Baldwin
Gordon, John L.	Baldwin	5	116/7	Wilkinson
Gordon, John L.	Baldwin	5	254/19	Baldwin
Gordon, Mary(Wid.)	Wilkes	Roreys	41/26	Wilkinson
Gordon, Moses	Burke	Burks	316/9	Wilkinson
Gordon, Sarah	Jefferson	Tarvers	242/17	Wilkinson
Gordon, Thomas	Hancock	Barnes	225/24	Wilkinson
Gordon, Thomas	Hancock	Barnes	53/18	Baldwin
Gordy, Benjamin	Burke	Hilliards	128/14	Wilkinson
Gordy, James	Burke	Hilliards	150/21	Wilkinson
Gordy, Thomas Sr.	Burke	Hilliards	59/12	Wilkinson
Gore, Elisha	Wilkinson		23/20	Baldwin
Gore, Mannan Sr.	Jackson	Johnsons	118/17	Baldwin
Gorman, Jane(Wid.)	Camden	Ashleys	174/16	Wilkinson
Gorman, John S.	Warren	Hills	57/8	Baldwin
Gorman, Samuel	Bulloch	Williams	124/27	Wilkinson
Gornto, Nathan	Bulloch	Williams	245/13	Wilkinson
Goss, Benjamin	Elbert	Mobleys	312/11	Wilkinson
Goss, Charles	Greene	Dawsons	256/6	Wilkinson
Goss, Isham	Oglethorpe	Moores	125/6	Wilkinson
Gotcher, Joshua	Franklin	Yowells	189/16	Wilkinson
Gotcher, Joshua	Franklin	Yowells	29/22	Wilkinson
Gotear, Margaret	Chatham	Abrahams	45/13	Baldwin
Gould, William	McIntosh		292/13	Wilkinson
Gowers, Abel	Oglethorpe	Hitchcocks	186/15	Wilkinson
Goyne, John	Wilkes	Youngs	218/20	Wilkinson
Goza, John	Washington	Holts	118/26	Wilkinson
Goza, Joshua Sr.	Warren	Newsoms	243/6	Wilkinson
Goza, Josiah	Washington	Holts	106/16	Baldwin
Goza, Peter	Warren	Newsoms	159/23	Wilkinson
Grace, James	Jackson	Wrights	58/22	Wilkinson
Grace, Thos.Sr.	Tattnall	Armstrongs	70/17	Baldwin
Grace, William	Tattnall	Halls	69/16	Baldwin
Graddy, William	Wilkes	Stovalls	312/21	Wilkinson

NAME	COUNTY	MIL.DIST.	LOT/DIST	DREW LAND
Graddy, William	Wilkinson		193/17	Baldwin
Graddy, William	Wilkinson		48/13	Wilkinson
Grady, Archibald	Franklin	Hollingsworths	235/17	Wilkinson
Gragg, Elender	Jackson	Hendersons	39/7	Wilkinson
Gragg, Henry	Jackson	Hendersons	104/11	Baldwin
Gramberry, Loamia	Jefferson		73/24	Wilkinson
Gramberry, Sarah	Jefferson		20/9	Baldwin
Grammar, John	Hancock	Barnes	231/19	Baldwin
Granger, Absalom	Oglethorpe	Hartsfields	151/7	Wilkinson
Grant's, Thos.(Orphs.)	Wilkes	M.Hendersons	310/24	Wilkinson
Grant, Isaac	Screven	Olivers	45/9	Wilkinson
Grant, James	Glynn		57/8	Wilkinson
Grant, William A.	Chatham		207/28	Wilkinson
Grant, William	Greene	Baxters	60/8	Wilkinson
Grantham, Daniel	Hancock	Thomas	24/15	Baldwin
Grantham, Matthew	Warren	Heaths	92/6	Wilkinson
Grantham, Nancy(Single)	Wilkinson		226/8	Wilkinson
Gravenstien, John	Effingham		182/13	Baldwin
Graves', Thos.(Orphs.)	Lincoln	Gartrells	231/14	Wilkinson
Graves, John	Wilkes	Heards	110/13	Baldwin
Graves, Perree	Columbia	7	108/6	Wilkinson
Graves, Robert	Baldwin	2	305/16	Wilkinson
Graves, Robert	Lincoln	Busseys	1/6	Wilkinson
Gray, Archibald	Greene	Armors	289/7	Wilkinson
Gray, Basil	Burke	Ballards	65/6	Wilkinson
Gray, Daniel	Lincoln	Kennons	124/20	Wilkinson
Gray, George	Clarke	Stewarts	15/16	Wilkinson
Gray, George	Clarke	Stewarts	4/13	Baldwin
Gray, George	Hancock	Smiths	207/13	Wilkinson
Gray, Isaac	Burke	Sandifords	408/8	Wilkinson
Gray, James	Warren	Neals	291/16	Wilkinson
Gray, John	Columbia	3	173/14	Baldwin
Gray, John	Greene	Dawsons	487/7	Wilkinson
Gray, John	Hancock	Smiths	11/27	Wilkinson
Gray, Joseph Sr.	Wilkes	Heards	51/11	Baldwin
Gray, Joshua	Burke	Sandifords	136/14	Wilkinson
Gray, Mary Ann McG.	Burke	Mulkeys	18/20	Wilkinson
Gray, Mary	Burke	Ballards	249/24	Wilkinson
Gray, Matthias	Warren	Devereuxs	131/23	Wilkinson
Gray, Moulton	Hancock	Weeks	133/7	Wilkinson
Gray, Moulton	Hancock	Weeks	7/25	Wilkinson
Gray, Robert	Elbert	Keelings	204/17	Wilkinson
Gray, Sarah	Wilkes	Heards	3/27	Wilkinson
Gray, Thomas	Greene	Carletons	168/8	Baldwin
Gray, William	Burke	Martins	108/25	Wilkinson
Grayham, Betsy Statem(S)	Wilkinson		60/18	Wilkinson
Grayham, Buckner	Oglethorpe	Smiths	301/11	Wilkinson
Grayham, David	Elbert	Moons	6/20	Baldwin
Grayham, James	Baldwin	2	269/20	Baldwin
Grayham, John	Franklin	Wems	21/8	Baldwin
Grayham, Joseph	Elbert	Groves	131/20	Wilkinson
Grayham, Joshua	Baldwin	1	216/14	Wilkinson
Grayham, Samuel	Baldwin	1	109/24	Wilkinson
Grayham, William	Franklin	Wems'	189/9	Wilkinson
Grayham, Wm.	Elbert	Groves	38/10	Baldwin
Grear, Richard	Wilkinson		21/1	Baldwin
Greason, John Sr.	Warren	Hills	305/14	Wilkinson
Greathouse, Jacob	Clarke	Robinsons	199/10	Wilkinson
Greecy, John	Oglethorpe	Moores	1/17	Baldwin
Greecy, Newell	Oglethorpe	Moores	64/14	Wilkinson
Green's, Hubbert(Orphs.)	Warren	Bakers	177/10	Wilkinson
Green's, Wm.(Orphs.)	Wilkes	Coopers	42/13	Wilkinson
Green, Benjamin	Burke	Hilliards	260/14	Baldwin
Green, Benjamin	Jefferson	Tarvers	278/19	Wilkinson
Green, Eliz.(Single)	Clarke	Silmans	105/7	Wilkinson
Green, Ephraim	Washington	Andersons	157/9	Baldwin
Green, James W.	Hancock	Barnes	230/20	Wilkinson

NAME	COUNTY	MIL.DIST.	LOT/DIST	DREW LAND
Green, James	Hancock	Smiths	100/23	Wilkinson
Green, Jesse	Wilkinson		19/14	Baldwin
Green, John(Orph.)	Camden	Hardees	496/7	Wilkinson
Green, Judith(Wid.)	Wilkes	Coopers	201/23	Wilkinson
Green, Lemuel	Greene	Watsons	108/24	Wilkinson
Green, Mathew	Burke	Forths	4/19	Wilkinson
Green, Michael	Chatham	Neyles	265/17	Wilkinson
Green, Richard	Bulloch	Godfreys	104/8	Baldwin
Green, Thomas	Lincoln	Kings	237/10	Wilkinson
Green, Thomas	Washington	Collins	145/19	Wilkinson
Green, Thomas	Washington	Collins	354/22	Wilkinson
Green, Thomas	Wilkes	M.Hendersons	126/12	Baldwin
Green, William	Burke	Hilliards	55/27	Wilkinson
Green, Wm.Jr.	Wilkes	Wellborns	174/6	Wilkinson
Greene, Alexander	Baldwin	1	196/19	Wilkinson
Greene, Allen	Baldwin	5	82/18	Wilkinson
Greene, Amos	Warren	Hills	105/10	Baldwin
Greene, Beneta	Jefferson	Tarvers	366/21	Wilkinson
Greene, Benjamin	Jefferson	Tarvers	116/9	Baldwin
Greene, Daniel	Baldwin	1	75/27	Wilkinson
Greene, Isaac	Camden	Hardees	231/7	Wilkinson
Greene, Jacob	Bryan	Birds	247/17	Wilkinson
Greene, Jacob	Bryan	Birds	57/17	Baldwin
Greene, James Sr.	Baldwin	1	174/25	Wilkinson
Greene, James	Clarke	Silmans	119/11	Wilkinson
Greene, John Jr.	Jefferson	Tarvers	137/26	Wilkinson
Greene, John	Jackson	Cockrans	147/27	Wilkinson
Greene, Phillip	Columbia	6	113/10	Wilkinson
Greene, Thomas	Lincoln	Gartrells	250/23	Wilkinson
Greene, William	Baldwin	1	147/24	Wilkinson
Greenleese, Eliz.	Elbert	Willifords	29/18	Baldwin
Greenwood's, John(Orphs.)	Elbert	Faulkners	109/10	Wilkinson
Greer, Aaron	Greene	Dawsons	120/26	Wilkinson
Greer, Aquilla	Oglethorpe	Beasleys	207/15	Wilkinson
Greer, Aquilla	Oglethorpe	Stewarts	66/6	Wilkinson
Greer, Asa	Oglethorpe	Stewarts	326/11	Wilkinson
Greer, David	Clarke	Hopkins	57/7	Wilkinson
Greer, George	Washington	Wiggins	133/10	Baldwin
Greer, Henry	Greene	Greers	221/11	Wilkinson
Greer, James	Clarke	Hopkins	205/9	Wilkinson
Greer, John Sr.	Clarke	Browns	193/25	Wilkinson
Greer, Josiah	Baldwin	1	112/11	Wilkinson
Greer, Priscilla	Clarke	Hopkins	120/16	Baldwin
Greer, Robert(Esq.)	Greene	Dawsons	168/19	Wilkinson
Greer, Sally	Washington	Wiggins	155/27	Wilkinson
Greer, William(Esq.)	Greene	Dawsons	371/7	Wilkinson
Greer, William	Oglethorpe	Hudsons	79/25	Wilkinson
Greer, William	Oglethorpe	Stewarts	68/18	Wilkinson
Greer, Wm.(Esq.)	Greene	Dawsons	60/9	Baldwin
Greesham, Edmund	Jackson	Wrights	198/14	Wilkinson
Gregg, Silas	Wilkes	Edges	235/24	Wilkinson
Greggory, John	Burke	Martins	170/9	Wilkinson
Greggory, Wm.G.	Columbia	4	271/7	Wilkinson
Grenade, John	Columbia	6	97/17	Baldwin
Grenstead, John	Wilkinson		74/10	Baldwin
Gresham's, Thos.(Orphs.)	Oglethorpe	Hartsfields	112/22	Wilkinson
Gresham's, Thos.(Orphs.)	Oglethorpe	Hartsfields	313/12	Wilkinson
Gresham's, Thos.(Orphs.)	Wilkes	J.Hendersons	377/7	Wilkinson
Gresham, Chas.Wms.	Wilkes	J.Hendersons	12/12	Wilkinson
Gresham, Harris	Oglethorpe	Bells	29/28	Wilkinson
Gresham, Harris	Oglethorpe	Bells	79/14	Wilkinson
Gresham, John Jr.	Oglethorpe	Hatchetts	354/9	Wilkinson
Gresham, John(Col.)	Oglethorpe	Hartsfields	158/18	Baldwin
Gresham, John	Wilkes	Wellborns	386/7	Wilkinson
Gresham, Kauffman	Wilkes	Parks	192/7	Wilkinson
Gresham, Kauffman	Wilkes	Parks	68/17	Baldwin
Gresham, Littleberry	Greene	Armors	194/12	Baldwin

NAME	COUNTY	MIL.DIST.	LOT/DIST	DREW LAND
Gresham, Sally	Oglethorpe	Stewarts	88/16	Wilkinson
Gresham, Young(Col.)	Greene	Greers	194/23	Wilkinson
Greson, Mathew	Tattnall	Armstrongs	208/8	Wilkinson
Grey, Robert	Warren	Hills	62/9	Wilkinson
Gribbin, Patrick	Chatham	Abrahams	11/13	Wilkinson
Grier, Aaron	Warren	Bakers	140/13	Wilkinson
Grier, Moses	Greene	Stewarts	364/22	Wilkinson
Griffin's, And.(Orphs.)	Baldwin	3	78/19	Wilkinson
Griffin's, Owen(Orphs.)	Wilkes	Heards	24/28	Wilkinson
Griffin's, Richard(Orphs.)	Lincoln	Jones	32/9	Wilkinson
Griffin, Avengton	Washington	Chivers	232/10	Baldwin
Griffin, Benjamin M.	Montgomery	51	13/7	Wilkinson
Griffin, Benjamin M.	Montgomery	51	218/19	Baldwin
Griffin, David (Orph.)	Bulloch	Parishs	110/18	Wilkinson
Griffin, David	Oglethorpe	Popes	234/10	Baldwin
Griffin, Dempsey	Washington	Garretts	239/10	Wilkinson
Griffin, James	Lincoln	Mays	88/18	Baldwin
Griffin, James	Washington	Blackshears	121/23	Wilkinson
Griffin, Jerry	Columbia	10	165/18	Baldwin
Griffin, John	Oglethorpe	Popes	86/17	Baldwin
Griffin, John	Warren	Devereuxs	167/16	Wilkinson
Griffin, John	Wilkes	Sheets	95/15	Wilkinson
Griffin, Joseph	Elbert	Dyes	191/27	Wilkinson
Griffin, Joshua	Montgomery	54	166/16	Wilkinson
Griffin, Lem	Wilkinson		95/20	Baldwin
Griffin, Leroy	Washington	Chivers	128/15	Wilkinson
Griffin, Mary	Burke	Mulkeys	112/17	Baldwin
Griffin, Phereby	Burke	Carswells	122/25	Wilkinson
Griffin, Polly	Wilkes	Heards	237/6	Wilkinson
Griffin, Richard	Richmond		318/9	Wilkinson
Griffin, Richard	Richmond		81/8	Wilkinson
Griffin, Silas	Oglethorpe	Hudsons	262/17	Wilkinson
Griffin, Thomas	Liberty		227/19	Baldwin
Griffin, Uphama	Richmond		113/14	Wilkinson
Griffin, William	Montgomery	51	4/22	Wilkinson
Griffin, William	Wilkinson		324/15	Baldwin
Griffin, Winnifred	Washington	Chivers	67/10	Wilkinson
Griffis, Charles	Montgomery	57	29/6	Baldwin
Griffith, Caleb	Franklin	Griffiths	68/17	Wilkinson
Griffith, James	Oglethorpe	Hudsons	81/22	Wilkinson
Griffith, Morgan	Oglethorpe	Hudsons	223/19	Baldwin
Griggs, John Sr.	Hancock	Barnes	360/8	Wilkinson
Griggs, Rhodum	Hancock	Barnes	210/23	Wilkinson
Griggs, William	Hancock	Barnes	6/13	Baldwin
Griggsby, Drusilla	Greene	Davenports	245/15	Wilkinson
Griggsby, Grizzel	Greene	Davenports	88/12	Baldwin
Grimball, Paul	Liberty		178/12	Wilkinson
Grimes', Wm.(Orphs.)	Elbert	Groves	211/22	Wilkinson
Grimes, Benjamin	Greene	Jenkins	3/11	Baldwin
Grimes, James	Montgomery	51	127/20	Baldwin
Grimes, John	Columbia	8	144/26	Wilkinson
Grimes, Thomas	Greene	Stewarts	164/20	Baldwin
Grimit, William	Clarke	Tramells	131/9	Baldwin
Grimmer, William	Clarke	Cooks	217/19	Baldwin
Grimsley, Joseph	Baldwin	2	125/22	Wilkinson
Griner, John	Screven	Williamsons	118/11	Baldwin
Griner, Sarah	Bulloch	Williams	180/24	Wilkinson
Grizzard, Marget	Warren	Flournoys	280/13	Wilkinson
Grizzel, Joel	Elbert	Thompsons	263/24	Wilkinson
Groce, John Jr.	Screven		285/8	Wilkinson
Groce, John Sr.	Screven		103/20	Baldwin
Groce, John Sr.	Screven		118/8	Wilkinson
Gromet, Jno.C.(Orph.)	Effingham		37/6	Baldwin
Gromet, John J.(Orph.)	Effingham		37/6	Baldwin
Gromet, Judy S.(Orph.)	Effingham		37/6	Baldwin
Gromet, Margaret M.(Orph.)	Effingham		37/6	Baldwin
Groms, Joseph	Bulloch	Williams	179/18	Wilkinson

NAME	COUNTY	MIL.DIST.	LOT/DIST	DREW LAND
Groom, Charles	Washington	Holts	12/8	Baldwin
Groom, Charles	Washington	Holts	226/25	Wilkinson
Gross, Joshua	Wilkes	Sheets	33/11	Baldwin
Grovenstine, Christoph.	Camden	Hardees	139/10	Wilkinson
Groves, Stephen	Elbert	Groves	86/11	Wilkinson
Grubbs', Thomas(Orphs.)	Burke	Carswells	253/21	Wilkinson
Grubbs, Francis	Burke	Carswells	21/20	Wilkinson
Grubbs, Thomas	Baldwin	1	120/22	Wilkinson
Gruber, Solomon	Effingham		23/18	Baldwin
Gruber, Solomon	Effingham		91/9	Wilkinson
Guerard, Peter	Chatham	Abrahams	9/25	Wilkinson
Guest, Moses Jr.	Franklin	Griffiths	261/15	Baldwin
Gugel, Christian	Chatham	Pettybones	17/26	Wilkinson
Gugel, Daniel	Chatham	Pettybones	10/12	Wilkinson
Guice, Delila(Wid.)	Lincoln	Jones	88/25	Wilkinson
Guice, John	Lincoln	Jones	169/8	Wilkinson
Guice, Jonas	Lincoln	Mays	230/8	Wilkinson
Guice, Nicholas	Lincoln	Mays	218/17	Wilkinson
Guice, Nicholas	Lincoln	Mays	95/15	Baldwin
Guinn, Lancelot B.	Chatham	Hardens	239/22	Wilkinson
Guinn, Richard	Chatham	Pettybones	273/7	Wilkinson
Guinn, Richard	Chatham	Pettybones	51/18	Baldwin
Gumm, Jacob	Hancock	Gumms	330/13	Wilkinson
Gunn, Daniel Sr.	Wilkes	M.Hendersons	46/26	Wilkinson
Gunn, Daniel Sr.	Wilkes	M.Hendersons	76/12	Baldwin
Gunn, Jesse	Burke	Ballards	273/16	Wilkinson
Gunn, Jesse	Burke	Ballards	63/26	Wilkinson
Gunn, Richard	Warren	Carters	182/10	Baldwin
Gunn, Richard	Warren	Carters	85/17	Baldwin
Gunnells, Daniel	Wilkes	Stovalls	306/17	Wilkinson
Gunnels, Nancy(Miss)	Warren	Heaths	105/8	Wilkinson
Gunter, Charles	Elbert	Morrisons	217/16	Baldwin
Gunter, Isham	Elbert	Morrisons	260/19	Baldwin
Gunter, Isham	Elbert	Morrisons	78/24	Wilkinson
Gunter, James	Elbert	Morrisons	275/19	Wilkinson
Gurgainas, Cooper	Screven		308/11	Wilkinson
Guttery, Beverly	Oglethorpe	Hartsfeilds	193/15	Baldwin
Guttery, Wm.	Greene	Baxters	24/19	Wilkinson
Hadaway, David	Wilkes	Hendrix	416/7	Wilkinson
Hadaway, Eliz.	Wilkes	Kendricks	74/12	Baldwin
Hadden, Wm.Jr.	Jefferson	Hardwichs	45/18	Wilkinson
Hadley, Benjamin	Burke	Gordons	168/6	Wilkinson
Hadley, Thomas	Washington	Renfroes	189/19	Baldwin
Hagan, Etheldred	Bulloch	Williams	160/9	Wilkinson
Hagan, Peter	Bulloch	Williams	272/10	Wilkinson
Hagan, Solomon	Bulloch	Williams	107/28	Wilkinson
Hagan, Thomas	Bulloch	Williams	43/18	Wilkinson
Hagerty, Abel	Baldwin	4	331/9	Wilkinson
Haggard, James	Jackson	Johnsons	62/10	Wilkinson
Haggard, Samuel	Franklin	Christians	244/10	Wilkinson
Hagin's, Edward(orphs.)	Baldwin	4	136/14	Baldwin
Hagins, Jno.(Orph.)	Richmond		212/14	Baldwin
Hagins, Kitty(Orph.)	Richmond		2/21	Wilkinson
Hagins, Mary(Orph.)	Richmond		212/14	Baldwin
Hail's, Joshua(Orphs.)	Burke	Hilliards	105/20	Wilkinson
Hail, Thomas	Oglethorpe	Watkins	245/21	Wilkinson
Hailey, Reubin	Elbert	Roebucks	250/20	Baldwin
Haithcock, John Jr.	Burke	Spains	143/16	Wilkinson
Haithcock, John Jr.	Burke	Spains	173/8	Baldwin
Halcombe, John Jr.	Franklin	Hollingsworth	299/16	Wilkinson
Halcombe, Joseph	Franklin	Henrys	296/11	Wilkinson
Halcombe, Joseph	Franklin	Henrys	46/8	Baldwin
Hale, Drusilla(Wid.)	Burke	Hilliards	25/18	Wilkinson
Hale, Jesse	Oglethorpe	Hatchetts	59/8	Baldwin
Hale, Jose	Oglethorpe	Hitchcocks	104/8	Wilkinson
Hale, Sarah	McIntosh		176/16	Wilkinson
Hale, William	Washington	Holts	6/9	Baldwin

NAME	COUNTY	MIL.DIST.	LOT/DIST	DREW LAND
Hales, John	Jackson	Johnsons	204/19	Baldwin
Hales, John	Oglethorpe	Hitchcocks	218/23	Wilkinson
Haley, James	Elbert	Faulkners	75/16	Baldwin
Hall, Alexander	Clarke	Tramells	155/8	Wilkinson
Hall, Boling	Hancock	Barnes	357/7	Wilkinson
Hall, David	Burke	Ballards	173/14	Wilkinson
Hall, David	Camden	Hardys	74/9	Baldwin
Hall, Enoch Sr.	Montgomery	54	152/10	Wilkinson
Hall, Enoch Sr.	Montgomery	54	207/18	Wilkinson
Hall, George Jr.	Jackson	Cockrans	206/12	Baldwin
Hall, Hugh Sr.	Greene	Reas	318/8	Wilkinson
Hall, Hugh	Hancock	Barnes	173/12	Wilkinson
Hall, James M.	Burke	Montgomerys	5/17	Baldwin
Hall, James Sr.	Jefferson		142/25	Wilkinson
Hall, Jas.(B.Smith)	Hancock	Barnes	156/16	Wilkinson
Hall, Jeremiah	Elbert	Groves	151/8	Wilkinson
Hall, Jethro	Hancock	Pinkstons	209/21	Wilkinson
Hall, John	Greene	Greers	296/14	Wilkinson
Hall, John	Liberty		78/23	Wilkinson
Hall, John	Washington	Renfroes	25/12	Baldwin
Hall, Lewis Sr.	Tattnall	Halls	51/17	Baldwin
Hall, Littleton	Montgomery	56	195/12	Baldwin
Hall, Mary(Wid.)	Greene	Greers	145/22	Wilkinson
Hall, Redding	Montgomery	57	18/13	Wilkinson
Hall, Robert Sr.	Elbert	Blackwells	156/17	Baldwin
Hall, Samuel	Warren	Flournoys	179/15	Wilkinson
Hall, Sion	Montgomery	54	234/9	Wilkinson
Hall, Thomas	Chatham	Pembertons	44/6	Wilkinson
Hall, Thomas	Jackson	Wrights	304/13	Wilkinson
Hall, Thomas	Jackson	Wrights	55/15	Wilkinson
Hall, Thomas	Tattnall	Halls	135/9	Wilkinson
Hall, Timothy	Camden	Smiths	196/12	Wilkinson
Hall, William	Tattnall	Halls	97/26	Wilkinson
Hall, Wingate	Hancock	Candlers	24/24	Wilkinson
Hall, Wm.Adams	Elbert	Mobleys	259/8	Wilkinson
Hallaway, John	Bulloch	Parishs	169/19	Wilkinson
Halmark, John	Columbia	4	221/9	Wilkinson
Ham, John	Elbert	Olivers	183/13	Wilkinson
Hambey, John	Clarke	Robinsons	67/16	Wilkinson
Hambleton, John	Oglethorpe	Moores	278/14	Baldwin
Hambleton, John	Warren	Willsons	169/17	Wilkinson
Hambrick, James Sr.	Lincoln	Gartrells	122/16	Baldwin
Hambrick, James	Lincoln	Kennons	45/22	Wilkinson
Hambrick, Joseph	Baldwin	5	248/15	Baldwin
Hambrick, Susannah(S.W.)	Clarke	Mitchells	273/19	Baldwin
Hamburgh, Nicholas	Lincoln	Kings	161/16	Baldwin
Hamby, Absalom	Jackson	Cockrans	140/7	Wilkinson
Hamby, Absalom	Jackson	Cockrans	80/28	Wilkinson
Hamill, Hugh	Oglethorpe	Watkins	48/14	Baldwin
Hamilton, John	Lincoln	Jones	192/8	Wilkinson
Hamilton, John	Wilkes	Normans	141/18	Wilkinson
Hamilton, John	Wilkes	Normans	41/16	Baldwin
Hamilton, Rachel(Wid.)	Chatham	Abrahams	188/18	Wilkinson
Hamilton, Wm.	Wilkes	Wellborns	25/21	Wilkinson
Hamlin, John	Hancock	Weeks	243/10	Baldwin
Hamlin, Richard	Hancock	Weeks	5/11	Baldwin
Hammett, Absalom	Oglethorpe	Bells	116/8	Baldwin
Hammett, James	Oglethorpe	Bells	139/16	Wilkinson
Hammett, James	Oglethorpe	Bells	185/19	Wilkinson
Hammock, Benedick	Wilkes	Wellborns	67/11	Baldwin
Hammock, Benjamin	Lincoln	Gartrells	43/12	Wilkinson
Hammock, Catharine	Wilkes	Youngs	54/6	Baldwin
Hammock, Daniel	Washington	Paces	10/11	Wilkinson
Hammock, Emanuel	Jefferson		23/10	Wilkinson
Hammock, James	Wilkes	Youngs	201/14	Wilkinson
Hammock, Jesse	Jefferson		4/28	Wilkinson
Hammock, John	Clarke	Robinsons	181/27	Wilkinson

NAME	COUNTY	MIL.DIST.	LOT/DIST	DREW LAND
Hammock, Lewis	Wilkes	Youngs	296/8	Wilkinson
Hammock, Milly(Wid.)	Wilkes	Youngs	85/12	Baldwin
Hammock, Robert	Wilkes	Youngs	126/24	Wilkinson
Hammock, Sam'l(Orps.)	Wilkes	Wellborns	281/20	Baldwin
Hammock, Samuel	Jefferson		93/8	Wilkinson
Hammock, William	Wilkes	Youngs	10/9	Baldwin
Hammock, Wm.	Wilkes	Wellborns	198/27	Wilkinson
Hammond, Abraham	Wilkes	Coopers	119/9	Baldwin
Hammond, Eve(Wid.)	Wilkes	Coopers	247/10	Wilkinson
Hammond, Henry	Hancock	Wallers	292/11	Wilkinson
Hammond, Robert	Greene	Owsleys	121/7	Wilkinson
Hammond, Sarah(Wid.)	Greene	Owsleys	22/6	Wilkinson
Hampton, Benjamin	Jackson	Cockrans	239/25	Wilkinson
Hampton, Geo.	Oglethorpe	Hitchcocks	194/20	Wilkinson
Hampton, Henry	Columbia	8	150/7	Wilkinson
Hampton, William	Wilkinson		199/22	Wilkinson
Hampton, Wm.	Wilkinson		276/9	Wilkinson
Hamrick, John	Wilkes	Wellborns	136/6	Baldwin
Hamrick, John	Wilkes	Wellborns	309/12	Wilkinson
Hams, Isaac Sr.	Lincoln	Busseys	304/12	Wilkinson
Hancock, Clem	Warren	Devereux	92/17	Wilkinson
Hancock, Isaac	Franklin	Hoopers	255/23	Wilkinson
Hancock, Isaac	Franklin	Hoopers	332/15	Baldwin
Hancock, James	Tattnall	McDonalds	113/26	Wilkinson
Hancock, James	Tattnall	McDonalds	159/16	Baldwin
Hancock, John Sr.	Wilkes	Milners	13/19	Baldwin
Hancock, Joseph	Warren	Devereux	26/7	Baldwin
Hancock, Sarah(Wid.)	Jefferson	Fultons	43/17	Baldwin
Hand, Eleazer	Chatham	Whites	96/7	Wilkinson
Hand, Henry Sr.	Columbia	9	115/15	Wilkinson
Hand, John	Columbia	9	319/14	Wilkinson
Hand, John	Warren	Willsons	67/17	Baldwin
Handley, Jarard	Richmond		88/17	Baldwin
Handley, Jarod	Burke	Forths	14/26	Wilkinson
Handoff, James(Orph.)	Glynn		293/22	Wilkinson
Haney's, Wm.(Orph.)	Elbert	Moons	63/13	Wilkinson
Haney, Charles	Elbert	Moons	143/11	Baldwin
Haney, George	Jackson	Wrights	342/8	Wilkinson
Hannah, Thomas	Jefferson	Hardwichs	86/6	Wilkinson
Hannah, William	Screven		200/10	Baldwin
Hanners, John	Burke	Thompsons	147/11	Wilkinson
Hannon, Henry	Columbia	5	134/9	Baldwin
Hannon, John	Columbia	5	184/26	Wilkinson
Hanson, Elizabeth	Wilkes	M.Henderson	146/16	Wilkinson
Hanson, Samuel	Columbia	1	73/20	Wilkinson
Hanson, Thomas Sr.	Jackson	Wrights	247/16	Wilkinson
Hanson, Wm.(Son/Saml.)	Columbia	5	149/7	Wilkinson
Haralson, Vincent	Baldwin	4	133/14	Wilkinson
Harbisson, Alexander	Clarke	Robinsons	327/20	Baldwin
Harbour, Esaias	Franklin	Allens	11/6	Wilkinson
Harbuck, Henry	Warren	Neals	198/18	Wilkinson
Harbuck, William	Warren	Neals	352/21	Wilkinson
Harcrow, Hugh	Elbert	McGuires	186/23	Wilkinson
Hardee, Allen	Washington	Renfroes	336/8	Wilkinson
Hardee, Thomas	Washington	Paces	140/10	Wilkinson
Harden's, Charles(Orphs.)	Bryan	Austins	19/19	Wilkinson
Harden, Ebenezer	Screven		3/7	Wilkinson
Harden, Edward	Oglethorpe	Stewarts	166/20	Baldwin
Harden, Josiah	Warren	Hills	115/14	Baldwin
Harden, Mark	Franklin	Thompsons	85/17	Wilkinson
Harden, Mark	Warren	Willsons	38/16	Wilkinson
Harden, Martin	Franklin	Thompsons	208/28	Wilkinson
Harden, Samuel	Hancock	Barnes	196/13	Wilkinson
Hardeway, Washington	Warren	Neals	244/13	Wilkinson
Hardiman's, John(Orphs.)	Oglethorpe	Beasleys	22/20	Wilkinson
Hardiman's, Jos.(Orphs.)	Washington	Willis	105/16	Wilkinson
Hardiman, Elizabeth	Washington	Willis	353/12	Wilkinson

NAME	COUNTY	MIL.DIST.	LOT/DIST	DREW LAND
Hardiman, Sarah	Washington	Willis	206/16	Wilkinson
Hardman, John	Oglethorpe	Hewells	92/27	Wilkinson
Hardman, Wm.(M.Stone)	Oglethorpe	Hewells	168/8	Wilkinson
Hardman, Wm.Sr.	Oglethorpe	Hewells	251/20	Baldwin
Hardwich, Geo.W.	Jefferson	Tarvers	48/27	Wilkinson
Hardwich, Wm.P.	Jefferson	Hardwichs	161/25	Wilkinson
Hardwick, Garland	Baldwin	3	280/12	Wilkinson
Hardwick, Garland	Baldwin	3	91/13	Baldwin
Hardy's, Chas.(Orphs.)	Baldwin	5	160/13	Wilkinson
Hardy, Elizabeth	Washington	Andersons	88/13	Wilkinson
Hardy, John Sr.	Lincoln	Flemings	225/20	Wilkinson
Hardy, John(Esq.)	Lincoln	Flemings	413/7	Wilkinson
Hardy, John(Son/John)	Lincoln	Flemings	340/8	Wilkinson
Hardy, John	Camden	Hardys	230/19	Wilkinson
Hardy, John	Washington	Renfroes	106/7	Wilkinson
Hardy, Miles	Lincoln	Busseys	178/16	Baldwin
Hardygree, Polly(Orp/Jno.)	Greene	Davenports	119/19	Wilkinson
Hare, Wm.	Jefferson	Thomas	320/22	Wilkinson
Hargrove's, Benj.(Orphs.)	Burke	Carswells	44/24	Wilkinson
Hargrove, Aley(Wid.)	Jefferson	Wrights	343/10	Wilkinson
Hargrove, Charity	Montgomery		50/26	Wilkinson
Hargrove, Eldridge	Jefferson	Colemans	314/17	Wilkinson
Hargrove, Jordan	Burke	Fields	66/21	Wilkinson
Hargrove, Randal	Montgomery	51	238/20	Wilkinson
Hargrove, Randal	Montgomery	51	78/12	Baldwin
Hargrove, Reubin	Jefferson	Wrights	277/13	Wilkinson
Hargrove, Richard	Oglethorpe	Moores	27/9	Wilkinson
Hargrove, William	Franklin	Wems	277/22	Wilkinson
Hargrove, Wm.	Franklin	Wems	151/10	Baldwin
Harkins, James	Columbia	4	146/18	Baldwin
Harkins, James	Columbia	4	363/8	Wilkinson
Harkins, Robert	Baldwin	5	232/15	Baldwin
Harkins, Roger	Columbia	8	297/21	Wilkinson
Harkins, Roger	Columbia	8	61/26	Wilkinson
Harkins, Walter	Jackson	Hendersons	294/22	Wilkinson
Harkins, Wm.	Columbia	10	25/14	Wilkinson
Harlow, Southworth	Burke	Sandifords	3/10	Baldwin
Harman, Wm.N.	Chatham	Pettybones	138/10	Wilkinson
Harn, William	Bryan	Birds	11/21	Wilkinson
Harnage, Mary(Wid.)	Liberty		241/24	Wilkinson
Harnisberger, Stephen	Lincoln	Jones	174/18	Baldwin
Harp, Arthur	Greene	Alfords	127/10	Wilkinson
Harp, William	Greene	Alfords	188/11	Baldwin
Harp, Wm.	Greene	Alfords	147/9	Baldwin
Harpe, Manning	Greene	Alfords	252/11	Wilkinson
Harpe, Samuel	Greene	Alfords	305/13	Wilkinson
Harper, Benjamin J.	Hancock	Weeks	163/12	Wilkinson
Harper, Charlotte B.	Elbert	Clarks	66/22	Wilkinson
Harper, Darcas(Wid.)	Clarke	Harpers	28/15	Baldwin
Harper, Drusilla	Elbert	Clarks	126/8	Baldwin
Harper, Edmund	Elbert	Clarks	206/26	Wilkinson
Harper, Edmund	Elbert	Clarks	58/9	Wilkinson
Harper, Edward	Hancock	Barnes	69/10	Wilkinson
Harper, Everett	Clarke	Harpers	150/14	Baldwin
Harper, Everett	Clarke	Harpers	183/17	Wilkinson
Harper, George	Clarke	Harpers	14/11	Baldwin
Harper, George	Clarke	Harpers	255/6	Wilkinson
Harper, Haywood	Clarke	Harpers	165/25	Wilkinson
Harper, Henry	Elbert	McGuires	165/6	Baldwin
Harper, John	Wilkes	Milners	205/27	Wilkinson
Harper, Mary(Single)	Wilkes	Sheets	177/8	Wilkinson
Harper, Robert	Greene	Jenkins	252/17	Wilkinson
Harper, Roderick	Elbert	McGuires	13/27	Wilkinson
Harper, Sally R.	Elbert	Clarks	135/11	Wilkinson
Harper, Samuel(Esq.)	Greene	Davenports	134/19	Wilkinson
Harper, Sarah	Greene	Butlers	73/27	Wilkinson
Harper, Thomas	Elbert	McGuires	90/6	Wilkinson

NAME	COUNTY	MIL.DIST.	LOT/DIST	DREW LAND
Harper, Wm.Sr.	Lincoln	Mays	267/19	Baldwin
Harrell, Bailey	Wilkinson		203/16	Wilkinson
Harrell, Bailey	Wilkinson		28/14	Wilkinson
Harrell, Etheldred	Burke	Blounts	311/16	Wilkinson
Harrell, Hardy	Wilkinson		155/11	Baldwin
Harrell, James	Hancock	Shivers	6/18	Baldwin
Harrell, Milly	Hancock	Shivers	63/18	Baldwin
Harrell, Samuel	Greene	Owsleys	262/6	Wilkinson
Harrell, Simon Jr.	Warren	Flournoys	134/6	Baldwin
Harrell, Simon Jr.	Warren	Flournoys	200/20	Wilkinson
Harrell, Thomas	Bulloch	Parishs	97/16	Baldwin
Harrell, Thomas	Warren	Neals	56/19	Wilkinson
Harrington, Drury	Lincoln	Jones	218/20	Baldwin
Harris', Edward(Orphs.)	Hancock	Pinkstons	85/16	Baldwin
Harris', Thos.(Orphs.)	Clarke	Hitchcocks	77/26	Wilkinson
Harris', Wm.(Orphs.)	Greene	Loves	97/24	Wilkinson
Harris, Absalom	Franklin	Cornelius	261/25	Wilkinson
Harris, Ann Maria	Chatham	Whites	224/19	Wilkinson
Harris, Catharine(Wid.)	Hancock	Pinkstons	109/20	Baldwin
Harris, Churchwell	Washington	Renfroes	193/16	Wilkinson
Harris, Daniel	Greene	Jenkins	176/9	Baldwin
Harris, David Jr.	Clarke	Hitchcocks	183/15	Wilkinson
Harris, David Sr.	Columbia	6	191/21	Wilkinson
Harris, David	Greene	Loves	231/16	Wilkinson
Harris, David	Hancock	Shivers	103/10	Wilkinson
Harris, Drury	Jefferson		90/11	Baldwin
Harris, Elizabeth	Elbert	Mobleys	35/16	Baldwin
Harris, Elizabeth	Lincoln	Jones	70/25	Wilkinson
Harris, Ezekiel	Columbia	2	115/21	Wilkinson
Harris, George	Baldwin	4	41/11	Wilkinson
Harris, Henry	Warren	Neals	62/28	Wilkinson
Harris, Henry	Washington	Paces	233/11	Wilkinson
Harris, Isbel	Greene	Loves	87/15	Baldwin
Harris, Isham	Clarke	Hitchcocks	347/22	Wilkinson
Harris, Jailes	Elbert	Willifords	152/20	Baldwin
Harris, Jailes-Giles	Elbert	Willifords	155/12	Baldwin
Harris, James	Greene	Moores	18/10	Wilkinson
Harris, James	Greene	Moores	32/8	Wilkinson
Harris, Jesse	Jackson	Cockrans	488/7	Wilkinson
Harris, John	Glynn		149/6	Wilkinson
Harris, John	McIntosh		155/23	Wilkinson
Harris, Joseph	Jackson	Johnsons	49/6	Baldwin
Harris, Joshua	Lincoln	Jones	5/24	Wilkinson
Harris, Jourdan	Greene	Jinkins	272/13	Wilkinson
Harris, Laird W.	Hancock	Huffs	66/24	Wilkinson
Harris, Lu-Allen	Glynn		136/23	Wilkinson
Harris, Martha(Single)	Hancock	Huffs	76/15	Baldwin
Harris, Micajah	Baldwin	4	63/7	Baldwin
Harris, Moses	Baldwin	5	233/14	Baldwin
Harris, Nathan	Hancock	Barksdales	177/21	Wilkinson
Harris, Patience(Wid.)	Clarke	Martindales	356/7	Wilkinson
Harris, Peter	Wilkes	Roreys	96/9	Wilkinson
Harris, Sampson	Jackson	Cockrans	283/6	Wilkinson
Harris, Samuel C.	Warren	Bakers	1/6	Baldwin
Harris, Samuel C.	Warren	Bakers	123/20	Baldwin
Harris, Sarah(S)	Hancock	Huffs	215/9	Wilkinson
Harris, Sarah(Wid.)	Greene	Moores	184/10	Wilkinson
Harris, Sarah	Greene	Moores	14/8	Baldwin
Harris, Sarah	Washington	Renfroes	215/25	Wilkinson
Harris, Thomas	Jackson	Cockrans	161/10	Wilkinson
Harris, Tryon	Elbert	Clarks	129/13	Baldwin
Harris, Walton Sr.	Greene	Davenports	60/19	Wilkinson
Harris, Walton	Jackson	Wrights	28/16	Wilkinson
Harris, William	Clarke	Robinsons	142/7	Wilkinson
Harris, Wm.	Greene	Moores	86/21	Wilkinson
Harris, Wm.D.	Clarke	Hitchcocks	263/22	Wilkinson
Harrison, Barzillai	Franklin	Cornelius	148/12	Wilkinson

NAME	COUNTY	MIL.DIST.	LOT/DIST	DREW LAND
Harrison, Benjamin	Montgomery	50	139/19	Baldwin
Harrison, Davis	Greene	Reas	86/16	Wilkinson
Harrison, Edward	Franklin	Everetts	106/20	Baldwin
Harrison, Elisha	Columbia	6	267/8	Wilkinson
Harrison, Elizabeth(Orph.)	Greene	Armors	124/17	Wilkinson
Harrison, Gadwell R.	Columbia	8	108/17	Wilkinson
Harrison, J.H.	McIntosh		80/23	Wilkinson
Harrison, John Jr.	Hancock	Birdsongs	224/12	Wilkinson
Harrison, John	Wilkes	Edges	102/9	Wilkinson
Harrison, Joseph	Jackson	Hendersons	182/16	Wilkinson
Harrison, Joseph	Jackson	Wrights	16/24	Wilkinson
Harrison, Margarett(Orph.)	Greene	Armors	124/17	Wilkinson
Harrison, Robt.(Orph.)	Greene	Armors	124/17	Wilkinson
Harrison, Samuel	Wilkinson		157/26	Wilkinson
Harrison, Vincent R.Sr.	Wilkes	Edges	226/21	Wilkinson
Harrison, Wm.(Orph.)	Greene	Armors	124/17	Wilkinson
Harrison, Wm.	Chatham	Hardens	321/13	Wilkinson
Harrison, Wm.	Washington	Holts	228/26	Wilkinson
Harrod, Susannah(Wid.)	Jackson	Cockrans	180/18	Wilkinson
Hart's, Saml.(Orphs.)	Washington	Kendricks	226/20	Baldwin
Hart, Archibald	Oglethorpe	Moores	161/20	Wilkinson
Hart, Archibald	Oglethorpe	Moores	194/21	Wilkinson
Hart, David	Jefferson	Bosticks	301/24	Wilkinson
Hart, Edwin	Burke	Martins	125/7	Wilkinson
Hart, Elizabeth(Wid.)	Franklin	Wems	122/27	Wilkinson
Hart, Henry	Burke	Forths	36/15	Baldwin
Hart, Henry	Camden	Crews	68/28	Wilkinson
Hart, Henry	Washington	Kendricks	21/15	Wilkinson
Hart, Nelly(Wid.)	Burke	Blounts	42/12	Wilkinson
Hart, Robert	Burke	Blounts	365/7	Wilkinson
Hart, Robert	Wilkinson		216/8	Wilkinson
Hart, Wm.(Orp/Anthony)	Screven	Hutchinsons	283/21	Wilkinson
Hartgrove's, Henry(Orphs.)	Franklin	Griffiths	80/20	Wilkinson
Hartley, Mary(Orph.)	Burke	Sharps	43/7	Baldwin
Hartley, Robert	Hancock	Barksdales	249/19	Baldwin
Hartley, Samuel	Montgomery	55	290/14	Baldwin
Harton, Lott	Hancock	Weeks	40/24	Wilkinson
Hartridge, John E.	Chatham	Pettybones	134/27	Wilkinson
Hartsfield, Henry	Oglethorpe	Hartsfields	193/11	Wilkinson
Hartsfield, Richd.	Oglethorpe	Hartsfields	259/16	Wilkinson
Harvell, James	Columbia	9	17/19	Wilkinson
Harvell, James	Columbia	9	269/13	Wilkinson
Harvey, Benjamin	Wilkinson		27/24	Wilkinson
Harvey, Evan	Baldwin	2	181/7	Wilkinson
Harvey, James Sr.	Hancock	Coopers	266/8	Wilkinson
Harvey, John P.	Jefferson	Wrights	265/9	Wilkinson
Harvey, Michael	Baldwin	3	149/22	Wilkinson
Harvey, Pinkethman	Baldwin	1	200/10	Wilkinson
Harvey, Thomas	Baldwin	2	409/7	Wilkinson
Harvey, Thomas	Hancock	Coopers	138/17	Wilkinson
Harvey, Zephenah	Hancock	Pinkstons	39/14	Baldwin
Harvill's, Jos.(Orphs.)	Warren	Devereux	93/13	Wilkinson
Harvill, Joseph	Warren	Willsons	52/8	Baldwin
Harvill, Wm.	Oglethorpe	Moores	72/18	Baldwin
Harville, James Sr.	Greene	Greers	20/19	Baldwin
Harwell, Anderson	Hancock	Barnes	227/12	Wilkinson
Harwell, Samuel	Hancock	Huffs	167/13	Wilkinson
Haskins, Rhoda(Wid.)	Burke	Hilliards	125/18	Wilkinson
Haswell, Thomas	Hancock	Thomas	155/6	Baldwin
Hatcher, Archibald	Richmond		51/14	Baldwin
Hatcher, Edward	Richmond		34/8	Wilkinson
Hatcher, Henry	Richmond		43/16	Wilkinson
Hatcher, James	Elbert	Hillyers	223/23	Wilkinson
Hatcher, John	Washington	Willis	10/8	Wilkinson
Hatcher, Josiah	Burke	Ballards	108/26	Wilkinson
Hatcher, Josiah	Burke	Ballards	21/8	Wilkinson
Hathcock, James	Franklin	Dixons	197/9	Baldwin

NAME	COUNTY	MIL.DIST.	LOT/DIST	DREW LAND
Hathcock, John	Elbert	Thompsons	113/6	Wilkinson
Hathcock, John	Franklin	Allens	22/22	Wilkinson
Hathcock, John	Franklin	Allens	65/18	Wilkinson
Hathcock, Oziah	Elbert	Olivers	252/8	Wilkinson
Hathhorn, Andrew	Jackson	Cockrans	161/22	Wilkinson
Hathhorn, Andrew	Jackson	Cockrans	93/16	Wilkinson
Hathhorn, Elizabeth	Warren	Devereux	293/13	Wilkinson
Hathhorn, Thomas	Washington	Garretts	168/18	Baldwin
Hathhorn, Wm.	Washington	Garretts	40/19	Wilkinson
Hatley, Bynum	Baldwin	4	311/13	Wilkinson
Haupt, George	Chatham	Herbs	433/7	Wilkinson
Haupt, John	Chatham	Neyles	303/7	Wilkinson
Haupt, John	Chatham	Neyles	52/18	Wilkinson
Hawk, Peter	Greene	Baxters	166/20	Wilkinson
Hawk, Peter	Greene	Baxters	311/15	Wilkinson
Hawkins, Hardress	Hancock	Shivers	89/17	Wilkinson
Hawkins, Mathew	Baldwin	2	243/7	Wilkinson
Hawkins, Wyatt Jr.	Elbert	Grovers	147/19	Wilkinson
Hawthorn, Aaron	Burke	Montgomerys	123/17	Wilkinson
Hawthorn, Eliz.(Wid.)	Elbert	Olivers	172/17	Baldwin
Hawthorn, James Sr.	Jackson	Johnsons	116/10	Wilkinson
Hay, David	Wilkes	Stovalls	8/24	Wilkinson
Hay, Polly(Single)	Wilkes	Sheets	81/15	Baldwin
Hayens, John	Clarke	Hitchcocks	104/26	Wilkinson
Hayes, Charles	Richmond		193/10	Baldwin
Haygood, James	Clarke	Browns	83/10	Wilkinson
Haygood, John	Clarke	Browns	71/17	Wilkinson
Hayles, George	Clarke	Cooks	279/19	Baldwin
Hayles, John	Clarke	Cooks	71/10	Wilkinson
Hayly, Ambrose	Clarke	Browns	70/7	Baldwin
Hayman, Jeremiah	Bulloch	Denmarks	52/13	Baldwin
Haymans, Wm.Jr.	Burke	Gordans	199/20	Baldwin
Haymans, Wm.Sr.	Burke	Gordans	72/17	Baldwin
Haynes, Charles E.	Warren	Hills	288/14	Baldwin
Haynes, Daniel	Greene	Carletons	136/20	Baldwin
Haynes, Henry Sr.	Greene	Davenports	255/14	Wilkinson
Haynes, Isaac	Jackson	Cockrans	352/22	Wilkinson
Haynes, James	Hancock	Wallers	204/6	Wilkinson
Haynes, Leven	Washington	Chivers	202/10	Wilkinson
Haynes, Mary(Wid.)	Washington	Chivers	107/9	Wilkinson
Haynes, Nathan	Washington	Chivers	96/15	Baldwin
Haynie, Dyskin	Elbert	Moons	122/7	Wilkinson
Haynie, William	Burke	Martins	206/25	Wilkinson
Hays, Adam(Esq.)	Greene	Jinkins	346/13	Wilkinson
Hays, Edith	Burke	Blounts	122/15	Baldwin
Hays, George	Tattnall	Armstrongs	187/8	Baldwin
Hays, George	Tattnall	Armstrongs	204/10	Wilkinson
Hays, Hugh	Greene	Jinkins	19/9	Wilkinson
Hays, Martin	Columbia	9	100/15	Wilkinson
Hays, Rebecca	Richmond		113/13	Baldwin
Hays, Thomas	Jackson	Cockrans	129/12	Wilkinson
Hazzard, William	McIntosh		292/9	Wilkinson
Head, John S.	Elbert	Clarks	103/10	Baldwin
Head, John	Glynn		357/10	Wilkinson
Head, Sarah(Orp/Rich'd)	Montgomery	59	32/28	Wilkinson
Head, William	Elbert	Roebucks	189/20	Wilkinson
Head, Wm.	Elbert	Roebucks	130/9	Baldwin
Head, Wm.Jr.	Baldwin	2	52/17	Baldwin
Headen, Jesse	Jackson	Wrights	131/15	Baldwin
Headen, Jesse	Jackson	Wrights	149/17	Wilkinson
Heard, Eliz.(Wid.)	Wilkes	J.Hendersons	180/19	Wilkinson
Heard, James	Greene	Loves	50/8	Wilkinson
Heard, John	Greene	Watts	64/11	Baldwin
Heard, Margarett(Wid.)	Wilkes	Heards	255/20	Baldwin
Heard, Mary	Wilkes	Heards	238/16	Wilkinson
Heard, Stephen	Elbert	Clarks	50/12	Wilkinson
Heard, Thomas Sr.	Greene	Watts	44/8	Wilkinson

NAME	COUNTY	MIL.DIST.	LOT/DIST	DREW LAND
Heard, William	Baldwin	5	141/9	Baldwin
Heard, Wm.	Greene	Greers	206/23	Wilkinson
Heard, Woodson	Greene	Watts	9/20	Wilkinson
Hearn, Asa	Jackson	Wrights	212/22	Wilkinson
Hearn, Benjamin	Baldwin	4	48/12	Wilkinson
Hearn, Wm.Jr.	Hancock	Wallers	73/16	Baldwin
Heath, Chappel	Warren	Bakers	151/14	Wilkinson
Heath, Chappell	Hancock	Huffs	156/10	Baldwin
Heath, James	Warren	Heaths	208/13	Baldwin
Heath, Joel	Baldwin	3	239/13	Wilkinson
Heath, Joel	Warren	Hills	456/7	Wilkinson
Heath, John	Washington	Renfroes	128/25	Wilkinson
Heath, Mary(Miss)	Warren	Heaths	159/8	Baldwin
Heath, Rebecca(Orph.)	Baldwin	3	215/16	Baldwin
Heath, Rhoda(Wid.)	Baldwin	3	92/7	Wilkinson
Heath, Richard(Orph.)	Baldwin	3	215/16	Baldwin
Heath, Sterling	Hancock	Barnes	119/25	Wilkinson
Heath, Thomas	Warren	Heaths	54/7	Baldwin
Heath, Thomas	Warren	Heaths	6/8	Wilkinson
Heathorn, Samuel	Clarke	Hitchcocks	308/7	Wilkinson
Heathorn, Samuel	Clarke	Hitchcocks	52/13	Wilkinson
Heaton, Thomas	Montgomery	53	414/7	Wilkinson
Heflin, James Sr.	Baldwin	5	261/14	Baldwin
Height, Howell Jr.	Warren	Hills	66/19	Baldwin
Height, Howell Sr.	Warren	Hills	74/7	Wilkinson
Heinamann, Mary(Wid.)	Chatham	Whites	16/15	Wilkinson
Heinley, Israel	Effingham		93/13	Baldwin
Heinley, John	Effingham		238/8	Wilkinson
Heisler, George	Chatham	Neyles	63/20	Wilkinson
Helmley, Eliz.(Single)	Effingham		367/22	Wilkinson
Helsebeck, Henry	Oglethorpe	Hudsons	178/11	Wilkinson
Helton, Richard	Washington	Collins	98/7	Wilkinson
Hemphill, John	Jackson	Cockrans	243/9	Wilkinson
Hemphill, Polly	Greene	Carltons	139/12	Baldwin
Hemphill, Samuel	Jackson	Hendersons	245/9	Wilkinson
Hemphill, Thompson	Greene	Carletons	43/28	Wilkinson
Hemphill, Wm.	Greene	Carletons	312/12	Wilkinson
Henderson's, Robt.(Orphs.)	Jackson	Hendersons	287/13	Wilkinson
Henderson, Betsy	Greene	Carletons	215/12	Baldwin
Henderson, Eliza(Wid.)	Chatham	Whites	114/18	Wilkinson
Henderson, Isbel	Greene	Carletons	174/9	Wilkinson
Henderson, John G.	Franklin	Everetts	166/10	Baldwin
Henderson, Jos.	Wilkes	J.Hendersons	31/18	Wilkinson
Henderson, Jos.Sr.	Greene	Carletons	232/16	Wilkinson
Henderson, Joseph	Clarke	Cooks	97/22	Wilkinson
Henderson, Joseph	Elbert	Blackwells	249/17	Wilkinson
Henderson, Joseph	Elbert	Blackwells	43/10	Wilkinson
Henderson, Major	Wilkes	M.Hendersons	65/8	Wilkinson
Henderson, Michael	Glynn		174/17	Wilkinson
Henderson, Randel	Tattnall	Sharrards	45/24	Wilkinson
Henderson, Samuel	Clarke	Browns	1/18	Baldwin
Henderson, Samuel	Clarke	Cooks	43/14	Wilkinson
Henderson, Simon	Warren	Carters	339/7	Wilkinson
Henderson, Wm.	Wilkes	Sovalls	227/26	Wilkinson
Hendley, John	Bulloch	Hendleys	178/14	Wilkinson
Hendley, John	Wilkes	J.Hendersons	230/6	Wilkinson
Hendon, Robertson	Oglethorpe	Hitchcocks	362/8	Wilkinson
Hendon, Thomas	Elbert	McGuires	201/15	Baldwin
Hendrick, Absalom	Elbert	Groves	60/16	Baldwin
Hendrick, Benj.	Wilkes	Parks	39/16	Baldwin
Hendrick, Daniel	Bulloch	Williams	41/22	Wilkinson
Hendrick, John	McIntosh		183/20	Wilkinson
Hendrick, Nimrod	Elbert	Morrisons	206/22	Wilkinson
Hendrickson, Catharine	Hancock	Barksdales	76/16	Baldwin
Hendrickson, Christian	Chatham	Abrahams	168/28	Wilkinson
Hendrix's, Isaac(Orphs.)	Franklin	Wems	498/7	Wilkinson
Hendrix, Abijah	Elbert	Olivers	234/9	Baldwin

NAME	COUNTY	MIL.DIST.	LOT/DIST	DREW LAND
Hendrix, Andrew	Jackson	Hendersons	15/12	Wilkinson
Hendrix, Jesse Sr.	Elbert	Morrisons	188/19	Wilkinson
Hendrix, John	Jackson	Hendersons	138/18	Wilkinson
Hendrix, John	Jackson	Hendersons	35/8	Wilkinson
Hendrix, Sarah(Wid.)	Elbert	Olivers	149/8	Baldwin
Hendry, Isaac	Washington	Kendricks	7/16	Baldwin
Hendry, John	Baldwin	1	173/15	Baldwin
Hendry, Micajah	Lincoln	Gartrells	173/27	Wilkinson
Henley, Abijah	Wilkes	Roreys	95/13	Baldwin
Henley, Alley	Columbia	9	346/22	Wilkinson
Henley, Edmund	Franklin	Bryants	221/18	Wilkinson
Henley, Philip	Lincoln	Kings	19/7	Wilkinson
Henley, Thomas	Columbia	9	23/12	Wilkinson
Henley, Wm.	Jackson	Cockrans	250/19	Baldwin
Henly's, John(Orphs.)	Wilkes	Roreys	126/9	Wilkinson
Hennindon, Jonathan	Washington	Paces	78/12	Wilkinson
Henry, George	Columbia	10	7/20	Baldwin
Henry, Jemina(Miss)	Warren	Hills	275/15	Baldwin
Henry, John	Hancock	Crowders	248/12	Wilkinson
Henry, Joseph Jr.	Hancock	Crowders	270/7	Wilkinson
Hensler, Hannah(Single)	Effingham		261/22	Wilkinson
Hensler, Jacob	Effingham		153/25	Wilkinson
Henson, Thomas	Hancock	Weeks	90/10	Wilkinson
Henton, James	Wilkes	Normans	398/8	Wilkinson
Henton, Noah	Wilkes	Normans	152/19	Wilkinson
Herb, Catharine(Wid.)	Chatham	Pembertons	32/12	Baldwin
Herdman, George	Richmond		170/9	Baldwin
Herendon, Stephen	Washington	Paces	101/8	Wilkinson
Herndon, Betsy(Orph.)	Elbert	Clarks	241/19	Baldwin
Herndon, Edw'd(Orph.)	Elbert	Clarks	241/19	Baldwin
Herndon, Fanny(Orph.)	Elbert	Clarks	241/19	Baldwin
Herndon, Joseph	Clarke	Browns	144/23	Wilkinson
Herndon, Mich'l(Orph.)	Elbert	Clarks	241/19	Baldwin
Herndon, Polly(Orph.)	Elbert	Clarks	241/19	Baldwin
Herndon, Susannah(Wid.)	Elbert	Clarks	65/7	Wilkinson
Herrin, Benjamin	Clarke	Martins	253/15	Wilkinson
Herrin, George	Jackson	Hendersons	21/11	Wilkinson
Herrin, Gresham	Clarke	Mitchells	207/27	Wilkinson
Herrington, Argent	Montgomery	53	5/6	Wilkinson
Herrington, David	Washington	Garretts	9/9	Baldwin
Herrington, Ephraim	Montgomery	53	66/15	Baldwin
Herrington, Luke	Hancock	Barnes	57/17	Wilkinson
Herrington, Richard	Screven	Hutchinsons	171/7	Wilkinson
Herrod, Jacob	Montgomery	50	199/20	Wilkinson
Herron, James	Richmond		170/7	Wilkinson
Hershman, Jacob	Chatham	Pettybones	214/26	Wilkinson
Hester's, Jas.(Orphs.)	Lincoln	Kings	262/14	Wilkinson
Hester's, John(Orph.)	Clarke	Butlers	149/21	Wilkinson
Hester, Mathew	Clarke	Butlers	28/11	Baldwin
Hester, Thomas	Clarke	Butlers	118/10	Wilkinson
Hewell, Wyatt	Oglethorpe	Hewells	200/14	Baldwin
Hewett, Sally(S.W.)	Clarke	Stewarts	150/19	Wilkinson
Hickey, Benjamin	Burke	Forths	125/9	Wilkinson
Hickman, Joseph	Clarke	Tramells	334/13	Wilkinson
Hickman, Uphe	Jackson	Hendersons	212/15	Baldwin
Hicks, Harrison	Elbert	Faulkners	2/20	Wilkinson
Hicks, Nathaniel	Columbia	7	173/12	Baldwin
Hicks, William	Baldwin	1	120/19	Wilkinson
Hide, Eliz.(Wid.)	Wilkes	Sheets	101/11	Baldwin
Hidle, Caty	Columbia	8	298/16	Wilkinson
Higdon, Charles	Wilkinson		27/6	Baldwin
Higdon, Robert	Burke	Sharps	132/8	Baldwin
Higgason, Larkin	Elbert	Thompsons	291/12	Wilkinson
Higginbotham, Benj.	Elbert	Olivers	26/13	Baldwin
Higginbotham, Gabriel	Elbert	Olivers	218/9	Wilkinson
Higginbotham, Jno.S.	Elbert	Blackwells	144/7	Baldwin
Higginbotham, Oliver	Clarke	Robinsons	270/19	Wilkinson

NAME	COUNTY	MIL.DIST.	LOT/DIST	DREW LAND
Higginbotham, Wm.	Elbert	Olivers	14/14	Wilkinson
Highnote, Betsy	Baldwin	1	24/17	Wilkinson
Highnote, Henry	Warren	Devereux	255/19	Wilkinson
Highsmith, Daniel	Tattnall	Halls	116/24	Wilkinson
Highsmith, Isaac	Tattnall	Halls	45/19	Wilkinson
Hightower, Charnell	Elbert	Morrisons	199/6	Baldwin
Hightower, Davis J.	Greene	Owsleys	120/12	Wilkinson
Hightower, James	Baldwin	3	495/7	Wilkinson
Hightower, Milly	Greene	Alfords	111/15	Baldwin
Hightower, Sally A.	Montgomery	50	318/21	Wilkinson
Hightower, Wm.Sr.	Baldwin	3	199/12	Wilkinson
Hill's, Wm.(Orphs.)	Burke	Gordans	271/11	Wilkinson
Hill, Benjamin	Baldwin	2	126/12	Wilkinson
Hill, Charles	Effingham		109/18	Baldwin
Hill, Eliz.H.	Hancock	Hudsons	69/8	Wilkinson
Hill, Francis L.	Greene	Stewarts	351/8	Wilkinson
Hill, George	Baldwin	3	17/22	Wilkinson
Hill, Gillum	Burke	Ballards	74/14	Baldwin
Hill, Gillum	Burke	Ballards	85/10	Baldwin
Hill, Isaac	Clarke	Browns	113/12	Baldwin
Hill, Isaac	Clarke	Browns	13/12	Wilkinson
Hill, Jacob	Elbert	McGuires	371/22	Wilkinson
Hill, Jane(Orph.)	Chatham	Abrahams	158/8	Baldwin
Hill, Jeremiah	Baldwin	1	65/13	Baldwin
Hill, John	Columbia	7	15/7	Baldwin
Hill, John	Columbia	7	57/20	Wilkinson
Hill, John	Screven		35/8	Baldwin
Hill, Jos.Logan	Baldwin	2	28/21	Wilkinson
Hill, Joseph	Warren	Bakers	312/14	Wilkinson
Hill, Lilly	Greene	Reas	120/9	Baldwin
Hill, Lucy	Jackson	Cockrans	30/28	Wilkinson
Hill, Mary Ann	Greene	Reas	140/20	Wilkinson
Hill, Mary J.	Hancock	Hudsons	60/14	Baldwin
Hill, Mary	Lincoln	Flemings	139/11	Wilkinson
Hill, Miles	Oglethorpe	Popes	98/13	Baldwin
Hill, Nancy(Miss)	Warren	Bakers	173/9	Wilkinson
Hill, Richard	Richmond		110/13	Wilkinson
Hill, Richard	Warren	Bakers	115/26	Wilkinson
Hill, Sally	Jackson	Cockrans	15/11	Wilkinson
Hill, Sarah(Wid.)	Baldwin	1	344/22	Wilkinson
Hill, Theoph.(Son/Henry)	Wilkes	M.Hendersons	24/13	Baldwin
Hill, Theoph.(Son/Henry)	Wilkes	M.Hendersons	34/17	Baldwin
Hill, Theophilus	Oglethorpe	Popes	253/19	Wilkinson
Hill, Thomas	Clarke	Browns	13/8	Baldwin
Hill, Thomas	Franklin	Dixons	150/20	Baldwin
Hill, Thomas	Oglethorpe	Watkins	157/13	Wilkinson
Hill, Thomas	Oglethorpe	Watkins	314/13	Wilkinson
Hill, William	Hancock	Smiths	269/19	Baldwin
Hill, Willie	Oglethorpe	Watkins	207/12	Baldwin
Hill, Wm.	Hancock	Gumms	140/25	Wilkinson
Hill, Wright	Hancock	Birdsongs	273/19	Wilkinson
Hillard, Kinchen	Washington	Andersons	89/6	Baldwin
Hillard, Major	Washington	Delks	270/15	Baldwin
Hillhouse, Mary	Wilkes	Roreys	109/17	Baldwin
Hilliard, Drury	Bryan	Birds	325/15	Baldwin
Hilliard, John	Bulloch	Godfreys	245/6	Wilkinson
Hilliard, Thos.H.C.	Greene	Carletons	66/14	Wilkinson
Hillsman, Micajah	Greene	Davenports	139/9	Wilkinson
Hillson, Diana	Warren	Devereux	119/13	Baldwin
Hillson, John	Warren	Devereux	265/20	Baldwin
Hilly, Francis	Wilkes	Roreys	21/13	Baldwin
Hillyer, Shaler	Elbert	Hillyers	276/20	Wilkinson
Hilton's, John(Orphs.)	Warren	Devereux	125/13	Baldwin
Hilton, Abraham	Franklin	Conners	147/17	Wilkinson
Hilton, Abraham	Washington	Collins	1/9	Baldwin
Hines, James Jr.	Greene	Watsons	159/19	Baldwin
Hines, Nancy	Burke	Fields	47/20	Wilkinson

NAME	COUNTY	MIL.DIST.	LOT/DIST	DREW LAND
Hines, Nathaniel	Greene	Alfords	420/7	Wilkinson
Hines, Richard	Burke	Ballards	61/14	Baldwin
Hines, Robert	Elbert	Clarks	128/10	Baldwin
Hines, William	Burke	Fields	105/14	Baldwin
Hines, William	Burke	Fields	303/20	Baldwin
Hines, William	Camden	Browns	212/6	Wilkinson
Hinesman, Mary(Orph.)	Glynn		190/19	Wilkinson
Hinson, John	Oglethorpe	Popes	124/16	Wilkinson
Hinson, Philip Jr.	Burke	Hilliards	45/7	Baldwin
Hinton's, Hardy(Orps.)	Oglethorpe	Popes	302/11	Wilkinson
Hinton, John(Son/Job)	Wilkes	Normans	294/8	Wilkinson
Hinton, Peter	Elbert	Roebucks	206/20	Baldwin
Hinton, Thomas	Clarke	Dukes	217/21	Wilkinson
Hister, Nancy(Wid.)	Lincoln	Kings	21/6	Baldwin
Hitchcock, Jesse	Oglethorpe	Hitchcocks	42/19	Baldwin
Hitchcock, Wm.Sr.	Oglethorpe	Hitchcocks	454/7	Wilkinson
Hite, James	Jackson	Wrights	335/20	Baldwin
Hix, Robert	Hancock	Birdsongs	15/15	Baldwin
Hobbs, John	Columbia	6	104/13	Baldwin
Hobbs, Joseph	Oglethorpe	Beasleys	81/25	Wilkinson
Hobbs, Lewis	Columbia	6	14/18	Wilkinson
Hobbs, Sarah	Greene	Greers	320/21	Wilkinson
Hobbs, William	Columbia	6	156/13	Wilkinson
Hobkirk, William	Chatham	Hardens	88/15	Wilkinson
Hobson, Caswell	Warren	Bakers	147/18	Wilkinson
Hobson, Nicholas	Jackson	Wrights	45/20	Wilkinson
Hobson, Nicholas	Jackson	Wrights	9/14	Wilkinson
Hodge's, Francis(Orphs.)	Jackson	Hendersons	22/14	Wilkinson
Hodge, Alexander	Oglethorpe	Hatchetts	205/22	Wilkinson
Hodge, Alexander	Oglethorpe	Hatchetts	96/18	Baldwin
Hodge, Archibald	Oglethorpe	Hatchetts	131/16	Wilkinson
Hodge, David	Columbia	6	10/9	Wilkinson
Hodge, John	Screven		235/26	Wilkinson
Hodges, Anne W.(Wid.)	Greene		127/9	Baldwin
Hodges, Fleming	Warren	Carters	74/8	Wilkinson
Hodges, Hanley	Burke	Forths	108/10	Baldwin
Hodges, John	Greene	Jenkins	118/19	Wilkinson
Hodges, Joshua Jr.	Bulloch	Williams	258/24	Wilkinson
Hodges, Joshua Jr.	Bulloch	Williams	89/16	Baldwin
Hodges, Mary	Tattnall	Staffords	6/19	Baldwin
Hodges, Mary	Washington	Paces	251/17	Wilkinson
Hodges, Nathan	Tattnall	McDonalds	27/27	Wilkinson
Hodges, Nathaniel	Bulloch	Williams	176/12	Wilkinson
Hodges, Nathaniel	Bulloch	Williams	186/19	Baldwin
Hodges, William	Tattnall	Staffords	136/16	Baldwin
Hodges, William	Tattnall	Staffords	45/20	Baldwin
Hodges, Wm.(Orph.)	Oglethorpe	Hudsons	63/6	Baldwin
Hodgins, Hannah	Warren	Willsons	53/20	Baldwin
Hodnett, Benj.	Oglethorpe	Stewarts	150/18	Wilkinson
Hoff, Charles	Wilkes	Heards	47/20	Baldwin
Hoff, Elizabeth	Wilkes	Heards	158/21	Wilkinson
Hoff, Mathias	Wilkes	Heards	135/7	Wilkinson
Hoffman, Jacob	Bulloch	Denmarks	58/6	Wilkinson
Hogan's, Wm.(Orphs.)	Lincoln	Busseys	23/14	Baldwin
Hogan, Isham T.	Hancock	Holts	171/19	Wilkinson
Hoges, Mary	Washington	Howards	236/21	Wilkinson
Hoges, Robert	Washington	Wiggins	256/14	Wilkinson
Hogg, John	Columbia	6	171/12	Baldwin
Hogg, John	Screven		171/6	Baldwin
Hogins, John R.	Washington	Holts	276/20	Baldwin
Hogins, Tabitha	Washington	Holts	90/12	Wilkinson
Hogue, Jonathan	Oglethorpe	Bells	325/24	Wilkinson
Holbrook's, (Orphs.)	Columbia	7	213/17	Baldwin
Holbrook, Edy	Elbert	Keelings	7/7	Baldwin
Holbrooks, Dorcus	Franklin	Cornelius	72/8	Baldwin
Holcmbe, Henry	Chatham	Pettybones	19/25	Wilkinson
Holcombe, Justis	McIntosh		160/22	Wilkinson

NAME	COUNTY	MIL.DIST.	LOT/DIST	DREW LAND
Holdbrook, Jesse	Franklin	Allens	212/14	Wilkinson
Holder, Thomas	Columbia	9	213/26	Wilkinson
Holland, David	Montgomery	58	274/8	Wilkinson
Holland, Dempsey	Warren	Neals	135/19	Baldwin
Holland, Eliz.	Washington	Chivers	32/10	Wilkinson
Holland, Henry	Montgomery	58	189/10	Baldwin
Holland, James	Glynn		176/6	Baldwin
Holland, Laban	Jackson	Wrights	62/14	Wilkinson
Holland, Thomas	Greene	Baxters	160/16	Wilkinson
Holley, Hazel	Montgomery	50	132/7	Wilkinson
Holley, Isaac	Washington	Willis	161/23	Wilkinson
Holley, Jonathan	Montgomery	50	241/14	Wilkinson
Holley, Wm.	Montgomery	50	92/28	Wilkinson
Holliday's, Jeremiah(Orps.)	Jackson	Wrights	260/25	Wilkinson
Holliday, Dickerson	Wilkes	Wellborns	174/27	Wilkinson
Holliday, Elizabeth	Warren	Neals	164/19	Wilkinson
Holliday, Guilford	Burke	Martins	142/17	Baldwin
Holliday, Isham	Greene	Armors	71/11	Baldwin
Holliday, Joseph Jr.	Effingham		187/12	Baldwin
Holliday, Mary	Bryan	Austins	223/7	Wilkinson
Holliday, Owen	Wilkes	Edges	175/18	Baldwin
Holliday, William	Burke	Ballards	138/9	Wilkinson
Holliday, William	Burke	Ballards	267/7	Wilkinson
Holliman, Blake	Greene	Reas	16/16	Baldwin
Holliman, Harmon	Hancock	Birdsongs	262/15	Wilkinson
Holliman, John	Clarke	Robinsons	249/21	Wilkinson
Hollinger, Eliz.	Burke	Spains	191/17	Baldwin
Hollinger, William	Burke	Spains	165/10	Wilkinson
Hollingsworth, Jacob	Burke	Thompsons	341/8	Wilkinson
Hollingsworth, James	Franklin	Hollingsworth	7/9	Baldwin
Hollingsworth, Stephen	Montgomery	57	187/21	Wilkinson
Hollingsworth, Wm.	Clarke	Robinsons	62/16	Baldwin
Holloman, John	Richmond		198/12	Baldwin
Hollomon, Samuel	Columbia	9	67/7	Baldwin
Hollomon, Thomas	Washington	Garretts	40/17	Wilkinson
Holloway's, Cado(Orphs.)	Clarke	Martins	154/14	Baldwin
Holloway, John	Elbert	Faulkners	148/21	Wilkinson
Holloway, Samuel	Clarke	Mitchells	158/11	Wilkinson
Holloway, Samuel	Greene	Carletons	200/16	Wilkinson
Holly, Martha(Wid.)	Jackson	Cockrans	152/15	Baldwin
Holmes', James(Orphs.)	Jackson	Johnsons	144/13	Baldwin
Holmes, David	Jackson	Cockrans	130/23	Wilkinson
Holmes, Elizabeth	Richmond		79/7	Wilkinson
Holmes, Gideon Jr.	Elbert	Barretts	247/12	Wilkinson
Holmes, James	Clarke	Stewarts	364/21	Wilkinson
Holmes, John(Son/John)	Wilkes	Milners	66/18	Wilkinson
Holmes, John	Glynn		26/19	Baldwin
Holmes, Joshua	Elbert	Barretts	8/14	Baldwin
Holmes, Pheneas	Clarke	Stewarts	136/28	Wilkinson
Holmes, Wm.J.	Washington	Howards	137/14	Baldwin
Holswriter, Wm.	Camden	Crews	198/16	Baldwin
Holt, Betsy(S.W.)	Oglethorpe	Hewells	63/9	Wilkinson
Holt, Peyton	Hancock	Wallers	307/21	Wilkinson
Holt, Raleigh	Baldwin	3	50/9	Baldwin
Holton's, Samuel(Orphs.)	Wilkinson		30/20	Baldwin
Holton, Francis	Burke	Hilliards	296/6	Wilkinson
Holton, James	Burke	Mulkeys	65/22	Wilkinson
Holton, Lalathael	Washington	Renfroes	95/24	Wilkinson
Holton, Robert	Wilkinson		182/23	Wilkinson
Holton, Thomas	Burke	Martins	326/14	Wilkinson
Holton, Thomas	Burke	Martins	88/19	Baldwin
Holwell, Luther	Screven		228/22	Wilkinson
Holwell, Sabiah(S.W.)	Screven		210/12	Wilkinson
Honeycutt, Myrick	Warren	Willsons	191/10	Wilkinson
Honiker, Benjamin	Camden	Smiths	238/14	Wilkinson
Hoobs, Jonathan	Franklin	Hoopers	182/10	Wilkinson
Hood, Alexander	Washington	Renfroes	140/11	Wilkinson

NAME	COUNTY	MIL.DIST.	LOT/DIST	DREW LAND
Hood, Nancy	Warren	Willsons	137/10	Wilkinson
Hood, William	Jackson	Cockrans	65/6	Baldwin
Hoofman, Caspar	Chatham	Pettybones	73/8	Baldwin
Hooker, Stephen	Bulloch	Denmarks	214/9	Wilkinson
Hooker, William	Elbert	Barretts	358/21	Wilkinson
Hooks, Jacob	Montgomery	59	345/7	Wilkinson
Hooks, James	Baldwin	4	85/7	Baldwin
Hooks, John	Wilkes	Coopers	173/20	Wilkinson
Hooks, Thomas	Baldwin	5	128/16	Baldwin
Hooks, Wm.	Washington	Renfroes	279/16	Wilkinson
Hooper, John	Franklin	Hoopers	10/20	Baldwin
Hooper, Richard	Franklin	Allens	56/19	Baldwin
Hooper, Sarah	Franklin	Hoopers	389/22	Wilkinson
Hooper, William	Franklin	Hoopers	77/10	Baldwin
Hooton, Polly	Hancock	Barksdales	109/27	Wilkinson
Hopgood's, Wm.(Orphs.)	Elbert	Keelings	158/9	Wilkinson
Hopkins', Lambeth(Orphs.)	Clarke	Silmans	83/12	Baldwin
Hopkins, E.B.	McIntosh		186/17	Baldwin
Hopkins, Elijah	Clarke	Harpers	45/19	Baldwin
Hopkins, Josiah	Elbert	Willifords	327/10	Wilkinson
Hopkins, Samuel	Clarke	Hopkins	193/7	Wilkinson
Hopkins, Timothy	Camden	Crews	208/19	Baldwin
Hopkins, Wm.	Wilkes	Coopers	244/16	Wilkinson
Hopper, Samuel	Oglethorpe	Hewells	254/17	Wilkinson
Hopper, Thomas	Oglethorpe	Hewells	108/7	Wilkinson
Hopper, Thomas	Oglethorpe	Hewells	295/12	Wilkinson
Hopson, Willie	Washington	Chivers	303/22	Wilkinson
Horn's, Jesse(Orphs.)	Warren	Flournoys	46/7	Wilkinson
Horn's, Joshua(Orps.)	Wilkinson		159/20	Baldwin
Horn, Joab Jr.	Jefferson		356/13	Wilkinson
Horn, John	Washington	Delks	119/26	Wilkinson
Horn, Levi	Hancock	Shivers	70/10	Wilkinson
Horn, Levi	Jackson	Johnsons	60/26	Wilkinson
Horn, Michael	Wilkinson		266/10	Wilkinson
Horn, Richard	Tattnall	Halls	156/10	Wilkinson
Horn, Willie	Jefferson		220/22	Wilkinson
Hornby, James	McIntosh		92/16	Baldwin
Horne, Isaac	Greene	Jenkins	113/9	Wilkinson
Hornsbey, John	Glynn		106/18	Wilkinson
Horton, Elijah	Hancock	Smiths	94/21	Wilkinson
Horton, Hugh	Hancock	Smiths	134/15	Baldwin
Horton, Samuel	Hancock	Gumms	224/24	Wilkinson
Horton, Samuel	Hancock	Gumms	7/15	Wilkinson
Horton, Sherwood	Jackson	Hendersons	240/21	Wilkinson
Houghton's, Alex'r(Orphs.)	Greene	Greers	137/8	Wilkinson
Houghton, Joshua Sr.	Greene	Dawsons	143/17	Baldwin
Houghton, Joshua Sr.	Greene	Dawsons	39/15	Wilkinson
House's, Britton(Orps.)	Oglethorpe	Smiths	295/15	Wilkinson
House, Delila	Elbert	Willifords	37/17	Wilkinson
House, James	Oglethorpe	Hitchcocks	32/15	Wilkinson
House, Lott	Lincoln	Kings	45/27	Wilkinson
House, Rebecca(Wid.)	Oglethorpe	Hartsfields	72/28	Wilkinson
House, Samuel	Jackson	Cockrans	67/9	Wilkinson
House, Willey(S.W.)	Oglethorpe	Smiths	2/23	Wilkinson
Housley, Sally	Baldwin	5	314/20	Wilkinson
Houston, James E.	McIntosh		155/10	Baldwin
Houston, Robert	McIntosh		132/9	Wilkinson
Howard, Abigail(Orph.)	Effingham		341/21	Wilkinson
Howard, Acceth(Wid.)	Montgomery	58	135/15	Baldwin
Howard, Benjamin	Jefferson	Tarvers	206/11	Wilkinson
Howard, Chloe	McIntosh		297/7	Wilkinson
Howard, Groves	Oglethorpe	Hewells	198/16	Wilkinson
Howard, Hardy	Jackson	Hendersons	290/20	Baldwin
Howard, Hezekiah	Screven		33/13	Baldwin
Howard, James S.	Baldwin	1	234/15	Baldwin
Howard, James(R.C.)	Baldwin	1	49/9	Wilkinson
Howard, James	Warren	Newsoms	302/21	Wilkinson

NAME	COUNTY	MIL.DIST.	LOT/DIST	DREW LAND
Howard, James	Washington	Collins	319/22	Wilkinson
Howard, James	Washington	Howards	119/12	Baldwin
Howard, John	Clarke	Dukes	247/15	Wilkinson
Howard, John	Warren	Flournoys	148/15	Baldwin
Howard, Joseph	Clarke	Silmans	127/19	Wilkinson
Howard, Joseph	Clarke	Silmans	223/20	Baldwin
Howard, Joseph	Elbert	Barretts	155/7	Wilkinson
Howard, Joseph	Elbert	Barretts	93/14	Wilkinson
Howard, Joseph	Warren	Flournoys	119/15	Wilkinson
Howard, Joseph	Warren	Flournoys	59/17	Wilkinson
Howard, Nathan	Screven		185/6	Baldwin
Howard, Nathan	Screven		307/16	Wilkinson
Howard, Samuel	Jackson	Cockrans	120/21	Wilkinson
Howard, Samuel	Washington	Collins	201/18	Wilkinson
Howard, Samuel	Wilkinson		101/19	Baldwin
Howard, Samuel	Wilkinson		94/12	Baldwin
Howard, Thamer(Wid.)	Warren	Newsoms	40/22	Wilkinson
Howard, Thomas	Lincoln	Busseys	120/11	Wilkinson
Howard, Thomas	Warren	Newsoms	206/15	Baldwin
Howard, Thomas	Wilkinson		89/7	Wilkinson
Howard, William	Burke	Fields	191/15	Baldwin
Howard, William	Jackson	Cockrans	187/19	Baldwin
Howell, Abel	Elbert	Faulkners	83/22	Wilkinson
Howell, Charlotte	Greene	Owsleys	109/12	Baldwin
Howell, Elizabeth(Wid.)	Baldwin	2	183/22	Wilkinson
Howell, Henry	Burke	Sharps	30/25	Wilkinson
Howell, James(Orph.)	Baldwin	2	195/20	Wilkinson
Howell, James	Hancock	Coopers	55/11	Baldwin
Howell, Jehu	Baldwin	2	246/25	Wilkinson
Howell, John Jr.	Hancock	Birdsongs	273/15	Baldwin
Howell, Joseph Jr.	Hancock	Birdsongs	47/9	Wilkinson
Howell, Joseph	Warren	Devereux	296/20	Wilkinson
Howell, Nathaniel	Greene	Owsleys	273/24	Wilkinson
Howell, William	Franklin	Allens	6/6	Wilkinson
Howell, William	Franklin	Allens	72/21	Wilkinson
Howell, Willie	Baldwin	5	204/16	Baldwin
Howenton, Wm.	Franklin	Christians	209/8	Wilkinson
Hubanks, Nancy	Burke	Fields	327/8	Wilkinson
Hubbard, Bennett	Oglethorpe	Smiths	43/7	Wilkinson
Hubbard, Jane	Elbert	Clarkes	118/25	Wilkinson
Hubbard, Richard	Elbert	Thompsons	115/25	Wilkinson
Hubbart, Hiram	Warren	Heaths	113/18	Baldwin
Hubbert, Thomas	Greene	Butlers	157/10	Baldwin
Hubert, James	Jackson	Cockrans	166/14	Baldwin
Huckaby's, Isham(Orphs.)	Hancock	Birdsongs	80/10	Wilkinson
Huckaby, Charles	Hancock	Barksdales	48/24	Wilkinson
Huckaby, David	Hancock	Barksdales	311/24	Wilkinson
Huckaby, Isham	Hancock	Barksdales	322/20	Baldwin
Huckaby, John	Jackson	Wrights	12/16	Wilkinson
Huckaby, Philip	Wilkes	Edges	18/22	Wilkinson
Huddleston, Isaac	Hancock	Barnes	20/6	Baldwin
Huddleston, Robt.	Oglethorpe	Moores	337/13	Wilkinson
Hudgins, Ansel	Baldwin	2	52/28	Wilkinson
Hudgins, Thornton	Wilkes	Wellborns	177/16	Baldwin
Hudgins, William	Lincoln	Gartrells	64/25	Wilkinson
Hudler, Timothy	Bulloch	Denmarks	114/14	Baldwin
Hudman, Garrett	Hancock	Smiths	115/14	Wilkinson
Hudman, John	Baldwin	3	102/15	Wilkinson
Hudman, William	Baldwin	3	170/18	Wilkinson
Hudnall, Amos	Montgomery	52	38/11	Wilkinson
Hudson's, Thomas(Orphs.)	Clarke	Simms	146/22	Wilkinson
Hudson, Ann	Richmond		176/23	Wilkinson
Hudson, Darcas	Richmond		270/12	Wilkinson
Hudson, Derrell	Hancock	Shivers	18/7	Wilkinson
Hudson, Elizabeth(Wid.)	Clarke	Sims	272/25	Wilkinson
Hudson, Isaac(Esq.)	Burke	Carswells	104/12	Baldwin
Hudson, James	Camden	Crews	72/12	Baldwin

NAME	COUNTY	MIL.DIST.	LOT/DIST	DREW LAND
Hudson, John	Hancock	Smiths	40/12	Wilkinson
Hudson, Nathaniel	Wilkinson		132/18	Baldwin
Hudson, Richard	Greene	Watsons	187/13	Baldwin
Hudson, Robert	Oglethorpe	Stewarts	255/20	Wilkinson
Hudson, Rowland	Oglethorpe	Hudsons	63/17	Baldwin
Hudson, Samuel	Screven		118/28	Wilkinson
Hudson, Samuel	Wilkinson		122/10	Baldwin
Hudson, Wm.	Hancock	Weeks	85/20	Wilkinson
Hudspeth, George	Oglethorpe	Smiths	222/19	Baldwin
Hudspeth, George	Oglethorpe	Smiths	33/17	Baldwin
Hudspeth, Richard	Wilkes	M.Henderson	38/20	Baldwin
Hudspeth, Richard	Wilkes	M.Hendersons	184/19	Baldwin
Huff, Silvia(Single)	Hancock	Barnes	209/18	Wilkinson
Huggins, Samuel	Jefferson	Colemans	61/13	Baldwin
Huggins, Samuel	Jefferson	Colemans	94/10	Wilkinson
Hughes, Robert H.	Effingham		286/7	Wilkinson
Hughes, Thomas	Chatham	McLeans	168/27	Wilkinson
Hughey, Jenny	Baldwin	5	152/14	Baldwin
Hughey, John	Clarke	Butlers	33/8	Baldwin
Hughey, Joseph	Baldwin	5	115/11	Baldwin
Hughey, Joseph	Baldwin	5	317/21	Wilkinson
Hughs', James(Orphs.)	Lincoln	Mays	131/16	Baldwin
Hughs, Dempsey	Hancock	Thomas	220/20	Wilkinson
Hughs, John	Jackson	Cockrans	259/10	Wilkinson
Hughs, Peter	Oglethorpe	Moores	155/25	Wilkinson
Hughs, Polly	Wilkes	Heards	151/10	Wilkinson
Hughs, Robert	Lincoln	Mays	140/22	Wilkinson
Hughs, Thomas	Camden	Crews	190/20	Wilkinson
Hugley, Job	Wilkes	Coopers	312/7	Wilkinson
Hugley, John	Wilkes	Coopers	107/6	Wilkinson
Huie, Robert	Jackson	Cockrans	214/7	Wilkinson
Huling, James	Wilkes	Roreys	39/12	Baldwin
Hull, Nathaniel	Effingham		100/11	Wilkinson
Hull, Thomas	Franklin	Wems	176/11	Wilkinson
Hullum, John	Elbert	Roebucks	54/6	Wilkinson
Hulsey, Adler	Franklin	Everetts	205/17	Baldwin
Humphress, Shadrack	Jackson	Cockrans	53/7	Baldwin
Humphrey, Benjamin	Clarke	Cooks	128/24	Wilkinson
Humphrey, Daniel(Orph.)	Burke	Spains	302/8	Wilkinson
Humphries, Isaac	Clarke	Silmans	217/13	Baldwin
Humphries, Isaac	Clarke	Silmans	304/20	Baldwin
Humphries, Jos.Jr.	Screven		105/21	Wilkinson
Humphries, Jos.Sr.	Screven	Williamsons	93/21	Wilkinson
Hunt, Benjamin	Baldwin	1	8/8	Wilkinson
Hunt, Fitz M.	Columbia	9	31/12	Wilkinson
Hunt, Henry	Greene	Flournoys	25/25	Wilkinson
Hunt, John	Greene	Flournoys	287/21	Wilkinson
Hunt, John	Hancock	Barnes	126/14	Baldwin
Hunt, Littleton	Jackson	Cockrans	226/6	Baldwin
Hunt, Littleton	Jackson	Cockrans	75/8	Baldwin
Hunt, Michael C.	Baldwin	1	83/10	Baldwin
Hunt, Rebecca(Wid.)	Washington	Chivers	123/9	Wilkinson
Hunt, Thomas	Columbia	8	294/13	Wilkinson
Hunt, Thomas	Columbia	8	95/16	Wilkinson
Hunt, William	Columbia	10	143/8	Wilkinson
Hunt, William	Oglethorpe	Jno.Smiths	162/6	Wilkinson
Hunter's, Miles(Orps.)	Washington	Kendricks	82/14	Wilkinson
Hunter, Abraham	Screven		277/8	Wilkinson
Hunter, Alexander	Clarke	Silmans	138/15	Baldwin
Hunter, Alexander	Clarke	Silmans	196/15	Wilkinson
Hunter, Elisha	Greene	Baxters	111/6	Wilkinson
Hunter, Isabella	Chatham	Herbs	178/20	Baldwin
Hunter, James	Chatham	Herbs	55/18	Baldwin
Hunter, Jesse	Baldwin	2	81/7	Wilkinson
Hunter, Job	Lincoln	Flemings	133/18	Wilkinson
Hunter, Job	Lincoln	Flemings	19/16	Baldwin
Hunter, John Jr.	Franklin	Christians	209/15	Baldwin

NAME	COUNTY	MIL.DIST.	LOT/DIST	DREW LAND
Hurley, Henry	Wilkes	Malones	168/23	Wilkinson
Hurley, Henry	Wilkes	Malones	52/17	Wilkinson
Hurley, Jas.(Son/Henry)	Wilkes	Malones	333/7	Wilkinson
Hurley, Jas.(Son/Henry)	Wilkes	Malones	92/15	Baldwin
Hurley, Jos.	Wilkes	Malones	139/12	Wilkinson
Hurley, Joseph	Wilkes	Malones	353/7	Wilkinson
Hurley, Polly	Jackson	Cockrans	271/19	Wilkinson
Hurly, David	Bulloch	Godfreys	31/26	Wilkinson
Hurst, Major	Screven	Olivers	354/7	Wilkinson
Hurst, Miller	Baldwin	3	120/18	Baldwin
Hurt, Elisha(Esq.)	Warren	Jones	296/7	Wilkinson
Hurt, Joel	Baldwin	2	203/19	Wilkinson
Hurt, Joel	Greene	Watsons	126/7	Baldwin
Hurt, William	Baldwin	5	108/12	Baldwin
Huskey, Clayton	Warren	Hills	116/23	Wilkinson
Huskey, Frederick	Warren	Hills	83/14	Wilkinson
Hust, Henry Jr.	Burke	Carswells	100/19	Baldwin
Hust, James	Burke	Carswells	200/23	Wilkinson
Hust, Jesse	Burke	Mulkeys	88/6	Wilkinson
Hust, Mary	Burke	Mulkeys	295/13	Wilkinson
Huston, John	Clarke	Hopkins	102/17	Wilkinson
Huston, John	Clarke	Hopkins	216/17	Baldwin
Huston, William	Glynn		51/22	Wilkinson
Hutchins, Edward	Hancock	Pinkstons	149/19	Wilkinson
Hutchins, Lewis	Montgomery	56	28/7	Baldwin
Hutchins, Robert	Hancock	Pinkstons	117/7	Baldwin
Hutchins, Thomas	Wilkes	Edges	36/26	Wilkinson
Hutchins, Willie	Baldwin	3	242/10	Baldwin
Hutchins, Willie	Baldwin	3	79/10	Wilkinson
Hutchinson, Daniel	Warren	Neals	98/19	Wilkinson
Hutchinson, John	Screven	Hutchinsons	299/8	Wilkinson
Hutchinson, Nathl.	Warren	Neals	51/7	Baldwin
Hutchinson, Parr	Hancock	Winsletts	47/24	Wilkinson
Hutchinson, Wm.	Hancock	Wallers	119/18	Baldwin
Hutson, Zadock	Washington	Andersons	201/18	Baldwin
Hwass(?), Sabre(Orph.)	Burke	Martins	383/8	Wilkinson
Ihley, Polly	Burke	Martins	283/7	Wilkinson
Ihly, Philip	Chatham	Hardens	213/25	Wilkinson
Ihly, Samuel	Chatham	Pembertons	132/22	Wilkinson
Ingle, Polly	Franklin	Yowells	64/10	Wilkinson
Inglish, Margaret	Baldwin	2	42/7	Wilkinson
Inglish, Vincey	Baldwin	2	111/18	Baldwin
Inglot, Michael	Baldwin	1	7/7	Wilkinson
Inglut, John(Son/Andrw.)	Columbia	6	283/14	Wilkinson
Ingraham, Samuel(Oprh.)	Burke	Sharps	274/19	Baldwin
Ingram, David	Jefferson	Hardwichs	271/22	Wilkinson
Ingram, John	Hancock	Crowders	280/22	Wilkinson
Ingram, Thomas	Lincoln	Busseys	99/24	Wilkinson
Ingram, William	Jefferson	Hardwichs	194/13	Baldwin
Inlow, Penelope(Miss)	Warren	Carters	212/23	Wilkinson
Inlow, Silvester	Warren	Carters	153/12	Baldwin
Inman's, Daniel	Burke	Hilliards	393/7	Wilkinson
Inman's, Daniel	Burke	Hilliards	63/18	Wilkinson
Inman's, Jesse(Orphs.)	Burke	Hilliards	113/12	Wilkinson
Inman, Pherebe(Orph.)	Burke	Sandifords	301/7	Wilkinson
Irvin, Benjamin	Baldwin	3	16/16	Wilkinson
Irvin, David	Baldwin	1	248/25	Wilkinson
Irvin, Samuel	Bulloch	Williams	117/14	Wilkinson
Irvin, William	Bulloch	Williams	190/28	Wilkinson
Irvine's, John(Orphs.)	Chatham	Abrahams	170/14	Wilkinson
Irvine, Kenneth	Chatham	Pettybones	135/16	Wilkinson
Irwell, Thomas	Washington	Wiggins	28/28	Wilkinson
Irwin's, Alexr.(Orphs.)	Washington	Paces	66/28	Wilkinson
Irwin's, John(Orphs.)	Wilkes	Edges	85/9	Baldwin
Irwin, Eliz.(Wid.)	Burke	Montgomery	210/14	Baldwin
Irwin, John	Wilkes	Edges	61/6	Baldwin
Isham, James	Jefferson	Thomas'	172/18	Baldwin

NAME	COUNTY	MIL.DIST.	LOT/DIST	DREW LAND
Isler, Ellender	Jefferson	Colemans	119/23	Wilkinson
Isom, Edward	Franklin	Everetts	143/22	Wilkinson
Ivey, Jesse	Greene	Reas'	295/17	Wilkinson
Ivey, Josiah	Greene	Baxters	293/17	Wilkinson
Ivey, Major	Greene	Armors	54/19	Wilkinson
Ivey, Winnifred(Wid.)	Wilkes	Parks	128/11	Baldwin
Ivie, Jehu	Franklin	Wems'	432/7	Wilkinson
Ivie, Jehu	Franklin	Wems'	85/24	Wilkinson
Ivie, Lott	Franklin	Wems'	37/17	Baldwin
Ivie, Lott	Franklin	Wems'	90/27	Wilkinson
Ivie, Thomas	Franklin	Wems'	56/15	Wilkinson
Ivy, Randolph	Warren	Neals	356/8	Wilkinson
Ivy, Robert	Warren	Devereux	120/28	Wilkinson
Ivy, Sampson	Warren	Neals	202/22	Wilkinson
Jack, James K.P.	Wilkes	Wellborns	210/26	Wilkinson
Jack, James W.	Wilkes	Sidwells	187/9	Baldwin
Jack, Patrick	Elbert	Mobleys	155/15	Wilkinson
Jack, Patrick	Elbert	Mobleys	20/17	Wilkinson
Jacks, Absalom	Columbia	10	14/10	Wilkinson
Jackson's, Jacob(Orph.)	Liberty		138/27	Wilkinson
Jackson's, Shadrack(Orphs.)	Clarke	Martindales	246/22	Wilkinson
Jackson, Absalom	Wilkinson		186/17	Wilkinson
Jackson, Charles	Washington	Delks	255/22	Wilkinson
Jackson, Daniel(S/Danl.)	Wilkes	Milners	211/10	Wilkinson
Jackson, Daniel	Baldwin	2	42/24	Wilkinson
Jackson, Daniel	Oglethorpe	Bells	118/17	Wilkinson
Jackson, Danl.(S/Danl.)	Wilkes	Milners	142/8	Wilkinson
Jackson, Drury	Baldwin	2	18/7	Baldwin
Jackson, Edward	Jackson	Cochrans	97/19	Wilkinson
Jackson, Enock	Baldwin	3	81/11	Baldwin
Jackson, Henry	Wilkes	Heards	91/25	Wilkinson
Jackson, James	Franklin	Hoopers	246/14	Wilkinson
Jackson, Jesse	Jefferson		161/21	Wilkinson
Jackson, Job	Hancock	Barksdales	150/25	Wilkinson
Jackson, Jobe	Jackson	Cochrans	181/28	Wilkinson
Jackson, Jobe	Jackson	Cochrans	42/12	Baldwin
Jackson, John Warren	Warren	Jones'	47/23	Wilkinson
Jackson, John Warren	Warren	Jones	57/19	Baldwin
Jackson, John	Chatham	Whites	298/14	Wilkinson
Jackson, John	Greene	Loves	177/15	Baldwin
Jackson, John	Screven		236/13	Wilkinson
Jackson, John	Wilkes	Heards	89/9	Wilkinson
Jackson, John	Wilkes	Roreys	330/24	Wilkinson
Jackson, Joseph	Baldwin	5	104/20	Baldwin
Jackson, Joshua	Wilkes	Milners	157/23	Wilkinson
Jackson, Joshua	Wilkes	Milners	206/8	Wilkinson
Jackson, Lewis	Jefferson		9/19	Wilkinson
Jackson, Mark	Greene	Butlers	257/19	Baldwin
Jackson, Martha(Wid.)	Hancock	Weeks	312/9	Wilkinson
Jackson, Mary	Franklin	Dicksons	468/7	Wilkinson
Jackson, Nathan	Lincoln	Flemings	201/13	Baldwin
Jackson, Reubin	Baldwin	3	229/9	Baldwin
Jackson, Richard	Jefferson	Bostwicks	129/20	Baldwin
Jackson, Rowland	Greene	Loves	231/26	Wilkinson
Jackson, Thomas	Warren	Devereux	259/12	Wilkinson
Jackson, Walter	Clarke	Mitchells	82/19	Baldwin
Jackson, Wilkins	Hancock	Weeks	27/13	Wilkinson
Jackson, Wm.	Clarke	Butlers	118/11	Wilkinson
Jackson, Wm.	Elbert	Hillyers	81/20	Wilkinson
Jackson, Wm.	Hancock	Gumms	6/12	Baldwin
Jackson, Wm.	Hancock	Gums	57/16	Wilkinson
Jackson, Wm.	Hancock	Weeks	344/11	Wilkinson
Jackson, Wm.	Wilkinson		457/7	Wilkinson
Jackson, Wm.R.	Franklin	Christians	331/7	Wilkinson
Jaco, Cornelius	Lincoln		10/16	Wilkinson
Jacob, John	Baldwin	2	90/12	Baldwin
Jacob, Mordicai	Baldwin	2	251/8	Wilkinson

NAME	COUNTY	MIL.DIST.	LOT/DIST	DREW LAND
James', David(Orphs.)	Columbia	7	6/15	Baldwin
James, Abel	Baldwin	1	270/16	Wilkinson
James, Enoch Jr.	Elbert	Olivers	166/13	Wilkinson
James, Enoch Sr.	Elbert	McGuires	110/12	Wilkinson
James, Francis	Hancock	Winsletts	286/15	Baldwin
James, Sally	Baldwin	1	140/13	Baldwin
James, Samuel	Elbert	McGuires	97/12	Wilkinson
Jamieson, Ellis	Wilkes	Sidwells	77/23	Wilkinson
Jamieson, Wm.	Elbert	Clarks	189/17	Wilkinson
Janes, Judith(Wid.)	Wilkes	Roreys	62/6	Baldwin
Jarrald, Arch'd.F.	Elbert	Barretts	301/16	Wilkinson
Jarrald, Wm.F.	Elbert	Barretts	13/10	Baldwin
Jarreld, Samuel F.	Elbert	Barretts	58/7	Wilkinson
Jarrell, George	Elbert	Groves	202/10	Baldwin
Jarrell, Thomas	Wilkes	Milners	37/23	Wilkinson
Jarvis, Edmund	Chatham	Herbs	46/15	Baldwin
Jarvis, Edmund	Chatham	Herbs	93/26	Wilkinson
Jarvis, Elisha	Wilkes	Hendersons	57/11	Baldwin
Jarvis, Elizabeth	Richmond		66/16	Wilkinson
Jean's, Jesse(Orphs.)	Washington	Renfroes	65/12	Baldwin
Jeffers, James	Screven		163/26	Wilkinson
Jeffers, John	Screven		133/15	Baldwin
Jeffers, Robert	Screven		307/9	Wilkinson
Jeffries, Lee(Orph.)	Greene	Baxters	129/17	Baldwin
Jeffries, Wm.	Greene	Moores	6/26	Wilkinson
Jelks, Etheldred	Greene	Moores	272/14	Baldwin
Jems, John	Clarke	Hitchcocks	249/15	Wilkinson
Jenkins, Arthur	Warren	Flournoys	0/18	Baldwin
Jenkins, Edmund B.	Clarke	Browns	163/11	Wilkinson
Jenkins, James	Warren	Bakers	210/25	Wilkinson
Jenkins, John J.	Bryan	Austins	101/22	Wilkinson
Jenkins, John	Greene	Watts	266/16	Wilkinson
Jenkins, Robert	Warren	Jones'	146/11	Baldwin
Jenkins, Thomas Jr.	Franklin	Hoopers	65/26	Wilkinson
Jenkins, Thomas Sr.	Franklin	Hoopers	95/16	Baldwin
Jernigan, David	Greene	Loves	102/15	Baldwin
Jernigan, Elias	Bulloch	Williams	28/25	Wilkinson
Jernigan, Henry	Hancock	Weeks	190/12	Wilkinson
Jernigan, James	Bulloch	Williams	233/17	Wilkinson
Jernigan, Jesse	Bulloch	Williams	286/20	Baldwin
Jernigan, Needham	Hancock	Coopers	293/14	Wilkinson
Jeter, Barnett	Elbert	Thompsons	81/10	Wilkinson
Jeter, Cornelius	Lincoln	Flemings	21/16	Wilkinson
Jeter, Cornelius	Lincoln	Flemings	256/11	Wilkinson
Jeter, John	Baldwin	2	180/25	Wilkinson
Jeter, Oliver	Lincoln	Flemings	30/19	Wilkinson
Jeter, Oliver	Lincoln	Flemings	9/10	Wilkinson
Jilcoat, John	Jackson	Wrights	152/18	Baldwin
Jiles, Mary(Wid.)	Baldwin	3	51/19	Baldwin
Jinckes, Ebenezer	Chatham	McLeans	93/19	Wilkinson
Jinkins', Daniel(Orphs.)	Chatham	Whites	183/23	Wilkinson
Jinkins', Philip(Orps.)	Burke	Fields	257/23	Wilkinson
Jinkins, Aquilla	Oglethorpe	Smiths	109/11	Baldwin
Jinkins, John	Franklin	Cleghorns	85/14	Baldwin
Jinkins, Lewis	Greene	Watts	189/22	Wilkinson
Jinkins, Owen	Screven		133/18	Baldwin
Jinkins, Owen	Screven		340/21	Wilkinson
Jinkins, Sampson	Burke	Martins	119/12	Wilkinson
Jinkins, Willie	Hancock	Thomas'	46/9	Wilkinson
Jinks, Abner	Oglethorpe	Moores	53/20	Wilkinson
Jinks, Abner	Oglethorpe	Moores	85/27	Wilkinson
Jinnings, Joshua	Oglethorpe	Moores	185/18	Wilkinson
Jinnings, Solomon	Oglethorpe	Smiths	216/7	Wilkinson
Jinnins, Priscilla(Wid.)	Baldwin	5	92/19	Baldwin
Johns', John(Orphs.)	Columbia	5	114/12	Wilkinson
Johns, John	Lincoln	Gartrells	87/16	Wilkinson
Johns, Robert	Columbia	10	121/9	Baldwin

NAME	COUNTY	MIL.DIST.	LOT/DIST	DREW LAND
Johnson's, Abraham(Orp.)	Columbia	10	33/21	Wilkinson
Johnson's, Rich'd.(Orphs.)	Greene	Davenports	58/16	Wilkinson
Johnson's, Wm.(Orphs.)	Hancock	Coopers	189/20	Baldwin
Johnson, Aaron	Warren	Devereux	164/17	Baldwin
Johnson, Alexander	Clarke	Cooks	155/26	Wilkinson
Johnson, Alexander	Greene	Davenports	37/28	Wilkinson
Johnson, Arch'd.	Elbert	McGuires	328/8	Wilkinson
Johnson, Bartholomew Sr.	Wilkes	J.Hendersons	31/19	Wilkinson
Johnson, Daniel	Jackson	Johnsons	50/20	Wilkinson
Johnson, Daniel	Liberty		167/18	Wilkinson
Johnson, Eliz.(Orph.)	Chatham	Pettybones	29/21	Wilkinson
Johnson, George	Burke	Blounts	128/10	Wilkinson
Johnson, George	Greene	Butlers	52/11	Baldwin
Johnson, Gilbert D.	Greene	Dawsons	98/20	Wilkinson
Johnson, Henry	Hancock	Coffees	179/15	Baldwin
Johnson, James Sr.	Burke	Hilliards	251/11	Wilkinson
Johnson, James Sr.	Chatham	Pembertons	297/15	Wilkinson
Johnson, James(Esq.)	Burke	Hilliards	309/15	Baldwin
Johnson, James	Elbert	Willifords	138/9	Baldwin
Johnson, James	Jefferson	Bosticks	334/8	Wilkinson
Johnson, Jane(Single)	Jefferson	Colemans	348/7	Wilkinson
Johnson, Jane	Jefferson	Wrights	230/12	Wilkinson
Johnson, Jehu	Clarke	Hitchcocks	263/14	Wilkinson
Johnson, Jemina	Washington	Delks	22/16	Baldwin
Johnson, Jesse(Orph.)	Richmond		305/20	Wilkinson
Johnson, Jesse	Wilkes	Hendersons	87/25	Wilkinson
Johnson, John A.	Hancock	Barksdales	252/21	Wilkinson
Johnson, John G.	Greene	Jinkins	82/15	Baldwin
Johnson, John	Hancock	Gumms	51/9	Wilkinson
Johnson, John	Jackson		252/14	Wilkinson
Johnson, Joseph P.	Wilkes	Edges	28/10	Wilkinson
Johnson, Joshua	Burke	Fields	167/13	Baldwin
Johnson, Leander(Wid.)	Lincoln	Gartrells	188/21	Wilkinson
Johnson, Lemuel	Richmond		28/17	Wilkinson
Johnson, Lewis	Warren	Neals	284/7	Wilkinson
Johnson, Lucy	Washington	Delks	107/19	Wilkinson
Johnson, Martha	Hancock	Birdsongs	167/10	Wilkinson
Johnson, Mary	Washington	Paces	130/17	Wilkinson
Johnson, Micajah	Hancock	Birdsongs	158/19	Baldwin
Johnson, Moses	Washington	Delks	291/15	Baldwin
Johnson, Needham	Elbert	Willifords	73/17	Wilkinson
Johnson, Nicholas	Oglethorpe	Smiths	111/14	Baldwin
Johnson, Penelope(Wid.)	Oglethorpe	Hartsfields	229/14	Wilkinson
Johnson, Penina(Orph.)	Richmond		305/20	Wilkinson
Johnson, Polly(Orp/James)	Oglethorpe	Hatchetts	171/26	Wilkinson
Johnson, Reubin Jr.	Oglethorpe	Hartsfields	61/14	Wilkinson
Johnson, Reubin Jr.	Oglethorpe	Hartsfields	66/15	Wilkinson
Johnson, Samuel Jr.	Jackson	Cochrans	47/14	Wilkinson
Johnson, Samuel	Burke	Forths	187/28	Wilkinson
Johnson, Samuel	Clarke	Cooks	317/22	Wilkinson
Johnson, Samuel	Greene	Owsleys	342/24	Wilkinson
Johnson, Samuel	Washington	Delks	39/15	Baldwin
Johnson, Stephen	Wilkes	M.Henderson	20/14	Wilkinson
Johnson, Thomas(295)	Baldwin	2	4/9	Baldwin
Johnson, Thomas	Elbert	Faulkners	173/18	Baldwin
Johnson, Thomas	Jackson	Johnsons	170/17	Baldwin
Johnson, Thos.	Oglethorpe	Hewells	94/20	Baldwin
Johnson, Thos.Sr.	Greene	Dawsons	189/14	Baldwin
Johnson, Washington	Franklin	Wems'	9/8	Wilkinson
Johnson, William	Burke	Burks	251/19	Wilkinson
Johnson, William	Lincoln	Busseys	15/10	Wilkinson
Johnson, William	Oglethorpe	Bells	279/8	Wilkinson
Johnson, Willson	Washington	Delks	165/28	Wilkinson
Johnson, Wm.	Baldwin	2	130/15	Wilkinson
Johnson, Wm.	Oglethorpe	Beasleys	133/12	Wilkinson
Johnson, Wm.	Tattnall	McDonalds	104/10	Wilkinson
Johnson, Wm.	Wilkes	Coopers	22/18	Baldwin

NAME	COUNTY	MIL.DIST.	LOT/DIST	DREW LAND
Johnson, Wm.	Wilkes	Coopers	79/24	Wilkinson
Johnson, Wm.	Wilkes	M.Hendersons	162/9	Baldwin
Johnson, Wm.	Wilkinson		118/7	Baldwin
Johnston, Anne(Orph.)	Chatham	Neyles	56/13	Wilkinson
Johnston, Benjamin	Jackson	Wrights	248/15	Wilkinson
Johnston, Eliza L.J.	Chatham	Pembertons	109/26	Wilkinson
Johnston, Isaac	Washington	Garretts	267/13	Wilkinson
Johnston, James(Orph.)	Chatham	Neyles	56/13	Wilkinson
Johnston, Jesse	Oglethorpe	Hewells	56/8	Wilkinson
Johnston, Jno.H.Sr.	Jackson	Hendersons	78/8	Baldwin
Johnston, John Jr.	Jackson	Hendersons	67/19	Baldwin
Johnston, John	Bulloch	Hendleys	232/15	Wilkinson
Johnston, John	Elbert	Roebucks	134/11	Wilkinson
Johnston, John	Elbert	Roebucks	212/9	Baldwin
Johnston, Joseph	Jackson	Hendersons	29/20	Wilkinson
Johnston, Lydia(Wid.)	Jefferson	Wrights	186/10	Baldwin
Johnston, Malcolm	Elbert	McGuires	150/12	Baldwin
Johnston, William	Bulloch	Hendleys	72/26	Wilkinson
Johnston, Willis	Columbia	7	165/11	Wilkinson
Johnston, Wm.	Columbia	10	71/8	Baldwin
Joice, Alexander	Oglethorpe	Stewarts	333/8	Wilkinson
Joice, Edward	Washington	Collins	116/20	Wilkinson
Joice, James	Tattnall	Armstrongs	154/23	Wilkinson
Joice, James	Tattnall	Armstrongs	224/16	Wilkinson
Joiner's, David(Orphs.)	Screven		125/16	Baldwin
Joiner, Gibson	Montgomery	52	61/24	Wilkinson
Joiner, Jacob	Bulloch	Hendleys	13/7	Wilkinson
Joiner, Jacob	Washington	Burneys	59/14	Baldwin
Joiner, John	Baldwin	1	47/16	Wilkinson
Joiner, John	Jefferson		8/11	Baldwin
Jollay, John Jr.	Clarke	Martins	166/6	Wilkinson
Jolly's, John(Orphs.)	Jefferson		33/7	Wilkinson
Jones', James(Orphs.)	Jackson	Wrights	6/13	Wilkinson
Jones', James(Orphs.)	Washington	Wiggins	64/13	Wilkinson
Jones', John(Orphs.)	Columbia	11	172/18	Wilkinson
Jones', John(Orphs.)	Liberty		107/13	Baldwin
Jones', John(Orps.)	Burke	Bynes	12/26	Wilkinson
Jones', Thomas(Orphs.)	Jackson	Wrights	362/22	Wilkinson
Jones, Aaron	Baldwin	2	195/13	Wilkinson
Jones, Agatha(Wid.)	Elbert	Clarks	11/7	Baldwin
Jones, Ambrose	Oglethorpe	Moores	44/11	Baldwin
Jones, Ambrose	Oglethorpe	Moores	482/7	Wilkinson
Jones, Bathsheba	Tattnall	Halls	35/26	Wilkinson
Jones, Batt	Burke	Spains	183/27	Wilkinson
Jones, Benjamin Sr.	Jackson	Cochrans	231/24	Wilkinson
Jones, Benjamin	Baldwin	2	62/18	Baldwin
Jones, Benjamin	Chatham	McLeans	61/12	Wilkinson
Jones, Benjamin	Columbia	7	68/7	Baldwin
Jones, Benjamin	Franklin	Dicksons	212/10	Wilkinson
Jones, Benjamin	Liberty		133/24	Wilkinson
Jones, Benjamin	Washington	Kendricks	16/17	Baldwin
Jones, Benjamin	Washington	Kendricks	38/13	Baldwin
Jones, Britton	Hancock	Coffees	463/7	Wilkinson
Jones, Catharine(Orph.)	Elbert	Hillyers	146/13	Baldwin
Jones, David G.	Camden	Smiths	282/19	Baldwin
Jones, David G.	Camden	Smiths	90/19	Wilkinson
Jones, David	Baldwin	5	174/6	Baldwin
Jones, David	Columbia	10	108/8	Wilkinson
Jones, David	Columbia	10	46/19	Wilkinson
Jones, David	Effingham		227/9	Wilkinson
Jones, David	Warren	Heaths	229/15	Baldwin
Jones, David	Warren	Newsoms	57/16	Baldwin
Jones, Edward	Greene	Stewarts	29/11	Baldwin
Jones, Edward	Oglethorpe	Moores	177/18	Baldwin
Jones, Edward	Oglethorpe	Moores	75/17	Baldwin
Jones, Eliz.(Wid/Tom)	Warren	Newsoms	47/28	Wilkinson
Jones, Ellis	Columbia	7	13/18	Wilkinson

NAME	COUNTY	MIL.DIST.	LOT/DIST	DREW LAND
Jones, Ephraim	Clarke	Hitchcocks	246/7	Wilkinson
Jones, Ephraim	Clarke	Hitchcocks	445/7	Wilkinson
Jones, Esther(Wid.)	Burke	Forths	128/28	Wilkinson
Jones, Evan	Baldwin	3	82/14	Baldwin
Jones, Ezra	Wayne	3	22/9	Wilkinson
Jones, Fanny	Warren	Newsoms	389/7	Wilkinson
Jones, Francis	Screven		183/25	Wilkinson
Jones, Francis	Screven		350/13	Wilkinson
Jones, Gabriel	Franklin	Wems'	320/11	Wilkinson
Jones, Gabriel	Oglethorpe	Hartsfields	5/12	Wilkinson
Jones, Goodrich	Clarke	Butlers	16/26	Wilkinson
Jones, Harrison	Hancock	Pinkstons	143/15	Wilkinson
Jones, Henry K.	Wilkes	Youngs	175/12	Baldwin
Jones, Henry	Baldwin	5	135/21	Wilkinson
Jones, Henry	Columbia	4	239/14	Wilkinson
Jones, Henry	Elbert	Moons	147/16	Baldwin
Jones, James K.	Columbia	10	211/25	Wilkinson
Jones, James	Elbert	Roebucks	119/28	Wilkinson
Jones, James	Oglethorpe	Hartsfields	107/15	Baldwin
Jones, James	Richmond		33/12	Baldwin
Jones, James	Warren	Jones'	88/9	Baldwin
Jones, James	Washington	Holts	141/14	Baldwin
Jones, James	Washington	Holts	143/20	Baldwin
Jones, James	Wayne	1	282/17	Wilkinson
Jones, Jesse	Jefferson	Colemans	288/22	Wilkinson
Jones, Joel	Hancock	Barksdales	67/26	Wilkinson
Jones, John A.C.	Jackson	Wrights	175/16	Baldwin
Jones, John P.	Wilkes	Youngs	78/17	Wilkinson
Jones, John Sr.	Greene	Jinkins	132/10	Wilkinson
Jones, John(Son/Richd.)	Columbia	10	31/8	Wilkinson
Jones, John	Baldwin	5	298/9	Wilkinson
Jones, John	Bulloch	Williams	208/11	Wilkinson
Jones, John	Camden	Crews	146/24	Wilkinson
Jones, John	Columbia	4	223/14	Wilkinson
Jones, John	Greene	Reas	26/11	Baldwin
Jones, John	Hancock	Coopers	145/28	Wilkinson
Jones, John	Jackson	Wrights	116/21	Wilkinson
Jones, John	Jefferson	Wrights	41/25	Wilkinson
Jones, Jonathan Jr.	Washington	Kendricks	186/27	Wilkinson
Jones, Joseph B.	Hancock	Crowders	143/23	Wilkinson
Jones, Joseph	Franklin	Hollingsworths	162/19	Wilkinson
Jones, Joseph	Franklin	Hollingsworths	171/13	Wilkinson
Jones, Joseph	Jackson	Cochrans	63/15	Wilkinson
Jones, Joseph	Oglethorpe	Moores	204/24	Wilkinson
Jones, Joshua(Orph.)	Washington	Garretts	186/13	Baldwin
Jones, Leonard	Washington	Wiggins	31/13	Wilkinson
Jones, Margarett(Wid.)	Glynn		272/7	Wilkinson
Jones, Mark Sr.	Wilkinson		140/8	Wilkinson
Jones, Martha(Wid.)	Warren	Heaths	47/15	Baldwin
Jones, Mary	Columbia	7	213/19	Baldwin
Jones, Mason	Lincoln	Jones'	64/21	Wilkinson
Jones, Mathew	Wayne	1	67/18	Wilkinson
Jones, Matthew	Wayne	1	17/7	Baldwin
Jones, Nancy	Columbia	4	183/12	Baldwin
Jones, Nancy	Jackson	Wrights	228/15	Wilkinson
Jones, Nicholas	Warren	Hills	28/6	Baldwin
Jones, Nimrod	Columbia	9	288/21	Wilkinson
Jones, Obadiah	Franklin	McDowells	25/27	Wilkinson
Jones, Patsey	Elbert	Clarks	1/16	Wilkinson
Jones, Patsy(Orph.)	Oglethorpe	Hartsfields	325/11	Wilkinson
Jones, Polly	Hancock	Wallers	47/26	Wilkinson
Jones, Rachel N.	Columbia	10	172/20	Wilkinson
Jones, Randal	Oglethorpe	Hartsfields	31/16	Baldwin
Jones, Reubin	Hancock	Shivers	36/7	Wilkinson
Jones, Richd(Son/Ambrose)	Columbia	11	98/16	Baldwin
Jones, Robert(Orph.)	Burke	Sharps	265/15	Baldwin
Jones, Robert(Son/Robt.)	Columbia	7	199/19	Baldwin

NAME	COUNTY	MIL.DIST.	LOT/DIST	DREW LAND
Jones, Robert(Son/Thos.)	Columbia	5	159/10	Wilkinson
Jones, Sam'l.(Orph.)	Elbert	Hillyers	146/13	Baldwin
Jones, Samuel	Baldwin	1	192/12	Baldwin
Jones, Samuel	Warren	Flournoys	184/18	Baldwin
Jones, Samuel	Wilkes	Malones	245/19	Baldwin
Jones, Simon	Burke	Carswells	31/13	Baldwin
Jones, Starling	Warren	Jones'	28/15	Wilkinson
Jones, Stephen	Elbert	Clarks	171/19	Baldwin
Jones, Susannah H.(Wid.)	Liberty		219/11	Wilkinson
Jones, Tammerland	Hancock	Crowders	197/25	Wilkinson
Jones, Thomas(Orph.)	Elbert	Hillyers	146/13	Baldwin
Jones, Thomas	Columbia	1	54/22	Wilkinson
Jones, Thomas	Columbia	4	160/8	Baldwin
Jones, Thomas	Warren	Willsons	26/20	Baldwin
Jones, Thos.B.(Son of J.)	Greene	Jenkins	375/8	Wilkinson
Jones, Tignall	Franklin	Griffiths	342/21	Wilkinson
Jones, William	Bulloch	Parishs	127/20	Wilkinson
Jones, William	Burke	Forths	189/8	Wilkinson
Jones, Willie	Burke	Forths	89/21	Wilkinson
Jones, Willie	Hancock	Birdsongs	77/14	Wilkinson
Jones, Willis	Lincoln	Normans	167/22	Wilkinson
Jones, Wingate	Greene	Loves	194/20	Baldwin
Jones, Wm.	Columbia	5	232/23	Wilkinson
Jones, Wm.	Oglethorpe	Moores	76/8	Wilkinson
Jones, Wm.G.	Greene	Jinkins	434/7	Wilkinson
Jones, Wm.Jr.	Camden	Smiths	111/11	Baldwin
Jones, Wm.Jr.	Camden	Smiths	227/14	Baldwin
Jones, Wm.R.	Wilkes	Youngs	173/28	Wilkinson
Jones, Wm.Sr.	Warren	Heaths	123/8	Baldwin
Jordan, Benajmin	Burke	Carswells	92/8	Wilkinson
Jordan, Benjamin	Greene	Watts	146/13	Wilkinson
Jordan, Burrell	Washington	Burneys	302/12	Wilkinson
Jordan, Charles	Lincoln	Flemings	303/21	Wilkinson
Jordan, Charles	Lincoln	Flemings	78/22	Wilkinson
Jordan, David	Hancock	Holts	22/10	Wilkinson
Jordan, Edmund	Oglethorpe	Hatchetts	104/19	Wilkinson
Jordan, Edward	Jefferson		66/9	Baldwin
Jordan, Isham	Wilkinson		68/10	Baldwin
Jordan, James	Camden	Crews	216/20	Wilkinson
Jordan, James	Elbert	Roebucks	185/24	Wilkinson
Jordan, Jesse	Washington	Burneys	32/9	Wilkinson
Jordan, John C.	Lincoln	Kennons	243/12	Wilkinson
Jordan, John	Elbert	Roebucks	2/8	Wilkinson
Jordan, Levi	Washington	Garretts	404/8	Wilkinson
Jordan, Nathan	Hancock	Coffees	210/21	Wilkinson
Jordan, Reubin	Oglethorpe	Smiths	270/14	Wilkinson
Jordan, Richard	Hancock	Candlers	80/14	Baldwin
Jordan, Robert	Chatham	Neyles	186/9	Wilkinson
Jordan, Samuel	Jackson	Cochrans	142/24	Wilkinson
Jordan, Thomas	Franklin	Allens	141/15	Wilkinson
Jordan, Thomas	Oglethorpe	Hatchetts	22/17	Wilkinson
Jordan, Thomas	Washington	Garretts	214/24	Wilkinson
Jordan, Zachariah	Clarke	Butlers	24/12	Wilkinson
Joseph, Sarah(Wid.)	Wilkes	Heards	215/26	Wilkinson
Jourdan's, John(Orphs.)	Bulloch	Hendleys	229/11	Wilkinson
Jourdan, Henry	Baldwin	1	305/24	Wilkinson
Jourdan, Margaret(Orp.)	Burke	Sandifords	152/16	Baldwin
Jourdan, Sterling	Burke	Carswells	179/20	Wilkinson
Joyner, Charles	McIntosh		238/19	Baldwin
Jurdine, Leonard	McIntosh		136/9	Baldwin
Jurnagin, Ezekiel	Tattnall	Sherrards	200/6	Baldwin
Jurnigan, Isaac	Tattnall	Armstrongs	355/21	Wilkinson
Justis, Isaac	Richmond		80/10	Baldwin
Kain, Wm.H.	Wilkes	Parks	172/8	Baldwin
Kannon, Reashey	Lincoln	Kings	197/8	Wilkinson
Kannon, Reashey	Lincoln	Kings	201/16	Wilkinson
Keal, Jacob	Chatham	Neals	20/17	Wilkinson

NAME	COUNTY	MIL.DIST.	LOT/DIST	DREW LAND
Kear, David	Wilkes	Hendersons	279/6	Wilkinson
Keath's, Lemuel(Orphs.)	Clarke	Cooks	215/11	Wilkinson
Keath, David	Columbia	3	136/19	Wilkinson
Keaton's, Cader(Orphs.)	Washington	Kendricks	98/12	Wilkinson
Keaton, Samuel	Washington	Kendricks	350/8	Wilkinson
Keeling, Edmund	Lincoln	Flemings	493/7	Wilkinson
Keeling, Leonard	Elbert	Keelings	136/24	Wilkinson
Keeling, Leonard	Elbert	Keelings	169/9	Baldwin
Keer, Larrence	Wilkes	Youngs	78/11	Baldwin
Keeton, Benjamin	Wilkinson		44/13	Wilkinson
Keeton, Charles	Wilkinson		127/6	Baldwin
Kein, Massey(Wid.)	Oglethorpe	Hatchetts	225/12	Wilkinson
Keith, George	Jackson	Wrights	138/12	Baldwin
Keith, Marshall	Columbia	1	41/17	Baldwin
Kellet, Solomon	Jackson	Wrights	204/28	Wilkinson
Kellet, William	Clarke	Hopkins	23/6	Baldwin
Kellum, Elender	Washington	Blackshears	200/16	Baldwin
Kellum, Jethro	Washington	Blackshears	100/17	Baldwin
Kelly's, Wm.(Orphs.)	Elbert	Keelings	134/11	Baldwin
Kelly's, Wm.(Orphs.)	Elbert	Keelings	96/17	Wilkinson
Kelly, Allen	Clarke	Robinsons	165/8	Baldwin
Kelly, Bernard	Wilkes	Roreys	27/28	Wilkinson
Kelly, Charles	Jackson	Cockrans	166/6	Baldwin
Kelly, Christopher	Franklin	Cornelius's	211/15	Wilkinson
Kelly, Daniel	Warren	Devereux's	276/16	Wilkinson
Kelly, David	Baldwin	1	337/10	Wilkinson
Kelly, Drury	Jackson	Cockrans	101/18	Baldwin
Kelly, Edward	Washington	Renfroes	174/24	Wilkinson
Kelly, Eliz.(Miss)	Warren	Hills	69/7	Baldwin
Kelly, Isabella(Orph.)	Camden	Johnsons	119/8	Baldwin
Kelly, Jacob Sr.	Clarke	Robinsons	158/17	Wilkinson
Kelly, James(Orph.)	Franklin	Cornelius	217/17	Wilkinson
Kelly, James	Greene	Armors	296/21	Wilkinson
Kelly, John J.	Baldwin	3	132/13	Baldwin
Kelly, John	Greene	Armors	100/21	Wilkinson
Kelly, John	Lincoln	Kennons	291/6	Wilkinson
Kelly, Maraim	Richmond		194/11	Wilkinson
Kelly, Mary(S)	Hancock	Smiths	194/9	Wilkinson
Kelly, Rachel	Jackson	Cockrans	66/17	Wilkinson
Kelly, Wm.(Orph.)	Camden	Johnsons	119/8	Baldwin
Kelly, Wm.	Baldwin	2	107/10	Wilkinson
Kelly, Wm.	Hancock	Hudsons	33/24	Wilkinson
Kelly, Wm.Sr.	Clarke	Robinsons	259/6	Wilkinson
Kemp, Keziah	Washington	Delks	179/25	Wilkinson
Kemp, Peggy(Orph.of John)	Screven	Ollivers	58/10	Wilkinson
Kemp, Reubin	Washington	Delks	204/15	Baldwin
Kemp, Samuel	Screven	Williamsons	47/12	Baldwin
Kemp, Wm.Sr.	Washington	Andersons	180/15	Baldwin
Kemple, Abraham	Richmond		31/16	Wilkinson
Kenan, Thomas H.	Baldwin	1	99/14	Wilkinson
Kendrick, Burrell	Wilkes	Parks	237/16	Wilkinson
Kendrick, James	Baldwin	2	155/17	Wilkinson
Kendrick, James	Washington	Kendricks	217/9	Baldwin
Kendrick, John	Columbia	7	222/15	Wilkinson
Kendrick, Jones	Washington	Kendricks	118/20	Baldwin
Kendrick, Jones	Washington	Kendricks	265/19	Wilkinson
Kendrick, Martin	Washington	Kendricks	252/16	Wilkinson
Kendrick, Nathaniel	Hancock	Huffs	279/19	Wilkinson
Kendrick, Sarah	Columbia	10	169/27	Wilkinson
Kendrick, Sheldrict	Columbia	10	167/18	Baldwin
Kendrick, Susannah	Wilkes	Parks	20/14	Baldwin
Kendrick, Thomas	Hancock	Wallers	14/10	Baldwin
Kenedy, Edward	Montgomery	54	168/20	Wilkinson
Kenedy, John	Tattnall	Staffords	199/14	Baldwin
Kennady, Elizabeth	Richmond		203/14	Wilkinson
Kennady, James	Glynn		91/26	Wilkinson
Kennady, Jane	Jefferson	Tarvers	171/25	Wilkinson

NAME	COUNTY	MIL.DIST.	LOT/DIST	DREW LAND
Kennady, John Sr.	Jefferson	Tarvers	15/23	Wilkinson
Kennady, John	Lincoln	Busseys	135/25	Wilkinson
Kennady, John	Richmond		96/20	Wilkinson
Kennady, Manfield	Jackson	Johnsons	35/20	Wilkinson
Kennady, Martha	Jefferson	Tarvers	28/19	Wilkinson
Kennady, Seth	Hancock	Winsletts	200/27	Wilkinson
Kennady, Wm.	Jefferson	Fultons	113/8	Baldwin
Kennady, Wm.	Richmond		86/26	Wilkinson
Kennebrew, Jacob	Lincoln	Gartrells	87/7	Wilkinson
Kenneday, Seth	Hancock	Winsletts	368/9	Wilkinson
Kenner, Jacob	Richmond		180/28	Wilkinson
Kennon, Charles	Lincoln	Kennons	334/21	Wilkinson
Kennon, Jane	Wilkes	Sidwells	80/24	Wilkinson
Kennon, John	Hancock	Barksdales	100/6	Wilkinson
Kenny's, James(Orphs.)	Jackson	Johnsons	149/8	Wilkinson
Kent, Henry	Wilkes	Hendricks	79/21	Wilkinson
Kent, Isaac	Bulloch	Hendleys	365/8	Wilkinson
Kent, James	Hancock	Shivers	206/13	Baldwin
Kent, Laban	Effingham		228/24	Wilkinson
Kent, Reubin	Screven	Hutchinsons	24/19	Baldwin
Kent, Reubin	Screven	Hutchinsons	9/27	Wilkinson
Kent, Stephen	Montgomery	55	172/9	Wilkinson
Kent, Thomas W.	Wilkes	Youngs	107/12	Baldwin
Kerby, Nancy(Orph.)	Oglethorpe	Popes	11/9	Baldwin
Kerlin, Wm.	Elbert	Moons	325/9	Wilkinson
Kerr, John	Greene	Dawsons	279/7	Wilkinson
Kerr, William	Greene	Kings	57/13	Wilkinson
Kerry, Elphisten	Warren	Bakers	78/6	Baldwin
Kerry, Robert	Warren	Bakers	2/7	Baldwin
Kersey, Elijah	Montgomery	57	42/28	Wilkinson
Kersey, Elijah	Montgomery	57	60/23	Wilkinson
Kersey, Thomas	Montgomery	59	66/20	Baldwin
Kerson, Sally	Warren	Hills	130/26	Wilkinson
Kersterson, Thomas	Chatham	Herbs	247/14	Wilkinson
Kersterson, Thomas	Chatham	Herbs	279/12	Wilkinson
Kettles, John	Wilkinson		385/9	Wilkinson
Key, Joseph	Greene	Carletons	172/25	Wilkinson
Key, Terrell	Elbert	Morrisons	181/20	Baldwin
Key, Wm.B.	Elbert	Morrisons	121/6	Wilkinson
Kidd's, Zachariah(Orphs.)	Oglethorpe	Hewells	226/22	Wilkinson
Kidd, Elizabeth M.	Elbert	Clarks	170/24	Wilkinson
Kidd, John Jr.	Oglethorpe	Hartsfields	115/22	Wilkinson
Kidd, John Sr.	Oglethorpe	Hatchetts	20/24	Wilkinson
Kidd, Martin	Elbert	Barretts	65/12	Wilkinson
Kidd, William	Oglethorpe	Hartsfields	248/21	Wilkinson
Kidd, William	Wayne	1	76/14	Wilkinson
Kieffer's, Ephraim(Orphs.)	Effingham		1/25	Wilkinson
Kilgo, Absalom	Clarke	Trammells	226/16	Wilkinson
Kilgo, Peter	Clarke	Trammells	189/11	Baldwin
Kilgo, Willis	Clarke	Trammells	149/9	Baldwin
Kilgore, Catharine	Lincoln	Normons	352/9	Wilkinson
Kilgore, John	Hancock	Shivers	291/22	Wilkinson
Kilgore, Wm.	Hancock	Shivers	180/23	Wilkinson
Killingsworth, Eliz.(Wid.)	Washington	Burneys	43/13	Wilkinson
Killingsworth, John	Columbia	6	219/14	Wilkinson
Kilpatrick, Spencer	Burke	Gordon's	198/20	Wilkinson
Kimball, Benj.(Orph.)	Burke	Thompsons	68/16	Baldwin
Kimball, Hazen	Chatham	Pettybones	181/9	Wilkinson
Kimball, James	Burke	Thompsons	123/14	Wilkinson
Kimbell, Buckner	Greene	Davenports	79/16	Wilkinson
Kimbro, John	Baldwin	3	76/24	Wilkinson
Kimbrough's, Wm.(Orphs.)	Wilkes	Heards	187/12	Wilkinson
Kinchin, Wm.Jr.	Montgomery	52	85/21	Wilkinson
Kindall, Isaac	Baldwin	5	168/16	Baldwin
Kindrick, Ann	Franklin	Henrys	270/10	Wilkinson
Kindrick, Obadiah	Franklin	Henrys	213/20	Wilkinson
King's, Alexander(Orphs.)	Greene	Dawsons	43/13	Baldwin

NAME	COUNTY	MIL.DIST.	LOT/DIST	DREW LAND
King's, Geo.(Orphs.)	Columbia	4	124/25	Wilkinson
King's, Thomas(Orphs.)	Liberty		300/24	Wilkinson
King's, Thomas(Orphs.)	Liberty		54/16	Baldwin
King's, Wm.(Orphs.)	Baldwin	4	51/12	Baldwin
King, Alexander	Greene	Dawsons	56/7	Wilkinson
King, Andrew	Warren	Heaths	12/6	Wilkinson
King, Azariah	Wilkes		122/18	Wilkinson
King, Curtis	Greene	Dawsons	198/25	Wilkinson
King, Curtis	Greene	Dawsons	35/7	Baldwin
King, David	Washington	Burneys	159/24	Wilkinson
King, Elijah	Hancock	Holts	334/12	Wilkinson
King, Elisha	Hancock	Holts	273/8	Wilkinson
King, Elizabeth	Franklin	Bryants	317/14	Wilkinson
King, George	Franklin	McDowells	1/17	Baldwin
King, Henry	Columbia	1	331/22	Wilkinson
King, Joel	Washington	Delks	236/10	Wilkinson
King, John Jr.	Washington	Burneys	250/13	Wilkinson
King, John W.	Chatham	Whites	287/19	Wilkinson
King, John	Effingham		491/7	Wilkinson
King, John	Greene	Moores	34/13	Baldwin
King, John	Jackson	Hendersons	163/27	Wilkinson
King, John	Jackson	Hendersons	66/17	Baldwin
King, John	Jackson	Wrights	76/19	Baldwin
King, Levi	Hancock	Holts	9/13	Wilkinson
King, Mary(Wid.)	Franklin	Hollingsworths	292/14	Wilkinson
King, Mary	Glynn		122/18	Baldwin
King, Mary	Washington	Willis's	123/9	Baldwin
King, Samuel	Chatham	Neals	199/24	Wilkinson
King, Thomas	Camden	Smiths	156/11	Wilkinson
King, Wm.(Dr.)	Greene	Dawsons	48/23	Wilkinson
Kingry, Daniel	Wilkinson		351/13	Wilkinson
Kinman's, Wm.(Orphs.)	Washington	Paces	106/9	Baldwin
Kinman, John	Greene	Alfords	243/19	Baldwin
Kinman, Samuel	Greene	Alfords	102/13	Baldwin
Kinman, Samuel	Greene	Alfords	112/9	Wilkinson
Kinnebrew's, Shadrack(Orps.)	Greene	Baxter	214/22	Wilkinson
Kinnebrew, Henry	Elbert	Mobleys	32/6	Wilkinson
Kinney's, James(Orph.)	Clarke	Trammells	204/12	Baldwin
Kinney's, James(Orphs.)	Clarke	Mitchells	46/22	Wilkinson
Kinsey, Edward	Warren	Neals	244/14	Wilkinson
Kirby, Moab	Bulloch	Williams	80/14	Wilkinson
Kirk, Jesse	Jackson	Wrights	290/20	Wilkinson
Kirk, Wm.	Jackson	Hendersons	241/15	Baldwin
Kirkland's, Richard(Orphs.)	Bulloch	Williams	151/20	Baldwin
Kirkland, Christiana(Wid.)	Liberty		169/29	Baldwin
Kirkland, John Sr.	Bulloch	Hendleys	315/15	Baldwin
Kirkland, Ralph	Bulloch	Hendleys	273/11	Wilkinson
Kirkland, Ralph	Bulloch	Hendleys	64/22	Wilkinson
Kirkland, Snoden	Wilkes	Coopers	170/27	Wilkinson
Kirkpatrick, James	Jackson	Wrights	102/28	Wilkinson
Kirkpatrick, James	Jackson	Wrights	97/28	Wilkinson
Kirkpatrick, Samuel	Hancock	Candlers	8/18	Wilkinson
Kirksey, Isaac	Tattnall	Sherrards	373/22	Wilkinson
Kitchen's, Joseph(Orphs.)	Greene	Watts	257/8	Wilkinson
Kitchens, Beaux	Warren	Flournoys	217/10	Baldwin
Kitchens, Samuel	Tattnall	Armstrongs	114/10	Baldwin
Kitchens, William	Warren	Newsoms	89/13	Baldwin
Kite, John	Tattnall	Staffords	230/7	Wilkinson
Knaphen, Thomas	Richmond		87/28	Wilkinson
Knave, John(Orph.)	Richmond		10/19	Wilkinson
Knave, Sally(Orph.)	Richmond		10/19	Wilkinson
Knight's, Joseph(Orphs)	Bulloch	Denmarks	435/7	Wilkinson
Knight, Calvery	Greene	Loves	169/17	Baldwin
Knight, Cofield	Jefferson		362/7	Wilkinson
Knight, Elizabeth	Greene	Reas	311/14	Wilkinson
Knight, Frederick	Jefferson		46/24	Wilkinson
Knight, James	Burke	Gordons	354/8	Wilkinson

NAME	COUNTY	MIL.DIST.	LOT/DIST	DREW LAND
Knight, James	Burke	Spain's	17/24	Wilkinson
Knight, James	Burke	Spain's	237/20	Baldwin
Knight, Joel	Hancock	Shivers	98/11	Baldwin
Knight, John	Burke	Carswells	312/20	Baldwin
Knight, John	Burke	Mongtomery's	80/22	Wilkinson
Knight, Mary	Columbia	9	120/9	Wilkinson
Knight, Robert	Bulloch	Denmarks	55/13	Baldwin
Knight, Silvanus	Washington	Collins	85/13	Baldwin
Knight, Stephen	Screven	Williamsons	38/26	Wilkinson
Knight, William	Burke	Ballards	121/14	Baldwin
Knotts, Nathaniel	Jefferson		202/9	Baldwin
Knowles, Joseph	Hancock	Shivers	116/11	Wilkinson
Knowles, Prettyman	Greene	Alfords	34/18	Baldwin
Knowles, Richard	Greene	Alfords	96/14	Baldwin
Knowles, Zachariah Sr.	Burke	Fields	200/25	Wilkinson
Knox's, John(Orphs.)	Wilkes	Wellborns	156/26	Wilkinson
Knox, George	Franklin	Hollingsworths	153/19	Wilkinson
Kulb, Joshua	Jackson	Hendersons	127/10	Baldwin
Kyle, James Jr.	Franklin	Christians	57/22	Wilkinson
Kyle, John	Franklin	Christians	233/13	Wilkinson
Kyle, Thomas Jr.	Franklin	Christians	182/8	Wilkinson
Lacky, Thomas Sr.	Wilkes	Heards	98/22	Wilkinson
Lacy's, Wm.(Orphs.)	Columbia	10	213/5	Baldwin
Lacy, Archibald	Warren	Heaths	148/16	Wilkinson
Lacy, James	Greene	Moores	87/7	Baldwin
Lacy, Noah	Oglethorpe	Smiths	31/6	Baldwin
Lacy, Stephen	Baldwin	4	189/18	Baldwin
Lahr, Ann	Franklin	Everetts	76/13	Wilkinson
Laidler, John	Burke	Carswells	226/15	Wilkinson
Lamar's, Bazil(Orphs.)	Lincoln	Kennons	122/21	Wilkinson
Lamar's, John(Orphs.)	Columbia	5	259/23	Wilkinson
Lamar, James	Wilkes	Edges	263/15	Baldwin
Lamar, John	Hancock	Gumms	19/8	Wilkinson
Lamar, Polly(Orph.)	Richmond		147/25	Wilkinson
Lamar, Zachariah	Columbia	1	274/16	Wilkinson
Lamar, Zachariah	Jefferson	Wrights	154/18	Baldwin
Lamar, Zachariah	Jefferson	Wrights	321/12	Wilkinson
Lamb, Isaac	Montgomery	57	247/21	Wilkinson
Lamb, Jacob	Burke	Gordans	53/25	Wilkinson
Lamb, Jacob	Burke	Gordons	242/24	Wilkinson
Lambert's, Jeremiah(Orphs.)	Montgomery	52	106/12	Baldwin
Lambert's, John(Orphs.)	Burke	Sharps	234/19	Wilkinson
Lambert, James	Burke	Blounts	152/23	Wilkinson
Lambert, John	Burke	Thompsons	120/7	Wilkinson
Lambertoz, A.D.	Chatham	Whites	280/16	Wilkinson
Lambirth, Elijah	Baldwin	5	276/11	Wilkinson
Lambirth, Wm.	Baldwin	5	138/17	Baldwin
Lambright, Wm.	Liberty		138/18	Baldwin
Lamkin, Cleophas	Richmond		93/10	Wilkinson
Lamkin, Griffin L.	Chatham	Whites	236/15	Wilkinson
Lamkin, James(Orp./Jerem.)	Columbia	3	102/24	Wilkinson
Lamkin, Sampson	Richmond		161/7	Wilkinson
Lamkin, Sarah	Wilkes	Parks	198/17	Wilkinson
Lancaster, Wm.S.	Burke	Hilliards	137/19	Baldwin
Land, Henry	Montgomery	53	80/13	Baldwin
Land, John	Jefferson	---	114/20	Wilkinson
Land, Margaret(Wid.)	Screven	Williamsons	337/21	Wilkinson
Land, Nathan	Montgomery	53	216/16	Baldwin
Landers, Claborn	Hancock	Barksdales	166/16	Baldwin
Landers, William	Columbia	4	74/25	Wilkinson
Landon, Daniel	Jefferson	Thomas	146/15	Baldwin
Landrom, Thomas	Oglethorpe	Hatchetts	112/28	Wilkinson
Landrom, Thomas	Oglethorpe	Hatchetts	237/24	Wilkinson
Landrum, Burton	Wilkes	Sheets	25/6	Wilkinson
Landrum, James	Franklin	Everetts	69/9	Baldwin
Landrum, Rebecca	Warren	Neals	87/14	Baldwin
Landrum, Samuel	Wilkes	Sheets	37/11	Wilkinson

NAME	COUNTY	MIL.DIST.	LOT/DIST	DREW LAND
Lane's, Richard(Orphs.)	Clarke	Mitchells	78/16	Baldwin
Lane, Bryan	Tattnall	Staffords	290/12	Wilkinson
Lane, Edmund	Baldwin	3	296/22	Wilkinson
Lane, Etheldred	Burke	Spains	461/7	Wilkinson
Lane, John Dade	Burke	Martins	208/9	Baldwin
Lane, John Jr.	Franklin	Cornelius	122/26	Wilkinson
Lane, John Jr.	Franklin	Cornelius	33/11	Wilkinson
Lane, John	Bulloch	Denmarks	24/20	Baldwin
Lane, Joshua Dade	Burke	Martins	258/7	Wilkinson
Lane, Lambert(Orph.)	Bryan	Birds	14/12	Baldwin
Lane, Sampson	Franklin	McDowells	136/7	Baldwin
Lane, Samuel	Clarke	Mitchells	287/8	Wilkinson
Lane, William	Montgomery	52	241/22	Wilkinson
Lane, Wm.Sr.	Elbert	Dyes	111/20	Baldwin
Lane, Wm.Sr.	Elbert	Dyes	181/20	Wilkinson
Lanear, Hardy	Camden	Ashleys	43/8	Baldwin
Lang, Charles	Richmond		136/22	Wilkinson
Lang, Cornelius	Richmond		136/22	Wilkinson
Lang, David(Orph.)	Richmond		136/22	Wilkinson
Lang, Isaac	Camden	Crews	277/19	Baldwin
Lang, James(Orph.)	Richmond		136/22	Wilkinson
Lang, Mary	Washington	Howards	152/9	Baldwin
Lang, Peggy	Baldwin	3	156/6	Wilkinson
Lang, Richard	Camden	Ashleys	339/8	Wilkinson
Lang, Robert(Orph.)	Richmond		136/22	Wilkinson
Langdon, Isaac	Wilkes	Roreys	21/16	Baldwin
Langdon, John Jr.	Wilkes	Hendricks	95/17	Baldwin
Langdon, John Sr.	Wilkes	Hendricks	73/18	Wilkinson
Langford, Euclid	Hancock	Huffs	250/12	Wilkinson
Langford, Francis	Hancock	Shivers'	103/12	Wilkinson
Langford, James	Jackson	Hendersons	131/18	Wilkinson
Langford, James	Jackson	Hendersons	136/8	Wilkinson
Langford, Thomas	Jackson	Hendersons	188/10	Wilkinson
Langham, Dorothy(Wid.)	Wilkes	Hendersons	84/26	Wilkinson
Langham, James	Baldwin	1	37/18	Wilkinson
Langham, Richard	Baldwin	1	296/17	Wilkinson
Langham, Thomas H.	Baldwin	5	135/18	Baldwin
Langley, Elizabeth	Chatham	Hardens	36/9	Baldwin
Langley, Isham	Tattnall	Sherrards	268/11	Wilkinson
Langston, Benjamin	Washington	Wiggins	20/22	Wilkinson
Langston, James	Columbia	8	11/9	Wilkinson
Langston, Samuel	Jackson	Cockrans	184/21	Wilkinson
Lanier's, Bird(Orphs.)	Screven		3/7	Baldwin
Lanier's, Nathaniel(Orphs.)	Baldwin	4	140/15	Wilkinson
Lanier, Amey(S.W.)	Screven		324/9	Wilkinson
Lanier, John Sr.	Bulloch	Denmarks	27/13	Baldwin
Lanier, John	Screven		27/10	Wilkinson
Lanier, Nancy(Wid.)	Screven		146/12	Wilkinson
Lankford, Joseph	Lincoln	Flemings	201/7	Wilkinson
Lans, Allen	Elbert	Thompsons	278/11	Wilkinson
Lantrip, John	Baldwin	1	240/19	Baldwin
Lard, Sarah Jr.	Washington	Andersons	11/8	Baldwin
Lard, Sarah(Wid)	Washington	Andersons	186/8	Wilkinson
Larey, Darby	Hancock	Barksdales	272/8	Wilkinson
Larey, George	Hancock	Birdsongs	341/10	Wilkinson
Larey, Jeremiah	Hancock	Birdsongs	169/14	Wilkinson
Larey, John	Hancock	Birdsongs	76/7	Wilkinson
Largent, Jesse	Baldwin	1	99/10	Baldwin
Larrance, William	Oglethorpe	Hartsfields	234/14	Wilkinson
Larrency, Nancy(S.W.)	Screven		216/18	Wilkinson
Larricy, Moses	Screven		314/10	Wilkinson
Larry, Larry	Warren	Flournoys	123/23	Wilkinson
Lartigue, Jarard	Richmond		73/12	Wilkinson
Lary's, Levi(Orphs.)	Hancock	Thomas'	40/17	Baldwin
Larymore, Robert	Liberty		28/10	Baldwin
Lasiter, Amos	Oglethorpe	Smiths	97/11	Wilkinson
Lasley, Thomas	Wilkes	Parks	70/21	Wilkinson

NAME	COUNTY	MIL.DIST.	LOT/DIST	DREW LAND
Lasley, William	Oglethorpe	Hatchetts	210/9	Baldwin
Lason, John F.(Orph.)	Greene	Armors	216/22	Wilkinson
Lassiter, Brinkley	Washington	Paces	303/8	Wilkinson
Lassiter, Emory	Burke	Sandifords	158/23	Wilkinson
Lassiter, James	Warren	Flournoys	194/13	Wilkinson
Lassiter, Jesse	Baldwin	3	74/22	Wilkinson
Lassiter, Jesse	Montgomery	52	136/18	Baldwin
Lassiter, Lemuel	Burke	Ballards	66/14	Baldwin
Lathrop, Asa	Camden	Smiths	32/27	Wilkinson
Laughan, Noel	Washington	Delks	233/19	Wilkinson
Laughter, Henry	Wilkes	Heards	143/6	Wilkinson
Laurence's, Miles(Orphs.)	Washington	Holts	198/14	Baldwin
Laurence, James	Hancock	Coffees	90/11	Wilkinson
Laurence, Joseph	Clarke	Mitchells	202/14	Wilkinson
Laurence, Joseph	Clarke	Mitchells	210/15	Baldwin
Laurence, Richard	Clarke	Mitchells	76/6	Wilkinson
Laurence, Stephen	Greene	Ousleys	141/22	Wilkinson
Laurence, Thomas	Greene	Alfords	162/28	Wilkinson
Laurence, Thomas	Greene	Alfords	195/16	Wilkinson
Laurence, William	Columbia	9	39/18	Wilkinson
Laurence, Wm.	Columbia	9	41/16	Baldwin
Lavender, George	Columbia	8	213/16	Wilkinson
Lavender, William	Chatham	Neals	170/16	Baldwin
Lavender, William	Chatham	Neals	225/14	Wilkinson
Law, Charles	Liberty	---	228/7	Wilkinson
Law, Joseph	Liberty		455/7	Wilkinson
Lawless', John(Orphs.)	Elbert	Olivers	121/15	Baldwin
Lawless', Reubin(Orph.)	Washington	Wiggins	37/15	Wilkinson
Lawrimore, Robert	Elbert	Keelings	128/6	Baldwin
Lawrimore, Robert	Elbert	Keelings	210/28	Wilkinson
Laws, John	Greene	Jinkins'	250/24	Wilkinson
Laws, Martin	Greene	Jinkins	5/13	Wilkinson
Lawson's, Hugh(Orphs.)	Washington	Blackshears	3/18	Wilkinson
Lawson, Adam	Wilkes	Malones	143/17	Wilkinson
Lawson, Andrew	Washington	Blackshears	44/12	Baldwin
Lawson, David	Hancock	Hudsons	451/7	Wilkinson
Lawson, Dudley	Hancock	Hudsons	359/7	Wilkinson
Lawson, Eliz.(Wid.)	Liberty		23/16	Wilkinson
Lawson, John	Liberty	---	271/8	Wilkinson
Lawson, John	Washington	Blackshears	213/23	Wilkinson
Lawson, John	Wilkes	Malones	223/13	Wilkinson
Lawson, Thompson	Washington	Wiggins	102/13	Wilkinson
Lawson, Wenwright	Wilkes	Malones	296/12	Wilkinson
Lawther, Charles	Screven		274/24	Wilkinson
Lay's, Emanuel(Orphs.)	Wilkes	Coopers	133/9	Baldwin
Lay, Richard	Chatham	Abrahams	194/18	Baldwin
Lay, William	Oglethorpe	Hudsons	109/13	Wilkinson
Layfoy, James	Franklin	Henrys	42/11	Baldwin
Lazenby, John	Columbia	7	201/14	Baldwin
Lazenby, Samuel I.	Columbia	7	60/19	Baldwin
Lea, Jonathan	Clarke	Harpers	249/20	Baldwin
Leach, Asa	Franklin	Conners	94/18	Baldwin
Leach, john	Franklin	Hoopers	50/16	Wilkinson
Leak, James(Orph.)	Clarke	Robinsons	125/24	Wilkinson
Leak, Robert	Clarke	Harpers	250/22	Wilkinson
Leak, Susannah	Clarke	Robinsons	96/16	Wilkinson
Leary, Dempsey	Tattnall	Sherrards	60/12	Baldwin
Ledbetter, Benjamin	Warren	Flournoys	124/18	Wilkinson
Ledbetter, Isaac	Warren	Flournoys	300/10	Wilkinson
Ledbetter, James(S.of Jno.)	Warren	Flournoys	182/14	Baldwin
Lee's, Joshua(Orphs.)	Clarke	Cooks	221/16	Wilkinson
Lee's, Joshua(Orphs.)	Screven		68/11	Baldwin
Lee, General	Bulloch	Williams	99/28	Wilkinson
Lee, James(F.Creek)	Greene	Davenports	80/6	Baldwin
Lee, James	Tattnall	Staffords	134/8	Wilkinson
Lee, James	Wilkes	Malones	9/11	Wilkinson
Lee, Jesse	Oglethorpe	Popes	104/27	Wilkinson

NAME	COUNTY	MIL.DIST.	LOT/DIST	DREW LAND
Lee, John Jr.	Hancock	Shivers'	203/17	Wilkinson
Lee, John	Tattnall	Staffords	205/7	Wilkinson
Lee, Lewis	Jefferson	Boswicks	351/24	Wilkinson
Lee, Mary	Oglethorpe	Popes	13/12	Baldwin
Lee, Priscilla(Wid.)	Screven		35/22	Wilkinson
Lee, Sion	Hancock	Crowders	338/20	Baldwin
Lee, Solomon P.	Wilkes	Hendersons	93/15	Wilkinson
Lee, Susannah	Wilkes	Hendersons	168/17	Wilkinson
Lee, Thomas	Baldwin	4	92/15	Wilkinson
Lee, Thomas	Wilkes	Hendersons	169/7	Wilkinson
Lee, William	Screven		104/11	Wilkinson
Lee, Wm.(T.Creek)	Greene	Watts	173/19	Baldwin
Leeper, James Sr.	Elbert	Groves	263/16	Wilkinson
Lefavor, Nancy	Jefferson	Thomas	92/8	Baldwin
Leggett, Benjamin	Clarke	Silmans	124/11	Baldwin
Leggett, Benjamin	Clarke	Silmans	176/22	Wilkinson
Legrand, Jesse	Elbert	Keelings	61/27	Wilkinson
Leiper, Allen	Elbert	Groves	77/12	Baldwin
Leiper, James Sr.	Elbert	Groves	109/18	Wilkinson
Leith, James W.(Orph/Wm.)	Columbia	6	288/13	Wilkinson
Leith, John	Columbia	1	267/15	Baldwin
Leon, David	Chatham	Pettybones	140/6	Baldwin
Leonard, Calvin	Tattnall	Staffords	160/13	Baldwin
Leonard, Coleman	Greene	Armors	113/10	Baldwin
Leonard, Davis	Wilkinson		23/10	Baldwin
Leonard, John	Wilkes	Roreys	259/13	Wilkinson
Lesley, Robert	Columbia		142/6	Baldwin
Lester, Celia	Burke	Martins	11/7	Wilkinson
Lesueur, James	Elbert	Thompsons	101/6	Wilkinson
Lesueur, James	Elbert	Thompsons	71/20	Wilkinson
Letlow, Adam	Columbia	2	50/19	Wilkinson
Letlow, James Jr.	Columbia	2	158/11	Baldwin
Letlow, James Sr.	Columbia	2	39/7	Baldwin
Letlow, James Sr.	Columbia	2	84/11	Baldwin
Lett's, James(Orphs.)	Clarke	Robinsons	113/18	Wilkinson
Lett, Polly(Wid.)	Greene	Alfords	139/20	Wilkinson
Level, Joseph	Franklin	Wems'	95/10	Baldwin
Levender, John	Screven	Hutchinsons	21/19	Wilkinson
Leveret, Henry	Lincoln	Kennons	283/9	Wilkinson
Leveret, John	Lincoln	Busseys	116/19	Baldwin
Leveret, John	Lincoln	Cartrells	57/15	Wilkinson
Leveret, Robert	Lincoln	Kennons	50/16	Baldwin
Leverett, Absalom	Wilkes	Wellborns	147/8	Wilkinson
Leverett, Patty	Wilkes	Malones	280/6	Wilkinson
Levi, Lewis	Camden	Ashleys	90/17	Baldwin
Leving's, Jacob(Orphs.)	Wilkinson		18/10	Baldwin
Levings, Nancy(Wid.)	Wilkinson		275/22	Wilkinson
Levingston, Joseph	Burke	Sharps	213/9	Wilkinson
Levingston, Joseph	Washington	Blackshears	136/16	Wilkinson
Lewis, Abel	Burke	Bynes	211/14	Baldwin
Lewis, Abraham Jr.	Screven		268/19	Baldwin
Lewis, Abraham Sr.	Screven		208/13	Wilkinson
Lewis, Ann	Jefferson	Fultons	150/17	Baldwin
Lewis, Anthony	Burke	Forths	172/22	Wilkinson
Lewis, Archibald	Hancock	Weeks'	93/18	Baldwin
Lewis, Daniel	Baldwin	1	194/28	Wilkinson
Lewis, David	Burke	Bynes	213/14	Wilkinson
Lewis, David	Camden	Smiths	82/11	Baldwin
Lewis, Eleazer	Burke	Hilliards	41/6	Wilkinson
Lewis, Eleazer	Burke	Hilliards	85/11	Wilkinson
Lewis, Esther	Elbert	Clarks	256/21	Wilkinson
Lewis, George	Hancock	Weeks	136/15	Wilkinson
Lewis, Henry	Greene	Alfords	218/19	Wilkinson
Lewis, Isaac	Hancock	Holts	16/13	Baldwin
Lewis, Isaac	Jefferson	Fultons	193/10	Wilkinson
Lewis, Isaac	Liberty		37/8	Baldwin
Lewis, Jacob Jr.	Wilkes	Edges	147/18	Baldwin

NAME	COUNTY	MIL.DIST.	LOT/DIST	DREW LAND
Lewis, Jacob Sr.	Wilkes	Edges	392/7	Wilkinson
Lewis, Jacob	Screven		61/11	Wilkinson
Lewis, James	Bulloch	Denmarks	25/6	Baldwin
Lewis, James	Burke	Forths	125/11	Wilkinson
Lewis, Jeremiah	Elbert	Clarks	26/9	Wilkinson
Lewis, Jesse	Columbia	9	6/16	Wilkinson
Lewis, John Jr.(M.T.)	Hancock	Hudsons	245/24	Wilkinson
Lewis, John	Burke	Sandifords	193/24	Wilkinson
Lewis, Johnson	Burke	Sandifords	243/22	Wilkinson
Lewis, Jonathan	Burke	Sharps	108/19	Baldwin
Lewis, Jonathan	Columbia	9	89/11	Wilkinson
Lewis, Keziah	Burke	Forths	186/16	Wilkinson
Lewis, Laton	Wilkinson		23/8	Baldwin
Lewis, Mary Ann(Orph.)	Chatham	Whites	170/18	Baldwin
Lewis, Patsy(S)	Hancock	Weeks	103/6	Wilkinson
Lewis, Peter	Clarke	Silmans	115/19	Baldwin
Lewis, Rebecca H.	Camden	Hardees	249/13	Wilkinson
Lewis, Samuel	Hancock	Wallers	39/19	Baldwin
Lewis, Sherrod	Burke	Burks	36/14	Baldwin
Lewis, Simon	Bulloch	Denmarks	197/13	Baldwin
Lewis, Sterling	Hancock	Huffs	24/10	Baldwin
Lewis, Thomas	Burke	Sandifords	279/14	Baldwin
Lewis, Thomas	Elbert	Clarks	33/10	Baldwin
Lewis, Walker	Greene	Loves	155/24	Wilkinson
Lewis, Walker	Greene	Loves	207/17	Baldwin
Lewis, William	Bulloch	Denmarks	265/14	Baldwin
Lifflee, John	Burke	Mulkeys	188/19	Baldwin
Lightfoot, Jesse	Tattnall	McDonalds	317/20	Wilkinson
Lightfoot, Thomas	Hancock	Coffees	282/13	Wilkinson
Lightfoot, William	Burke	Martins	94/9	Baldwin
Liles', Levi(Orphs.)	Jackson	Hendersons	180/20	Baldwin
Liles, Lemuel	Glynn		44/8	Baldwin
Liles, Sherwood	Jackson	Cockrans	327/22	Wilkinson
Lillibridge, Henrietta	Chatham	Neals	497/7	Wilkinson
Lillibridge, John	Chatham	Pettybones	136/13	Wilkinson
Lillibridge, John	Chatham	Pettybones	337/22	Wilkinson
Lincecum, Asa	Baldwin	3	70/23	Wilkinson
Linder, George	Glynn		299/17	Wilkinson
Linder, Jacob Jr.	Glynn		185/26	Wilkinson
Linder, Jacob Jr.	Glynn		23/6	Wilkinson
Lindsey, Abraham	Wilkes	Malones	116/22	Wilkinson
Lindsey, Benjamin	Burke	Martins	311/21	Wilkinson
Lindsey, Jacob Sr.	Wilkes	Harris	56/10	Baldwin
Lindsey, James	Wilkes	Harris	167/28	Wilkinson
Lindsey, Martha(Wid.)	Burke	Sharps	137/6	Baldwin
Lindsey, Thomas	Burke	Martins	85/15	Baldwin
Lingo, Elijah	Hancock	Candlers	208/17	Wilkinson
Linn, Nathan	Clarke	Stewarts	131/10	Wilkinson
Linsey, David	Washington	Holts	5/17	Wilkinson
Linsey, Jeremiah	Greene	Watsons	183/20	Baldwin
Linsey, Reubin	Elbert	Dyes	164/6	Wilkinson
Linson, Elizabeth	Burke	Sandifords	209/11	Wilkinson
Linton, John Jr.	Washington	Garretts	126/7	Wilkinson
Linton, John Sr.	Washington	Garretts	39/11	Wilkinson
Linville, Wm.	Lincoln	Flemings	120/16	Wilkinson
Linzy, John	Bulloch	Godfreys	130/24	Wilkinson
Lions, Norris	Oglethorpe	Smiths	147/15	Wilkinson
Liptrot, Auilla	Burke	Hilliards	191/12	Wilkinson
Liptrot, James	Burke	Hilliards	264/13	Wilkinson
Little's, Frederick(Orphs.)	Washington	Collins	76/17	Wilkinson
Little, Harmon	Burke	Carswells	108/18	Wilkinson
Little, James	Franklin	Henrys	20/16	Baldwin
Little, John	Jefferson	Hardwichs	13/9	Baldwin
Little, Mary(Orph.)	Camden	Crews	216/12	Wilkinson
Little, Micajah	Wilkes	Youngs	3/15	Wilkinson
Little, Nancy(Wid.)	Washington	Collins	219/24	Wilkinson
Little, Reubin	Elbert	Willifords	112/13	Wilkinson

NAME	COUNTY	MIL.DIST.	LOT/DIST	DREW LAND
Little, Sarah	Jefferson	Hardwichs	321/22	Wilkinson
Little, William	Washington	Burneys	143/21	Wilkinson
Littlejohn, John	Greene	Armors	67/11	Wilkinson
Littleton, Alexander	Warren	Bakers	215/10	Wilkinson
Littleton, Henry	Wilkes	Normans	260/9	Wilkinson
Littleton, Jacob	Wilkes	Normans	265/15	Wilkinson
Littleton, Lucretia(Miss)	Warren	Bakers	182/6	Baldwin
Lively, Mathew	Burke	Mulkeys	261/14	Wilkinson
Lively, Mathew	Burke	Mulkeys	95/22	Wilkinson
Lively, Samuel	Jackson	Hendersons	160/27	Wilkinson
Liverman, Conrod	Bulloch	Williams	177/9	Baldwin
Liverman, Conrod	Bulloch	Williams	86/23	Wilkinson
Liverman, Mary	Bulloch	Williams	63/15	Baldwin
Lloyd, Levi	Greene	Stewarts	363/9	Wilkinson
Lochridge, James	Clarke	Hitchcocks	12/20	Wilkinson
Lock, John	Warren	Jones	69/18	Baldwin
Lock, John	Warren	Jones	95/7	Baldwin
Lock, Jonathan	Warren	Jones	385/7	Wilkinson
Lock, Lydia(Miss)	Warren	Jones	126/11	Baldwin
Locker, Polly	Hancock	Shivers'	105/24	Wilkinson
Locket, Abner	Hancock	Barnes'	81/16	Wilkinson
Locket, Solomon	Warren	Bakers	255/21	Wilkinson
Lockett, Jacob	Hancock	Weeks	38/6	Baldwin
Lockett, Thomas	Warren	Bakers	238/23	Wilkinson
Lockhart, James	Elbert	Roebucks	19/13	Baldwin
Lockhart, Reuben	Baldwin	1	274/22	Wilkinson
Lockhart, Samuel	Bulloch	Hendleys	56/6	Wilkinson
Locklin, John	Columbia		194/14	Wilkinson
Lofley's, Jesse(Orphs.)	Jefferson	Hardwichs	72/18	Wilkinson
Lofley, Pittman	Jefferson	Hardwichs	27/9	Baldwin
Loflin, James	Lincoln	Cartrells	54/13	Wilkinson
Loflin, Nancy	Lincoln	Busseys	174/22	Wilkinson
Loftin, John	Hancock	Holts	314/12	Wilkinson
Loftin, Vann	Clarke	Silmans	306/9	Wilkinson
Loftin, Vann	Jackson	Cockrans	318/20	Wilkinson
Lofton, Asa	Washington	Howards	172/18	Wilkinson
Lofton, Elkanah	Wilkinson		183/26	Wilkinson
London, Eliz.(Wid.)	Effingham		289/10	Wilkinson
Long, Eliz.(Wid.)	Jefferson	Thomas	76/19	Wilkinson
Long, Henry	Hancock	Coopers	214/9	Baldwin
Long, James	Screven		305/8	Wilkinson
Long, James	Washington	Burneys	335/22	Wilkinson
Long, Richard	Washington	Renfroes	182/16	Baldwin
Long, Samuel	Jackson	Hendersons	173/9	Baldwin
Long, Samuel	Jackson	Hendersons	60/9	Wilkinson
Long, Short	Tattnall	Sherrards	153/8	Wilkinson
Long, William	Burke	Bynes	214/17	Baldwin
Longley, Miles	Washington	Burneys	321/11	Wilkinson
Longley, Miles	Washington	Burneys	58/8	Baldwin
Loper, Abel G.	Effingham		262/16	Wilkinson
Loper, Asa	Effingham		182/17	Baldwin
Loper, Curtis	Effingham		169/22	Wilkinson
Loper, Curtis	Effingham		226/13	Wilkinson
Lorance, Samuel	Oglethorpe	Hartsfields	500/7	Wilkinson
Lord, Hezekiah	Chatham	Whites	237/13	Wilkinson
Lord, Samuel	Hancock	Crowders	277/15	Baldwin
Lord, Sarah	Washington	Kendricks	60/6	Baldwin
Lord, Wheatles	Baldwin	1	224/8	Wilkinson
Lord, Wm.	Burke	Thompsons	299/13	Wilkinson
Lott, Arthur	Tattnall	Sherrards	155/19	Baldwin
Lott, Arthur	Tattnall	Sherrards	96/12	Wilkinson
Lott, Elizabeth	Tattnall	Sherrards	342/11	Wilkinson
Lott, John Sr.	Tattnall	Sherrards	147/18	Wilkinson
Lott, Mary	Tattnall	Sherrards	223/22	Wilkinson
Lott, Robert	Tattnall	Armstrongs	144/13	Wilkinson
Lott, William Sr.	Bulloch	Hendleys	34/6	Wilkinson
Louremore, Samuel	Elbert	Olivers	40/7	Baldwin

NAME	COUNTY	MIL.DIST.	LOT/DIST	DREW LAND
Louremore, Samuel	Elbert	Olivers	74/18	Baldwin
Louridge, James	Jackson	Cockrans	14/19	Baldwin
Love's, David(Orphs.)	Greene	Stewarts	115/24	Wilkinson
Love, Alexander	Jefferson	Tarvers	150/11	Wilkinson
Love, Benjamin	Franklin	Dixons	218/18	Wilkinson
Love, John(Dr.)	Chatham	Pettybones	51/15	Wilkinson
Loveless, Allen	Columbia	4	180/12	Wilkinson
Loveless, William	Columbia	4	15/21	Wilkinson
Lovett, James	Warren	Flournoys	68/10	Wilkinson
Lovett, Lemuel	Hancock	Birdsongs	91/20	Wilkinson
Lovett, Richard	Warren	Devereux's	163/17	Wilkinson
Loving, Adam	Wilkes	Heards	253/24	Wilkinson
Lovorn, Edmund	Franklin	McDowells	153/6	Baldwin
Lovvorn, James	Clarke	Robinsons	206/16	Baldwin
Low, Curtis	Columbia	10	110/10	Wilkinson
Low, William Sr.	Warren	Heaths	174/8	Baldwin
Low, William(Uchee)	Columbia	2	59/9	Wilkinson
Lowe, Beverly Sr.	Columbia	1	77/8	Baldwin
Lowe, John(Of Ralph)	Hancock	Huffs	335/7	Wilkinson
Lowe, Lunsford	Burke	Montgomerys	179/23	Wilkinson
Lowe, Ralph	Baldwin	2	158/20	Wilkinson
Lowe, Thomas	Baldwin	1	151/9	Wilkinson
Lowe, Vincent	Wilkes	Harris	42/17	Wilkinson
Lowery, Henry	Franklin	Cornelius'	62/7	Baldwin
Lowremore, Alexander	Elbert	Olivers	82/6	Baldwin
Lowremore, Anna	Elbert	Olivers	60/13	Wilkinson
Lowremore, Sarah(Wid.)	Elbert	Olivers	147/22	Wilkinson
Lowrie's, Patrick(Orphs.)	Columbia	7	229/10	Wilkinson
Lowry, Christopher	Franklin	McDowells	287/24	Wilkinson
Lowry, John R.	Bulloch	Parishs	63/14	Baldwin
Lowry, John	Jefferson	Fultons	5/10	Wilkinson
Lowry, Margaret	Wayne	1	159/13	Baldwin
Lowry, Meshack	Elbert	Dyes	111/16	Baldwin
Lowry, Robert	Jefferson	Thomas	219/6	Baldwin
Lowry, Simeon	Burke	Spains	233/15	Wilkinson
Lowther, Edward	Bulloch	Williams	62/10	Baldwin
Lowther, John	Bulloch	Williams	304/6	Wilkinson
Loy, William	Columbia	5	106/10	Baldwin
Loyal's, Francis(Orphs.)	Clarke	Hitchcocks	89/25	Wilkinson
Loyd, Charles	Clarke	Robinsons	92/24	Wilkinson
Loyd, Daniel	Washington	Kendricks	12/24	Wilkinson
Loyd, George	Clarke	Robinsons	252/14	Baldwin
Loyd, John	Hancock	Coopers	92/18	Wilkinson
Loyd, Thomas	Clarke	Silmans	249/12	Wilkinson
Loyd, Willam(Capt.)	Clarke	Robinsons	321/24	Wilkinson
Loyd, Wm.W.	Clarke	Silmans	220/13	Baldwin
Lucas', James(Orphs.)	Hancock	Crowders	65/10	Baldwin
Lucas', Polly(Miss)	Warren	Heaths	228/18	Wilkinson
Lucas', Thomas(Orphs.)	Jackson	Wrights	217/16	Wilkinson
Lucas', Wm.(Orphs.)	Warren	Heaths	264/6	Wilkinson
Lucas, John	Screven		6/10	Wilkinson
Lucas, Robert	Hancock	Coopers	177/25	Wilkinson
Lucker, Joseph	Jackson	Hendersons	68/19	Baldwin
Luckey, Susannah	Oglethorpe	Hitchcocks	141/13	Wilkinson
Luckie, John	Columbia	4	77/20	Wilkinson
Lucky, John	Greene	Stewarts	265/19	Baldwin
Lucky, John	Oglethorpe	Hitchcocks	193/13	Baldwin
Luis, Elender(Orph.of Jno.)	Jackson	Hendersons	141/11	Wilkinson
Luke, Joseph D.W.	Columbia	2	65/27	Wilkinson
Luke, William	Burke	Blounts	143/13	Wilkinson
Luke, William	Burke	Blounts	187/16	Wilkinson
Luker, Isaac	Clarke	Stewarts	112/11	Baldwin
Luker, Joshua	Wilkes	Coopers	226/10	Baldwin
Luker, William	Jackson	Johnsons	278/20	Wilkinson
Lumpkin, Ann(Wid.of Geo.)	Oglethorpe	Popes	205/16	Wilkinson
Lumpkin, Ann(Wid.of Jos.)	Oglethorpe	Beasleys	115/13	Baldwin
Lumpkin, George	Baldwin	4	343/22	Wilkinson

NAME	COUNTY	MIL.DIST.	LOT/DIST	DREW LAND
Lumpkin, Joseph	Oglethorpe	Moores	17/21	Wilkinson
Lumpkin, Polly(Orph.)	Oglethorpe	Moores	205/6	Baldwin
Lumsdale, Elijah	Baldwin	4	195/23	Wilkinson
Lunday, Nathaniel	Screven	Williamsons	61/20	Wilkinson
Lungeno, Hugh	Burke	Spains	276/14	Baldwin
Lunsford, Enoch	Baldwin	1	298/8	Wilkinson
Luper, William	Wilkinson		186/7	Wilkinson
Lutgert, Mary	Richmond		304/20	Wilkinson
Lyles, Dilmus	Jackson	Cockrans	159/9	Baldwin
Lyles, John	Jackson	Cockrans	207/7	Wilkinson
Lyles, John	Jackson	Cockrans	307/13	Wilkinson
Lynch, James Sr.	Hancock	Weeks	252/18	Wilkinson
Lynch, John	Washington	Garretts	298/6	Wilkinson
Lyner, James S.	Franklin	Hoopers	52/9	Baldwin
Lyner, James S.	Franklin	Hoopers	8/27	Wilkinson
Lynn, William	Warren	Flournoys	175/15	Wilkinson
Lyon, Castleton	Franklin	Griffiths	24/9	Wilkinson
Lyon, Castleton	Franklin	Griffiths	242/9	Wilkinson
Lyon, Dison	Columbia	4	47/10	Wilkinson
Lyon, Edmund	Lincoln	Kings	274/25	Wilkinson
Lyon, James	Baldwin	3	21/26	Wilkinson
Lyon, James	Baldwin	3	52/11	Wilkinson
Lyon, John	Chatham	McLeans	303/13	Wilkinson
Lyon, John	Columbia	3	135/16	Baldwin
Lyon, John	Lincoln	Kennons	197/16	Wilkinson
Lyon, John	Wilkes	Hendersons	439/7	Wilkinson
Lyon, Martha(Wid.)	Chatham	Pettybones	173/11	Baldwin
Lyon, Peter	Burke	Carswells	201/12	Wilkinson
Lyon, Robert	Lincoln	Kennons	108/7	Baldwin
Lyon, William	Richmond		157/15	Wilkinson
Lyon, William	Richmond		269/24	Wilkinson
Lyons, James	Warren	Devereux's	125/10	Wilkinson
Lyons, William	Jefferson	Colemans	113/19	Baldwin
Lysle, Charles	Columbia	10	260/20	Wilkinson
Maberry, Ephraim	Franklin	Dixons	223/17	Wilkinson
Mabrey, Ann L.	Camden	Crews	236/26	Wilkinson
Mabrey, Jamison	Wilkes	Welborns	358/9	Wilkinson
Mackay, Henry	Chatham	Neyles	187/7	Wilkinson
Mackey, John	Washington	Wiggins	294/15	Wilkinson
Macon, Nathaniel G.	Greene	Reas	264/19	Wilkinson
Maddieux, Richard	Warren	Hills	125/14	Baldwin
Maddieux, Richard	Warren	Hills	181/21	Wilkinson
Maddison, James	Oglethorpe	.Hewells	69/7	Wilkinson
Maddox's, Linney(Orphs.)	Montgomery	53	168/17	Baldwin
Maddox, Alexander	Jackson	Cockrans	69/14	Baldwin
Maddox, Alexander	Wilkinson		48/7	Wilkinson
Maddox, Alexander	Wilkinson		61/20	Baldwin
Maddox, Andrew	Clarke	Robinsons	44/7	Baldwin
Maddox, Benjamin	Columbia	5	97/10	Baldwin
Maddox, Clayborne	Jackson	Cockrans	140/23	Wilkinson
Maddox, Hardridge	Jackson	Cockrans	225/20	Baldwin
Maddox, John	Jackson	Cockrans	118/18	Wilkinson
Maddox, John	Jackson	Cockrans	233/18	Wilkinson
Maddox, Leah	Hancock	Wallers	20/10	Wilkinson
Maddox, Leaven	Jackson	Cockrans	261/7	Wilkinson
Maddox, Spencer	Lincoln	Busseys	68/27	Wilkinson
Maddox, Spencer	Lincoln	Busseys	87/8	Baldwin
Maddox, Thomas	Warren	Neals	197/10	Baldwin
Madry, Milly(Wid.)	Burke	Sharps	193/17	Wilkinson
Madry, Richard	Burke	Sharps	10/17	Wilkinson
Madry, William	Burke	Sharps	296/13	Wilkinson
Magbee, James	Clarke	Martindales	361/8	Wilkinson
Magee, Francis	Baldwin	5	330/7	Wilkinson
Magee, Wm.Sr.	Elbert	Blackwells	221/21	Wilkinson
Magnan, John B.	Richmond		344/10	Wilkinson
Magse, William	Elbert	Blackwells	503/7	Wilkinson
Magwier, David	Jackson	Hendersons	205/17	Wilkinson

NAME	COUNTY	MIL.DIST.	LOT/DIST	DREW LAND
Magwier, Frederick	Jackson	Hendersons	166/12	Baldwin
Magwier, Thompson	Jackson	Hendersons	140/14	Wilkinson
Mahoney, Wm.O.	Burke	Hilliards	267/11	Wilkinson
Mahoonee, Peter	Baldwin	2	68/12	Baldwin
Major, John	Chatham	Herbs	103/28	Wilkinson
Majors, James	Hancock	Barksdales	138/19	Wilkinson
Malcome, David	Lincoln	Jones'	36/14	Wilkinson
Mallard, John	Bulloch	Godfreys	102/7	Wilkinson
Mallett, Gideon	Effingham		337/8	Wilkinson
Mallory's, James(Orph.)	Burke	Forths	46/18	Wilkinson
Mallory, Wm.Sr.	Wilkes	Stovalls	8/6	Baldwin
Malone, James	Columbia	7	235/9	Baldwin
Malone, John	Clarke	Hitchcocks	52/26	Wilkinson
Malone, William	Columbia	7	322/13	Wilkinson
Malphurs, Jesse	Tattnall	Staffords	131/28	Wilkinson
Malryne, Jane	McIntosh		293/11	Wilkinson
Manion's, Francis(Orphs.)	Greene	Carletons	57/11	Wilkinson
Manley, Elizabeth	Franklin	Allens	41/11	Baldwin
Manley, Henry	Bryan	Austins	53/12	Wilkinson
Manley, Isaac D.	Franklin	Bryants	13/24	Wilkinson
Manley, John	Bryan	Austins	104/15	Baldwin
Mann, Cader	Montgomery	57	101/9	Wilkinson
Mann, Elizabeth J.	Elbert	Clarks	256/19	Baldwin
Mann, Francis	Richmond		225/22	Wilkinson
Mann, Harriett(Or.of Luke)	Bryan	Austins	38/9	Baldwin
Mann, James Sr.	Elbert	Clarks	204/9	Wilkinson
Mann, James Sr.	Elbert	Clarks	59/17	Baldwin
Mann, Jeremiah	Elbert	Clarkes	66/8	Baldwin
Mann, John	Elbert	Clarks	255/14	Baldwin
Mann, John	Oglethorpe	Smiths	212/11	Wilkinson
Mann, John	Oglethorpe	Smiths	80/13	Wilkinson
Mann, Margaret(Orph.)	Chatham	Pettybones	71/19	Baldwin
Mann, William	Tattnall	Halls	127/16	Baldwin
Mannen, Dury	Wilkinson		59/15	Baldwin
Mannen, John	Glynn		99/11	Baldwin
Mannen, John	Wilkinson		164/20	Wilkinson
Mannen, Lucy(Single)	Effingham		121/6	Baldwin
Mannen, Robert	Wilkinson		130/15	Baldwin
Manning, Benjamin	Washington	Collins	91/18	Wilkinson
Manning, James	Elbert	Hillyers	196/16	Baldwin
Manning, James	Elbert	Hillyers	82/24	Wilkinson
Manning, Lucy M.(Orph.)	Chatham	Whites	58/15	Baldwin
Manningore, -	Franklin	Winns	37/19	Wilkinson
Manson, James	Jefferson	Hardwichs	126/13	Wilkinson
Mapp, John	Greene	Owsleys	207/10	Wilkinson
Mapp, Robert H.	Hancock	Hudsons	197/23	Wilkinson
Mara, Morgan	Liberty		241/12	Wilkinson
Marable, Campbell	Oglethorpe	Hudsons	160/25	Wilkinson
Marable, -	Clarke	Hitchcocks	14/8	Wilkinson
Marable, William	Oglethorpe	Hudsons	64/13	Baldwin
Marbury, Horatio	Jefferson	Wrights	324/12	Wilkinson
Marchman, James	Hancock	Wallers	316/7	Wilkinson
Marcum, William	Camden	Ashleys	156/13	Baldwin
Marks, Anna(Single)	Effingham		179/13	Wilkinson
Marks, John H.	Elbert	Groves	109/11	Wilkinson
Markum, James	Baldwin	4	163/16	Wilkinson
Marsh, Edith(Wid.)	Burke	Montgomerys	149/6	Baldwin
Marsh, Hannah	Warren	Willsons	351/21	Wilkinson
Marsh, Henry	Chatham	Hardens	102/12	Baldwin
Marsh, James	Burke	Montgomerys	2/26	Wilkinson
Marsh, John	Columbia	9	248/11	Wilkinson
Marsh, Littleberry	Burke	Montgomerys	188/20	Wilkinson
Marsh, Nathan	Warren	Newsoms	23/11	Wilkinson
Marsh, Nathan	Warren	Newsoms	46/12	Baldwin
Marshall, Abraham	Columbia	2	137/16	Baldwin
Marshall, James	Lincoln	Busseys	87/18	Baldwin
Marshall, Jno.	Chatham	Abrahams	142/12	Baldwin

NAME	COUNTY	MIL.DIST.	LOT/DIST	DREW LAND
Marshall, Jno.	Tattnall	Sherrards	319/17	Wilkinson
Marshall, John	Lincoln	Busseys	106/27	Wilkinson
Marshall, Joseph Jr.	Columbia	2	138/14	Baldwin
Marshall, Mary(Wid.)	Hancock	Gumms	159/26	Wilkinson
Marshall, William	Greene	Butlers	157/22	Wilkinson
Marshall, Zachariah	Columbia	2	147/9	Wilkinson
Marston's, Samuel(Orphs.)	Hancock	Crowders	257/13	Wilkinson
Martin's, Catharine	Greene	Alfords	237/7	Wilkinson
Martin's, Jos.(Orphs.)	Wilkes	Malones	279/15	Baldwin
Martin's, Joshua Sr.(Orphs.)	Greene	Watsons	118/6	Baldwin
Martin's, Philemon(Orphs.)	Franklin	Griffiths	50/15	Baldwin
Martin's, Wylie(Orph.)	Greene	Butlers	143/6	Baldwin
Martin, Alexander	Hancock	Barnes	109/14	Baldwin
Martin, Angus	Richmond		274/14	Wilkinson
Martin, Anthony	Oglethorpe	Watkins	27/7	Wilkinson
Martin, Betsy(Orph.)	Elbert	Mobleys	139/15	Wilkinson
Martin, Elijah	Franklin	Griffiths	315/14	Wilkinson
Martin, Francis S.	Greene	Alfords	14/13	Baldwin
Martin, George	Columbia	7	199/23	Wilkinson
Martin, George	Franklin	Allens	23/7	Baldwin
Martin, Isaac	Clarke	Silmans	175/26	Wilkinson
Martin, James	Bryan	Birds	117/6	Baldwin
Martin, James	Jackson	Hendersons	26/18	Wilkinson
Martin, James	Warren	Devereux's	113/15	Baldwin
Martin, Jane	Tattnall	Sherrards	11/20	Wilkinson
Martin, John A.	Bulloch	Denmarks	58/12	Baldwin
Martin, John F.	Elbert	Thompsons	169/10	Baldwin
Martin, John Sr.	Liberty		108/20	Wilkinson
Martin, John	Burke	Burks	215/19	Baldwin
Martin, John	Burke	Montgomerys	34/14	Wilkinson
Martin, John	Jackson	Wrights	191/19	Baldwin
Martin, John	Jackson	Wrights	72/8	Wilkinson
Martin, John	Washington	Chivers	162/24	Wilkinson
Martin, John	Washington	Chivers	199/7	Wilkinson
Martin, Joseph	Franklin	Yowells	147/17	Baldwin
Martin, Julius	Washington	Howards	172/6	Wilkinson
Martin, Leonard	Columbia	7	24/8	Wilkinson
Martin, Levi	Washington	Howards	273/6	Wilkinson
Martin, Lewis	Effingham		40/8	Baldwin
Martin, Martin	Liberty		76/14	Baldwin
Martin, Mary	Tattnall	Sherrards	137/19	Wilkinson
Martin, Merritt	Franklin	Yowells	3/8	Baldwin
Martin, Murdoch	Jackson	Wrights	125/16	Wilkinson
Martin, Noah	Washington	Howards	77/6	Baldwin
Martin, Richard	Washington	Andersons	81/28	Wilkinson
Martin, Robert D.	Greene	Carletons	84/25	Wilkinson
Martin, Robert Sr.	Clarke	Silmans	106/13	Baldwin
Martin, Robert(Capt.)	Clarke	Martins	259/15	Baldwin
Martin, Robert	Jackson	Cockrans	143/27	Wilkinson
Martin, Sally	Oglethorpe	Bells	172/21	Wilkinson
Martin, Samuel	Richmond		104/6	Baldwin
Martin, Stephen	Wilkes	Heards	117/11	Baldwin
Martin, Thomas	Washington	Howards	20/28	Wilkinson
Martin, William	Oglethorpe	Hitchcocks	135/24	Wilkinson
Mason, David	Montgomery	56	150/15	Wilkinson
Mason, Gideon	Lincoln	Cartrells	62/11	Baldwin
Mason, James	Washington	Andersons	71/13	Wilkinson
Mason, Nancy(Wid.)	Wilkes	Sidwells	14/23	Wilkinson
Mason, William	Hancock	Shivers	204/14	Baldwin
Massee, Needham	Wilkes	Youngs	112/8	Baldwin
Massee, Needham	Wilkes	Youngs	56/21	Wilkinson
Massinggale, Daniel	Columbia	9	284/10	Wilkinson
Massinggale, Daniel	Columbia	9	29/16	Baldwin
Mastin, James	Clarke	Trammells	314/15	Baldwin
Mathew, John	Liberty		253/11	Wilkinson
Mathews', Edmond(Orphs.)	Hancock	Crowders	100/9	Wilkinson
Mathews', Peter(Orphs.)	Burke	Ballards	65/9	Baldwin

NAME	COUNTY	MIL.DIST.	LOT/DIST	DREW LAND
Mathews', Richard(Orphs.)	Columbia	9	233/9	Wilkinson
Mathews', Stephen(Orph.)	Baldwin	5	56/20	Wilkinson
Mathews, Charles	Warren	Newsoms	82/7	Baldwin
Mathews, Edmond	Bulloch	Parishs	134/9	Wilkinson
Mathews, Gracy	Columbia	10	71/15	Baldwin
Mathews, Henry	Wilkinson		223/25	Wilkinson
Mathews, Isham	Washington	Kendricks	195/15	Wilkinson
Mathews, James(Rev.)	Wilkes	Heards	42/13	Baldwin
Mathews, James	Jefferson	Tarvers	231/8	Wilkinson
Mathews, James	Warren	Jones	106/6	Baldwin
Mathews, James	Warren	Jones	27/14	Wilkinson
Mathews, Jeremiah	Hancock	Gumms	249/23	Wilkinson
Mathews, Joel	Warren	Bakers	27/8	Baldwin
Mathews, John	Bulloch	Parish	384/7	Wilkinson
Mathews, John	Columbia	7	261/19	Wilkinson
Mathews, Joseph	Clarke	Dukes	90/14	Wilkinson
Mathews, Mathew	Hancock	Smiths	174/26	Wilkinson
Mathews, Mathew	Hancock	Smiths	19/19	Wilkinson
Mathews, Michael	Wilkinson		39/11	Baldwin
Mathews, Nancy	Warren	Newsoms	136/17	Wilkinson
Mathews, Robert	Wilkes	Edges	212/18	Wilkinson
Mathews, Sarah	Wilkes	Edges	109/9	Wilkinson
Mathews, Solomon	Wilkes	Edges	24/6	Wilkinson
Mathews, William	Hancock	Smiths	122/7	Baldwin
Mathews, Wm.H.	Hancock	Crowders	192/8	Wilkinson
Mathis, John	Washington	Wiggins	359/21	Wilkinson
Matt, Zapheniah	Wilkinson		336/7	Wilkinson
Matthews, Elijah	Warren	Flournoys	99/13	Wilkinson
Matthews, Henry	Chatham	Pembertons	270/11	Wilkinson
Matthews, Joel	Warren	Bakers	142/8	Baldwin
Matthews, Josiah	Burke	Gordons	159/14	Baldwin
Matthews, Polly	Warren	Neals	239/6	Wilkinson
Matthews, Sally	Warren	Neals	119/17	Wilkinson
Matthews, William	Warren	Wilsons	194/18	Wilkinson
Mattock, Charles	Wilkes	Hendricks	306/14	Wilkinson
Mattocks, Lewis	Washington	Blackshears	207/11	Wilkinson
Mauk, Barbara(Wid.)	Wilkes	Hendersons	282/16	Wilkinson
Mauk, Matthias	Wilkes	Hendersons	301/13	Wilkinson
Mauper, Jesse	Elbert	Thompsons	175/6	Wilkinson
Maurice, Benjamin	Chatham	Whites	136/21	Wilkinson
Maxcey, Jeremiah Jr.	Oglethorpe	Hudsons	164/21	Wilkinson
Maxcey, John	Clarke	Dukes	1/15	Wilkinson
Maxcey, John	Clarke	Dukes	131/12	Baldwin
Maxcey, Pounce	Oglethorpe	Stewarts	89/15	Wilkinson
Maxcey, Walter	Oglethorpe	Stewarts	129/6	Baldwin
Maxcey, Walter	Oglethorpe	Stewarts	78/15	Baldwin
Maxey, John	Oglethorpe	Beasleys	144/19	Wilkinson
Maxwell, Hester(Orph.)	Bryan	Austins	55/16	Baldwin
Maxwell, Jane(Orph.)	Bryan	Austins	55/16	Baldwin
Maxwell, John J.	Bryan	Austins	78/16	Wilkinson
Maxwell, Margaret	Wilkes	Hendersons	365/22	Wilkinson
Maxwell, Mary(Orph.)	Bryan	Austins	55/16	Baldwin
Maxwell, Richard	Clarke	Martindales	61/13	Wilkinson
Maxwell, Stephen	Bryan	Austins	142/10	Baldwin
Maxwell, Susan(Orph.)	Bryan	Austins	55/16	Baldwin
Maxwell, Thomas Jr.	Elbert	Blackwells	245/17	Wilkinson
Maxwell, Thomas Sr.	Elbert	Blackwells	370/9	Wilkinson
Maxwell, William Jr.	Bryan	Austins	177/9	Wilkinson
Maxwell, William	Jefferson		174/7	Wilkinson
Maxwell, William	Jefferson		245/20	Wilkinson
Maxwell, Wm.(S.of Thos.)	Wilkes	Hendersons	34/19	Wilkinson
Maxwell, Wm.B.	Chatham	Abrahams	314/24	Wilkinson
Maxwell, Wm.Sr.	Bryan	Austins	120/19	Baldwin
May, John	McIntosh		326/9	Wilkinson
May, Lewis	Baldwin	2	70/15	Baldwin
Maybunk, Andrew	Liberty		88/15	Baldwin
Maycock's, Wm.(Orphs.)	Baldwin	2	237/14	Wilkinson

NAME	COUNTY	MIL.DIST.	LOT/DIST	DREW LAND
Mayes, James	Jackson	Johnsons	134/19	Baldwin
Mayes, John	Jackson	Johnsons	198/20	Baldwin
Mayfield, Luke	Jackson	Johnsons	55/10	Wilkinson
Mayfield, Mary(Wid.)	Jackson	Hendersons	236/23	Wilkinson
Maynard, Edward	Franklin	Thompsons	77/20	Baldwin
Maynard, James	Franklin	Thompsons	158/12	Wilkinson
Maynard, Richard	Franklin	Thompsons	343/13	Wilkinson
Mayo's, Samuel(Orphs.)	Jefferson		326/13	Wilkinson
Mayo's, Wm.(Orphs.)	Wilkinson		124/13	Baldwin
Mayo, Benjamin	Jefferson		174/11	Wilkinson
Mayo, Benjamin	Jefferson		70/9	Baldwin
Mayo, Britton	Jefferson		226/17	Wilkinson
Mayo, Harmon	Montgomery	57	294/6	Wilkinson
Mayo, Joseph	Jefferson		150/26	Wilkinson
Mayo, William	Washington	Garretts	90/15	Wilkinson
Mays, James	Jackson	Johnsons	91/14	Wilkinson
Mays, John	Franklin	Dixons	99/20	Wilkinson
Mays, William	Lincoln	Mays	190/14	Wilkinson
Mays, William	Lincoln	Mays	239/12	Wilkinson
McAllister, David	Hancock	Winsletts	124/16	Baldwin
McAllister, John	Oglethorpe	Beasleys	184/15	Wilkinson
McAlphin, Mary(Wid.)	Elbert	Roebucks	230/14	Baldwin
McAlpin, Alexander	Clarke	Butlers	32/22	Wilkinson
McAlpin, Wm.A.	Clarke	Butlers	102/11	Wilkinson
McAuley, Niel	McIntosh		278/21	Wilkinson
McBride, Mary	Jefferson	Tarvers	32/25	Wilkinson
McBride, William	Jefferson	Tarvers	65/19	Wilkinson
McBurnett, James	Clarke	Hopkins	72/19	Wilkinson
McBurnett, Thomas	Clarke	Hopkins	273/21	Wilkinson
McCain, Hamilton	Wilkes	Youngs	110/15	Baldwin
McCain, Hugh Jr.	Wilkes	Hendricks'	221/7	Wilkinson
McCain, Hugh	Clarke	Mitchells	132/27	Wilkinson
McCalister, John	Baldwin	1	254/12	Wilkinson
McCall, Francis	Bulloch	Williams	170/26	Wilkinson
McCall, George	Bulloch	Williams	269/15	Baldwin
McCall, James	Baldwin	4	181/12	Baldwin
McCall, Jesse	Liberty		20/13	Wilkinson
McCall, Robert	Bulloch	Williams	19/9	Baldwin
McCall, William	Montgomery	54	297/10	Wilkinson
McCall, William	Screven	Olivers	54/10	Baldwin
McCallaghan, Jane(Orph.)	Chatham	Pettybones	397/21	Wilkinson
McCane, Mary	Greene	Carletons	159/9	Wilkinson
McCann, James	Jackson	Johnsons	84/20	Wilkinson
McCann, Joshua	Screven		242/8	Wilkinson
McCann, Peggy	Burke	Carswells	12/27	Wilkinson
McCant, James	Burke	Forths	89/23	Wilkinson
McCardel, John	Screven		137/10	Baldwin
McCardell, Charles	Warren	Devereux's	192/23	Wilkinson
McCardell, Charles	Warren	Devereux's	49/11	Baldwin
McCardell, Keziah(Wid.)	Lincoln	Busseys	246/24	Wilkinson
McCarroll, James	Baldwin	4	148/28	Wilkinson
McCarter, James Sr.	Franklin	Allens	55/14	Wilkinson
McCarter, James	Franklin	Allens	238/11	Wilkinson
McCarthy's, John(Orphs.)	Columbia	9	263/8	Wilkinson
McCartney, Charles	Jackson	Johnsons	222/9	Wilkinson
McCartney, Charles	Jackson	Johnsons	296/10	Wilkinson
McCartney, James	Jackson	Johnsons	74/27	Wilkinson
McCartney, Jane	Jackson	Johnsons	236/15	Baldwin
McCarty, Hannah(Wid.)	Jackson	Hendersons	65/16	Wilkinson
McCarty, John	Oglethorpe	Hudsons	32/14	Wilkinson
McCaskel, Affa	Chatham	Whites	14/15	Wilkinson
McClain, Reubin	Oglethorpe	Beasleys	145/24	Wilkinson
McClendon, Ephraim	Montgomery	52	190/18	Wilkinson
McClendon, Lovin S.	Hancock	Candlers	36/8	Wilkinson
McClendon, Nancy	Montgomery	52	287/16	Wilkinson
McCloud, John	Baldwin	2	14/15	Baldwin
McCloyd, John	Baldwin	2	105/11	Baldwin

NAME	COUNTY	MIL.DIST.	LOT/DIST	DREW LAND
McCluskey, David H.	Jackson	Hendersons	306/22	Wilkinson
McCluskey, William	Jackson		175/15	Baldwin
McClusky, David H.	Jackson	Hendersons	53/15	Baldwin
McClusky, James	Jackson	Hendersons	14/27	Wilkinson
McClusky, James	Jackson	Hendersons	177/19	Wilkinson
McCoil, Gideon	Burke	Mulkeys	35/6	Baldwin
McCollister, Margaret	Wilkinson		123/16	Baldwin
McCollom, Joseph	Burke	Ballards	276/10	Wilkinson
McCollom, Joseph	Burke	Ballards	389/8	Wilkinson
McColpin, Niel	Montgomery	51	130/14	Wilkinson
McCombs, Andrew	Greene	Armors	236/6	Wilkinson
McCook, Elizabeth	Hancock	Thomas'	237/21	Wilkinson
McCook, Mary	Hancock	Thomas'	47/11	Baldwin
McCord, David	Jackson	Johnsons	192/19	Wilkinson
McCorkle, James	Lincoln	Cartrells	77/10	Wilkinson
McCormack, David	Clarke	Dukes	37/26	Wilkinson
McCormick's, Henry(Orphs.)	Clarke	Hitchcocks	176/10	Baldwin
McCormick's, Jos'h. (Orphs.)	Lincoln	Kennons	72/13	Wilkinson
McCormick, Nancy(Dau/Jno.)	Columbia	3	277/9	Wilkinson
McCormick, Thomas	Wilkes	Youngs	262/20	Wilkinson
McCoy's, Daniel(Orphs.)	Baldwin	2	153/21	Wilkinson
McCoy's, James(Orphs.)	Burke	Mulkeys	100/16	Baldwin
McCoy, David	Wilkes	Sidwells	15/17	Wilkinson
McCoy, Henry	Greene	Greers	270/22	Wilkinson
McCoy, Jeremiah	Clarke	Silmans	26/13	Wilkinson
McCoy, John Jr.	Montgomery	52	114/20	Baldwin
McCoy, John	Baldwin	2	170/22	Wilkinson
McCoy, John	Clarke	Silmans	111/10	Baldwin
McCoy, John	Warren	Devereux's	149/16	Baldwin
McCoy, Lewis	Richmond		184/22	Wilkinson
McCoy, Nealy	Clarke	Robinsons	5/15	Wilkinson
McCoy, Reubin	Elbert	Olivers	225/23	Wilkinson
McCoy, Thomas	Clarke	Dukes	7/27	Wilkinson
McCoy, William	Elbert	Olivers	36/17	Baldwin
McCracken, Wm.	Franklin	Dixons	99/25	Wilkinson
McCravey, John	Jackson	Johnsons	453/7	Wilkinson
McCrea, Anable(S.W.)	Screven		98/18	Wilkinson
McCree, Benjamin	Clarke	Trammell's	14/22	Wilkinson
McCuin, Robert	Jackson	Cockrans	191/14	Baldwin
McCullers, Amey(Wid.)	Warren	Neals	77/14	Baldwin
McCullers, Colson	Jefferson		336/22	Wilkinson
McCullers, Drury	Warren	Neals	133/13	Baldwin
McCullers, Mary	Jefferson		117/8	Wilkinson
McCullers, Simon	Jefferson	Thomas'	294/12	Wilkinson
McCullers, Susannah(Wid.)	Jefferson	Tarvers	303/15	Wilkinson
McCullers, William	Jefferson	Tarvers	121/15	Wilkinson
McCulloch, John	McIntosh		302/9	Wilkinson
McCullogh, James	Liberty		188/24	Wilkinson
McCulloh, John	Hancock	Smiths	283/10	Wilkinson
McCullough's, Jas.(Orphs.)	Baldwin	5	78/7	Wilkinson
McCullough, Ann(Orph.)	Richmond		27/11	Baldwin
McCullough, Ann	Richmond		86/25	Wilkinson
McCullough, Christ'r.(Orph.)	Richmond		27/11	Baldwin
McCullough, Jacob Jr.	Richmond		108/21	Wilkinson
McCullough, James(Orph.)	Richmond		27/11	Baldwin
McCullough, Nathaniel	Camden	Crews	163/10	Baldwin
McCullough, Saml.(Orph.)	Richmond		27/11	Baldwin
McCune's, Wm.(Orphs by Jane)	Elbert	Roebucks	193/18	Wilkinson
McCune's, Wm.(Orphs.by Mary)	Elbert	Roebucks	90/9	Baldwin
McCune, Jane(Wid.)	Elbert	Roebucks	147/28	Wilkinson
McCune, Sally(S.W.)	Clarke	Mitchells	206/10	Baldwin
McCune, Sarah(Wid.)	Clarke	Martins	111/8	Wilkinson
McCurdy, James	Elbert	Groves	121/8	Wilkinson
McCurdy, James	Elbert	Groves	24/18	Baldwin
McCurry, Angus	Elbert	McGuires	261/19	Baldwin
McCurry, Lauchlin	Chatham	Pettybones	307/11	Wilkinson
McCutchen, Robert	Jackson	Hendersons	125/17	Baldwin

NAME	COUNTY	MIL.DIST.	LOT/DIST	DREW LAND
McCutchen, Sarah	Jackson	Cockrans	81/13	Wilkinson
McCutchin's, Patr.(Orphs.)	Tattnall	Halls	208/15	Wilkinson
McDade, William	Richmond		5/23	Wilkinson
McDaniel's, Jno.(Orphs.)	Warren	Heaths	228/17	Wilkinson
McDaniel, Ailcy(Miss)	Warren	Hills	176/12	Baldwin
McDaniel, Alexander	Greene	Owsleys	2/27	Wilkinson
McDaniel, Archibald	Wilkinson		187/6	Baldwin
McDaniel, Braddock	Jackson	Hendersons	39/23	Wilkinson
McDaniel, Bryant	Montgomery	54	150/16	Baldwin
McDaniel, Daniel	Warren	Flournoys	486/7	Wilkinson
McDaniel, Elizabeth	Burke	Gordons	319/7	Wilkinson
McDaniel, John	Washington	Holts	167/27	Wilkinson
McDaniel, John	Washington	Holts	175/16	Wilkinson
McDaniel, John	Wayne	2	105/6	Baldwin
McDaniel, John	Wayne	2	175/24	Wilkinson
McDaniel, Jonathan	Montgomery	54	84/22	Wilkinson
McDonald's, James(Orphs.)	Columbia	10	234/23	Wilkinson
McDonald's, John(Orphs.)	Burke	Spains	341/24	Wilkinson
McDonald, Daniel	Liberty		133/8	Wilkinson
McDonald, Donald Jr.	Elbert	McGuires	165/26	Wilkinson
McDonald, Donald Jr.	Elbert	McGuires	200/15	Baldwin
McDonald, Donald Sr.	Elbert	McGuires	12/28	Wilkinson
McDonald, Donald Sr.	Elbert	McGuires	71/17	Baldwin
McDonald, Donald	Columbia	7	136/19	Baldwin
McDonald, Donald	McIntosh		16/11	Baldwin
McDonald, Elspy	McIntosh		391/7	Wilkinson
McDonald, James	Chatham	Whites	174/15	Wilkinson
McDonald, James	Washington	Renfroes	206/7	Wilkinson
McDonald, John	Elbert	McGuires	304/22	Wilkinson
McDonald, Stephen	Columbia	4	218/8	Wilkinson
McDonald, William	Burke	Fields	197/10	Wilkinson
McDonald, William	Columbia	4	120/15	Baldwin
McDonald, William	Columbia	4	41/20	Wilkinson
McDonald, William	McIntosh		204/23	Wilkinson
McDougall, Robert	Chatham	Whites	300/14	Wilkinson
McDowell, Robert	Jackson	Cockrans	313/22	Wilkinson
McDuffee, John	Columbia	9	95/8	Wilkinson
McElrath, John	Oglethorpe	Popes	68/13	Wilkinson
McElroy, Elizabeth	Oglethorpe	Bells	334/14	Wilkinson
McEver, Robert	Jackson	Cockrans	353/24	Wilkinson
McFarland, Betsy(Orph.)	Jefferson	Bostwicks	26/8	Wilkinson
McFarland, Charles(Orph.)	Jefferson	Bostwicks	26/8	Wilkinson
McFarland, Edw.(Orph.)	Richmond		220/23	Wilkinson
McFarland, James H.	Warren	Carters	173/24	Wilkinson
McFarland, James	Columbia	10	237/8	Wilkinson
McFarland, Mary(Orph.)	Richmond		220/23	Wilkinson
McFarland, Nancy(Orph)	Jefferson	Bostwicks	26/8	Wilkinson
McFarland, Peter	Baldwin	2	168/21	Wilkinson
McFarland, Robert	Franklin	Bryants	159/16	Wilkinson
McFarland, Sarah(Orph.)	Richmond		220/23	Wilkinson
McFarlane, Peter	Chatham	Whites	85/13	Wilkinson
McFerran, Martha(Wid.)	Wilkes	Parks'	211/19	Wilkinson
McGaughey, James H.	Baldwin	2	23/13	Wilkinson
McGaughy, John M.Sr.	Columbia	7	227/18	Wilkinson
McGaughy, Martha	Hancock	Wallers	19/11	Baldwin
McGaughy, William	Columbia	7	216/16	Wilkinson
McGee's, Hugh(Orphs.)	Jefferson		304/14	Wilkinson
McGee, William	Warren	Hills	91/16	Baldwin
McGehee, James	Oglethorpe	Smiths	54/8	Wilkinson
McGehee, Nathan(s.of Dan'l.)	Columbia	1	308/20	Wilkinson
McGehee, Samuel	Elbert	Thompsons	136/25	Wilkinson
McGehee, William	Jefferson	Wrights	494/7	Wilkinson
McGehee, William	Jefferson	Wrights	81/7	Baldwin
McGiles, John	Clarke	Butlers	73/20	Baldwin
McGill, Susannah	Lincoln	Flemmings	156/6	Baldwin
McGill, Thomas	Lincoln	Flemings	352/8	Wilkinson
McGinnis, Felix	Columbia	8	215/20	Baldwin

NAME	COUNTY	MIL.DIST.	LOT/DIST	DREW LAND
McGinnis, Felix	Columbia	8	4/15	Wilkinson
McGinnis, James	Jackson	Johnsons	42/15	Baldwin
McGirt's, Daniel(Orphs.)	Camden	Crews	301/21	Wilkinson
McGowan, James Jr.	Screven	Olivers	158/15	Wilkinson
McGowen, Robert	Clarke	Mitchells	174/23	Wilkinson
McGregory, Dempsey	Washington	Willis'	186/22	Wilkinson
McGriff, Elizabeth	Montgomery	53	56/20	Baldwin
McGriff, Richard	Montgomery	53	172/8	Wilkinson
McGuire, Allegany	Elbert	Roebucks	339/19	Wilkinson
McGuire, John	Greene	Flournoys	71/8	Wilkinson
McGuire, Timothy	Jackson	Cockrans	282/24	Wilkinson
McHargue, Alexander	Jackson	Wrights	333/22	Wilkinson
McHargue, James	Greene	Dawsons	141/16	Wilkinson
McIntosh, Barbara	McIntosh		204/15	Wilkinson
McIntosh, Daniel	Greene	Flournoys	58/23	Wilkinson
McIntosh, Hemp	McIntosh		38/23	Wilkinson
McIntosh, Lach	McIntosh		179/6	Wilkinson
McIntosh, Lach	McIntosh		48/18	Wilkinson
McIntosh, Lydia	Greene	Flournoys	281/11	Wilkinson
McIntosh, Sarah(Wid.)	Chatham	Pettybones	147/10	Wilkinson
McIntyre, Archibald	Wilkinson		60/6	Wilkinson
McIver, Brice	Franklin	Wems'	152/22	Wilkinson
McKelroy, Reubin	Clarke	Cooks	118/22	Wilkinson
McKelroy, Reubin	Clarke	Cooks	93/8	Baldwin
McKenney, Hix	Hancock	Shivers	70/19	Baldwin
McKenzie, John	Hancock	Candlers	103/13	Baldwin
McKey, Wm.(Wid.of)	Chatham	Pettybones	257/7	Wilkinson
McKie, Kitty(Orph.)	Richmond		194/22	Wilkinson
McKie, Peter(Orph.)	Richmond		194/22	Wilkinson
McKie, Sally(Orph.)	Richmond		194/22	Wilkinson
McKie, Samuel	Franklin	Allens	118/13	Wilkinson
McKingney, Beatia	Clarke	Mitchells	285/21	Wilkinson
McKinley, Mary	Washington	Wiggins	91/18	Baldwin
McKinne, John(B.L.)	Richmond		107/16	Wilkinson
McKinney's, Tilman(Orphs.)	Washington	Wiggins'	41/12	Baldwin
McKinnie, Barney	Richmond		145/14	Wilkinson
McKinsey's, Wm.(Orphs.)	Washington	Holts	136/13	Baldwin
McKinzie, Daniel W.	Chatham	Abrahams	99/6	Wilkinson
McKinzie, John	Washington	Willis'	134/10	Baldwin
McKissac, James	Hancock	Weeks'	294/17	Wilkinson
McKissac, James	Hancock	Weeks	208/21	Wilkinson
McKleroy, Louis	Jackson	Johnsons	39/26	Wilkinson
McLaws, Alexander	Richmond		98/17	Wilkinson
McLean's, Jas. (Orphs.)	Wilkes	Heards	166/10	Wilkinson
McLean, Andrew	Camden	Hardees	47/21	Wilkinson
McLean, Andrew	Chatham	McLeans	3/12	Wilkinson
McLean, James	Franklin	Thompsons	40/9	Baldwin
McLean, James	Franklin	Thompsons	69/24	Wilkinson
McLean, Thomas	Chatham	Herbs	243/14	Wilkinson
McLean, Wm.	Richmond		107/16	Wilkinson
McLee, John	Burke	Mulkeys	12/25	Wilkinson
McLeland, John	Tattnall	Halls	188/12	Wilkinson
McLellan, John	Hancock	Coffees	80/19	Wilkinson
McLemore, Wm.	Hancock	Smiths	279/20	Wilkinson
McLendon, Dennis	Washington	Andersons	118/8	Baldwin
McLendon, Jacob	Wilkes	Normans	64/18	Baldwin
McLendon, Lewis	Jackson	Hendersons	195/10	Wilkinson
McLendon, Lewis	Wilkes	Harris'	208/27	Wilkinson
McLendon, Mason	Washington	Kendricks	135/8	Wilkinson
McLendon, Penyma	Washington	Andersons	101/21	Wilkinson
McLendon, Willis	Wilkinson		165/15	Baldwin
McLeod, Ann	McIntosh		53/18	Wilkinson
McLeod, Eliz.(Wid.)	Chatham	Pettybones	227/10	Wilkinson
McLeod, Francis H.	Chatham	Pettybones	121/18	Baldwin
McLeod, James	Glynn		286/14	Baldwin
McLeod, John	Wilkes	Heards	256/8	Wilkinson
McLeod, Norman	Chatham	Pettybones	162/16	Baldwin

NAME	COUNTY	MIL.DIST.	LOT/DIST	DREW LAND
McLeroy, Fanny	Elbert	Moons	3/10	Wilkinson
McLeroy, Henry Jr.	Elbert	Moons	105/10	Wilkinson
McMahan, Elizaeth	Burke	Montgomerys	102/8	Baldwin
McManis, Samuel	Richmond		132/19	Baldwin
McManis, Samuel	Richmond		9/6	Wilkinson
McMath, Philip	Wilkinson		208/16	Wilkinson
McMichael, James(Orph.)	Baldwin	3	286/22	Wilkinson
McMichael, John	Greene	Owsleys	110/7	Baldwin
McMillan, Arch'd.	Washington	Collins	142/14	Wilkinson
McMillian, William	Franklin	Cleghorns	136/15	Baldwin
McMullen's, James(Orphs.)	Burke	Montgomerys	102/25	Wilkinson
McMurphey, John	Greene	Alfords	222/2	Wilkinson
McMurray, Frances	Jefferson	Wrights	11/15	Wilkinson
McMurray, William	Washington	Howards	303/12	Wilkinson
McMurren, John	Warren	Flournoys	192/27	Wilkinson
McNabb, Elizabeth	Wilkes	Hendersons	40/11	Wilkinson
McNair, Daniel	Richmond		79/14	Baldwin
McNair, John Jr.	Columbia	6	257/11	Wilkinson
McNair, John(Orph.)	Liberty		120/7	Baldwin
McNatt, Benjamin	Chatham	Pettybones	236/8	Wilkinson
McNear, Daniel	Warren	Wilsons	345/9	Wilkinson
McNear, Jennett	Columbia	7	245/23	Wilkinson
McNear, Mary	Columbia	7	81/24	Wilkinson
McNeas', Henry(Orphs.)	Warren	Neals	240/25	Wilkinson
McNeel, Dann	Burke	Burks	158/7	Wilkinson
McNeely, Adam(Orph.)	Liberty		11/8	Wilkinson
McNeely, Hugh	Jefferson	Tarvers	7/23	Wilkinson
McNeil, Jane(Wid.)	Jefferson	Hardwicks	5/9	Wilkinson
McNeil, Sarah	Columbia	7	3/17	Baldwin
McNeiley, Robert	Baldwin	2	91/23	Wilkinson
McNiel, Daniel	Jefferson	Hardwicks	90/8	Wilkinson
McNorril's, Wm.(Orphs.)	Burke	Gordons	100/14	Wilkinson
McOwn, Daniel	Warren	Hills	242/22	Wilkinson
McQueen, Sally	Chatham	Neyles	109/7	Baldwin
McQueen, William	Chatham	Herbs	2/15	Wilkinson
McRea's, Robert(Orphs.)	Wilkes	Roreys	218/13	Baldwin
McTyre, Frizzell	Burke	Carswells	141/8	Baldwin
McTyre, John	Richmond		178/25	Wilkinson
McVay, David	Washington	Howards	3/19	Baldwin
McWhir, Wm.	Liberty		214/11	Wilkinson
McWright, Mary	Jefferson		343/14	Wilkinson
McWright, Mary	Jefferson		345/14	Wilkinson
Meaders, William	Warren	Carters	240/6	Wilkinson
Meador, Jonas	Greene	Carletons	37/7	Wilkinson
Meadows, Barnett	Franklin	Wims'	228/23	Wilkinson
Meadows, Dicey	Burke	Fields	197/11	Wilkinson
Meadows, Isham Jr.	Greene	Moores	61/17	Wilkinson
Meadows, Lydia	Greene	Moores	129/24	Wilkinson
Meals, Joshua Jr.	Richmond		12/14	Baldwin
Means, Hugh	Elbert	Roebucks	145/16	Baldwin
Means, John	Baldwin	5	255/11	Wilkinson
Means, Samuel	Baldwin	4	22/20	Baldwin
Means, Samuel	Baldwin	4	65/21	Wilkinson
Mears, William(Orph.)	Washington	Collins	196/15	Baldwin
Medders, Reubin	Baldwin	1	25/28	Wilkinson
Meeks, Nasse	Franklin	Hollingsworths	238/12	Wilkinson
Meeler, William	Wilkes	Youngs	196/6	Wilkinson
Meers, Elizabeth	Burke	Blounts	161/9	Baldwin
Meers, John	Burke	Blounts	197/15	Baldwin
Meers, John	Burke	Blounts	67/14	Baldwin
Megee, Felix	Clarke	Silmans	40/27	Wilkinson
Megee, Patrick	Clarke	Silmans	233/12	Wilkinson
Megrady, Polly	Franklin	Christians	76/6	Wilkinson
Megrady, Robert	Franklin	Christians	47/25	Wilkinson
Megrady, Silas	Franklin	Christians	41/20	Baldwin
Meigs, Joseph	Chatham		64/10	Baldwin
Mell's, John(Orphs.)	Liberty		95/18	Baldwin

NAME	COUNTY	MIL.DIST.	LOT/DIST	DREW LAND
Mell, Mary(Wid.)	Liberty		21/9	Wilkinson
Melson, Daniel	Hancock	Weeks	49/18	Baldwin
Melton's, Joshua(Orphs.)	Washington	Kendricks	137/13	Wilkinson
Melton, Nathaniel	Bulloch	Denmarks	78/17	Baldwin
Melton, Timothy	Montgomery	57	176/19	Baldwin
Melton, Wm.(Col.)	Greene	Greers	186/15	Baldwin
Melvill, Thomas	Liberty		115/28	Baldwin
Mendenhall's, Marmad.(Orps.)	Columbia	10	72/10	Wilkinson
Mendenhall, Thos.Jr.	Chatham	Whites	26/11	Wilkinson
Mendenhall, Thos.Sr.	Chatham	Whites	473/7	Wilkinson
Mercer, James	Franklin	Dixons	111/24	Wilkinson
Mercer, John	Wilkes	Hendricks	406/8	Wilkinson
Mercer, Solomon	Montgomery	58	96/16	Baldwin
Mercer, Stephen	Screven		307/7	Wilkinson
Mercer, Stephen	Screven	Williamsons	308/15	Wilkinson
Merchant, Isaac	Warren	Newsoms	277/16	Wilkinson
Merchant, Jacob	Warren	Newsoms	228/10	Wilkinson
Meridith's, Jas.(Orphs.)	Clarke	Butlers	251/7	Wilkinson
Meriwether, David(Gen.)	Clarke	Harpers	38/13	Wilkinson
Meriwether, David(m)	Clarke	Browns	41/6	Baldwin
Meriwether, James	Jefferson	Wrights	43/6	Wilkinson
Meriwether, Mary(Wid.)	Wilkes	Sheets	92/13	Baldwin
Meriwether, Sally(Orph.)	Oglethorpe	Smiths	121/7	Baldwin
Meriwether, Thomas Sr.	Columbia	3	122/19	Baldwin
Meriwether, William Sr.	Columbia	3	131/11	Baldwin
Merony, Nathan	Oglethorpe	Hitchcocks	24/13	Wilkinson
Messer, Wm.	Clarke	Browns	247/15	Baldwin
Messer, Wm.	Richmond		135/13	Baldwin
Metzger, John	Effingham		49/14	Wilkinson
Michael, Joseph	Clarke	Butlers	23/14	Wilkinson
Micklejohn, George	Burke	Montgomerys	9/24	Wilkinson
Mickler, Jacob	Camden	Smiths	429/7	Wilkinson
Mickler, Peter	Camden	Smiths	169/11	Baldwin
Mickler, Peter	Camden	Smiths	316/10	Wilkinson
Middlebrooks, John	Hancock	Holts	2/16	Wilkinson
Middlebrooks, John	Hancock	Holts	99/6	Baldwin
Middleton, James	Wayne	3	128/21	Wilkinson
Middleton, Nanny(Wid.)	Greene	Greers	144/27	Wilkinson
Middleton, Robert	Clarke	Robinsons	25/10	Wilkinson
Middleton, Robert	Elbert	Thompsons	76/7	Baldwin
Middleton, Zacceus	Clarke	Robinsons	273/13	Wilkinson
Miears, Thomas	Washington	Chivers	289/12	Wilkinson
Miers, Joshua	Greene	Stewarts	286/8	Wilkinson
Mikell's, John(Orphs.)	Bulloch	Denmarks	149/9	Wilkinson
Mikell, Alexander	Bulloch	Williams	59/8	Wilkinson
Mikell, James	Liberty		84/9	Wilkinson
Mikell, James	Liberty		95/18	Baldwin
Mikell, William	Bulloch	Williams	151/23	Wilkinson
Milam, Benjamin	Jackson	Cockrans	17/13	Baldwin
Milburn, Rebecca	Greene	Carltons	147/15	Baldwin
Miles, Rebecca	Columbia	7	230/16	Wilkinson
Miles, Thomas	Washington	Holts	58/25	Wilkinson
Miles, William	Columbia	10	122/23	Wilkinson
Miles, William	Wilkes	Coopers	258/21	Wilkinson
Miles, William	Wilkes	Coopers	40/10	Wilkinson
Millagan, Hugh Sr.	Columbia	6	54/16	Wilkinson
Milledge, Philip	Chatham	Neyles	185/10	Wilkinson
Millen, George	Chatham	Whites	106/28	Wilkinson
Miller's, Philip(Orphs.)	Burke	Mulkeys	5/25	Wilkinson
Miller's, Philips(Orphs.)	Burke	Mulkeys	165/16	Baldwin
Miller, Andrew	Wilkinson		32/17	Wilkinson
Miller, Benjamin	Bulloch	Parishs	141/20	Wilkinson
Miller, Cynthia	Screven	Williamsons	166/17	Baldwin
Miller, Daniel	Burke	Mulkeys	44/16	Baldwin
Miller, David(Orph.)	Chatham	Pettybones	241/7	Wilkinson
Miller, David	Franklin	Everetts	240/14	Wilkinson
Miller, David	Franklin	Everetts	84/9	Baldwin

NAME	COUNTY	MIL.DIST.	LOT/DIST	DREW LAND
Miller, Eliz.L.(Orph.)	Chatham	Abrahams	214/17	Wilkinson
Miller, Ezekiel	Warren	Hills	226/20	Wilkinson
Miller, Henry	Hancock	Hudsons	79/19	Baldwin
Miller, Hugh	Liberty		188/16	Wilkinson
Miller, James Jr.	Franklin	Everetts	56/7	Baldwin
Miller, James Sr.	Hancock	Birdsongs	260/11	Wilkinson
Miller, James Sr.	Hancock	Birdsongs	98/19	Baldwin
Miller, James	Baldwin	1	250/21	Wilkinson
Miller, James	Wilkinson		163/12	Baldwin
Miller, Jane(Wid.)	Baldwin	1	79/16	Baldwin
Miller, Jeremiah	Burke	Martins	29/11	Wilkinson
Miller, Jeremiah	Burke	Martins	68/24	Wilkinson
Miller, John	Glynn		324/21	Wilkinson
Miller, John C.	Effingham		24/12	Baldwin
Miller, John P.	Wilkes	Hendersons	57/7	Baldwin
Miller, John(B.S.)	Hancock	Thomas'	205/14	Wilkinson
Miller, John	Bulloch	Parishs	58/18	Wilkinson
Miller, John	Jackson	Hendersons	179/24	Wilkinson
Miller, John	Screven	Olivers	21/10	Wilkinson
Miller, John	Washington	Renfroes	150/10	Baldwin
Miller, John	Washington	Renfroes	279/14	Wilkinson
Miller, Joseph	Columbia	10	402/7	Wilkinson
Miller, Joseph	Wilkinson		172/17	Wilkinson
Miller, Lewis	Washington	Wiggins	31/28	Wilkinson
Miller, Lewis	Wilkes	Hendricks	77/11	Baldwin
Miller, Mark	Baldwin	4	167/19	Wilkinson
Miller, Peter	Chatham	Pembertons	82/7	Wilkinson
Miller, Richard W.	Screven	Williamsons	59/9	Baldwin
Miller, Samuel	Clarke	Dukes	5/18	Wilkinson
Miller, Thomas B.	Liberty		239/24	Wilkinson
Miller, William Sr.	Screven		332/7	Wilkinson
Miller, William	Jackson	Wrights	95/8	Baldwin
Millican, Andrew	Franklin	Cleghorns	169/6	Wilkinson
Millican, Jane(Wid.)	Jackson	Johnsons	155/13	Baldwin
Millican, Wm.C.	Franklin	Cleghorns	176/17	Baldwin
Millirons, Christian C.	Columbia	7	150/23	Wilkinson
Millis', James(Orphs.)	Liberty		38/17	Baldwin
Mills, Ansil	Franklin	Cornelius'	86/12	Baldwin
Mills, Elijah	Jefferson		41/9	Baldwin
Mills, James	Lincoln	Kings	17/18	Wilkinson
Mills, John	Screven		149/13	Baldwin
Mills, Stephen	Screven	Hutchinsons	162/18	Wilkinson
Mills, Thomas	Chatham	Neils	38/7	Wilkinson
Mills, William	Chatham	Pembertons	163/17	Baldwin
Mills, William	Chatham	Pembertons	30/13	Wilkinson
Mills, Wm.Jr.	Lincoln	Kings	68/7	Wilkinson
Milner, John Jr.	Wilkes	Milners	62/13	Baldwin
Milner, Jonathan	Oglethorpe	Beasleys	95/11	Wilkinson
Mimms, David	Tattnall	Halls	10/26	Wilkinson
Mims, Benjamin	Montgomery	50	364/7	Wilkinson
Mims, David	Tattnall	Halls	197/14	Wilkinson
Mims, David	Warren	Jones	260/13	Wilkinson
Mims, Drury	Baldwin	1	49/24	Wilkinson
Mims, John	Wilkinson	3	268/12	Wilkinson
Mims, Leory	Warren	Carters	317/13	Wilkinson
Mims, Mary	Tattnall	Halls	164/9	Baldwin
Mims, Shadrack	Lincoln	Kennons	39/6	Wilkinson
Mims, William	Wilkinson		87/13	Wilkinson
Minis, Abigail	Chatham	Pembertons	91/16	Wilkinson
Minis, Judith	Chatham	Abrahams	10/7	Wilkinson
Minter, Anthony	Washington	Renfroes	168/24	Wilkinson
Minter, Berry	Warren	Bakers	169/14	Baldwin
Minter, Morgan	Washington	Renfroes	63/14	Wilkinson
Minton's, Joseph(Orphs.)	Hancock	Crowders	161/11	Wilkinson
Minton, James	Jefferson	Thomas'	313/9	Wilkinson
Minton, Wm.J.(S.of Jno.)	Wilkes	Roreys	135/28	Wilkinson
Mitchell's, Alexn.(Orphs.)	Columbia	9	110/21	Wilkinson

NAME	COUNTY	MIL.DIST.	LOT/DIST	DREW LAND
Mitchell's, Chas.(Orphs.)	Jackson	Wrights	212/26	Wilkinson
Mitchell's, John(Orphs.)	Oglethorpe	Beasleys	28/23	Wilkinson
Mitchell, Benjamin	Warren	Newsoms	4/12	Wilkinson
Mitchell, Henry	Greene	Alfords	267/14	Wilkinson
Mitchell, Jane(Wid.)	Clarke	Stewarts	188/27	Wilkinson
Mitchell, John F.	Burke	Forths	181/17	Wilkinson
Mitchell, John	Franklin	Allens	145/8	Wilkinson
Mitchell, John	Hancock	Shivers	29/15	Baldwin
Mitchell, John	Warren	Willsons	67/8	Baldwin
Mitchell, Joseph(Spanish)	Clarke	Butlers	228/8	Wilkinson
Mitchell, Joshua	Greene	Alfords	22/7	Wilkinson
Mitchell, Nancy	Oglethorpe	Popes	207/14	Baldwin
Mitchell, Ransom	Baldwin	3	18/11	Baldwin
Mitchell, Solomon	Warren	Newsoms	30/16	Wilkinson
Mitchell, Uriah G.	Washington	Andersons	175/14	Baldwin
Mitchell, Uriah G.	Washington	Andersons	7/28	Wilkinson
Mitchell, William	Chatham	Pettybones	355/10	Wilkinson
Mitchem, Elijah	Wilkes	Harris'	205/12	Baldwin
Mixon's, John(Orphs.)	Burke	Ballards	272/12	Wilkinson
Mixon, Jesse Sr.	Bulloch	Parishs	97/7	Wilkinson
Mixon, Nancy	Burke	Ballards	225/7	Wilkinson
Mize, James	Lincoln	Jones	84/14	Baldwin
Mizell, Charlton Jr.	Camden	Browns	156/12	Wilkinson
Mizell, James	Bulloch	Hendleys	53/9	Wilkinson
Mizell, William Jr.	Bulloch	Williams	489/7	Wilkinson
Mizelle, Eliz.(Wid.)	Screven		8/12	Wilkinson
Moaler, Frederick	Wilkes	Welborns	163/20	Wilkinson
Mobley, Alexander	Burke	Mulkeys	25/7	Baldwin
Mobley, Edward	Hancock	Holts	178/24	Wilkinson
Mobley, Eleazer	Jackson	Cockrans	351/7	Wilkinson
Mobley, Jethro	Jackson	Wrights	19/22	Wilkinson
Mobley, Solomon	Tattnall	Armstrongs	166/23	Wilkinson
Mobley, Stephen	Elbert	Mobleys	134/18	Wilkinson
Mock, John Jr.	Jefferson	Boswicks	84/28	Wilkinson
Molich, Jan	Liberty		131/20	Baldwin
Moncrief's, Caleb(Orphs.)	Columbia	3	101/15	Wilkinson
Moncrief, Josiah	Wilkes	Hendricks'	165/12	Baldwin
Moncrief, Noah	Wilkes	Hendricks	72/19	Baldwin
Money, Mary	Columbia	10	271/16	Wilkinson
Monk, Elizabeth	Bulloch	Parishs	26/8	Baldwin
Monk, Menon	Bulloch	Parishs	71/18	Wilkinson
Monk, Richard	Bulloch	Parishs	136/10	Wilkinson
Monk, William	Hancock	Candlers	13/8	Wilkinson
Montcrief, William Sr.	Lincoln	Gartrells	86/9	Baldwin
Montford, Joseph	Wilkinson		8/13	Wilkinson
Montfort, James	Wilkes	Roreys	243/23	Wilkinson
Montfort, John K.	McIntosh		279/13	Wilkinson
Montgomery's, Jas.(Orphs.)	Wilkes	Heards	256/9	Wilkinson
Montgomery, David	Wilkes	Malones	171/18	Baldwin
Montgomery, Eliz.(Single)	Hancock	Weeks'	214/15	Wilkinson
Montgomery, Hugh	Jackson	Wrights	25/18	Baldwin
Montgomery, Hugh	Jackson	Wrights	97/25	Wilkinson
Montgomery, Hugh	Jefferson	Bostwicks	117/24	Wilkinson
Montgomery, James	Jackson	Johnsons	70/14	Wilkinson
Montgomery, Jane	Jefferson	Tarvers	67/21	Wilkinson
Montgomery, Robert	Jackson	Cockrans	24/9	Baldwin
Montgomery, Robert	Jefferson	Tarvers	146/16	Baldwin
Montgomery, Samuel	Burke	Montgomerys	176/8	Wilkinson
Moody, Benjamin	Greene	Carletons	310/11	Wilkinson
Moody, Benjamin	Liberty		36/16	Baldwin
Moody, Daniel	Washington	Willis'	210/18	Wilkinson
Moody, Granville	Warren	Bakers	249/7	Wilkinson
Moody, James	Liberty		260/14	Wilkinson
Moody, Samuel	Franklin	Cleghorns	42/9	Wilkinson
Moody, Solomon	Camden	Hardees	33/18	Baldwin
Moon's, Jacob(Orphs.)	Hancock	Holts	132/10	Baldwin
Moon, Archelaus	Elbert	Moons	140/12	Wilkinson

NAME	COUNTY	MIL.DIST.	LOT/DIST	DREW LAND
Moon, Archelaus	Elbert	Moons	209/26	Wilkinson
Moon, Olive(Wid.)	Warren	Newsoms	154/11	Baldwin
Moon, William Sr.	Elbert	Moons	6/12	Wilkinson
Moon, William Sr.	Elbert	Moons	85/28	Wilkinson
Moonaham, Wilson	Warren	Jones	176/18	Baldwin
Mooney, Agrippa(Orph.)	Richmond		299/15	Baldwin
Mooney, Charlotte(Orph.)	Richmond		299/15	Baldwin
Mooney, Jas.(Orph.)	Richmond		299/15	Baldwin
Mooney, Jno.(Orph.)	Richmond		299/15	Baldwin
Mooney, Marian(Orph.)	Richmond		299/15	Baldwin
Mooney, Richard(Orph.)	Richmond		299/15	Baldwin
Mooney, Sarah(Orph.)	Richmond		299/15	Baldwin
Mooney, Sophia(Orph.)	Richmond		299/15	Baldwin
Mooney, Valentine	Jackson	Cockrans	164/24	Wilkinson
Moore's, Ephraim(Orphs.)	Hancock	Gumms	131/7	Wilkinson
Moore's, Frederick(Orphs.)	Clarke	Martindales	190/12	Baldwin
Moore's, Jesse(Orphs.)	Columbia	7	32/26	Wilkinson
Moore's, John(Orphs.)	Wilkes	Hendersons	288/7	Wilkinson
Moore's, Jonas(Orphs.)	Clarke	Robinsons	112/9	Baldwin
Moore's, Richard(Orphs.)	Columbia	10	167/8	Baldwin
Moore's, Samuel (Orphs.)	Baldwin	4	8/21	Wilkinson
Moore, Alexander	Columbia	10	93/11	Baldwin
Moore, Andrew	Jefferson	Wrights	228/9	Baldwin
Moore, Andrew	Jefferson	Wrights	241/16	Wilkinson
Moore, Anthony	Richmond		61/18	Wilkinson
Moore, Augustus	Richmond		283/15	Wilkinson
Moore, Augustus	Richmond		76/10	Wilkinson
Moore, Charity	Chatham	McLeans	255/16	Wilkinson
Moore, Charles	Oglethorpe	Hudsons	153/20	Wilkinson
Moore, Charles	Oglethorpe	Hudsons	297/16	Wilkinson
Moore, Davis	Burke	Forths	1/15	Baldwin
Moore, Ebenezer	Hancock	Gumms	28/19	Baldwin
Moore, Elijah Sr.	Hancock	Gumms	18/18	Baldwin
Moore, Eliza(Orph.)	Bryan	Austins	28/16	Baldwin
Moore, George	Oglethorpe	Beasleys	320/20	Baldwin
Moore, Hartwell	Baldwin	1	42/25	Wilkinson
Moore, Hartwell	Baldwin	1	99/26	Wilkinson
Moore, Henry	Burke	Burks	150/12	Wilkinson
Moore, Hiram	Baldwin	3	55/16	Wilkinson
Moore, Isaac	Greene	Flournoys	164/13	Wilkinson
Moore, Jacob	Burke	Blounts	38/7	Baldwin
Moore, Jacob	Hancock	Candlers	224/16	Baldwin
Moore, James	Burke	Forths	236/14	Baldwin
Moore, James	Greene	Stewarts	272/9	Wilkinson
Moore, James	Jackson	Cockrans	46/27	Wilkinson
Moore, James	Montgomery	53	176/8	Wilkinson
Moore, James	Montgomery	53	240/10	Wilkinson
Moore, Jeremiah	Hancock	Huffs	267/19	Wilkinson
Moore, Jermiah	Hancock	Huffs	249/20	Wilkinson
Moore, Jesse B.	Burke	Forths	218/15	Baldwin
Moore, Jesse	Montgomery	51	229/20	Baldwin
Moore, Jethro	Richmond		147/20	Wilkinson
Moore, Joel	Clarke	Martindales	228/19	Baldwin
Moore, John C.	Oglethorpe	Hudsons	1/10	Wilkinson
Moore, John Jr.	Oglethorpe	Hewells	164/13	Baldwin
Moore, John	Baldwin	3	79/12	Wilkinson
Moore, John	Columbia	10	48/21	Wilkinson
Moore, John	Columbia	10	99/16	Wilkinson
Moore, John	Greene	Loves	47/27	Wilkinson
Moore, John	Screven		8/20	Wilkinson
Moore, John	Warren	Neals	108/18	Baldwin
Moore, Joseph J.	Columbia	10	333/10	Wilkinson
Moore, Joseph	Elbert	Clarks	110/17	Baldwin
Moore, Joseph	Jackson	Johnsons	133/17	Wilkinson
Moore, Leven	Hancock	Candlers	75/16	Wilkinson
Moore, Levy	Columbia	9	185/14	Baldwin
Moore, Mary Ann(Orph.)	Chatham	Whites	20/11	Wilkinson

NAME	COUNTY	MIL.DIST.	LOT/DIST	DREW LAND
Moore, Morris	Washington	Blackshears	188/22	Wilkinson
Moore, Morris	Washington	Blackshears	82/28	Wilkinson
Moore, Nathaniel	Oglethorpe	Hartsfields	103/22	Wilkinson
Moore, Richard H.	Oglethorpe	Hewells	125/7	Baldwin
Moore, Risdon Sr.	Hancock	Coopers	93/12	Baldwin
Moore, Robert	Warren	Hills	178/6	Wilkinson
Moore, Shadrack Sr.	Washington	Burneys	189/15	Baldwin
Moore, Shadrack Sr.	Washington	Burneys	25/24	Wilkinson
Moore, Thomas	Burke	Forths	212/28	Wilkinson
Moore, Thomas	Jackson	Johnsons	92/16	Wilkinson
Moore, William Sr.	Jackson	Johnsons	145/17	Wilkinson
Moore, William	Wilkes	Hendersons	162/20	Baldwin
Moore, Wm.	Greene	Greers	129/17	Wilkinson
Mooreman, Jacob	Hancock	Hudsons	38/21	Wilkinson
Moran, Elisha	Hancock	Candlers	117/17	Wilkinson
Moran, Susannah(S)	Hancock	Candlers	81/14	Baldwin
Morarity, Susannah D.	Richmond		49/23	Wilkinson
Mordecai, Samuel M.	Baldwin	1	202/12	Baldwin
More, Barnett	Wilkes	Malones	48/17	Baldwin
Moreland, Elizabeth	Jefferson	Hardwichs	101/12	Baldwin
Moreland, Jesse	Baldwin	2	31/15	Baldwin
Moreland, Mary	Greene	Carletons	53/9	Baldwin
Moreland, Turner	Hancock	Huffs	46/10	Wilkinson
Morell, Sarah(Wid.)	Montgomery	54	83/26	Wilkinson
Moreman, Thomas	Wilkes	Wellborns	86/24	Wilkinson
Morgan's, Wm.(Orphs.)	Columbia	8	144/28	Wilkinson
Morgan's, Wm.(Orphs.)	Wilkes	Heards	182/20	Wilkinson
Morgan, Daniel	Oglethorpe	Moores	238/13	Wilkinson
Morgan, David	Baldwin	1	119/13	Wilkinson
Morgan, David	Franklin	Christians	141/20	Baldwin
Morgan, George	Baldwin	4	376/7	Wilkinson
Morgan, Hardy	Oglethorpe	Watkins	61/18	Baldwin
Morgan, John (F.C.)	Oglethorpe	Hudsons	158/13	Baldwin
Morgan, Lewis	Effingham		335/11	Wilkinson
Morgan, Samuel Jr.	Franklin	Dicksons	55/22	Wilkinson
Morgan, Stephen	Elbert	Thompsons	160/9	Baldwin
Morgan, Stephen	Jefferson	Colemans	271/9	Wilkinson
Morgan, Thomas	Effingham		224/25	Wilkinson
Morgan, Thomas	Jackson	Hendersons	166/13	Baldwin
Morgan, William	Baldwin	2	95/18	Wilkinson
Morgan, William	Effingham		165/16	Wilkinson
Morgan, William	Jackson	Johnsons	244/7	Wilkinson
Morgan, William	Lincoln	Normans	184/14	Baldwin
Morgan, Wm.B.	Baldwin	5	107/8	Wilkinson
Morran, Jesse	Hancock	Candlers	230/14	Wilkinson
Morrell, James	Chatham	Pembertons	141/27	Wilkinson
Morrell, James	Chatham	Pembertons	157/11	Baldwin
Morrell, Richard	Chatham	Pettybones	137/11	Wilkinson
Morris's, Thomas(Orphs.)	Screven	Hutchinsons	54/26	Wilkinson
Morris, Chesley Jr.	Jackson	Wrights	152/12	Wilkinson
Morris, Chesley Sr.	Jackson	Wrights	72/7	Wilkinson
Morris, Henry	Baldwin	1	199/13	Wilkinson
Morris, James	Greene	Carletons	312/8	Wilkinson
Morris, James	Jackson	Cockrans	52/20	Baldwin
Morris, Jeremiah	Hancock	Candlers	273/23	Wilkinson
Morris, John	Jackson	Cockrans	256/25	Wilkinson
Morris, Mary	Warren	Willsons	151/6	Baldwin
Morris, Moses	Burke	Sharps	200/20	Baldwin
Morris, Robert(Orph.)	Baldwin	3	154/17	Baldwin
Morris, Winey	Baldwin	5	263/13	Wilkinson
Morrison, Alexander	Jackson		104/9	Baldwin
Morrison, Buncan	Elbert	Willifords	234/8	Wilkinson
Morrison, Donald	Hancock	Weeks'	131/14	Baldwin
Morrison, Donald	Hancock	Weeks	172/11	Baldwin
Morrison, Francis(Orph.)	Elbert	Morrisons	175/22	Wilkinson
Morrison, Jane	Elbert	Morrisons	231/13	Wilkinson
Morrison, Thomas	Elbert	Morrisons	114/8	Baldwin

NAME	COUNTY	MIL.DIST.	LOT/DIST	DREW LAND
Morrison, Washington	Elbert	Thompsons	225/16	Baldwin
Morriss, Wm.	Wilkes	Youngs	208/17	Baldwin
Morrow's, Wm.(Orphs.)	Camden	Ashleys	98/20	Baldwin
Morrow, Ewing	Greene	Moores	239/19	Wilkinson
Morrow, Robert	Baldwin	4	184/15	Baldwin
Morrow, Robert	Baldwin	4	32/13	Baldwin
Morse, Fountain(Orph.)	Burke	Sandifords	156/12	Baldwin
Morse, George	Richmond		139/10	Baldwin
Morton, Joel	Jackson	Cockrans	126/13	Baldwin
Morton, Joseph Jr.	Oglethorpe	Hatchetts	149/10	Wilkinson
Morton, Olympia M.(Orph.)	Franklin	Hoopers	90/24	Wilkinson
Moses, Joshua	Washington	Paces	34/15	Baldwin
Mosley, Benjamin	Greene	Greers	224/17	Wilkinson
Mosley, Maury	Elbert	Morrisons	140/15	Baldwin
Mosly, Jonathan	Baldwin	4	120/14	Wilkinson
Moss, Alexander	Lincoln	Kings	104/21	Wilkinson
Moss, Dempsey D.	Jefferson	Colemans	7/14	Wilkinson
Moss, Dempsey D.	Jefferson	Colemans	83/18	Baldwin
Moss, John Jr.	Lincoln	Kings	198/24	Wilkinson
Moss, John Sr.	Lincoln	Kings	83/27	Wilkinson
Moss, Lewis	Jefferson	Tarvers	227/8	Wilkinson
Moss, Lewis	Jefferson	Tarvers	298/22	Wilkinson
Moss, Nancy	Warren	Devereux's	188/10	Baldwin
Moss, Peter	Jefferson	Tarvers	212/12	Wilkinson
Moss, Samuel Jr.	Franklin	Griffiths	234/20	Baldwin
Moss, Samuel Jr.	Franklin	Griffiths	28/12	Wilkinson
Moss, Stephen	Oglethorpe	Hudsons	119/18	Wilkinson
Mote, Benjamin	Jackson	Cockrans	144/10	Wilkinson
Motley, Wilson	Washington	Howards	215/7	Wilkinson
Mott, Abraham	Screven		164/18	Wilkinson
Mott, Isaac	Screven	Hutchinsons	341/13	Wilkinson
Mounger, Edwin	Jefferson	Fultons	313/10	Wilkinson
Mountain, Robert	Jefferson	Fultons	74/9	Wilkinson
Moxley, Daniel	Burke	Blounts	34/9	Baldwin
Moy, Elijah	Burke	Thompsons	134/12	Wilkinson
Mozley, Brantley	Montgomery	54	329/22	Wilkinson
Mozley, Wm.	Lincoln	Jones'	140/21	Wilkinson
Mucklehannon, Christopher	Jackson	Henderson	64/16	Baldwin
Mucklehannon, Christopher	Jackson	Hendersons	121/13	Wilkinson
Muckleroy's, Jno.(Orphs.)	Oglethorpe	Smiths	35/15	Wilkinson
Muckleroy, Chas.	Oglethorpe	Hartsfields	287/15	Baldwin
Muckleroy, Edward	Oglethorpe	Hartsfields	129/10	Wilkinson
Muckleroy, Isaac	Oglethorpe	Moores	110/25	Wilkinson
Mulkey, Philip Jr.	Franklin	Cornelius'	174/8	Wilkinson
Mulkey, Philip	Burke	Fields	118/20	Wilkinson
Mulkey, Philip	Burke	Fields	75/14	Baldwin
Mulkey, Wm.	Burke	Ballards	47/17	Wilkinson
Mullair, Lewis	Liberty		150/6	Baldwin
Mullens, Thomas	Baldwin	2	151/12	Baldwin
Mullens, Thomas	Warren	Carters	2/17	Wilkinson
Mullican, Amsey	Wilkes	Sidwells	85/14	Wilkinson
Mullican, John	Wilkes	Coopers	1/12	Baldwin
Mullikin, Fielder	Wilkes	Sidwells	95/12	Wilkinson
Mullins', Peter(Orphs.)	Warren	Carters	218/14	Baldwin
Mullins, Jeremiah Jr.	Hancock	Smiths	286/13	Wilkinson
Mullins, Jeremiah Sr.	Hancock	Smiths	199/19	Wilkinson
Mullins, Priscilla	Baldwin	2	49/17	Wilkinson
Mullons, Geon	Baldwin	2	244/14	Baldwin
Mumford, Susannah	Greene	Carletons	216/25	Wilkinson
Munroe, Niel Sr.	Montgomery	54	85/6	Baldwin
Munroe, Peter	Montgomery	54	220/8	Wilkinson
Munroe, Sarah(Wid.)	Montgomery	54	344/13	Wilkinson
Murphey's, Thos.(Orphs.)	Burke	Sharps	178/28	Wilkinson
Murphey, Ambrose	Washington	Collins'	247/19	Wilkinson
Murphey, Ambrose	Washington	Collins	309/24	Wilkinson
Murphey, Charity	Burke	Hilliards	29/19	Wilkinson
Murphey, James	Hancock	Thomas'	174/9	Baldwin

NAME	COUNTY	MIL.DIST.	LOT/DIST	DREW LAND
Murphey, James	Richmond		193/23	Wilkinson
Murphey, James	Washington	Garretts	250/11	Wilkinson
Murphey, John	Wilkes	Welborns	246/23	Wilkinson
Murphey, John	Wilkes	Welborns	54/23	Wilkinson
Murphey, Mills	Burke	Hilliards	110/11	Baldwin
Murphey, William	Burke	Blounts	317/9	Wilkinson
Murphey, William	Hancock	Thomas'	356/22	Wilkinson
Murray's, Thos.(Orphs.)	Oglethorpe	Hartsfields	201/25	Wilkinson
Murray, David	Lincoln	Mays	239/17	Wilkinson
Murray, William	Oglethorpe	Hartsfields	197/22	Wilkinson
Murray, Wm.	Wilkes	Coopers	59/27	Wilkinson
Murrey, Catherine(Wid.)	Burke	Thompsons	471/7	Wilkinson
Murry, Sarah(Wid.)	Oglethorpe	Hartsfields	219/15	Wilkinson
Murry, Stephen Jr.	Burke	Thompsons	85/6	Wilkinson
Murry, Stephen Sr.	Burke	Thompsons	277/7	Wilkinson
Murry, Tabitha	Elbert	Blackwells	130/7	Wilkinson
Musgrove's, Harrison(Orphs.)	Greene	Baxters	174/21	Wilkinson
Musgrove, John	Jefferson	Bostwicks	11/15	Baldwin
Muzzall, Anne B.	Greene	Carletons	197/6	Wilkinson
Myers', Daniel(Orphs.)	Liberty		211/15	Baldwin
Myers, George Sr.	Chatham	Whites	190/13	Wilkinson
Myers, George Sr.	Chatham	Whites	266/7	Wilkinson
Myers, Sarah	Glynn		218/12	Wilkinson
Myers, William	Glynn		198/10	Wilkinson
Myhand, James	Warren	Jones	123/11	Wilkinson
Myhand, James	Warren	Jones	130/19	Baldwin
Myhand, John	Warren	Jones	143/11	Wilkinson
Nail, Reubin	Tattnall	Halls	153/16	Baldwin
Naish, John	Elbert	Thompsons	235/6	Wilkinson
Nale, Julian Sr.	Elbert	Blackwells	183/6	Baldwin
Nall, Richard	Jackson	Wrights	123/21	Wilkinson
Napier's, Thomas(Orphs.)	Columbia	8	101/9	Baldwin
Napper, Priscilla(Wid.)	Wilkinson		58/8	Wilkinson
Nash's, Henry(Orph.)	Oglethorpe	Smiths	318/22	Wilkinson
Nash, Acton	Wilkes	Hendersons	199/25	Wilkinson
Nash, Betsy H.(S.W.)	Oglethorpe	Smith	193/12	Wilkinson
Nash, James	Jackson	Johnsons	257/10	Wilkinson
Nash, Peggy(Wid.)	Oglethorpe	Smiths	197/12	Wilkinson
Nasworthey, John	Hancock	Pinkstons	10/13	Baldwin
Neal, Ann(D.of Basil)	Columbia	11	12/13	Baldwin
Neal, Stephen	Franklin	Wems'	139/17	Wilkinson
Neal, Thomas	Montgomery	56	17/28	Wilkinson
Neel, Joseph	Elbert	Keelings	210/24	Wilkinson
Neely, John	Jefferson	Thomas	34/25	Wilkinson
Neely, Thomas	Washington	Paces	205/16	Baldwin
Neely, Thomas	Washington	Willis'	75/14	Wilkinson
Nees, Gotthelf I.	Effingham		141/23	Wilkinson
Neesman, Mary	Chatham	McLeans	272/15	Wilkinson
Neidlinger, John G.	Effingham		164/12	Baldwin
Neidlinger, John G.	Effingham		45/8	Wilkinson
Neil, Julan	Clarke	Hopkins	206/27	Wilkinson
Neill, John	Washington	Paces	140/9	Wilkinson
Neilson, John	Richmond		40/20	Baldwin
Nelams, Jacob	Elbert	Keelings	159/19	Wilkinson
Nelms', Wm.(Orphs.)	Elbert	Blackwells	138/8	Baldwin
Nelms, Jacob	Elbert	Keelings	176/17	Wilkinson
Nelson, John Jr.	Screven		140/12	Baldwin
Nelson, Jonathan	Hancock	Holts	21/18	Wilkinson
Nelson, Polly	Hancock	Hudsons	383/7	Wilkinson
Nelson, Samuel	Jackson	Hendersons	48/18	Baldwin
Nelson, Sylvester	Jackson	Wrights	52/18	Baldwin
Nelson, Wm.Jr.	Montgomery	52	96/25	Wilkinson
Nelson, Wm.T.	Montgomery	52	49/20	Baldwin
Nephew, James	McIntosh		50/14	Wilkinson
Neron, Eli	Clarke	Martins	105/17	Wilkinson
Nesbett, Andrew B.	Franklin	Christians	135/7	Baldwin
Nesbitt, Allen	Richmond		88/18	Wilkinson

NAME	COUNTY	MIL.DIST.	LOT/DIST	DREW LAND
Nessler, Frederick	Burke	Spains	284/11	Wilkinson
Netherclift, Alexander	Bryan	Austins	221/13	Wilkinson
Nettles, James	Franklin	Allens	148/11	Baldwin
Nevils, Nelly(Orph.)	Richmond		252/15	Baldwin
Nevis, John	Warren	Neals	121/12	Wilkinson
New, John	Clarke	Stewarts	302/7	Wilkinson
Newall, Samuel	Greene	Stewarts	65/14	Baldwin
Newberry, Joshua H.	Franklin	Yowells	33/6	Wilkinson
Newberry, Thomas	Hancock	Gumms	51/14	Wilkinson
Newberry, Thomas	Hancock	Gumms	89/20	Baldwin
Newborn, Archibald	Elbert	Blackwells	180/10	Wilkinson
Newborn, Archibald	Elbert	Blackwells	252/20	Baldwin
Newby, Jesse	Hancock	Weeks	160/12	Baldwin
Newdigate, Penelope(Wid.)	Chatham	Pettybones	120/23	Wilkinson
Newman's, Samuel(Orphs.)	Warren	Flournoys	258/19	Wilkinson
Newman, Fanny	Hancock	Barksdales	75/19	Wilkinson
Newman, James Jr.	Bulloch	Denmarks	56/15	Baldwin
Newman, John	Warren	Flournoys	180/14	Baldwin
Newman, Thomas	Columbia	6	199/8	Wilkinson
Newnon, Eleanor(Wid.)	Clarke	Robinsons	177/13	Wilkinson
Newsom's, Carter(Orphs.)	Washington	Blackshears	126/21	Wilkinson
Newsom's, Joeday	Warren	Newsoms	178/19	Wilkinson
Newsom's, Robt.(Orphs.)	Hancock	Wallers	63/7	Wilkinson
Newsom's, Solomon(Orph.)	Warren	Newsoms	94/11	Wilkinson
Newsom, Hardy	Warren	Willsons	144/20	Baldwin
Newsom, Hardy	Warren	Willsons	19/26	Wilkinson
Newsom, Joel	Greene	Watsons	191/19	Wilkinson
Newsom, Ricks	Warren	Newsoms	46/14	Wilkinson
Newsom, William	Baldwin	4	213/21	Wilkinson
Newsom, William	Baldwin	4	233/14	Wilkinson
Newton, Joseph	Baldwin	1	216/26	Wilkinson
Newton, Joseph	Baldwin	1	35/7	Wilkinson
Newton, Joshua	Montgomery	54	168/12	Baldwin
Newton, Moses(Dr.)	Jefferson	Colemans	177/6	Baldwin
Newton, Philip	Screven		152/8	Wilkinson
Newton, Thomas	Franklin	Christians	310/22	Wilkinson
Neyland, Gilbert	Burke	Bynes	65/18	Baldwin
Neyland, John	Burke	Ballard	20/12	Wilkinson
Neyland, John	Washington	Kendricks	8/12	Baldwin
Neyland, Joshua	Burke	Carswells	291/9	Wilkinson
Neyland, Nancy	Washington	Kendricks	200/24	Wilkinson
Niblack, William	Camden	Crews	12/15	Wilkinson
Niblack, William	Camden	Crews	233/26	Wilkinson
Niblet, Nancy	Clarke	Robinsons	339/12	Wilkinson
Niblitt, Tilman	Warren	Bakers	106/25	Wilkinson
Nicholas, Jonathan	Jackson	Wrights	252/13	Wilkinson
Nicholes, Jonathan	Hancock	Pinkstons	223/19	Wilkinson
Nicholes, Ramsom	Clarke	Hitchcocks	41/16	Wilkinson
Nichols, James Jr.	Burke	Blounts	107/26	Wilkinson
Nichols, James	Clarke	Trammells	294/15	Baldwin
Nichols, William	Burke	Blounts	113/7	Wilkinson
Nichols, William	Burke	Blounts	37/12	Wilkinson
Nicholson, Davis	Baldwin	4	31/21	Wilkinson
Nicholson, Harris	Wilkinson		157/13	Baldwin
Nicholson, James H.	Greene	Carletons	170/15	Baldwin
Nicholson, John	Oglethorpe	Hudsons	154/27	Wilkinson
Nicholson, John	Screven	Williamsons	94/6	Wilkinson
Nicholson, Joseph	Wilkes	Parks	110/20	Wilkinson
Nicks, David	Oglethorpe	Smiths	151/11	Wilkinson
Nicks, Robert	Oglethorpe	Watkins	293/16	Wilkinson
Nicolls, Henry	Effingham		60/11	Wilkinson
Nicolls, Henry	Effingham		60/24	Wilkinson
Nipper's, (Orphs.)	Bulloch	Hendleys	211/14	Wilkinson
Nix, John	Franklin	Hollingsworths	361/22	Wilkinson
Nix, Joseph	Elbert	Clarks	206/9	Wilkinson
Nix, Lucy	Elbert	Blackwells	96/19	Baldwin
Nix, Sarah(Wid.)	Franklin	Yowells	122/9	Baldwin

NAME	COUNTY	MIL.DIST.	LOT/DIST	DREW LAND
Nixon, John	Clarke	Mitchells	102/14	Baldwin
Nixon, Joshua	Screven		7/22	Wilkinson
Nixon, Robert Jr.	Baldwin	3	19/19	Baldwin
Nixon, Robert	Baldwin	3	92/25	Wilkinson
Nixson, Hurial	Franklin	Everetts	379/7	Wilkinson
Nixson, John	Franklin	Everetts	93/23	Wilkinson
Nixson, Joseph	Franklin	Everetts	301/22	Wilkinson
Nobles, Leonard	Richmond		124/26	Wilkinson
Nobles, Lucretia(Wid.)	Burke	Burks	290/22	Wilkinson
Nobles, Solomon	Washington	Delks	105/7	Baldwin
Noland, James	Wilkes	Coopers	13/17	Wilkinson
Noleman, Anthony	Oglethorpe	Hatchetts	22/10	Baldwin
Nongazer, George Sr.	Chatham	Neyles	20/15	Wilkinson
Norman's, Rebecca	Liberty		133/22	Wilkinson
Norman's, Wm.(Orph.)	Liberty		168/9	Baldwin
Norman, Elijah	Wilkes	Sheets	170/20	Wilkinson
Norman, Jesse Sr.	Wilkes	Normans	253/19	Baldwin
Norman, Joseph	Jackson	Johnsons	187/27	Wilkinson
Norman, Lettice(Wid.)	Wilkes	Sheets	95/9	Wilkinson
Norman, Lewis	Wilkes	Normans	221/20	Baldwin
Norrington, Nancy(Wid.)	Hancock	Barnes	218/13	Wilkinson
Norris, James	Oglethorpe	Smiths	102/16	Baldwin
Norris, James	Warren	Neals	22/13	Wilkinson
Norris, Josiah	Oglethorpe	Moores	264/25	Wilkinson
Norris, Nancy(S.W.)	Oglethorpe	Moores	129/20	Wilkinson
Norris, Thomas	Wilkes	Hendricks	192/15	Wilkinson
Norris, William	Baldwin	2	35/27	Wilkinson
Norris, William	Richmond		42/18	Baldwin
Northington, David	Franklin	Bryants	278/8	Wilkinson
Northington, David	Franklin	Bryants	350/21	Wilkinson
Norton's, John(Orphs.)	Oglethorpe	Hatchetts	86/8	Wilkinson
Norton, William	Washington	Andersons	185/17	Baldwin
Norwood, James	Burke	Martins	403/7	Wilkinson
Nottage, Thomas	Bulloch	Parishs	241/9	Baldwin
Nowland's, John(Orphs.)	Wilkes	Normans	107/7	Wilkinson
Nun, Thomas	Franklin	Allens	317/7	Wilkinson
Nunley, Eliz.	Oglethorpe	Smiths	277/17	Wilkinson
Nunley, Moses	Oglethorpe	Smiths	247/22	Wilkinson
Nunley, Patsy(S.W.)	Oglethorpe	Smiths	246/20	Wilkinson
Nunn's, James(Orphs.)	Washington	Olivers	36/24	Wilkinson
Nunn, Francis	Jackson	Hendersons	153/10	Wilkinson
Nunn, Nimrod	Warren	Newsoms	93/9	Wilkinson
Nunn, William	Baldwin	1	2/25	Wilkinson
Nunn, William	Washington	Olivers	155/10	Wilkinson
Nunn, Zepheniah	Elbert	Keelings	64/9	Wilkinson
O'Bannon, Elijah	Baldwin	1	116/18	Baldwin
O'Barr, John	Oglethorpe	Hudsons	215/17	Baldwin
O'Barr, John	Oglethorpe	Hudsons	39/21	Wilkinson
O'Berry, Henry	Effingham		111/22	Wilkinson
O'Berry, James	Baldwin	1	241/23	Wilkinson
O'Berry, John	McIntosh		181/10	Baldwin
O'Berry, Solomon	McIntosh		118/27	Wilkinson
O'Nail, Zachariah	Baldwin	3	164/6	Baldwin
O'Neal, Benjamin	Jackson	Hendersons	6/7	Baldwin
O'Neal, Daniel	Jackson	Cockrans	310/16	Wilkinson
O'Neal, Edward	Columbia	3	276/23	Wilkinson
O'Neal, Ferd	McIntosh		53/16	Wilkinson
O'Neal, Jesse	Washington	Howards	256/19	Wilkinson
O'Neal, John Jr.	Hancock	Gumms	92/20	Wilkinson
O'Neal, John	Warren	Neals	149/14	Wilkinson
O'Neal, Wooten	Greene	Moores	189/10	Wilkinson
O'Niel, Joseph	Oglethorpe	Smiths	50/11	Baldwin
O'Rear, John	Clarke	Robinsons	162/11	Wilkinson
O'Rear, Mariam(Wid.)	Clarke	Robinsons	334/7	Wilkinson
Oakes, John	Oglethorpe	Hatchetts	176/27	Wilkinson
Oaks, Isaac	Oglethorpe	Hatchetts	151/16	Wilkinson
Oaks, John	Camden	Hardees	16/8	Wilkinson

NAME	COUNTY	MIL.DIST.	LOT/DIST	DREW LAND
Odam's, John(Orphs.)	Screven		157/20	Wilkinson
Odam, Elizabeth	Glynn		99/10	Wilkinson
Odam, Jacob	Elbert	Moons	26/7	Wilkinson
Odam, Richard	Elbert	Moons	235/14	Baldwin
Odam, Richard	Elbert	Moons	70/12	Wilkinson
Odam, William	Elbert	Moons	215/14	Baldwin
Odum, Celia(Wid.)	Burke	Burks	137/17	Baldwin
Offutt, Jesse	Columbia	7	209/10	Wilkinson
Ofil, Elijah	Jackson	Cockrans	212/16	Wilkinson
Ogden, Mary(Orph.)	Elbert	Hillyers	264/15	Baldwin
Ogden, Sarah(Orph.)	Elbert	Hillyers	264/15	Baldwin
Oglesbie, Benjamin	Effingham		299/22	Wilkinson
Oglesby, William	Elbert	Faulkners	213/11	Wilkinson
Oglethorpe, John	Wilkes	Parks	118/16	Wilkinson
Ogletree, Clayton	Wilkes	Youngs	345/10	Wilkinson
Ogletree, Thomas	Wilkes	Youngs	235/20	Baldwin
Ogletree, Thomas	Wilkes	Youngs	79/15	Wilkinson
Oldfield, Wm.	Jackson	Johnsons	188/18	Baldwin
Olive, John	Columbia	7	277/24	Wilkinson
Olive, Samuel	Oglethorpe	Moores	80/26	Wilkinson
Oliver, Caleb	Baldwin	2	275/19	Baldwin
Oliver, Charles	Hancock	Shivers	327/15	Baldwin
Oliver, Dionesius	Elbert	Olivers	161/9	Wilkinson
Oliver, James B.	Richmond		135/6	Wilkinson
Oliver, John Sr.	Screven	Olivers	103/25	Wilkinson
Oliver, McCarty	Elbert	Morrisons	5/21	Wilkinson
Oliver, McDaniel	Screven	Olivers	142/21	Wilkinson
Oliver, McDaniel	Screven	Olivers	234/20	Wilkinson
Oliver, Peter	Warren	Flournoys	64/26	Wilkinson
Oliver, Rebecca(Orph.)	Richmond		275/9	Wilkinson
Oliver, Risdon Jr.	Screven	Olivers	22/19	Baldwin
Oliver, William	Elbert	Thompsons	130/10	Baldwin
Olliff's, John(Orphs.)	Bulloch	Williams	154/24	Wilkinson
Olliphant, Robert	Franklin	Everetts	203/15	Wilkinson
Oneyland, David	Washington	Kendricks	10/14	Wilkinson
Orr, James	Jackson	Cockrans	239/20	Baldwin
Orr, John	Jackson	Hendersons	76/26	Wilkinson
Orr, Rebecca	Jackson	Hendersons	80/15	Wilkinson
Orrick, James Sr.	Hancock	Smiths	93/18	Wilkinson
Osborn, George	Warren	Flournoys	77/25	Wilkinson
Osborn, John	Hancock	Pinkstons	94/7	Wilkinson
Osborn, William	Elbert	Mobleys	14/16	Wilkinson
Osborn, William	Elbert	Mobleys	184/25	Wilkinson
Osborn, William	Warren	Flournoys	224/19	Baldwin
Osborne's, Henry(Orphs.)	Camden	Smiths	138/11	Wilkinson
Osbourne's, Wm.(Orphs.)	Wilkes	Hendersons	163/14	Baldwin
Osgood, John Sr.	Liberty		86/9	Wilkinson
Osgoods, Josiah Jr.(Orphs.)	Liberty		228/11	Wilkinson
Osteen, Jesse	Oglethorpe	Hitchcocks	186/21	Wilkinson
Osteen, Jesse	Oglethorpe	Hitchcocks	193/15	Wilkinson
Osteen, Samuel	Oglethorpe	Hitchcocks	62/20	Baldwin
Oswald, Ann(Wid.)	Liberty		268/14	Wilkinson
Ounsell's, Daniel(Orphs.)	Burke	Sandifords	215/15	Wilkinson
Ousley, John	Elbert	Hillyers	172/14	Baldwin
Outlaw, Elizabeth	Montgomery	56	121/14	Wilkinson
Outlaw, Jeremiah	Montgomery	56	246/10	Wilkinson
Outlaw, John	Burke	Martins	167/9	Baldwin
Outlaw, John	Montgomery	56	127/15	Baldwin
Outley, Ginny	Washington	Burneys	118/10	Baldwin
Overstreet, Brassel	Tattnall	McDonalds	321/7	Wilkinson
Overstreet, Mary	Montgomery	57	245/15	Baldwin
Owen, David Sr.	Burke	Carswells	201/9	Baldwin
Owen, George	Greene	Baxters	58/20	Baldwin
Owen, Glenn	Oglethorpe	Bells	142/15	Baldwin
Owen, Henry	Greene	Jinkins	116/11	Baldwin
Owen, John	Oglethorpe	Hudsons	237/17	Wilkinson
Owen, Philamon	Greene	Baxters	152/11	Baldwin

NAME	COUNTY	MIL.DIST.	LOT/DIST	DREW LAND
Owen, Philamon	Greene	Baxters	222/7	Wilkinson
Owen, William	Oglethorpe	Hudsons	146/23	Wilkinson
Owen, William	Wilkes	Roreys	302/16	Wilkinson
Owens, John	Elbert	Thompsons	25/19	Wilkinson
Owens, Sam'l	McIntosh		195/17	Wilkinson
Owens, Thomas	Oglethorpe	Hartsfields	175/23	Wilkinson
Owsley, Weldon	Baldwin	2	265/14	Wilkinson
Oxford, Edward	Baldwin	2	136/12	Baldwin
Pace, Drury	Clarke	Martins	103/9	Wilkinson
Pace, Isaac	Clarke	Stewarts	197/14	Baldwin
Pace, James	Richmond		60/25	Wilkinson
Pace, Thomas	Elbert	Hillyers	360/21	Wilkinson
Pace, Wm.Sr.	Clarke	Martins	177/13	Baldwin
Page, Lemuel	Washington	Andersons	100/24	Wilkinson
Page, Solomon	Washington	Burneys	52/27	Wilkinson
Page, Thomas	Hancock	Winsletts	23/11	Baldwin
Page, William	Glynn		136/26	Wilkinson
Page, Wm.	Columbia	8	78/14	Wilkinson
Paine, Sylvanyne(Wid./Saml.)	Columbia	3	173/19	Wilkinson
Painter, John	Greene	Carletons	6/8	Baldwin
Pall, James	Wilkinson		176/21	Wilkinson
Palmer's, Samuel(Orphs.)	Screven		269/9	Wilkinson
Palmer, George	Burke	Carswells	120/6	Wilkinson
Palmer, John	Montgomery	54	48/20	Wilkinson
Palmer, Sally	Hancock	Gumms	197/20	Wilkinson
Palmore, Mary	Washington	Paces	29/8	Wilkinson
Paradise, James	Lincoln		208/10	Baldwin
Paradise, Wm.	Lincoln	Mays	162/16	Wilkinson
Paradise, Wm.	Lincoln	Mays	221/19	Baldwin
Parce, George	Franklin	Griffiths	196/8	Baldwin
Pare, Benjamin	Clarke	Martins	117/18	Baldwin
Parham, Haddon	Washington	Renfroes	130/19	Wilkinson
Parham, Mathew	Warren	Hills	199/16	Baldwin
Parham, Milly	Elbert	Faulkners	99/9	Baldwin
Parham, Thomas	Warren	Hills	290/9	Wilkinson
Parish, Ezekiel	Camden	Browns	280/10	Wilkinson
Parish, Henry	Bulloch	Parishs	239/15	Wilkinson
Parish, Hezekiah	Bulloch	Parishs	346/12	Wilkinson
Parish, Joel	Greene	Loves	2/13	Wilkinson
Parish, Mary	Bulloch	Parishs	10/8	Baldwin
Parish, Polly	Greene	Loves	257/25	Wilkinson
Parish, Thomas	Warren	Flournoys	213/6	Wilkinson
Parish, Wiatt	Hancock	Gumms	460/7	Wilkinson
Park, Joseph	Franklin	Allens	8/19	Baldwin
Parkard, Nathaniel	Screven		138/24	Wilkinson
Parker's, Simon(Orphs.)	Burke	Ballards	240/13	Wilkinson
Parker, Ann(Wid.)	Hancock	Weeks	101/18	Wilkinson
Parker, Asa	Jefferson		180/14	Wilkinson
Parker, Benj.	Hancock	Holts	9/23	Wilkinson
Parker, Caleb	Screven		188/9	Baldwin
Parker, Elisha	Tattnall	McDonalds	228/15	Baldwin
Parker, Gabriel	Screven		300/7	Wilkinson
Parker, Genus	Lincoln	Busseys	43/23	Wilkinson
Parker, Isaac	Hancock	Coffees	177/24	Wilkinson
Parker, Isaiah	Hancock	Weeks	114/17	Wilkinson
Parker, Jacob(S.of Jno.)	Baldwin	1	315/21	Wilkinson
Parker, John	Baldwin	5	106/15	Baldwin
Parker, John	Hancock	Birdsongs	73/19	Baldwin
Parker, John	Warren	Hills	46/10	Baldwin
Parker, Joseph	Wilkinson		123/12	Baldwin
Parker, Mary(Wid.)	Hancock	Winsletts	141/10	Wilkinson
Parker, Peter	Hancock	Winsletts	186/19	Wilkinson
Parker, Polly	Greene	Greers	138/19	Baldwin
Parker, Richard	Jefferson	Tarvers	264/15	Wilkinson
Parker, Samuel	Baldwin	1	202/20	Wilkinson
Parker, William	Chatham	Pettybones	138/11	Baldwin
Parks, Abraham	Elbert	McGuires	102/16	Wilkinson

NAME	COUNTY	MIL.DIST.	LOT/DIST	DREW LAND
Parks, Charles	Jackson	Hendersons	36/22	Wilkinson
Parks, Erastus	Glynn		344/21	Wilkinson
Parks, Henry	Franklin	Allens	43/20	Wilkinson
Parks, John B.	Jackson	Wrights	112/10	Wilkinson
Parks, John B.	Jackson	Wrights	160/11	Baldwin
Parks, John	Wilkes	Parks	1/23	Wilkinson
Parks, Lewis	Wilkes	Parks	24/15	Wilkinson
Parks, Marshel(Orph.)	Franklin	Cornelius	111/6	Baldwin
Parks, Mary(Wid.)	Elbert	Barretts	27/22	Wilkinson
Parmer, Ephraim	Baldwin	2	340/13	Wilkinson
Parmer, Joseph	Hancock	Winsletts	179/6	Baldwin
Parnell, Cyrus	Baldwin	2	132/17	Baldwin
Parnell, Daniel	Baldwin	2	243/17	Wilkinson
Parnell, James	Baldwin	4	159/14	Wilkinson
Parnell, James	Baldwin	4	206/24	Wilkinson
Parnell, Moses	Franklin	Bryans	74/23	Wilkinson
Parr, James	Richmond		60/25	Wilkinson
Parramore, James	Screven		87/22	Wilkinson
Parramore, John Jr.	Screven		236/17	Wilkinson
Parramore, John Sr.	Screven		112/12	Baldwin
Parramore, Thomas	Screven		164/22	Wilkinson
Parramore, Wm.	Screven		123/19	Baldwin
Parret, Susannah(Wid.)	Washington	Blackshears	65/25	Wilkinson
Parrett, Henry	Greene	Greers	375/22	Wilkinson
Parris, Jinny(Wid.)	Franklin	Yowells	48/8	Baldwin
Parrott, James	Baldwin	2	124/14	Wilkinson
Parsons', Josiah(Orphs.)	Warren	Jones	182/15	Baldwin
Parsons, Amos	Warren	Jones'	225/13	Wilkinson
Parsons, Amos	Warren	Jones	22/8	Wilkinson
Parsons, Thomas	Glynn		57/25	Wilkinson
Parsons, Thomas	Jefferson	Thomas'	384/22	Wilkinson
Parsons, Wm.	Jefferson	Fultons	168/11	Baldwin
Partin, Charles	Tattnall	Staffords	178/14	Baldwin
Partin, Charles	Tattnall	Staffords	40/7	Wilkinson
Partrick, Ephraim	Jackson	Johnsons	233/8	Wilkinson
Partridge's, Jesse(Orphs.)	Wilkes	Malones	51/20	Wilkinson
Pascal, Thomas	Lincoln	Gartrells	299/10	Wilkinson
Pascal, Wm.	Lincoln	Gartrells	129/22	Wilkinson
Paschal, Samuel	Wilkes	Wellborns	122/13	Baldwin
Pass, William	Baldwin	3	72/12	Wilkinson
Pate, James	Lincoln	Mays	57/18	Baldwin
Pate, Thomas	Baldwin	5	127/27	Wilkinson
Pate, Thomas	Jackson	Hendersons	211/21	Wilkinson
Pate, William	Hancock	Pinkstons	211/12	Wilkinson
Paterson, Milly(Orph.)	Greene	Watts	179/10	Baldwin
Patrick, David	Oglethorpe	Hudsons	121/11	Baldwin
Patrick, Ephraim	Jackson	Johnsons	161/18	Wilkinson
Patrick, Esther	Greene	Jinkens	137/7	Wilkinson
Patrick, John C.	Greene	Jinkins	56/26	Wilkinson
Patrick, John	Columbia	1	222/24	Wilkinson
Patrick, Jonathan	Greene	Jinkens	48/9	Baldwin
Patrick, Joseph	Greene	Carletons	162/8	Baldwin
Patrick, Joshua	Greene	Carletons	188/28	Wilkinson
Patrick, Margaret	Greene	Carletons	18/12	Wilkinson
Patrick, Robert	Greene	Carletons	242/19	Baldwin
Patrick, William	Oglethorpe	Popes	324/13	Wilkinson
Patten, Thomas	Clarke	Mitchells	275/13	Wilkinson
Patterson, Alexander	Elbert	Roebucks	226/23	Wilkinson
Patterson, Anna	Wilkes	Sidwells	170/8	Wilkinson
Patterson, Arthur	McIntosh		143/10	Wilkinson
Patterson, Chas.	Chatham	Hardens	164/8	Baldwin
Patterson, David	Richmond		217/25	Wilkinson
Patterson, David	Richmond		68/19	Wilkinson
Patterson, Francis	Bulloch	Hendleys	210/20	Wilkinson
Patterson, Isabella(Wid.)	Wilkes	Coopers	224/10	Wilkinson
Patterson, Isabella	Wilkes	Coopers	2/14	Wilkinson
Patterson, James	Elbert	Roebucks	50/18	Baldwin

NAME	COUNTY	MIL.DIST.	LOT/DIST	DREW LAND
Patterson, James	McIntosh		16/20	Wilkinson
Patterson, Jane	Greene	Carletons	63/27	Wilkinson
Patterson, John Jr.	Burke	Blounts	76/10	Baldwin
Patterson, John Sr.	Burke	Blounts	176/25	Wilkinson
Patterson, John Sr.	Burke	Blounts	256/13	Wilkinson
Patterson, John Sr.	Elbert	Roebucks	254/20	Baldwin
Patterson, Jos'h.	Elbert	Roebucks	4/23	Wilkinson
Patterson, Joseph	Burke	Blounts	49/7	Wilkinson
Patterson, Mary	Bulloch	Williams	127/17	Baldwin
Patterson, Nancy	Richmond		265/16	Wilkinson
Patterson, Peggy Ann	Richmond		72/16	Baldwin
Patterson, Polly	Bulloch	Williams	212/19	Wilkinson
Patterson, Tryon	Franklin	Yowells	49/19	Baldwin
Patterson, William	Burke	Blounts	320/17	Wilkinson
Patton, James	Jackson	Johnsons	203/20	Wilkinson
Patton, Samuel	Clarke	Silmans	190/9	Baldwin
Patton, Samuel	Elbert	Moons	40/9	Wilkinson
Paul, William	Lincoln	Kennons	162/6	Baldwin
Paulk, John	Columbia	6	191/26	Wilkinson
Paulk, Micajah	Montgomery	52	191/9	Wilkinson
Paxson, John	Elbert	Hillyers	69/8	Baldwin
Paxton, Joseph	Jackson	Hendersons	5/20	Baldwin
Paxton, Robert	Elbert	Willifords	241/10	Wilkinson
Paxton, Samuel	Elbert	Dyes	228/13	Wilkinson
Payne, Archibald	Clarke	Silmans	254/14	Baldwin
Payne, Benjamin	Richmond		177/12	Baldwin
Payne, Cleveland	Franklin	Thompsons	288/20	Wilkinson
Payne, Hensley	Franklin	Cornelius'	241/13	Wilkinson
Payne, John	Greene	Watsons	234/22	Wilkinson
Payne, Moses	Franklin	Yowells	398/7	Wilkinson
Payne, Poyndexter	Franklin	Thompsons	74/10	Wilkinson
Payne, Robert	Glynn		73/10	Wilkinson
Payne, William Sr.	Franklin	Cornelius'	91/15	Wilkinson
Peace, John	Hancock	Barksdales	16/21	Wilkinson
Peace, Major	Hancock	Barksdales	273/9	Wilkinson
Peacock's, Thomas A.	Liberty		103/15	Wilkinson
Peacock's, Wm.(Orphs.)	Liberty		182/28	Wilkinson
Peacock's, Wm.B.	Liberty		33/26	Wilkinson
Peacock, Abraham	Washington	Kendricks	140/18	Wilkinson
Peacock, Isham	Bulloch	Denmarks	126/19	Wilkinson
Peacock, Mary	Washington	Kendricks	334/15	Baldwin
Peacock, Samuel Jr.	Bulloch	Denmarks	40/16	Wilkinson
Peacock, Samuel Sr.	Bulloch	Godfreys	31/19	Baldwin
Peacock, Wm.	Oglethorpe	Smiths	177/11	Wilkinson
Peak, Abel	Franklin	Wems	98/14	Wilkinson
Peak, William	Baldwin	3	190/9	Wilkinson
Peake, Leonard	Columbia	3	114/13	Baldwin
Pearce, John Jr.	Greene	Greers	26/15	Wilkinson
Pearce, Joshua Sr.	Screven		121/20	Wilkinson
Pearre, John O.	Columbia	3	107/21	Wilkinson
Pearre, John Sr.	Columbia	5	194/25	Wilkinson
Pearson, Enoch	Elbert	Moons	90/23	Wilkinson
Pearson, Eoch	Elbert	Moons	176/14	Baldwin
Pearson, James	McIntosh		2/10	Wilkinson
Pearson, Thomas	Liberty		228/25	Wilkinson
Pearson, William	Washington	Kendricks	70/28	Wilkinson
Peddy, Polly	Washington	Kendricks	45/11	Wilkinson
Peddy, Rachel(Wid.)	Washington	Kendricks	215/18	Wilkinson
Peebles, Betsey(Miss)	Warren	Jones'	44/10	Baldwin
Peebles, Henry	Warren	Jones'	275/14	Baldwin
Peek, Solomon	Jackson	Hendersons	126/17	Baldwin
Peeke, Leonard	Hancock	Coffees	20/20	Baldwin
Peel, Richard	Jefferson	Hardwicks	56/16	Wilkinson
Peel, William	Jefferson	Bosticks	245/19	Wilkinson
Peeples, David(Orph.of N.)	Greene	Watts	218/26	Wilkinson
Peeples, Joseph	Greene	Watts	153/14	Wilkinson
Peeples, Joseph	Greene	Watts	18/13	Baldwin

NAME	COUNTY	MIL.DIST.	LOT/DIST	DREW LAND
Peevey, Abraham Jr.	Warren	Heaths	26/19	Wilkinson
Peevey, Abraham	Warren	Heaths	151/6	Baldwin
Peevey, Abraham	Warren	Heaths	98/23	Wilkinson
Peevy, Jane	Wilkes	Edges	79/9	Baldwin
Peign, Joseph	Wilkinson		209/23	Wilkinson
Pelton, Wm.	Warren	Jones'	177/12	Wilkinson
Pemblerton, Joshua	Greene	Moores	290/16	Wilkinson
Penington, Thomas	Burke	Bynes	168/12	Wilkinson
Penn, Benjamin	Elbert	Olivers	259/11	Wilkinson
Penn, Edmond	Oglethorpe	Beasleys	155/21	Wilkinson
Penn, Edmund	Oglethorpe	Beasleys	63/10	Wilkinson
Penn, Frances(Wid.)	Oglethorpe	Stewart	160/8	Wilkinson
Penn, Lucy	Elbert	Olivers	87/14	Wilkinson
Penn, Moses	Oglethorpe	Stewarts	250/9	Wilkinson
Penn, Sally	Elbert	Olivers	162/23	Wilkinson
Penn, Wilson	Elbert	Willifords	253/12	Wilkinson
Pennington, Isaac	Jackson	Wrights	307/24	Wilkinson
Pennington, Stephen	Montgomery	50	38/15	Baldwin
Pennington, William	Jefferson	Hardwicks	92/9	Wilkinson
Penrose, Ralph	Burke	Montgomerys	100/27	Wilkinson
Peoples, Henry	Jackson	Wrights	82/10	Baldwin
Peoples, Joel	Oglethorpe	Hudsons	146/12	Baldwin
Pepper's, (Orphs.)	Greene	Carletons	173/13	Baldwin
Perdew, James	Jefferson	Bosticks	65/10	Wilkinson
Perdew, Wm.Sr.	Jefferson	Bosticks	124/21	Wilkinson
Perdew, Wm.Sr.	Jefferson	Bosticks	226/14	Wilkinson
Perkins', Eirie(Orphs.)	Jefferson	Wrights	152/25	Wilkinson
Perkins, Benjamin	Washington	Renfroes	91/15	Baldwin
Perkins, Celiah	Burke	Spains	81/17	Baldwin
Perkins, Joseph	Washington	Renfroes	42/16	Baldwin
Perkins, Moses	Washington	Wiggins'	40/12	Baldwin
Perrett, Nathaniel	Hancock	Barksdales	13/20	Wilkinson
Perry, Ambrose	Washington	Blackshears	146/6	Baldwin
Perry, Benjamin	Warren	Hills	129/18	Wilkinson
Perry, Geo.C.(Orph.)	Burke	Mulkeys	380/7	Wilkinson
Perry, Jeremiah	Warren	Hills	467/7	Wilkinson
Perry, John	Hancock	Weeks	189/19	Wilkinson
Perry, Micajah	Warren	Hills	129/13	Wilkinson
Perry, Milly(Wid.)	Washington	Willis'	179/28	Wilkinson
Perry, Rebecca	Washington	Blackshears	203/18	Wilkinson
Perry, Richardson	Clarke	Martins	142/23	Wilkinson
Perry, Thomas	Jackson	Johnsons	154/22	Wilkinson
Perry, Thornton	Montgomery	50	40/10	Baldwin
Perry, Walter	Wilkes	Edges	379/8	Wilkinson
Perry, William	Greene	Armors	17/6	Baldwin
Perry, William	Greene	Armors	49/21	Wilkinson
Perryman, Daniel	Greene	Jinkins	223/18	Wilkinson
Perryman, David	Baldwin	3	278/9	Wilkinson
Perryman, Elisha	Columbia	5	105/9	Wilkinson
Perryman, Harmon	Warren	Jones	13/28	Wilkinson
Perryman, John	Columbia	10	85/25	Wilkinson
Petard, Thompson	Elbert	Moons	116/13	Baldwin
Peteet, John	Wilkes	Hendersons	201/10	Baldwin
Peters, Jemima	Wilkes	Coopers	244/24	Wilkinson
Peters, Jeremiah	Wilkes	Coopers	244/24	Wilkinson
Peters, John	Greene	Davenports	205/26	Wilkinson
Peters, Lewis	Wilkes	Coopers	59/21	Wilkinson
Peterson, John	Montgomery	51	2/22	Wilkinson
Petigrew, George	Jackson	Hendersons	164/17	Wilkinson
Petigrew, George	Jackson	Hendersons	53/17	Baldwin
Petigrew, John	Jackson	Hendersons	219/15	Baldwin
Petman, Jeremiah	Jefferson	Colemans	93/6	Baldwin
Pettee, Sally	Wilkes	Coopers	221/2	Wilkinson
Pettee, Susannah	Wilkes	Coopers	11/26	Wilkinson
Petters', Stephen(Orps.)	Wilkes	Roreys	332/9	Wilkinson
Petties, John	Clarke	Mitchells	149/15	Wilkinson
Pettybone, John	Chatham	Pettybones	4/16	Baldwin

NAME	COUNTY	MIL.DIST.	LOT/DIST	DREW LAND
Pettybone, John	Chatham	Pettybones	96/27	Wilkinson
Pettyjohn, Reubin	Jackson	Wrights	349/9	Wilkinson
Pevey's, Isaac(Orphs.)	Screven		69/25	Wilkinson
Pevy, Diall	Wilkes	Edges	187/22	Wilkinson
Pharr, Edward	Jackson	Hendersons	64/12	Wilkinson
Pharr, Peter	Jefferson	Wrights	411/7	Wilkinson
Phelps, James	Elbert	Faulkners	229/26	Wilkinson
Phelps, Thomas	Clarke	Silmans	111/26	Wilkinson
Phelps, Thomas	Clarke	Silmans	26/18	Baldwin
Philips, John	Burke	Blounts	103/16	Baldwin
Phillips', Wm.(Orphs.)	Bulloch	Godfreys	173/15	Wilkinson
Phillips, Aaron	Oglethorpe	Hitchcocks	70/12	Baldwin
Phillips, Benjamin	Clarke	Silmans	248/13	Wilkinson
Phillips, Budd	Columbia	6	62/17	Baldwin
Phillips, Daniel	Columbia	8	207/21	Wilkinson
Phillips, Elijah	Wilkes	Malones	43/24	Wilkinson
Phillips, George	Oglethorpe	Hatchetts	197/20	Baldwin
Phillips, Hardy	Greene	Flournoys	62/15	Baldwin
Phillips, Isaac	Clarke	Butlers	55/25	Wilkinson
Phillips, Isham	Wilkinson		249/19	Wilkinson
Phillips, James	Clarke	Cooks	174/18	Wilkinson
Phillips, James	Clarke	Cooks	342/20	Baldwin
Phillips, Jane(Wid.)	Montgomery	54	2/11	Baldwin
Phillips, Joel	Baldwin	5	48/25	Wilkinson
Phillips, John	Clarke	Butlers	430/7	Wilkinson
Phillips, John	Jackson	Wrights	74/13	Wilkinson
Phillips, Joseph Sr.	Wilkinson		36/19	Wilkinson
Phillips, Joseph	Jackson	Wrights	60/28	Wilkinson
Phillips, Lemuel B.	Greene	Jinkins	111/9	Wilkinson
Phillips, Levi	Oglethorpe	Hitchcocks	213/24	Wilkinson
Phillips, Levy	Oglethorpe	Beasleys	217/18	Wilkinson
Phillips, Mark	Greene	Jinkins	61/7	Baldwin
Phillips, Mathew	Greene	Watts	68/26	Wilkinson
Phillips, Nancy	Wilkes	Coopers	292/15	Wilkinson
Phillips, Solomon	Hancock	Barksdales	185/9	Wilkinson
Phillips, Thomas	Baldwin	2	86/15	Wilkinson
Phillips, William	Greene	Butlers	66/26	Wilkinson
Phillips, Wm.	Greene	Armors	25/20	Baldwin
Phips, Benjamin	Jackson	Hendersons	63/13	Baldwin
Pichard, Nancy	Baldwin	1	323/11	Wilkinson
Pickard, Micajah	Hancock	Barksdales	294/11	Wilkinson
Pickens, Gabriel	Elbert	Willifords	287/22	Wilkinson
Pickert, John H.	Warren	Devereux's	409/8	Wilkinson
Pickett, James Jr.	Lincoln	Flemings	130/11	Baldwin
Pickett, James Sr.	Lincoln	Flemings	127/16	Wilkinson
Pickett, James Sr.	Lincoln	Flemings	64/9	Baldwin
Pickring, Gabriel	Clarke	Silmans	62/21	Wilkinson
Pierce's, Abner(Orphs)	Jackson	Cockrans	171/8	Baldwin
Pierce, Benjamin	Richmond		404/7	Wilkinson
Pierce, George	Jackson	Cockrans	157/7	Wilkinson
Pierce, James C.	Chatham	Pembertons	75/7	Baldwin
Pierce, Joel	Jackson	Cockrans	244/15	Baldwin
Pierce, John	Burke	Sharps	252/24	Wilkinson
Pierce, John	Jackson	Cockrans	15/14	Baldwin
Pierce, John	Wilkes	Youngs	195/9	Baldwin
Pierce, Joseph	Burke	Blounts	1/12	Wilkinson
Pierce, Lewis	Oglethorpe	Stewarts	192/10	Wilkinson
Pierson, Jeremiah	Warren	Newsoms	81/13	Baldwin
Pike, Lewis	Jackson	Wrights	37/27	Wilkinson
Pilcher, Edward Sr.	Glynn		222/13	Baldwin
Pile, John	Oglethorpe	Beasleys	36/20	Baldwin
Pinchard, Thomas	Greene	Watts	220/20	Baldwin
Pinder, Joseph Wm.	Chatham	Pembertons	98/9	Wilkinson
Pinkard, John	Greene	Carletons	127/14	Baldwin
Pinkerton, David	Baldwin	5	121/24	Wilkinson
Pinkston, Basel	Washington	Collins	90/25	Wilkinson
Pinkston, Greenberry(Orp/J.)	Wilkes	Parks	55/14	Baldwin

NAME	COUNTY	MIL.DIST.	LOT/DIST	DREW LAND
Pinkston, John Jr.	Washington	Renfroes	131/26	Wilkinson
Pinkston, John Jr.	Washington	Renfroes	300/11	Wilkinson
Pinkston, John	Hancock	Barksdales	68/20	Wilkinson
Pinkston, John	Hancock	Barksdales	94/18	Wilkinson
Pinkstone, Greenberry	Wilkes	Coopers	48/15	Wilkinson
Pinkum's, Philip(Orphs.)	Tattnall	Armstrongs	15/17	Baldwin
Pinson, Isaac	Washington	Howards	229/15	Wilkinson
Pinson, James	Oglethorpe	Moores	222/17	Wilkinson
Pinson, James	Oglethorpe	Moores	67/15	Baldwin
Pinson, Joab	Washington	Howards	139/18	Baldwin
Pior, Edmund	Burke	Bynes	36/10	Baldwin
Pipkin, Harvey(Orph.)	Jefferson	Thomas'	60/14	Wilkinson
Pipkin, Sally(Orph.)	Jefferson	Thomas'	60/14	Wilkinson
Pipkin, Uriah(Orph.)	Jefferson	Thomas'	60/14	Wilkinson
Piquette, Lewis	Wilkes	Roreys	38/9	Wilkinson
Pitman, James	Jackson	Johnsons	114/7	Wilkinson
Pitman, Mary(Wid.of John)	Columbia	2	173/10	Baldwin
Pittman, Edward	Elbert	Morrisons	44/11	Wilkinson
Pittman, William	Baldwin	5	167/23	Wilkinson
Pitts', Lewis(Orph.)	Warren	Jones'	15/24	Wilkinson
Pitts, Anthony	Effingham		56/18	Baldwin
Pitts, Anthony	Effingham		61/16	Baldwin
Pitts, Hardy(Orph.)	Effingham		117/13	Wilkinson
Pitts, William	Clarke	Mitchells	55/24	Wilkinson
Pitts, William	Warren	Jones'	172/13	Wilkinson
Pitts, Wm.	Clarke	Mitchells	179/17	Wilkinson
Playle, Daniel	Screven	Olivers	214/25	Wilkinson
Pleasants, William	Hancock	Smiths	444/7	Wilkinson
Poe, Matilda(Orph.)	Richmond		29/8	Baldwin
Poe, Robt.(Orph.)	Richmond		29/8	Baldwin
Poe, Stephen	Franklin	Dixons	151/21	Wilkinson
Poe, Washington(Orph.)	Richmond		29/8	Baldwin
Poe, Wm.(Orph.)	Richmond		29/8	Baldwin
Pogue, David	Greene	Carletons	168/15	Baldwin
Poindexter, John	Bulloch	Parishs	166/12	Wilkinson
Poindexter, John	Bulloch	Parishs	63/9	Baldwin
Polhill, Thomas Jr.	Effingham		324/22	Wilkinson
Polk, Wm.	Clarke	Stewarts	111/8	Baldwin
Polk, Wm.	Clarke	Stewarts	83/21	Wilkinson
Pollard, Joseph	Wilkes	Hendersons	35/13	Wilkinson
Pollard, Joseph	Wilkes	Hendersons	55/9	Wilkinson
Pollard, Silvia	Elbert	Clarks	10/23	Wilkinson
Polock, John	Screven	Olivers	263/17	Wilkinson
Ponder, James	Oglethorpe	Hitchcocks	112/15	Baldwin
Ponder, James	Screven		95/28	Wilkinson
Ponder, Reubin	Elbert	Blackwells	33/14	Wilkinson
Ponder, Wm.L.	Oglethorpe	Hitchcocks	170/19	Wilkinson
Pool, Baxter	Richmond		107/10	Baldwin
Pool, Baxter	Richmond		21/14	Baldwin
Pool, Henry	Warren	Neals	232/13	Wilkinson
Pool, James J.	Lincoln	Normans	79/18	Baldwin
Pool, James	Jackson	Hendersons	50/6	Baldwin
Pool, James	Jackson	Hendersons	7/11	Wilkinson
Pool, Jilmon	Greene	Jinkins	316/15	Baldwin
Pool, Joseph(Orph.)	Jefferson	Bosticks	131/27	Wilkinson
Pool, Joseph	Jefferson	Bosticks	84/19	Wilkinson
Pool, Mary(Orph.)	Jefferson	Bosticks	131/27	Wilkinson
Pool, Nicholas	Warren	Bakers	347/21	Wilkinson
Pool, Sam'l.(Orph.)	Jefferson	Bosticks	131/27	Wilkinson
Pool, Stovall	Wilkes	Heards	193/22	Wilkinson
Pool, Tempey	Warren	Bakers	123/26	Wilkinson
Pool, William Jr.	Bulloch	Denmarks	60/20	Baldwin
Poole, Jeremiah	Baldwin	1	119/6	Baldwin
Pooler, John	Chatham	Abrahams	20/12	Baldwin
Pooler, Olivia M.	Chatham	Abrahams	148/12	Baldwin
Poore, Elisha	Wilkes	Malones	22/28	Wilkinson
Poore, Thomas	Warren	Carters	59/16	Wilkinson

NAME	COUNTY	MIL.DIST.	LOT/DIST	DREW LAND
Pope's, Henry(Orphs.)	Wilkes	Normans	37/24	Wilkinson
Pope, Alexander	Elbert	Hillyers	22/27	Wilkinson
Pope, Archelus	Oglethorpe	Hatchetts	3/23	Wilkinson
Pope, Barnaby	Hancock	Pinkstons	165/9	Baldwin
Pope, Burwell(Orph.)	Oglethorpe	Popes	170/10	Wilkinson
Pope, Isaac R.	Hancock	Pinkstons	286/11	Wilkinson
Pope, Jesse McKinny	Hancock	Weeks	35/10	Baldwin
Pope, John Sr.	Washington	Collins	115/7	Wilkinson
Pope, Saml.(S.of Chas.)	Columbia	1	145/12	Baldwin
Pope, Samuel	Hancock	Shivers	325/17	Wilkinson
Pope, Willie	Washington	Collins	25/13	Baldwin
Pope, Wylie	Oglethorpe	Popes	380/8	Wilkinson
Porch, Hartwell	Hancock	Huffs	271/15	Baldwin
Porch, Henry	Hancock	Crowders	138/8	Wilkinson
Porch, Henry	Hancock	Huffs	130/11	Wilkinson
Porch, Wm.	Clarke	Hopkins	66/7	Wilkinson
Porter, Annie(Orph)	Effingham		44/15	Baldwin
Porter, Benjamin	Wilkes	Sidwells	177/6	Wilkinson
Porter, John A.	Oglethorpe	Bells	213/19	Wilkinson
Porter, John T.	Warren	Neals	30/18	Baldwin
Porter, Nathaniel	Oglethorpe	Bells	316/14	Wilkinson
Porter, Nobles	Washington	Paces	309/9	Wilkinson
Porter, Richard	Warren	Jones'	284/16	Wilkinson
Porter, William	Warren	Newsoms	240/18	Wilkinson
Porter, Wm.Jr.	Wilkes	Wellborns	285/6	Wilkinson
Posner, Joseph G.	Jefferson	Wrights	189/18	Wilkinson
Poss, Chris.Sr.	Wilkes	Wellborns	2/17	Baldwin
Poss, Henry	Wilkes	Coopers	235/12	Wilkinson
Poss, Nicholas	Wilkes	Coopers	194/15	Baldwin
Post, John	Elbert	Faulkners	298/15	Baldwin
Post, Wm.	Clarke	Robinsons	69/18	Wilkinson
Poste, Samuel Sr.	Jackson	Wrights	271/17	Wilkinson
Potter, Pleasant	Hancock	Coffees	119/8	Wilkinson
Potts, Stephen Jr.	Oglethorpe	Beasleys	54/20	Wilkinson
Potts, Stephen	Jackson	Hendersons	35/9	Wilkinson
Potts, William	Jackson	Hendersons	63/28	Wilkinson
Pound, David	Hancock	Birdsongs	37/10	Wilkinson
Pounds, Richard	Clarke	Robinsons	148/10	Baldwin
Pounds, Richard	Clarke	Robinsons	87/10	Baldwin
Powell's, Edward(Orphs.)	Oglethorpe	Beasleys	49/16	Baldwin
Powell's, Hugh	Hancock	Huffs	135/23	Wilkinson
Powell's, John(Orphs.)	Hancock	Wallers	146/8	Baldwin
Powell's, John(Orphs.)	Jefferson		167/7	Wilkinson
Powell, Alexander	McIntosh		52/14	Baldwin
Powell, Benjamin	Columbia		10/21	Wilkinson
Powell, Benjamin	Montgomery	55	148/6	Wilkinson
Powell, Chas.Jr.	Washington	Delks	284/22	Wilkinson
Powell, Drury	Oglethorpe	Beasleys	321/10	Wilkinson
Powell, Elizabeth	Columbia	7	68/22	Wilkinson
Powell, Francis	Wilkes	Harris'	15/22	Wilkinson
Powell, George	Burke	Gordons	387/21	Wilkinson
Powell, Henry	Clarke	Browns	282/14	Wilkinson
Powell, Jesse	Washington	Blackshears	155/28	Wilkinson
Powell, John	Clarke	Hitchcocks	32/6	Baldwin
Powell, John	Oglethorpe	Beasleys	164/16	Wilkinson
Powell, Lewis	Burke	Gordons	61/28	Wilkinson
Powell, Mary(Blind)	Jefferson		227/16	Wilkinson
Powell, Phillip	Wayne	2	208/7	Wilkinson
Powell, Rachel	Columbia	7	205/23	Wilkinson
Powell, Reubin	Wilkinson		204/22	Wilkinson
Powell, Sampson	Montgomery	55	393/21	Wilkinson
Powell, Wm.	Warren	Newsoms	16/7	Baldwin
Power, David	Elbert	Groves	224/18	Wilkinson
Power, William	Elbert	Groves	107/11	Wilkinson
Powers, Wm.	Greene	Carletons	151/15	Baldwin
Poythres', Thomas(Orphs.)	Burke	Sharps	44/22	Wilkinson
Poythress', Francis(Orphs.)	Hancock	Coffees	290/24	Wilkinson

NAME	COUNTY	MIL.DIST.	LOT/DIST	DREW LAND
Poythress, Elizabeth	Hancock	Coffees	31/6	Wilkinson
Prater, Edward	Columbia	7	95/27	Wilkinson
Prather, Edward	Richmond		148/6	Baldwin
Prather, James W.	Wilkes	Coopers	200/17	Wilkinson
Pratt, Hillery	Columbia	11	24/7	Wilkinson
Presscoat, Thomas	Screven	Olivers	216/9	Wilkinson
Prestidge, John	Franklin	Henrys	216/9	Baldwin
Prestidge, Larkin	Franklin	Henrys	17/9	Wilkinson
Prestidge, Samuel	Franklin	Henrys	211/9	Wilkinson
Prevatt, James Jr.	Camden	Ashleys	323/9	Wilkinson
Prevatt, Peter	Camden	Browns	60/27	Wilkinson
Prewett, William	Elbert	Roebucks	211/26	Wilkinson
Price, Daniel	Wilkes	Hendricks	146/9	Wilkinson
Price, Edward(Orph.)	Greene	Armors	52/15	Wilkinson
Price, Eliz.(Wid.)	Chatham	Whites	271/25	Wilkinson
Price, Ephraim	Greene	Watts	160/14	Wilkinson
Price, Ephraim	Greene	Watts	296/9	Wilkinson
Price, Evan	Wilkes	Malones	17/27	Wilkinson
Price, Evan	Wilkes	Malones	313/8	Wilkinson
Price, John	Burke	Ballards	154/12	Wilkinson
Price, John	Burke	Fields	19/18	Baldwin
Price, John	Montgomery	50	96/28	Wilkinson
Price, Sarah	McIntosh		163/13	Baldwin
Price, Stephen	Clarke	Hitchcocks	69/16	Wilkinson
Price, William Sr.	Burke	Fields	2724/20	Wilkinson
Price, William	Washington	Collins	126/23	Wilkinson
Prichett, George	Elbert	Barretts	101/13	Baldwin
Prickett, Israel	Franklin	Cornelius'	59/19	Baldwin
Prickett, Jacob	Franklin	Bryans	210/14	Wilkinson
Prickett, John	Franklin	Dixons	326/21	Wilkinson
Prickett, Mary(Wid.)	Franklin	Cornelius'	14/17	Baldwin
Pridgen, Thomas	Bulloch	Williams	183/21	Wilkinson
Pridgen, William(Orph.)	Bulloch	Williams	56/13	Baldwin
Prignet, Helena(Orph.)	Richmond		211/13	Baldwin
Prince, John	Greene	Owsleys	49/14	Baldwin
Prine, Joseph	Franklin	Griffiths	167/6	Wilkinson
Prine, Joseph	Franklin	Griffiths	261/6	Wilkinson
Prior, Obadiah	Clarke	Tramells	169/28	Wilkinson
Pritchart, Rodum(Orph.)	Jefferson	Tarvers	262/21	Wilkinson
Proctor, Samuel	Burke	Martins	1/7	Baldwin
Proctor, Starling	Warren	Newsoms	224/21	Wilkinson
Proctor, William	Baldwin	1	231/9	Baldwin
Proctor, Wm.	Jefferson	Bosticks	92/11	Baldwin
Proctor, Wm.	Washington	Chivers'	158/6	Baldwin
Prophet, James	Greene	Flournoys	56/11	Wilkinson
Provost, Wm.	Chatham	Herbs	15/6	Wilkinson
Pruitt, Benjamin	Franklin	Christians	167/20	Wilkinson
Pruitt, James	Baldwin	2	103/14	Baldwin
Pruitt, Martin	Baldwin	2	438/7	Wilkinson
Pruitt, Samuel	Franklin	Wems'	80/12	Wilkinson
Prussell, Jacob(Russell)	Franklin	Hoopers	126/22	Wilkinson
Prussell, Jacob	Franklin	Hoopers	127/8	Baldwin
Pryor, Absalom	Jefferson	Thomas'	23/18	Wilkinson
Pryor, Allen	Greene	Watsons	11/15	Wilkinson
Pryor, Archibald	Elbert	Moons	59/28	Wilkinson
Pryor, John(Orph.)	Baldwin	1	20/27	Wilkinson
Pryor, John	Greene	Watsons	123/6	Baldwin
Pryor, Marlow L.	Baldwin	1	277/14	Baldwin
Pugh's, Jesse(Orphs.)	Wilkes	Edges	88/6	Baldwin
Pugh, Francis	Bulloch	Hendleys	156/27	Wilkinson
Pugh, Isaac	Jackson	Cockrans	185/14	Wilkinson
Pugsley, John	Jefferson	Thomas'	155/16	Wilkinson
Pullen, Elisha	Wilkes	Sheets	117/25	Wilkinson
Pullen, Robert	Greene	Dawsons	170/13	Wilkinson
Pullen, Robert	Greene	Dawsons	176/10	Wilkinson
Pullen, Thomas Sr.	Washington	Blackshears	225/16	Wilkinson
Pullen, William	Wilkes	Normans	96/20	Baldwin

NAME	COUNTY	MIL.DIST.	LOT/DIST	DREW LAND
Pullen, Wm.Sr.	Columbia	3	266/15	Wilkinson
Pumfey, John	Richmond		209/16	Baldwin
Purcel, Ignatius	Franklin	Hollingsworths	145/11	Baldwin
Purgason, Drury	Greene	Owsleys	202/9	Wilkinson
Purgason, Drury	Greene	Owsleys	336/11	Wilkinson
Purgason, William	Greene	Owsleys	253/17	Wilkinson
Purkin's, John(Orphs.)	Hancock	Holts	170/25	Wilkinson
Purkins, Benjamin	Jackson	Cockrans	4/24	Wilkinson
Purkins, Elizabeth	Oglethorpe	Hartsfields	323/8	Wilkinson
Purkins, Jenks	Chatham	McLenns	20/26	Wilkinson
Purkins, John	Hancock	Barksdales	15/14	Wilkinson
Purkins, Samuel	Montgomery	59	138/15	Wilkinson
Purkins, Samuel	Montgomery	59	254/23	Wilkinson
Purkins, Solomon	Wilkes	Hendricks	95/26	Wilkinson
Purkins, Uriah	Hancock	Barksdales	155/6	Wilkinson
Purnell, John P.	Chatham	Pembertons	144/21	Wilkinson
Purvis, William	Bulloch	Hendleys	169/24	Wilkinson
Putnam, Benj.(Orph.)	Chatham	Hardens	7/18	Wilkinson
Putnam, Caroline(Orph.)	Chatham	Hardens	7/18	Wilkinson
Putnam, Chas.(Orph.)	Chatham	Hardens	7/18	Wilkinson
Putnam, Jno.(Orph.)	Chatham	Hardens	7/18	Wilkinson
Pye, Edward	Screven	Williamsons	243/16	Wilkinson
Pye, James Jr.	Oglethorpe	Smiths	254/11	Wilkinson
Pye, James Sr.	Oglethorpe	Smiths	163/25	Wilkinson
Pyor, Absalom	Jefferson	Thomas'	126/28	Wilkinson
Pyron, Lewis	Greene	Davenports	206/13	Wilkinson
Quarterman, Elizabeth(Wid.)	Liberty		119/7	Wilkinson
Quarterman, Robert	Liberty		20/11	Baldwin
Quartermans, Robt.(Orph.)	Liberty		387/7	Wilkinson
Quigly, Charles	Liberty	Roreys	319/13	Wilkinson
Quinn, Joseph C.	Columbia	10	237/20	Wilkinson
Quinn, Margaret	Columbia	10	126/25	Wilkinson
Rabun, Burwell	Warren	Devereux's	136/12	Wilkinson
Rabun, Joel	Franklin	Griffiths	283/19	Wilkinson
Rabun, Mathew	Hancock	Shivers'	17/17	Baldwin
Rabun, Richard	Warren	Neals	145/23	Wilkinson
Raburn's, John(Orphs.)	Hancock	Holts	106/16	Wilkinson
Raby, Richard	Bulloch	Godfreys	177/14	Wilkinson
Rachel, James	Washington	Garretts	54/28	Wilkinson
Rackley, Mary(Orph.)	Burke	Thompsons	79/20	Baldwin
Rackley, Mills	Franklin	Henrys	121/16	Baldwin
Raddock, Wm.R.	Baldwin	1	38/12	Wilkinson
Radford's, Henry(Orphs.)	Clarke	Dukes	129/14	Wilkinson
Radford, Shadrack	Hancock	Birdsongs	123/10	Baldwin
Radford, William	Oglethorpe	Popes	56/18	Wilkinson
Radford, Wm.	Oglethorpe	Popes	107/13	Wilkinson
Raefield's, Chas.(Orphs.)	Hancock	Wallers	154/6	Wilkinson
Raffity's, Rich.(Orphs.)	Oglethorpe	Bells	111/12	Baldwin
Ragain, Thomas	Jackson		87/19	Wilkinson
Ragan, John	Baldwin	2	205/25	Wilkinson
Ragan, John	Baldwin	2	308/10	Wilkinson
Ragland's, John(Orphs.)	Montgomery	57	168/18	Wilkinson
Ragland, Hudson	Jefferson	Colemans	89/16	Wilkinson
Ragland, Thompson	Elbert	Thompsons	112/27	Wilkinson
Raiford, John	Jefferson		294/24	Wilkinson
Railey, Frances	Warren	Flournoys	79/19	Wilkinson
Raines', Frederick(Orphs.)	Wilkinson		234/15	Wilkinson
Raines, Benjamin	Chatham	McLeans	202/15	Baldwin
Raines, Delilah	Franklin	Everetts	58/11	Wilkinson
Raines, Henry	Wilkes	Stovalls	152/17	Baldwin
Raines, Sarah	Franklin	Everetts	159/28	Wilkinson
Raines, Winnefred(Wid.)	Wilkinson		30/24	Wilkinson
Rainey, Isham	Oglethorpe	Watkins	223/16	Wilkinson
Raley, Josiah	Washington	Howards	16/8	Baldwin
Ramey's, Presly(Orphs.)	Clarke	Hitchcocks	249/6	Wilkinson
Ramey, Absalom	Clarke	Hitchcocks	248/14	Wilkinson
Ramey, Absalom	Clarke	Hitchcocks	91/10	Wilkinson

NAME	COUNTY	MIL.DIST.	LOT/DIST	DREW LAND
Ramey, John Sr.	Clarke	Hitchcocks	271/14	Wilkinson
Ramey, Wm.	Clarke	Hitchcocks	17/7	Wilkinson
Ramsey, Abraham	Oglethorpe	Bells	214/14	Baldwin
Ramsey, Henry	Jackson	Johnsons	167/17	Baldwin
Ramsey, James	Columbia	4	269/14	Wilkinson
Ramsey, James	Columbia	4	330/10	Wilkinson
Ramsey, James	Franklin	Allens	465/7	Wilkinson
Ramsey, James	Oglethorpe	Moores	175/19	Wilkinson
Ramsey, John	Columbia	2	189/9	Baldwin
Ramsey, John	Franklin	Allens	56/22	Wilkinson
Ramsey, Randal	Baldwin	1	10/12	Baldwin
Randal's, Beverly(Orphs.)	Burke	Forths	46/17	Wilkinson
Randal, Abel	Franklin	Wems'	117/28	Wilkinson
Randal, Abel	Franklin	Wems'	7/10	Baldwin
Randal, Johnson	Franklin	Wems'	150/20	Wilkinson
Randal, Johnson	Franklin	Wems'	53/19	Wilkinson
Randal, Patsy	Burke	Forths	214/15	Baldwin
Randle's, James(Orphs.)	Hancock	Coopers	62/8	Wilkinson
Randle's, John(Orphs.)	Hancock	Coopers	80/27	Wilkinson
Randle, Josias(Rev.)	Warren	Jones	146/20	Wilkinson
Randolph, Jno.	Chatham	Pembertons	320/14	Wilkinson
Randolph, Mary	Chatham	Pembertons	320/14	Wilkinson
Randolph, Wm.	Chatham	Pembertons	320/14	Wilkinson
Raney, Benjamin	Washington	Willis'	34/10	Baldwin
Rankin, Ezekiel	Greene	Dawsons	185/8	Wilkinson
Ransom, Ambrose	Hancock	Coffees	18/8	Baldwin
Ransom, Ambrose	Hancock	Coffees	264/14	Baldwin
Ransom, Henry	Hancock	Coffees	11/22	Wilkinson
Rasberry, Benjamin	Baldwin	4	89/12	Baldwin
Rasberry, Thomas	Baldwin	4	288/14	Wilkinson
Rasco, James	Chatham	McLeans	120/8	Wilkinson
Ratchford, Joseph	Jackson	Wrights	148/10	Wilkinson
Ratchford, Wm.	Oglethorpe	Hudsons	208/15	Baldwin
Ratcliff, Gabriel(Orph.)	Bryan	Birds	31/11	Wilkinson
Ratcliff, James	Liberty		49/13	Wilkinson
Ratcliff, John	Liberty		105/23	Wilkinson
Ratcliff, Margarett(Orph.)	Glynn		175/13	Baldwin
Ratcliff, Redden	Baldwin	2	251/12	Wilkinson
Ratliff's, Robert(Orphs.)	Lincoln	Jones	331/24	Wilkinson
Rawlings, Mark	Bulloch	Williams	187/24	Wilkinson
Rawls, Allen	Tattnall	Staffords	142/28	Wilkinson
Rawls, Cotton	Screven		167/10	Baldwin
Rawls, Isaac	Jefferson	Wrights	258/11	Wilkinson
Ray's, George(Orphs.)	Columbia	8	31/8	Baldwin
Ray, Benjamin	Columbia	9	235/15	Baldwin
Ray, Charles Sr.	Wilkinson		117/8	Baldwin
Ray, George	Clarke	Hitchcocks	222/16	Baldwin
Ray, Isabella(Orph.)	Chatham	Pembertons	320/7	Wilkinson
Ray, John	Columbia	8	75/19	Baldwin
Ray, Julia(Wid.)	Greene	Watsons	340/7	Wilkinson
Ray, Mary(Single)	Clarke	Silmans	29/24	Wilkinson
Ray, Samuel	Clarke	Hitchcocks	35/19	Wilkinson
Ray, Thomas	Clarke	Silmans	41/27	Wilkinson
Ray, Ussery	Wilkes	Youngs	171/18	Wilkinson
Ray, William	Columbia	7	88/8	Baldwin
Ray, William	Washington	Andersons	124/23	Wilkinson
Ray, William	Washington	Renfroes	32/17	Baldwin
Raymond, Rebecca(Wid.)	Jefferson	Bosticks	254/9	Wilkinson
Raynes, Benjamin	Chatham	McLeans	98/8	Baldwin
Reach, Shadrack	Montgomery	57	150/27	Wilkinson
Read, Judity(Wid.)	Baldwin	2	41/7	Baldwin
Read, Thomas Jr.	Columbia	10	167/25	Wilkinson
Read, Thomas Sr.	Columbia	8	198/21	Wilkinson
Readen, Wm.	Washington	Renfroes	364/9	Wilkinson
Readick, Peter	Burke	Mulkeys	25/17	Wilkinson
Ready, Benjamin	Baldwin	2	217/8	Wilkinson
Ready, Lee	Baldwin	2	274/11	Wilkinson

NAME	COUNTY	MIL.DIST.	LOT/DIST	DREW LAND
Reagan, James	Elbert	Dyes	55/11	Wilkinson
Reaney, Mary(Wid.)	Jackson	Hendersons	183/13	Baldwin
Reckel, Elizabeth	Oglethorpe	Hatchetts	196/19	Baldwin
Reckell, John	Oglethorpe	Hatchetts	131/21	Wilkinson
Reckell, John	Oglethorpe	Hatchetts	88/28	Wilkinson
Red, Joseph	Burke	Ballards	211/16	Baldwin
Red, Samuel	Burke	Ballards	54/12	Wilkinson
Redden, Archibald	Washington	Renfroes	60/12	Wilkinson
Redden, Arthur	Baldwin	3	221/19	Wilkinson
Redding, Henry H.(Orph.)	Burke	Sandifords	91/19	Baldwin
Redding, Nancy	Franklin	Griffiths	90/26	Wilkinson
Reddock, David	Baldwin	1	217/22	Wilkinson
Reddock, David	Baldwin	1	253/13	Wilkinson
Reddock, Wm.R.	Baldwin	1	75/10	Baldwin
Reddy's, Nicholas(Orphs.)	Screven	Hutchinsons	181/10	Wilkinson
Reed's, Geo.(Orphs.)	Baldwin	4	28/13	Wilkinson
Reed's, John(Orph.)	Hancock	Barnes	311/8	Wilkinson
Reed's, Joseph(Orphs.)	Jackson	Hendersons	221/16	Baldwin
Reed, Alex.S.(Orph.)	Green	Alfords	144/16	Wilkinson
Reed, Alexander	Hancock	Barnes'	71/14	Wilkinson
Reed, Alexander	Oglethorpe	Popes	6/20	Wilkinson
Reed, Allick(Orph.)	Greene	Alfords	144/16	Wilkinson
Reed, Andrew	Hancock	Barnes	305/20	Baldwin
Reed, Cullin A.(Orph.)	Greene	Alfords	144/16	Wilkinson
Reed, Fanny(Single)	Hancock	Weeks'	46/28	Wilkinson
Reed, Henry	Jackson	Johnsons	158/18	Wilkinson
Reed, Hugh	Jackson	Johnsons	71/11	Wilkinson
Reed, Jacob	Oglethorpe	Hatchetts	129/26	Wilkinson
Reed, James	Camden	Smiths	401/8	Wilkinson
Reed, James	Columbia	2	207/20	Wilkinson
Reed, James	Greene	Carltons	240/10	Baldwin
Reed, James	Hancock	Coffees	201/16	Baldwin
Reed, John	Greene	Stewarts	272/19	Wilkinson
Reed, John	Hancock	Barnes'	148/17	Wilkinson
Reed, John	Hancock	Weeks	300/9	Wilkinson
Reed, John	Oglethorpe	Popes	248/9	Wilkinson
Reed, Joseph	Greene	Stewarts	77/19	Wilkinson
Reed, Joseph	Oglethorpe	Popes	148/17	Baldwin
Reed, Joseph	Oglethorpe	Popes	442/7	Wilkinson
Reed, Margaret	Jackson	Cockrans	290/14	Wilkinson
Reed, Mary Eliz.(Orph)	Greene	Alfords	144/16	Wilkinson
Reed, Robert	Richmond		122/14	Baldwin
Reed, Samuel Sr.	Hancock	Barnes'	196/20	Baldwin
Reed, William	Baldwin	2	91/17	Wilkinson
Reed, Zachariah	Greene	Armors	250/15	Wilkinson
Reese, Hugh Jr.	Warren	Willsons	30/22	Wilkinson
Reese, James Jr.	Hancock	Smiths	230/17	Wilkinson
Reese, Joel	Hancock	Barnes	173/26	Wilkinson
Reese, John	Jefferson	Hardwichs	240/9	Wilkinson
Reese, William Jr.	Hancock	Smiths	291/17	Wilkinson
Reese, Wm.Sr.	Hancock	Hudsons	308/12	Wilkinson
Reeves', John(Orphs.)	Franklin	Dixons	99/23	Wilkinson
Reeves, Greene	Washington	Howards	15/25	Wilkinson
Reeves, Ichabud	Wilkes	Milners	152/10	Baldwin
Reeves, Ichabud	Wilkes	Milners	310/15	Baldwin
Reeves, James	Wilkes	Milners	103/23	Wilkinson
Reeves, Jane(Wid.)	Wilkes	Milners	15/16	Baldwin
Reeves, Joel	Burke	Hilliards	18/12	Baldwin
Reeves, Joseph	Burke	Martins	166/7	Wilkinson
Reeves, Nancy	Liberty		195/10	Baldwin
Reeves, Simon	Washington	Wiggins'	138/16	Wilkinson
Reeves, Spires	Burke	Gordons	26/16	Wilkinson
Reeves, Thomas	Warren	Willsons	113/7	Baldwin
Register, Mary(Wid.)	Washington	Blackshears	32/7	Wilkinson
Reich, Martin	Montgomery	57	185/17	Wilkinson
Reid, Elizabeth(Wid.)	Hancock	Barnes	50/11	Wilkinson
Reighly's, Ferrel(Orphs.)	Columbia	7	164/15	Wilkinson

NAME	COUNTY	MIL.DIST.	LOT/DIST	DREW LAND
Reingeard, Mathurin	Chatham	Abrahams	225/10	Wilkinson
Reisser, Dorothy	Chatham	Pettybones	21/7	Baldwin
Reisser, Nathan	Chatham	Pettybones	21/7	Baldwin
Reisser, Saml.	Chatham	Pettybones	21/7	Baldwin
Reisser, Sarah	Chatham	Pettybones	316/22	Wilkinson
Remson, Rem	Lincoln	Mays	49/22	Wilkinson
Renfroe, Elisha	Washington	Renfroes	94/7	Baldwin
Renfroe, Eliz.(Wid.)	Washington	Collins	137/12	Baldwin
Renfroe, George	Baldwin	4	220/16	Baldwin
Renfroe, George	Baldwin	4	333/12	Wilkinson
Renfroe, John	Washington	Renfroes	399/7	Wilkinson
Renfroe, Nathan	Washington	Renfroes	312/16	Wilkinson
Renfroe, Stephen Jr.	Washington	Renfroes	195/7	Wilkinson
Renfroe, Wm.	Washington	Renfroes	53/8	Wilkinson
Restor, Frederick	Bulloch	Denmarks	215/8	Wilkinson
Reynolds', Richard(Orphs.)	Wilkes	Roreys	170/23	Wilkinson
Reynolds, Lewis	Burke	Martins	17/23	Wilkinson
Reynolds, Redman	Wilkes	Hendersons	113/13	Wilkinson
Reynolds, Robert	Columbia	6	38/15	Wilkinson
Reynolds, Samuel	Elbert	Keelings	307/10	Wilkinson
Reynolds, Stephen Jr.	Burke	Martins	36/18	Wilkinson
Reynolds, Thomas	Wilkes	Roreys	113/13	Wilkinson
Reynolds, Thomas	Wilkes	Roreys	47/8	Wilkinson
Reynolds, Wm.	Burke	Martins	159/27	Wilkinson
Reynolds, Wm.Sr.	Burke	Martins	285/12	Wilkinson
Rhodes, Charles	Washington	Andersons	118/7	Wilkinson
Rhodes, James	Elbert	Groves	34/7	Wilkinson
Rhodes, James	Wilkes	Youngs	318/7	Wilkinson
Rhodes, James	Wilkinson		63/16	Baldwin
Rhodes, James	Wilkinson		93/11	Wilkinson
Rhodes, Smith	Washington	Wiggins'	112/7	Wilkinson
Rhodes, Wm.	Washington	Holts	322/8	Wilkinson
Rhymes, Alexander	Warren	Carters	133/15	Wilkinson
Rice's, Benjamin(Orphs.)	Clarke	Hitchcocks	166/8	Baldwin
Rice's, Edward(Orphs.)	Franklin	Hollingsworths	154/6	Baldwin
Rice, Gabriel	Clarke	Harpers	229/21	Wilkinson
Rice, John	Baldwin	1	274/21	Wilkinson
Rice, John	Wilkes	Roreys	132/17	Wilkinson
Rice, Sarah(Single)	Clarke	Hitchcocks	96/6	Wilkinson
Rice, Sarah(Wid.)	Franklin	Hollingsworths	350/7	Wilkinson
Rich, Samuel	Burke	Carswells	20/6	Wilkinson
Richard, James	Clarke	Tramell's	77/11	Wilkinson
Richards', Wm.(Orphs.)	Elbert	Willifords	251/10	Wilkinson
Richards, John	Chatham	Neyles	83/20	Wilkinson
Richards, Silas	Chatham	Whites	154/14	Wilkinson
Richards, Wm.	Greene	Loves	113/21	Wilkinson
Richardson's, Daniel(Orphs.)	Hancock	Wallers	71/19	Wilkinson
Richardson, Daniel	Jefferson	Bosticks	38/10	Wilkinson
Richardson, Enoch	Lincoln	Kings	249/10	Wilkinson
Richardson, Jane(Orph.)	Chatham	Pettybones	240/17	Wilkinson
Richardson, John	Bulloch	Hendleys	274/10	Wilkinson
Richardson, John	Oglethorpe	Hartsfields	111/14	Wilkinson
Richardson, Randall(Orph.)	Washington	Burneys	22/12	Wilkinson
Richardson, Robt.E.	Washington	Kendricks	9/13	Baldwin
Richardson, Sarah	Bulloch	Hendleys	187/18	Wilkinson
Richardson, Thomas	Columbia	11	101/6	Baldwin
Richardson, Thomas	Greene	Owsleys	149/7	Baldwin
Richardson, William	Oglethorpe	Hartsfields	257/22	Wilkinson
Richardsons, Wm.(Orph.)	Bulloch	Hendleys	100/22	Wilkinson
Riche, Joseph	Jackson	Cockrans	143/28	Wilkinson
Riche, William	Oglethorpe	Stewarts	78/19	Baldwin
Ricketson, Gordius	Columbia		19/21	Wilkinson
Richmond, Silas	Camden	Hardys	101/8	Baldwin
Ricks, Jesse	Montgomery	56	59/13	Baldwin
Ricks, Richard	Wilkinson		58/13	Baldwin
Ridgedell, Penelope	Warren	Neals	128/26	Wilkinson
Ridgeway, Sally	Elbert	Faulkners	200/26	Wilkinson

NAME	COUNTY	MIL.DIST.	LOT/DIST	DREW LAND
Ridgsdill, David	Elbert	Olivers	196/27	Wilkinson
Ridon, Elizabeth	Greene	Baxters	185/27	Wilkinson
Rigdon, Thomas	Baldwin	1	180/12	Baldwin
Right, Solomon	Chatham	McLeans	44/27	Wilkinson
Riland, John	Washington	Howards	52/6	Wilkinson
Riley, John	Greene	Dawsons	223/15	Baldwin
Riley, John	Richmond		27/21	Wilkinson
Riley, Joseph	Washington	Wiggins'	122/20	Baldwin
Riley, Joseph	Washington	Wiggins'	308/16	Wilkinson
Riley, William	Wilkes	Hendersons	288/24	Wilkinson
Ringo, John	Oglethorpe	Hudsons	112/18	Wilkinson
Risspess, Richard Jr.	Hancock	Barnes	194/10	Baldwin
Ritch, Charles	Oglethorpe	Hitchcocks	84/14	Wilkinson
Ritchy, Daniel	Lincoln	Kennons	214/21	Wilkinson
Ritter, Mathew	Chatham	Pembertons	244/6	Wilkinson
Rivers, John	Columbia	7	88/12	Wilkinson
Rivers, Jones	Washington	Paces	103/17	Baldwin
Rivers, Joseph(Orph.)	Chatham	Pembertons	82/17	Wilkinson
Rivers, Rosetta(Orph.)	Chatham	Pembertons	82/17	Wilkinson
Rivers, Thomas	Hancock	Smiths	80/9	Wilkinson
Rivers, Wm.	Hancock	Pinkstons	126/18	Baldwin
Rives, Rebecca	Screven		101/20	Baldwin
Rivier, John	Wilkes	Sidwells	248/17	Wilkinson
Roach, James C.	Greene	Dawsons	149/15	Baldwin
Roach, James	Greene	Moores	152/16	Wilkinson
Roach, Samuel	Hancock	Barnes'	90/13	Baldwin
Roan, Lewis D.	Jackson	Wrights	342/22	Wilkinson
Robarts, John	Liberty		241/9	Wilkinson
Robarts, Wm.	Liberty		18/14	Wilkinson
Roberts', Burwell(Orphs.)	Burke	Sharps	198/23	Wilkinson
Roberts', Olive(Orphs.)	Elbert	Keelings	247/19	Baldwin
Roberts', Sally(Wid.)	Elbert	Keelings	174/14	Baldwin
Roberts', Shadrack(Orphs.)	Columbia	4	19/18	Wilkinson
Roberts, Abraham	Bulloch	Denmarks	137/15	Baldwin
Roberts, Abraham	Washington	Collins	104/14	Baldwin
Roberts, Daniel	Greene	Baxters	4/26	Wilkinson
Roberts, Darcus(Wid.)	Burke	Sharps	168/10	Wilkinson
Roberts, David(Orph.)	Bulloch	Denmarks	301/15	Wilkinson
Roberts, David(S./Shadrack)	Columbia		212/21	Wilkinson
Roberts, David	Chatham	Abrahams	221/20	Wilkinson
Roberts, Faithy(W.of Josiah)	Columbia	3	224/11	Wilkinson
Roberts, Frederick	Wilkinson		177/20	Baldwin
Roberts, Frederick	Wilkinson		73/13	Baldwin
Roberts, Gay S.	Montgomery	50	239/23	Wilkinson
Roberts, Hugh	Wilkes	Heards	130/6	Wilkinson
Roberts, James	Columbia	3	121/17	Baldwin
Roberts, James	Jefferson	Bosticks	114/15	Baldwin
Roberts, James	Jefferson	Bosticks	39/9	Wilkinson
Roberts, James	Screven	Williamsons	109/6	Wilkinson
Roberts, Jesse Jr.	Columbia	4	161/12	Wilkinson
Roberts, Jesse Jr.	Columbia	4	320/12	Wilkinson
Roberts, John	Baldwin	1	158/6	Wilkinson
Roberts, John	Baldwin	1	3/14	Wilkinson
Roberts, John	Bulloch	Williams'	141/18	Wilkinson
Roberts, John	Burke	Fields	77/13	Wilkinson
Roberts, John	Clarke	Hopkins	318/10	Wilkinson
Roberts, John	Greene	Greers	122/17	Wilkinson
Roberts, John	Greene	Greers	38/27	Wilkinson
Roberts, Patience	Columbia	4	125/13	Wilkinson
Roberts, Patty	Elbert	Faulkners	315/16	Wilkinson
Roberts, Richard	Greene	Armors	285/19	Baldwin
Roberts, Sarah(Orph.)	Franklin	Hollingsworths	119/9	Wilkinson
Roberts, Thomas	Screven		70/15	Wilkinson
Roberts, Wm.(Orph.)	Bulloch	Denmarks	301/15	Wilkinson
Robertson's, Edward(Orphs.)	Washington	Howards	57/27	Wilkinson
Robertson's, John(Orphs.)	Franklin	Allens	61/15	Baldwin
Robertson's, John(Orphs.)	Jackson	Cockrans	201/19	Wilkinson

NAME	COUNTY	MIL.DIST.	LOT/DIST	DREW LAND
Robertson, Bailey	Baldwin	2	173/7	Wilkinson
Robertson, Benjamin	Washington	Howards	171/6	Wilkinson
Robertson, Eli	Wilkes	Malones	199/17	Wilkinson
Robertson, Elijah	Oglethorpe	Hartsfields	318/14	Wilkinson
Robertson, Henry	Jackson	Hendersons	23/19	Baldwin
Robertson, James M.	Chatham	Pettybones	13/14	Baldwin
Robertson, James	Wilkes	Malones	275/16	Wilkinson
Robertson, Jno. (Sparta)	Hancock	Barnes	19/24	Wilkinson
Robertson, John Jr.	Warren	Flournoys	117/6	Wilkinson
Robertson, John M.S.	Clarke	Stewarts	61/8	Wilkinson
Robertson, John R.	Washington	Holts	67/20	Wilkinson
Robertson, John	Bulloch	Williams	112/8	Wilkinson
Robertson, Lazarus	Warren	Heiths	80/18	Baldwin
Robertson, Mary C.	Columbia	4	169/11	Wilkinson
Robertson, Norvell	Warren	Devereux's	212/16	Baldwin
Robertson, Richard	Jackson	Hendersons	60/17	Wilkinson
Robertson, Tabitha	Washington	Renfroes	181/14	Baldwin
Robertson, Thomas	Chatham	Pembertons	73/23	Wilkinson
Robertson, Thomas	Greene	Armors	110/7	Wilkinson
Robertson, Thomas	Greene	Armors	212/17	Wilkinson
Robertson, Thomas	Wilkes	Malones	117/14	Baldwin
Robertson, William	Montgomery	52	287/20	Wilkinson
Robertson, William	Warren	Flournoys	128/12	Baldwin
Robertson, Willis	Greene	Jenkins	145/9	Wilkinson
Robertson, Wm.	Baldwin	3	152/6	Wilkinson
Robertson, Wm.	Clarke	Martindales	91/24	Wilkinson
Robertson, Zachariah	Greene	Owsleys	250/10	Wilkinson
Robey, Mathew	Wilkes	Hendersons	85/15	Wilkinson
Robey, Williamson	Jackson	Johnsons	13/15	Baldwin
Robins, Arthur	Burke	Thompsons	381/9	Wilkinson
Robins, George	Screven		101/7	Wilkinson
Robins, Nicholas	Hancock	Wallers	258/22	Wilkinson
Robins, Sarah(Wid.)	Screven		114/7	Baldwin
Robinson, David(J.J.C.)	Burke	Sandifords	205/28	Wilkinson
Robinson, Fryer	Clarke	Robinsons	42/22	Wilkinson
Robinson, James B.	Richmond		237/11	Wilkinson
Robinson, James	Jefferson	Wrights	179/10	Wilkinson
Robinson, John B.	Washington	Collins	208/14	Wilkinson
Robinson, Peter	Greene	Carltons	395/8	Wilkinson
Robinson, Sarah	Greene	Armors	97/27	Wilkinson
Robinson, Willis	Washington	Collins	313/16	Wilkinson
Robinson, Wm.(Crusoe)	Baldwin	1	87/21	Wilkinson
Robinson, Wm.	Burke	Thompsons	5/16	Baldwin
Robinson, Wm.Sr.	Washington	Collins	218/16	Baldwin
Robison, John C.	Glynn		60/13	Baldwin
Rockmore, Eliza	Baldwin	2	219/19	Baldwin
Rockmore, James	Warren	Newsoms	227/13	Wilkinson
Rockmore, James	Warren	Newsoms	259/17	Wilkinson
Rockmore, Peter	Warren	Newsoms	199/27	Wilkinson
Rockmore, Thomas	Baldwin	2	5/20	Wilkinson
Rodes, Benjn.	Wilkes	Youngs	48/16	Baldwin
Rodes, James	Wilkes	Youngs	147/1	Baldwin
Roe, James	Baldwin	1	135/9	Baldwin
Roe, James	Baldwin	1	63/12	Baldwin
Roe, John	Hancock	Weeks'	205/11	Wilkinson
Roe, Lydda	Hancock	Barnes	2/10	Baldwin
Roe, Mary(W.of Isaac)	Columbia	1	144/22	Wilkinson
Roe, Shadrack	Hancock	Barnes'	275/17	Wilkinson
Roe, Susannah	Elbert	McGuires	114/17	Baldwin
Roebuck, Mary	Wilkes	Sheets	492/7	Wilkinson
Roebuck, Robt.Jr.	Elbert	Roebucks	162/27	Wilkinson
Roebuck, Robt.Sr.	Elbert	Clarks	266/19	Baldwin
Rogason, Richard	Chatham	McLeans	293/15	Baldwin
Rogers', Abel(Orphs.)	Jefferson	Tarvers	42/18	Wilkinson
Rogers', John(Orphs.)	Hancock	Coffees	93/7	Wilkinson
Rogers', John(Orphs.)	Hancock	Coopers	43/19	Baldwin
Rogers', John(Orphs.)	Jackson	Johnsons'	55/7	Baldwin

NAME	COUNTY	MIL.DIST.	LOT/DIST	DREW LAND
Rogers', Nathaniel(Orphs.)	Washington	Delks	47/18	Baldwin
Rogers', Wm.(Orphs.)	Franklin	Cornelius'	49/16	Wilkinson
Rogers, Benjamin	Jefferson	Hardwicks	129/16	Wilkinson
Rogers, Braxton	Washington	Wiggins'	219/13	Baldwin
Rogers, Burwell	Hancock	Weeks	157/12	Baldwin
Rogers, Clarey(Miss)	Warren	Bakers	293/24	Wilkinson
Rogers, Elizabeth	Hancock	Coopers	166/15	Wilkinson
Rogers, Henry	Hancock	Holts	253/8	Wilkinson
Rogers, Henry	Hancock	Holts	85/18	Baldwin
Rogers, Hugh	Clarke	Hitchcocks	111/17	Wilkinson
Rogers, Hugh	Clarke	Hitchcocks	92/4	Baldwin
Rogers, Jacob	Bulloch	Denmarks	272/24	Wilkinson
Rogers, John	Jackson	Hendersons	143/9	Wilkinson
Rogers, John	Jefferson	Colemans	107/16	Baldwin
Rogers, Joseph	Warren	Bakers	42/21	Wilkinson
Rogers, Mary(Wid.)	Montgomery	50	140/20	Baldwin
Rogers, Mary(Wid.)	Washington	Delks	122/8	Wilkinson
Rogers, Mary	Columbia	9	9/20	Baldwin
Rogers, Mathew	Burke	Mulkeys	77/16	Wilkinson
Rogers, Micajah	Hancock	Weeks'	169/12	Wilkinson
Rogers, Peleg	Hancock	Candlers	17/9	Baldwin
Rogers, Pleasant	Greene	Davenports	95/7	Wilkinson
Rogers, Reddock	Burke	Martins	141/26	Wilkinson
Rogers, Robert	Baldwin	4	11/23	Wilkinson
Rogers, Robert	Baldwin	4	263/14	Baldwin
Rogers, Ruth	Jackson	Hendersons	55/12	Wilkinson
Rogers, Susannah(Wid.)	Chatham	Pettybones	355/7	Wilkinson
Rogers, Thomas	Warren	Devereux's	417/7	Wilkinson
Rogers, Whitmell	Burke	Martins	188/13	Wilkinson
Rogers, Zachariah	Washington	Wiggins'	76/22	Wilkinson
Roland, William	Warren	Newsoms	44/25	Wilkinson
Rolley, Isaac	Washington	Kendricks	86/7	Wilkinson
Rollston, Ezekiel	Jackson	Cockrans	311/9	Wilkinson
Roma, Francis	Chatham	Abrahams	149/20	Wilkinson
Rooc, Mitchell	Warren	Heaths	33/20	Baldwin
Rook, Rachel	Richmond		124/20	Baldwin
Rook, William	Jackson	Wrights	111/13	Baldwin
Rooke's, Wm.(Orphs.)	Jackson	Wrights	148/19	Wilkinson
Rooke, Belithia	Warren	Willsons	155/18	Baldwin
Rooks, Vardiman	Screven		234/26	Wilkinson
Rorey's, John(Orphs.)	Wilkes	Roreys	129/15	Wilkinson
Rorey, John	Wilkes	Roreys	34/9	Wilkinson
Rose, Burwell	Screven		203/24	Wilkinson
Rose, Hutson	Baldwin	1	151/18	Wilkinson
Rose, Winneford	Franklin	Griffiths	217/13	Wilkinson
Ross', John(Orphs.)	Columbia	9	166/22	Wilkinson
Ross, Edward	Columbia	8	156/25	Wilkinson
Ross, Etheldred	Jackson	Wrights	114/13	Wilkinson
Ross, John Sr.	Jackson	Wrights	149/18	Baldwin
Ross, Nancy(Orp/Harmon)	Montgomery	59	23/28	Wilkinson
Ross, Richard	Elbert	Keelings	33/16	Wilkinson
Ross, Richard	Franklin	Henrys	93/9	Baldwin
Ross, Wylie	Jackson	Wrights	172/20	Baldwin
Rosser, Elijah	Baldwin	1	298/7	Wilkinson
Rossiter, Appleton	Warren	Devereux's	125/11	Baldwin
Roswell, Pherebe	Burke	Sandifords	140/27	Wilkinson
Roundtree, Arthur	Jefferson		339/22	Wilkinson
Roundtree, Wm.Sr.	Burke	Spains	190/10	Baldwin
Rowan, George	Wilkes	Hendricks	49/11	Wilkinson
Rowden, Pleasant	Jackson	Hendersons	184/6	Baldwin
Rowden, Pleasant	Jackson	Hendersons	239/21	Wilkinson
Rowe, Alexander S.	Chatham	Whites	266/20	Baldwin
Rowe, Alexander S.	Chatham	Whites	346/24	Wilkinson
Rowe, Wm.	Bulloch	Godfreys	78/11	Wilkinson
Rowell, Henry V.(Orph.)	Jefferson	Wrights	188/26	Wilkinson
Rowell, Henry	Baldwin	4	10/10	Baldwin
Rowell, Richard	McIntosh		449/7	Wilkinson

NAME	COUNTY	MIL.DIST.	LOT/DIST	DREW LAND
Rowell, Robert	Washington	Howards	81/15	Wilkinson
Rowell, Wm.	Washington	Howards	75/9	Baldwin
Rowland, Eleazer	Screven		44/19	Wilkinson
Rowland, Elizabeth	Greene	Baxters	125/14	Wilkinson
Rowland, Frederick	Greene	Baxters	208/19	Wilkinson
Rowland, James	Montgomery	56	220/7	Wilkinson
Rowland, Martha	Warren	Newsoms	36/21	Wilkinson
Rowland, Willis	Jackson	Cockrans	4/13	Wilkinson
Rowsey, John Sr.	Elbert	Olivers	62/25	Wilkinson
Rowton, Abraham E.	Jackson	Wrights	186/6	Baldwin
Rowton, Penny	Jackson	Wrights	294/10	Wilkinson
Royal, John Jr.	Elbert	Morrisons	128/19	Baldwin
Royal, John Sr.	Elbert	Morrisons	232/18	Wilkinson
Royal, John Sr.	Elbert	Morrisons	75/24	Wilkinson
Royal, John	Burke	Mulkeys	282/11	Wilkinson
Royals, Stephen	Burke	Thompsons	135/11	Baldwin
Royston, Richard C.	Greene	Rays	118/21	Wilkinson
Rozar, Aaron	Glynn		248/8	Wilkinson
Rozar, Alexander	Columbia	8	31/27	Wilkinson
Rozar, Robert	Columbia	8	187/14	Wilkinson
Rucker, Asmond	Elbert	Blackwells	166/17	Wilkinson
Rucker, Jane(Wid.)	Elbert	Hillyers	92/9	Baldwin
Rudolph, Eliza(Orph.)	Chatham	Abrams	22/14	Baldwin
Rumbley, Leven	Clarke	Martins	134/6	Wilkinson
Rumbly, Smith	Oglethorpe	Hitchcocks	140/17	Baldwin
Rumph, David	Glynn		292/6	Wilkinson
Rumsey, Fanny	Elbert	Barretts	165/15	Wilkinson
Rumsey, James	Wilkes	Hendersons	222/12	Wilkinson
Rumsey, James	Wilkes	Hendersons	247/20	Baldwin
Rumsey, John	Elbert	Barretts	162/19	Baldwin
Rumsey, Richard	Elbert	Barretts	2/19	Wilkinson
Runnells, Coleman	Clarke	Browns	325/14	Wilkinson
Rushen, William	Washington	Renfroes	148/15	Wilkinson
Rusher, John Sr.	Elbert	Blackwells	107/15	Wilkinson
Rushin, Eli	Washington	Renfroes	13/23	Wilkinson
Rushin, James	Washington	Renfroes	278/14	Wilkinson
Rushin, Wm.Sr.	Screven		321/21	Wilkinson
Rushton, John S.	Jackson	Cockrans	29/7	Baldwin
Russau, Peggy	Oglethorpe	Popes	155/12	Wilkinson
Russau, William	Columbia	8	251/14	Wilkinson
Russau, Wm.Jr.	Oglethorpe	Popes	190/16	Wilkinson
Russel, Andrew	Baldwin	2	231/9	Wilkinson
Russel, Jacob	Franklin	Hoopers	127/8	Baldwin
Russel, Philemon	Bulloch	Denmarks	261/20	Baldwin
Russell's, Wm.Sr.(Orphs.)	Lincoln	Flemings	216/12	Baldwin
Russell, Caleb	Wilkes	Wellborns	49/19	Wilkinson
Russell, Eliz.(Wid.)	Wilkes	Coopers	17/17	Wilkinson
Russell, Henry Trent	Wilkes	Malones	53/12	Baldwin
Russell, Jacob	Franklin	Hoopers	126/22	Wilkinson
Russell, James	Lincoln	Kings	263/23	Wilkinson
Russell, Jane(Wid.)	Oglethorpe	Stewarts	44/28	Wilkinson
Russell, Jas.G.	Hancock	Candlers	398/21	Wilkinson
Russell, John	Richmond		47/7	Baldwin
Russell, Miram(Wid.)	Wilkes	Parks	255/15	Wilkinson
Russell, Nathaniel	Franklin	Conners	125/10	Baldwin
Russell, Robert	Elbert	Moons	263/10	Wilkinson
Russell, Solomon	Glynn		86/14	Baldwin
Russell, Wm.	Burke	Spains	10/25	Wilkinson
Russel, Andrew	Baldwin	2	116/17	Baldwin
Rutherford, Thomas B.	Washington	Howards	110/14	Wilkinson
Rutledge, George	Franklin	Cleghorns	226/9	Wilkinson
Rutledge, John	Burke	Bynes	120/8	Baldwin
Rutledge, John	Jackson	Johnsons'	28/9	Wilkinson
Rutledge, John	Jackson	Johnsons	180/27	Wilkinson
Rutledge, Robert	Jackson	Johnsons	110/18	Baldwin
Rutledge, Thomas	Baldwin	5	202/6	Wilkinson
Rutledge, Thomas	Greene	Owsleys	162/9	Wilkinson

NAME	COUNTY	MIL.DIST.	LOT/DIST	DREW LAND
Ryals, Lewis	McIntosh		101/20	Wilkinson
Ryals, Lewis	McIntosh		39/9	Baldwin
Ryan, Dannis L.	Hancock	Barnes'	147/13	Baldwin
Ryan, Edward	Burke	Fields'	87/26	Wilkinson
Ryan, Elisha	Columbia	2	131/11	Wilkinson
Ryan, Peter	Columbia	10	150/19	Baldwin
Ryan, Richard	Columbia	10	259/15	Wilkinson
Ryan, Richard	Columbia	10	336/20	Baldwin
Ryle, James	Baldwin	2	359/9	Wilkinson
Rylee, James	Franklin	Christians	260/17	Wilkinson
Rynnolds, Sharp(Heirs)	Lincoln		159/11	Baldwin
Rynnolds, Sharp(Heirs/1809)	Lincoln		132/20	Wilkinson
Sacket, Simon	Richmond		199/11	Wilkinson
Sadler, Henry	Burke	Smiths	34/24	Wilkinson
Saffold, Reubin	Wilkes	Sheets'	61/21	Wilkinson
Saffold, Samuel	Washington	Renfroes	151/12	Baldwin
Saffold, Samuel	Washington	Renfroes	168/7	Wilkinson
Saffold, Wm.Sr.	Washington	Willis'	201/17	Wilkinson
Safford, Adam G.	Washington	Howards	38/19	Baldwin
Safford, Polly(Single)	Oglethorpe	Smiths	188/15	Baldwin
Sailors, Eliz.(Wid.)	Jackson	Johnsons	102/22	Wilkinson
Salisbury, John R.	Burke	Gordons	188/13	Baldwin
Sallard, William	Hancock	Weeks'	15/19	Baldwin
Sallis, David	Warren	Willsons	327/17	Wilkinson
Salter, James	Montgomery	58	50/21	Wilkinson
Salter, James	Washington	Collins	16/26	Wilkinson
Salter, Samuel	Washington	Garretts	171/11	Baldwin
Sammons, Benjamin	Jefferson	Colemans	355/24	Wilkinson
Sammons, Richard	Warren	Jones	2/15	Baldwin
Sample, Nathaniel	Jefferson	Hardwicks	37/9	Baldwin
Sample, Thomas B.	Jackson		479/7	Wilkinson
Sams, John	Oglethorpe	Beasleys	35/24	Wilkinson
Sanders', Hardy(Orphs.)	Elbert	Willifords	211/12	Baldwin
Sanders', John(Orphs.)	Washington	Collins	164/12	Wilkinson
Sanders, Alsey	Baldwin	2	181/11	Baldwin
Sanders, Daniel	Hancock	Huffs	72/51	Wilkinson
Sanders, Daniel	Warren	Jones	152/21	Wilkinson
Sanders, James	Oglethorpe	Hitchcocks	8/10	Baldwin
Sanders, John	Glynn		484/7	2
Sanders, Joseph	Oglethorpe	Hitchcocks	244/19	Wilkinson
Sanders, Mark	Hancock	Weeks	235/21	Wilkinson
Sanders, Moses Jr.	Franklin	Wems'	79/17	Wilkinson
Sanders, Samuel	Liberty		18/27	Wilkinson
Sanders, Samuel	Liberty		185/16	Wilkinson
Sanders, Thomas	Columbia	10	192/10	Baldwin
Sanders, Wm.	Oglethorpe	Hitchcocks	13/11	Wilkinson
Sandes, Aaron	Franklin	Wems'	114/19	Baldwin
Sandes, David	Franklin	Wems'	217/8	Wilkinson
Sandiford, James	Columbia	8	106/8	Baldwin
Sandiford, John	Burke	Sandifords	138/20	Wilkinson
Sandiford, John	Columbia	11	159/18	Wilkinson
Sandiford, John	Columbia	11	213/7	Wilkinson
Sands, John	Tattnall	McDonalds	188/16	Baldwin
Sands, Ray	Burke	Johnsons	229/18	Wilkinson
Sandwich, Thomas K.	Lincoln	Mays	338/9	Wilkinson
Sanford, Benjamin	Hancock	Smiths	73/19	Wilkinson
Sanford, Judith(Wid.)	Wilkes	Hendricks	233/6	Wilkinson
Sanford, Thornton	Hancock	Smiths	335/9	Wilkinson
Sanford, Wm.	Hancock	Barnes'	110/28	Wilkinson
Sansom, Archbald	Baldwin	4	123/10	Wilkinson
Sansom, Jacob	Baldwin	4	299/11	Wilkinson
Sansom, Micajah	Greene	Jenkins	70/22	Wilkinson
Sansom, Micajah	Greene	Jinkins	109/16	Baldwin
Sansom, Wm.Jr.	Baldwin	4	144/11	Wilkinson
Sansom, Wm.Sr.	Baldwin	4	119/16	Baldwin
Sapp, Abraham Jr.	Burke	Thompsons	310/20	Baldwin
Sapp, James	Burke	Thompsons	28/8	Wilkinson

NAME	COUNTY	MIL.DIST.	LOT/DIST	DREW LAND
Sapp, Luke Jr.	Burke	Thompsons	39/12	Wilkinson
Sapp, Luke Sr.	Burke	Thompsons	6/27	Wilkinson
Sapp, Mark	Burke	Thompsons	248/6	Wilkinson
Sapp, Philip	Burke	Thompsons	140/10	Baldwin
Sappington, John	Wilkes	J.Hendersons	186/28	Wilkinson
Sarp, Hiram(Orph.)	Baldwin	2	232/20	Baldwin
Sartain, James	Franklin	Wems'	23/21	Wilkinson
Sartain, James	Tattnall	Sherrards	204/16	Wilkinson
Sartain, James	Tattnall	Sherrards	6/17	Wilkinson
Sartain, Josiah Sr.	Elbert	Morrisons	22/13	Wilkinson
Sasser, Thomas	Burke	Gordons	35/15	Wilkinson
Sasser, Thomas	Burke	Gordons	69/17	Wilkinson
Satterwhite, David	Columbia	4	70/7	Wilkinson
Satterwhite, Nancy	Elbert	Olivers	153/6	Wilkinson
Satterwhite, William	Columbia	11	294/21	Wilkinson
Sauls, Patience(Wid.)	Liberty		154/16	Baldwin
Saunders, James	Baldwin	3	186/24	Wilkinson
Saunders, James	Baldwin	3	188/20	Baldwin
Saunders, John	Warren	Willsons	319/8	Wilkinson
Saunders, Mary G.(Wid.)	Chatham	Pettybones	103/11	Wilkinson
Saunders, Reubin	Columbia	10	246/20	Baldwin
Savage, Mary(Wid.)	Washington	Chivers	148/7	Wilkinson
Savage, Thomas	Franklin	Wems'	181/19	Wilkinson
Savage, Zebulon	Franklin	Wems'	15/18	Wilkinson
Savidge, Zachariah	Columbia	1	205/19	Baldwin
Sawyer, Charles	Clarke	Butlers	281/24	Wilkinson
Sawyer, John	Clarke	Butlers	126/14	Wilkinson
Sawyer, Stephen	Baldwin	1	40/25	Wilkinson
Saxon, John	Baldwin	1	44/21	Wilkinson
Saxon, John	Burke	Forths	119/27	Wilkinson
Saxon, Lewis W.	Elbert	Thompsons	93/27	Wilkinson
Saxon, Solomon	Jackson	Wrights	353/10	Wilkinson
Saxon, Wiley	Wilkes	Edges	110/27	Wilkinson
Saxon, William	Burke	Forths	331/13	Wilkinson
Say, James	Jackson	Johnsons	183/17	Baldwin
Sayers, David Sr.	Greene	Watts'	60/20	Wilkinson
Sayers, Hally(Woman)	Greene	Watts'	100/28	Wilkinson
Sayvill, Moses	Franklin	Wems'	345/11	Wilkinson
Scales, John Jr.	Elbert	Barretts	55/28	Wilkinson
Scarborough, David	Glynn		163/28	2
Scarborough, Hardy	Screven		229/8	Wilkinson
Scarborough, Jonathan	Bulloch	Hendleys	183/9	Baldwin
Scarborough, Jonathan	Bulloch	Hendleys	22/12	Baldwin
Scarborough, Jonathan	Burke	Fields	123/11	Baldwin
Scarborough, Samuel	Bulloch	Hendleys	37/19	Baldwin
Scarbrough, Addison	Burke	Spains	304/17	Wilkinson
Scarbrough, Moses	Burke	Hilliards	304/11	Wilkinson
Scarbrough, Thomas	Burke	Mulkeys	81/9	Baldwin
Scarth's, Jonathan(Orphs.)	Liberty		140/16	Baldwin
Scherraus, Gottlief	Effingham		128/25	Wilkinson
Scherraus, John	Effingham		205/21	Wilkinson
Schley, John	Jefferson	Wrights	359/22	Wilkinson
Schmidt, Christiana(Wid.)	Liberty		82/8	Baldwin
Schmidt, Georgia D.H.	Chatham	McLeans	21/28	Wilkinson
Schneider, Gottlieb	Effingham		153/15	Baldwin
Schweighoffer, Mary(Orph.)	Chatham	Pembertons	160/7	Wilkinson
Schweighoffer, Thos.(Orph.)	Effingham		220/18	Wilkinson
Scillavent, William	Montgomery	54	4/7	Wilkinson
Scoggin, Alexander	Oglethorpe	Moores	347/24	Wilkinson
Scoggin, Gillum	Oglethorpe	Moores	109/12	Wilkinson
Scoggin, Gresham	Oglethorpe	Moores	235/19	Wilkinson
Scoggin, Humphrey Jr.	Oglethorpe	Watkins	139/6	Wilkinson
Scott's, Francis(Orphs.)	Burke	Montgomerys	180/21	Wilkinson
Scott, Ann(Orph.)	Chatham	Whites	313/14	Wilkinson
Scott, Archibald	Franklin	Hollingsworths	106/19	Baldwin
Scott, Francis	Warren	Carters	160/12	Wilkinson
Scott, Frederick	Hancock	Hudsons	233/10	Baldwin

NAME	COUNTY	MIL.DIST.	LOT/DIST	DREW LAND
Scott, Harriet(Miss)	Warren	Carters	102/23	Wilkinson
Scott, John S.	Screven	Olivers	169/21	Wilkinson
Scott, John Sr.	Burke	Forths	1/14	Baldwin
Scott, John	Warren	Hills	276/13	Wilkinson
Scott, Rhodda	Richmond		274/20	Wilkinson
Scott, Richard	Baldwin	2	39/28	Wilkinson
Scott, Thomas B.	Elbert	Mobleys	127/25	Wilkinson
Scott, Thomas W.	Oglethorpe	Hitchcocks	105/17	Baldwin
Scott, Thomas	Hancock	Hudsons	27/25	Wilkinson
Scott, Thomas	Washington	Wiggins	139/7	Wilkinson
Scott, Thomas	Washington	Wiggins	148/20	Baldwin
Scott, Thomas	Wilkes	Youngs	323/15	Baldwin
Scott, Vaughan	Baldwin	4	347/13	Wilkinson
Scott, Vaughan	Baldwin	4	90/13	Wilkinson
Scott, William	Burke	Fields	1/16	Baldwin
Scott, William	Jackson	Wrights	18/8	Wilkinson
Scott, William	Jackson	Wrights	192/19	Baldwin
Screven, Charles O.	Bryan	Austins	71/7	Baldwin
Scrimmeger, Ann(Wid.)	Chatham	Whites	328/7	Wilkinson
Scrivner, Mary(S.W.)	Clarke	Stewarts	109/19	Wilkinson
Scroggin, Humphrey	Clarke	Mitchells	206/19	Wilkinson
Scruggs, Edward	Lincoln	Mays	303/16	Wilkinson
Scruggs, Gross	Effingham		62/11	Wilkinson
Scruggs, Mary(Wid.)	Effingham		195/6	Wilkinson
Scruggs, Mary	Burke	Sandifords	157/10	Wilkinson
Scruggs, Theodorick	Lincoln	Normans	217/15	Baldwin
Scrutchins', Saml.(Orphs.)	Jefferson	Tarvers	92/28	Wilkinson
Scurry, David	Burke	Martins	96/17	Baldwin
Scurry, Richardson G.	Oglethorpe	Moores	99/22	Wilkinson
Seal, Anthony	Lincoln	Kings	188/14	Baldwin
Seal, Thomas	Hancock	Weeks'	54/11	Wilkinson
Seale, Littleton	Baldwin	2	320/8	Wilkinson
Seale, Nancy(Wid.)	Lincoln	Normons	291/11	Wilkinson
Seale, Richard	Lincoln	Kings	109/14	Wilkinson
Seals, Sophia	Hancock	Thomas'	153/24	Wilkinson
Seals, Spencer	Warren	Carters	77/7	Baldwin
Seamore, Youngs	Warren	Carters	184/18	Wilkinson
Sears, John	Montgomery	52	303/11	Wilkinson
Sears, John	Richmond		154/16	Wilkinson
Seckinger, Caty(Orph.)	Effingham		84/12	Baldwin
Seckinger, Christ'r(Orph.)	Effingham		84/12	Baldwin
Seckinger, John G.(Orph.)	Effingham		84/12	Baldwin
Seckinger, Salome(Orph.)	Effingham		84/12	Baldwin
Segar's, George(Orphs.)	Burke	Sandifords	184/20	Baldwin
Self, Isaac	Oglethorpe	Popes	421/7	Wilkinson
Self, William	Oglethorpe	Hudsons	7/21	Wilkinson
Selfner, Dougherty	Chatham	Neals	187/17	Baldwin
Sell's, Thomas(Orphs.)	Warren	Willsons	96/13	Baldwin
Sell, Lodowick	Washington	Collins	1/8	Baldwin
Sellers, Samuel	Jackson	Johnsons	45/10	Baldwin
Sellson, William	Wilkes	Heards	89/14	Wilkinson
Selman, Abner	Franklin	Cleghorns	336/14	Wilkinson
Selman, Eli	Franklin	Cleghorns	136/27	Wilkinson
Selman, Stafford	Franklin	Cleghorns	140/24	Wilkinson
Sessions, Asa	Jackson	Hendersons	69/20	Baldwin
Sessions, Delilah	Washington	Paces	229/10	Baldwin
Sessions, Joseph	Washington	Kendricks	57/24	Wilkinson
Settle, Francis	Burke	Johnsons	146/26	Wilkinson
Sewell, Josiah	Screven	Williamsons	289/22	Wilkinson
Sewell, Lewis	Clarke	Martins	100/12	Wilkinson
Sewell, Samuel	Franklin	Cleghorns	155/17	Baldwin
Shackleford's, Leo(Orphs.)	Hancock	Coffees	202/12	Wilkinson
Shackleford, Edmond Sr.	Elbert	Faulkners	91/28	Wilkinson
Shackleford, Henry Jr.	Elbert	Clarks	22/24	Wilkinson
Shackleford, Henry Sr.	Elbert	Clarks	108/27	Wilkinson
Shackleford, James	Elbert	Roebucks	247/24	Wilkinson
Shackleford, John Sr.	Jackson	Cockrans	5/9	Baldwin

NAME	COUNTY	MIL.DIST.	LOT/DIST	DREW LAND
Shadiek, William	Columbia	4	170/17	Wilkinson
Shaffer, Jacob	Chatham	Abrahams	230/10	Wilkinson
Shaffer, James	Chatham	Pettybones	237/12	Wilkinson
Shaffer, Jno.W.	Chatham	Abrahams	117/16	Wilkinson
Shaffer, John W.	Chatham	Abrahams	40/15	Wilkinson
Shank, John	Wilkes	Coopers	168/14	Wilkinson
Shankle, Abraham	Jackson	Johnsons	205/15	Baldwin
Shankle, Eli	Jackson	Johnsons	36/25	Wilkinson
Shankle, Jacob	Franklin	Christians	203/23	Wilkinson
Shankle, John Jr.	Jackson	Johnsons	261/17	Wilkinson
Shankle, John Sr.	Jackson	Johnsons	50/10	Baldwin
Sharbrew, James Jr.	Screven	Williamsons	328/17	Wilkinson
Sharman, Catharine	Wilkes	Roreys	142/22	Wilkinson
Sharman, James	Wilkes	Coopers	213/13	Baldwin
Sharman, Robert Sr.	Wilkes	Roreys	23/9	Wilkinson
Sharp, Henry H.	Greene	Jinkins'	121/20	Baldwin
Sharp, James(Orph.)	Burke	Sharps	97/10	Wilkinson
Sharp, Joseph(Orph.)	Burke	Sharps	97/10	Wilkinson
Sharp, Joshua	Tattnall	Armstrongs	70/10	Baldwin
Sharp, Robert	Baldwin	4	79/11	Baldwin
Sharp, Samuel Jr.	Baldwin	4	247/8	Wilkinson
Sharp, Samuel Sr.	Baldwin	4	238/9	Wilkinson
Sharp, Thomas H.	Baldwin	4	119/22	Wilkinson
Sharp, William	Baldwin	2	109/10	Baldwin
Sharp, William	Baldwin	4	140/9	Baldwin
Shaun, George	Richmond		74/21	Wilkinson
Shave's, Richard(Orphs.)	Liberty		5/11	Wilkinson
Shave, Amy(Wid.)	Liberty		107/22	Wilkinson
Shavers, Philip	Clarke	Dukes	11/10	Baldwin
Shaw, Amos	Baldwin	2	221/15	Wilkinson
Shaw, Amos	Baldwin	2	64/19	Wilkinson
Shaw, Charles(S.of Robt.)	Columbia	6	82/16	Wilkinson
Shaw, Daniel	Baldwin	1	55/9	Baldwin
Shaw, Eli(Orph.)	Richmond		51/16	Baldwin
Shaw, George	Warren	Newsoms	151/24	Wilkinson
Shaw, Harriet(Orphs.)	Richmond		116/14	Baldwin
Shaw, Jno.(Orph.)	Richmond		116/14	Baldwin
Shaw, John	Greene	Davenports	161/10	Baldwin
Shaw, John	Hancock	Gumms	267/15	Wilkinson
Shaw, William	Chatham	Pettybones	149/14	Baldwin
Shaw, William	Clarke		56/17	Wilkinson
Shaw, William	Clarke	Harpers	113/6	Baldwin
Sheapard, Thomas	Clarke	Martins	118/9	Wilkinson
Sheely, Henry Godlove	Burke	Mulkeys	44/14	Wilkinson
Sheffield, John C.	Montgomery	56	187/8	Wilkinson
Sheflett, Powell	Elbert	McGuires	184/13	Baldwin
Sheftall, Benjamin	Chatham	Pembertons	226/12	Wilkinson
Sheftall, Emanuel	Chatham		10/22	Wilkinson
Sheftall, Frances(Wid.)	Chatham	Pembertons	196/26	Wilkinson
Shellman, Catharine	Chatham	Whites	39/14	Wilkinson
Shellman, John	Chatham	Whites	149/10	Baldwin
Shelton, Charlotte	Warren	Neals	122/28	Wilkinson
Shelvy's, John(Orphs.)	Washington	Holts	175/9	Baldwin
Shepard, John	Clarke	Martins	204/20	Baldwin
Shepers, James	Screven	Hutchinsons	202/24	Wilkinson
Sheppard, Andrew	Wilkes	Sidwells	203/6	Baldwin
Sheppard, Andrew	Wilkes	Sidwells	305/9	Wilkinson
Sheppard, Charles	Washington	Chivers	2/25	Wilkinson
Sheppard, James	Burke	Carswells	171/8	Wilkinson
Sheppard, James	Washington	Burneys	260/15	Baldwin
Sheppard, Thomas	Liberty		282/9	Wilkinson
Sheppard, William	Screven		10/15	Baldwin
Shepparson, Bartley	Screven		126/8	Wilkinson
Shepparson, Bartley	Screven		153/12	Wilkinson
Shepparson, Nathaniel	Screven		11/16	Baldwin
Shepparson, Nathaniel	Screven		52/7	Wilkinson
Sherley, Recardis	Hancock	Barksdales	200/9	Baldwin

NAME	COUNTY	MIL.DIST.	LOT/DIST	DREW LAND
Sherley, William	Burke	Carswells	205/12	Wilkinson
Sherman, Jared	McIntosh		255/10	Wilkinson
Sherrard, Simon	Burke	Hilliards	128/7	Wilkinson
Sherwood, Robert	McIntosh		136/7	Wilkinson
Shi, Simeon	Hancock	Barksdales	341/12	Wilkinson
Shick, Elizabeth	Chatham	Hardens	160/15	Baldwin
Shields', Robt.(Orphs.)	Burke	Smiths	307/15	Baldwin
Shields, James	Columbia	10	400/8	Wilkinson
Shields, Josiah	Clarke	Hitchcocks	57/20	Baldwin
Shields, Littleberry	Franklin	Christians	195/8	Wilkinson
Shields, Littleberry	Franklin	Christians	39/20	Baldwin
Shields, Thomas	Lincoln	Kennons	136/11	Wilkinson
Shiflet, Pickett	Elbert	Roebucks	192/24	Wilkinson
Shinholster, John U.	Richmond		118/15	Baldwin
Ship's, Benj.(Orphs.)	Hancock	Shivers	4/18	Baldwin
Ship, David	Hancock	Coffees	73/15	Wilkinson
Ship, John	Jackson	Wrights	62/17	Baldwin
Ship, Richard	Hancock	Shivers	310/20	Wilkinson
Ship, Richard	Hancock	Shivers	54/14	Baldwin
Ship, Wm.	Jackson	Wrights	55/19	Baldwin
Ship, Wm.	Jackson	Wrights	58/9	Baldwin
Shivers, Barnaby	Hancock	Shivers'	48/15	Baldwin
Shivers, Jonas	Warren	Heaths	127/15	Wilkinson
Shivers, William	Hancock	Shivers'	6/10	Baldwin
Shockley, Michael L.	Greene	Stewarts	112/13	Baldwin
Shockley, Wm.	Jackson	Hendersons	30/26	Wilkinson
Shockley, Zelpa(Single)	Hancock	Weeks'	71/21	Wilkinson
Shoemake, Joseph	Burke	Mulkeys	156/14	Baldwin
Sholar, John	Washington	Garretts	144/16	Baldwin
Shores, Mary(Wid.)	Montgomery	55	63/10	Baldwin
Shores, Nancy	Montgomery	53	107/8	Baldwin
Short, David	Oglethorpe	Hudsons	170/14	Baldwin
Short, Francis	Wilkes	M.Hendersons	173/16	Wilkinson
Short, James	Oglethorpe	Hudsons	147/16	Wilkinson
Short, Jonas	Jackson	Cockrans	295/14	Wilkinson
Short, William	Columbia	8	84/16	Wilkinson
Shorter, James	Wilkes	J.Hendersons	104/6	Wilkinson
Shorter, Mary	Wilkes	J.Hendersons	189/17	Baldwin
Shows, Jacob	Warren	Willsons	7/10	Wilkinson
Shrimph, Wm.	Effingham		98/21	Wilkinson
Shropshire, Jane(Wid.)	Oglethorpe	Stewarts	43/18	Baldwin
Shropshire, Spencer	Oglethorpe	Stewarts	153/27	Wilkinson
Shubart, Frederick(C.C.O.)	Burke	Sandifords	265/11	Wilkinson
Shubtain, Gottlieb(Orph.)	Effingham		70/20	Baldwin
Shubtain, Han(Orph.)	Effingham		70/20	Baldwin
Shuffield's, John(Orphs.)	Jackson	Wrights	4/7	Baldwin
Shuffield's, Mark(Orphs.)	Burke	Fields	180/11	Baldwin
Shuffield, Aaron	Wayne	2	275/12	Wilkinson
Shuffield, Austin	Bulloch	Denmarks	238/15	Baldwin
Shuffield, John C.	Montgomery	56	142/12	Wilkinson
Shuffield, Robert	Warren	Carters	222/18	Wilkinson
Shuffield, Sherrard	Burke	Browns	173/18	Wilkinson
Shuffield, Zaccheus	Warren	Carters	143/19	Baldwin
Shuffle's, John(Orphs.)	Wilkinson		41/13	Baldwin
Shuman, James	Effingham		241/14	Baldwin
Shurley, William Jr.	Warren	Flournoys	285/14	Wilkinson
Shurley, William	Warren	Devereux's	369/7	Wilkinson
Shurley, Wm.Jr.	Warren	Flournoys	257/19	Wilkinson
Sibert, John	Lincoln	Jones'	108/8	Baldwin
Sibert, John	Lincoln	Jones'	374/21	Wilkinson
Sibley, Robert(Orph.)	Chatham	Pettybones	54/18	Wilkinson
Sidwell, David(Capt.)	Wilkes	Sidwells	14/6	Baldwin
Sikes, Frances	Wilkinson		49/7	Baldwin
Sikes, Jacob	Washington	Burneys	56/11	Baldwin
Sikes, William	Richmond		43/26	Wilkinson
Sikes, Willoughby	Wilkinson		187/16	Baldwin
Sills, Edward	Baldwin	2	355/9	Wilkinson

NAME	COUNTY	MIL.DIST.	LOT/DIST	DREW LAND
Silman, William	Baldwin	5	211/13	Wilkinson
Silman, William	Baldwin	5	228/21	Wilkinson
Silvia, Betsy	Greene	Loves	36/20	Wilkinson
Simmons, Adam Sr.	Oglethorpe	Hewells	253/23	Wilkinson
Simmons, Charles	Baldwin	2	99/15	Wilkinson
Simmons, Henry	Bulloch	Parishs	35/15	Baldwin
Simmons, James	Baldwin	5	64/15	Wilkinson
Simmons, James	Hancock	Weeks'	95/10	Wilkinson
Simmons, James	Hancock	Weeks	78/13	Wilkinson
Simmons, Jesse	Greene	Moores	266/15	Baldwin
Simmons, Jesse	Jackson	Wrights	264/20	Wilkinson
Simmons, John Sr.	Hancock	Weeks	234/16	Wilkinson
Simmons, John	Warren	Carters	297/6	Wilkinson
Simmons, Sterns	Lincoln	Normans	132/11	Wilkinson
Simmons, Thomas	Hancock	Crowders	213/18	Wilkinson
Simmons, Thomas	Hancock	Weeks	397/8	Wilkinson
Simmons, William	Hancock	Candlers	199/28	Wilkinson
Simmons, William	Warren	Flournoys	106/20	Wilkinson
Simmons, Wm.(B.C.)	Baldwin	2	69/19	Baldwin
Simmons, Wm.	Greene	Davenports	52/14	Wilkinson
Simmons, Wm.	Hancock	Crowders	67/8	Wilkinson
Simms', John(Orphs.)	Wilkes	Parks	6/19	Wilkinson
Simms, Aggy(D.of Wm.)	Columbia	2	222/16	Wilkinson
Simms, George	Lincoln	Jones	283/11	Wilkinson
Simms, Green	Greene	Alfords	303/6	Wilkinson
Simms, Leonard	Burke	Bynes	106/24	Wilkinson
Simms, Leonard	Lincoln	Jones	92/20	Baldwin
Simms, Nathan	Franklin	Cornelius'	322/15	Baldwin
Simms, Robert	Clarke	Cooks	16/13	Wilkinson
Simms, Sarah M.	Columbia	1	82/12	Wilkinson
Simms, Wylie	Oglethorpe	Hitchcocks	18/16	Baldwin
Simons, Abraham	Wilkes	Wellborns	66/9	Wilkinson
Simons, John	Clarke	Butlers	32/24	Wilkinson
Simons, Saul	Chatham	Pettybones	298/21	Wilkinson
Simonton, Abner	Greene	Dawsons	50/13	Wilkinson
Simonton, Joel	Greene	Dawsons	20/21	Wilkinson
Simonton, Theophilus	Clarke	Hitchcocks	3/13	Baldwin
Simpson, David	Wilkes	Hendricks'	114/16	Wilkinson
Simpson, John N.	Wilkes	Coopers	116/27	Wilkinson
Simpson, Malachi	Oglethorpe	Moores	209/13	Wilkinson
Simpson, Nathan	Washington	Jones Kendrick	201/6	Baldwin
Simpson, Nathan	Washington	Kendricks	1/9	Wilkinson
Simpson, Robert	Wilkes	Malones	154/13	Wilkinson
Simpson, Thomas	Jackson	Johnsons	217/20	Baldwin
Simpson, Thomas	Montgomery	57	161/14	Wilkinson
Simpson, William	Baldwin	5	175/20	Wilkinson
Simpson, William	Clarke	Martins	169/16	Wilkinson
Simpson, William	Clarke	Martins	263/20	Wilkinson
Simpson, Wm.(Orph.)	Chatham	Abrahams	135/14	Baldwin
Simpson, Wm.N.	Wilkes	Malones	138/14	Wilkinson
Sims, Benjamin	Richmond		225/15	Wilkinson
Sims, Catharine(Wid.)	Warren	Flournoys	295/21	Wilkinson
Sims, David	Clarke	Browns	94/23	Wilkinson
Sims, James	Chatham	Hardens	105/28	Wilkinson
Sims, James	Oglethorpe	Hartsfields	151/18	Baldwin
Sims, Leonard	Lincoln	Jones	139/8	Wilkinson
Sims, Margaret	Washington	Andersons	89/22	Wilkinson
Singleton, David	Bulloch	Parishs	107/18	Wilkinson
Singleton, David	Bulloch	Parishs	90/9	Wilkinson
Singleton, Hezekiah	Hancock	Huffs	217/15	Wilkinson
Siquefield, Samuel Jr.	Baldwin	1	237/15	Baldwin
Sisson, Richard	Greene	Baxters	363/22	Wilkinson
Skelly, Samuel	Warren	Devereux's	184/17	Wilkinson
Skelton, Reecy	Elbert	Barretts	126/10	Wilkinson
Skinner, Jane(Wid.of Isaac)	Columbia	1	220/19	Baldwin
Skinner, John H.	Jackson	Wrights	89/9	Baldwin
Skinner, Phenehas	Clarke	Hopkins	225/15	Baldwin

NAME	COUNTY	MIL.DIST.	LOT/DIST	DREW LAND
Skinner, Redding	Burke	Montgomerys	30/11	Wilkinson
Skinner, Uriah	Burke	Sandifords	185/10	Baldwin
Skinner, William	Baldwin	2	128/13	Baldwin
Skipwith, Peyton	Burke	Ashleys	14/7	Wilkinson
Skipwith, Peyton	Burke	Ashleys	25/22	Wilkinson
Sky, Thomas	Chatham	McLeans	137/8	Baldwin
Slade's, Nicholas(Orph.)	Warren	Bakers	73/8	Wilkinson
Slade, Belinda(Miss)	Warren	Bakers	83/25	Wilkinson
Slade, Jeremiah	Liberty		192/16	Baldwin
Slade, Jeremiah	Liberty		70/11	Wilkinson
Slappy, Jacob	Washington	Renfroes	125/16	Baldwin
Slappy, Jacob	Washington	Renfroes	13/16	Wilkinson
Slater, James	Screven		135/18	Wilkinson
Slater, John	Chatham	Pettybones	75/25	Wilkinson
Slaton, Mary	Jackson	Wrights	33/25	Wilkinson
Slaton, Solomon	Tattnall	Halls	168/15	Wilkinson
Slatter, Joel	Warren	Jones	78/20	Wilkinson
Slatter, John	Warren	Jones	235/15	Wilkinson
Slaughter, Beverly	Greene	Alfords	64/17	Baldwin
Slaughter, Martin	Greene	Owsleys	113/8	Wilkinson
Slaughter, Martin	Greene	Owsleys	305/7	Wilkinson
Slaughter, Thomas S.	Hancock	Holts	225/25	Wilkinson
Slaughter, William	Greene	Alfords	204/11	Wilkinson
Slaughter, William	Greene	Alfords	267/24	Wilkinson
Slauter, Reubin	Hancock	Coffees	93/12	Wilkinson
Slauter, Samuel	Hancock	Candlers	201/13	Wilkinson
Slauter, Sarah	Hancock	Coffees	163/16	Baldwin
Slaven, Nancy(Wid.)	Wilkes	Edges	180/8	Wilkinson
Sledge's, Nathaniel(Orphs.)	Hancock	Huffs	26/22	Wilkinson
Sledge's, Payton(Orphs.)	Hancock	Huffs	132/9	Baldwin
Sledge, John	Hancock	Huffs	112/19	Baldwin
Sledge, John	Hancock	Huffs	207/13	Baldwin
Sledge, Polly(Wid.)	Hancock	Huffs	234/6	Wilkinson
Sleigh, John	Burke	Smiths	158/12	Baldwin
Sleigh, Mary(Wid.)	Bryan	Austins	199/13	Baldwin
Sloan, David	Chatham	McLeans	71/25	Wilkinson
Sloan, John	Columbia	11	258/17	Wilkinson
Slocum, Samuel	Jefferson	Bosticks	35/23	Wilkinson
Smallwood, Elisha Jr.	Wilkes	Edges	174/12	Baldwin
Smallwood, Polly	Wilkes	Hendricks	251/23	Wilkinson
Smallwood, William	Wilkes	Edges	40/18	Wilkinson
Smart, Naomi	Liberty		223/16	Baldwin
Smedley, Thomas	Baldwin	4	60/15	Wilkinson
Smelt, Dennis	Richmond		237/15	Wilkinson
Smiley, James	Baldwin	2	106/11	Wilkinson
Smilie, Jacob	Montgomery	52	308/22	Wilkinson
Smith's, Benj.(Orphs.)	Elbert	Blackwells	154/10	Wilkinson
Smith's, David(Orphs.)	Baldwin	1	139/17	Baldwin
Smith's, Esaw(Orphs.)	Columbia	7	58/14	Baldwin
Smith's, Jacob(Orphs.)	Greene	Baxters	105/15	Baldwin
Smith's, Jesse(Orphs.)	Washington	Collins	230/24	Wilkinson
Smith's, John T.(Orphs.)	Wilkes	Normans	286/70	Wilkinson
Smith's, John(Orph.)	Washington	Renfroes	38/18	Baldwin
Smith's, John(Orphs.)	Clarke	Robinsons	189/13	Baldwin
Smith's, Robert(Orphs.)	Washington	Willis	140/11	Baldwin
Smith's, S.(Orphs.)	Montgomery	51	22/21	Wilkinson
Smith's, Thomas(Orphs.)	Burke	Gordons	132/11	Baldwin
Smith's, Thomas(Orphs.)	Hancock	Barksdales	385/21	Wilkinson
Smith's, Thomas(Orphs.)	Jefferson		196/20	Wilkinson
Smith, Abraham	Baldwin	2	137/28	Wilkinson
Smith, Alexander	Washington	Holts	131/17	Baldwin
Smith, Anderson	Oglethorpe	Popes	200/11	Wilkinson
Smith, Anthony	Wilkinson		231/10	Baldwin
Smith, Anthony	Wilkinson		62/6	Wilkinson
Smith, Archibald	Chatham	Whites	181/6	Wilkinson
Smith, Arthur	Screven	Olivers	144/12	Wilkinson
Smith, Benjamin	Hancock	Winsletts	248/19	Baldwin

NAME	COUNTY	MIL.DIST.	LOT/DIST	DREW LAND
Smith, Bennett	Jefferson	Wrights	243/13	Wilkinson
Smith, Betsy	Baldwin	5	124/6	Wilkinson
Smith, Bird	Baldwin	5	174/17	Baldwin
Smith, Boling	Wilkes	J.Hendersons	134/22	Wilkinson
Smith, Bradley	Jackson	Johnsons	266/21	Wilkinson
Smith, Bradley	Jackson	Johnsons	75/11	Baldwin
Smith, Brinkley	Oglethorpe	Hewells	72/17	Wilkinson
Smith, Britton	Montgomery	56	154/11	Wilkinson
Smith, Catharine(Wid.)	Elbert	Dyes	103/6	Baldwin
Smith, Catharine	Greene	Alfords	16/10	Baldwin
Smith, Charles	Jackson	Hendersons	266/25	Wilkinson
Smith, Charles	Jackson	Hendersons	88/14	Baldwin
Smith, Charles	Wayne	1	74/15	Baldwin
Smith, Clayton	Oglethorpe	Hitchcocks	72/9	Baldwin
Smith, Colebay	Washington	Kendricks	23/8	Wilkinson
Smith, Daniel	Chatham	Pettybones	62/13	Wilkinson
Smith, David D.	Hancock	Crowders	37/14	Wilkinson
Smith, David	Hancock	Birdsongs	88/22	Wilkinson
Smith, David	Wilkes	Sidwells	80/16	Baldwin
Smith, Delilah	Elbert	Moons	172/23	Wilkinson
Smith, Ebenezer	Wilkes	Heards	28/13	Baldwin
Smith, Elijah	Wilkes	Hendricks	88/13	Baldwin
Smith, Eliz.(Orph.)	Richmond		149/18	Wilkinson
Smith, Francis	Lincoln	Kennons	180/7	Wilkinson
Smith, George	Wilkes	Malones	94/14	Baldwin
Smith, Griffin	Wilkes	Milners	368/21	Wilkinson
Smith, Griffin	Wilkes	Milners	52/19	Wilkinson
Smith, Guy	Oglethorpe	Smith	132/16	Wilkinson
Smith, Haley	Oglethorpe	Moores	78/13	Baldwin
Smith, Henry	Elbert	Moons	17/11	Wilkinson
Smith, Hill	Oglethorpe	Popes	309/20	Wilkinson
Smith, Isham	Oglethorpe	Hatchetts	258/6	Wilkinson
Smith, Isiah	Wilkinson		141/9	Wilkinson
Smith, Jacob	Burke	Martins	119/19	Baldwin
Smith, Jacob	Montgomery	56	138/12	Wilkinson
Smith, Jacob	Warren	Willsons	347/9	Wilkinson
Smith, Jacob	Washington	Andersons	123/13	Wilkinson
Smith, James	Baldwin	5	156/9	Baldwin
Smith, James	Burke	Thompsons	252/15	Wilkinson
Smith, James	Columbia	7	163/23	Wilkinson
Smith, James	Columbia	7	51/16	Wilkinson
Smith, James	Jefferson	Thomas'	130/14	Baldwin
Smith, James	Liberty		87/16	Baldwin
Smith, James	Oglethorpe	Smiths	129/8	Wilkinson
Smith, James	Tattnall	McDonalds	245/16	Wilkinson
Smith, James	Warren	Neals	184/20	Wilkinson
Smith, Jane(Wid.)	Oglethorpe	Beasleys	202/21	Wilkinson
Smith, Jane	Chatham	Whites	301/14	Wilkinson
Smith, Jeremiah	Baldwin	5	258/15	Baldwin
Smith, Jeremiah	Lincoln	Gartrells	77/19	Baldwin
Smith, Jeremiah	Washington	Wiggins	58/18	Baldwin
Smith, Jesse	Franklin	Yowells	173/17	Baldwin
Smith, Jesse	Jackson	Johnsons	295/16	Wilkinson
Smith, John G.	Elbert	Keelings	254/13	Wilkinson
Smith, John G.	Oglethorpe	Smiths	27/18	Baldwin
Smith, John Jr.	Franklin	Christians	59/14	Wilkinson
Smith, John Jr.	Lincoln	Kennons	35/9	Baldwin
Smith, John	Baldwin	2	29/16	Wilkinson
Smith, John	Franklin	Yowells	105/27	Wilkinson
Smith, John	Hancock	Smiths	28/18	Wilkinson
Smith, John	Jefferson	Colemans	26/16	Baldwin
Smith, John	Jefferson	Colemans	84/15	Wilkinson
Smith, Jonathan	Columbia	9	262/10	Wilkinson
Smith, Jordan	Washington	Burneys	127/12	Baldwin
Smith, Joseph	Baldwin	1	78/26	Wilkinson
Smith, Joseph	Baldwin	1	97/12	Baldwin
Smith, Joseph	Baldwin	4	164/26	Wilkinson

NAME	COUNTY	MIL.DIST.	LOT/DIST	DREW LAND
Smith, Lemuel	Baldwin	2	304/7	Wilkinson
Smith, Leonard B.	Columbia	6	160/17	Baldwin
Smith, Lewis	Baldwin	3	212/24	Wilkinson
Smith, Lovett	Hancock	Birdsongs	53/11	Wilkinson
Smith, Margaret(Wid.)	Wilkes	Heards	97/17	Wilkinson
Smith, Mary B.	Burke	Martins	53/17	Wilkinson
Smith, Mary(Wid.)	Liberty		76/15	Wilkinson
Smith, Milly	Franklin	Dixons	101/27	Wilkinson
Smith, Moses	Jefferson	Fultons	168/20	Baldwin
Smith, Moses	Lincoln	Kennons	171/16	Baldwin
Smith, Moses	Lincoln	Kennons	203/7	Wilkinson
Smith, Nancy(Wid.)	Baldwin	1	470/7	Wilkinson
Smith, Needham	Washington	Paces	109/22	Wilkinson
Smith, Nicholas	Clarke	Hopkins	127/18	Baldwin
Smith, Noah	Burke	Carswells	67/12	Wilkinson
Smith, Patsy(Wid.)	Warren	Newsoms	115/10	Wilkinson
Smith, Peter	Elbert	Willifords	222/11	Wilkinson
Smith, Peter	Oglethorpe	Moores	93/22	Wilkinson
Smith, Rachel	Hancock	Barksdales	150/6	Wilkinson
Smith, Rebecca(Wid.)	Washington	Paces	300/8	Wilkinson
Smith, Reddick	Greene	Greers	244/25	Wilkinson
Smith, Reddick	Washington	Paces	169/10	Wilkinson
Smith, Richard	Elbert	Roebucks	4/11	Wilkinson
Smith, Richard	Greene	Reas	158/25	Wilkinson
Smith, Robert	Elbert	Keelings	149/24	Wilkinson
Smith, Sally(Wid.)	Clarke	Robinsons	14/11	Wilkinson
Smith, Sarah Lane	Washington	Renfroes	167/14	Baldwin
Smith, Sarah(Orph)	Richmond		149/18	Wilkinson
Smith, Shadrack	Oglethorpe	Hatchetts	132/15	Wilkinson
Smith, Shadrack	Wilkes	Youngs	74/20	Wilkinson
Smith, Simon	Screven		101/14	Wilkinson
Smith, Thomas Sr.	Warren	Hills	142/10	Wilkinson
Smith, Thomas	Jackson	Hendersons	302/20	Baldwin
Smith, Thomas	Oglethorpe	Moores	238/25	Wilkinson
Smith, Thomas	Warren	Neals	90/20	Baldwin
Smith, Tobias	Clarke	Robinsons	45/12	Wilkinson
Smith, William C.	Oglethorpe	Moores	96/8	Baldwin
Smith, William Sr.	Clarke	Stewarts	408/7	Wilkinson
Smith, William Sr.	Lincoln	Flemings	92/11	Baldwin
Smith, William	Baldwin	3	127/11	Baldwin
Smith, William	Clarke	Robinsons	251/24	Wilkinson
Smith, William	Greene	Jinkins'	306/15	Baldwin
Smith, William	Greene	Loves	175/7	Wilkinson
Smith, William	Jackson	Johnsons	90/17	Wilkinson
Smith, William	Jefferson	Colemans	219/25	Wilkinson
Smith, William	Warren	Bakers	183/8	Wilkinson
Smith, William	Washington	Andersons	213/14	Baldwin
Smith, William	Washington	Paces	230/11	Wilkinson
Smith, Wm. Jr.	Clarke	Martins	89/24	Wilkinson
Smith, Wm.	Baldwin	4	131/10	Baldwin
Smith, Wm.	Hancock	Wallers	48/6	Baldwin
Smith, Wm.S.	Greene	Carltons	175/19	Baldwin
Smith, Wm.Sr.	Clarke	Martins	241/21	Wilkinson
Smith, Wm.Sr.	Clarke	Stewarts	190/22	Wilkinson
Smith, Wm.Sr.	Lincoln	Flemings	211/20	Wilkinson
Smith, Wm.Sr.	Lincoln	Normans	123/7	Wilkinson
Smithson, Benjamin	Columbia	8	18/17	Baldwin
Smithwick, William	Elbert	Keelings	178/15	Baldwin
Smylie, James	Liberty		212/25	Wilkinson
Snead, Eliz.(Wid.)	Burke	Spains	133/19	Baldwin
Snead, Nancy(D.of Dudly)	Columbia	1	186/12	Wilkinson
Snead, Samuel	Greene	Alfords	214/28	Wilkinson
Snead, Wm.Jr.	Clarke	Robinsons	135/8	Baldwin
Snell, Christopher	Montgomery	56	30/6	Wilkinson
Snellings, George	Elbert	Morrisons	137/14	Wilkinson
Snellson, Nathaniel	Wilkes	Heards	146/10	Wilkinson
Snow, Samuel G.	Greene	Owsleys	224/15	Baldwin

NAME	COUNTY	MIL.DIST.	LOT/DIST	DREW LAND
Snow, Thomas	Greene	Owsleys	27/16	Baldwin
Snow, Thomas	Greene	Owsleys	7/13	Baldwin
Snow, Winnifred(Wid.)	Wilkes	J.Hendersons	128/14	Baldwin
Snyder, John	Chatham	Pettybones	292/10	Wilkinson
Snyder, John	Richmond		172/24	Wilkinson
Solomon, Lazarus	Montgomery	53	33/28	Wilkinson
Somarsall, George	Liberty		282/12	Wilkinson
Somarsall, Stafford	Liberty		146/20	Baldwin
Sorrel's, George(Orphs.)	Greene	Davenports	47/22	Wilkinson
Sorrel, Mary	Clarke	Browns	200/28	Wilkinson
Sorrow, Elijah	Oglethorpe	Hitchcocks	440/7	Wilkinson
Sorrow, John	Oglethorpe	Smiths	59/10	Wilkinson
Sorrow, Randle	Oglethorpe	Hewells	156/24	Wilkinson
Sorsby, Thomas	Burke	Gordons	286/16	Wilkinson
Sorsby, Thomas	Burke	Gordons	59/20	Baldwin
Sotherland, John	Columbia	7	12/18	Wilkinson
Sotherland, John	Columbia	7	23/12	Baldwin
Southall's, John(Orphs.)	Hancock	Huffs	281/9	Wilkinson
Sowell, Abihugh	Greene	Loves	195/13	Baldwin
Sowell, Zadock	Wilkes	Hendricks'	66/18	Baldwin
Spain's, John(Orphs.)	Burke	Spains	19/28	Wilkinson
Spain, Levy	Burke	Spains	57/14	Baldwin
Spalding, Isham	Burke	Johnsons	51/6	Wilkinson
Spalding, John	Columbia	4	130/13	Wilkinson
Spalding, John	Columbia	4	5/8	Wilkinson
Spalding, Thomas	McIntosh		141/16	Baldwin
Spalding, Thomas	McIntosh		226/24	Wilkinson
Spalding, Wm.	Baldwin	2	200/12	Baldwin
Span, Frances	Baldwin	1	78/9	Wilkinson
Sparks, Bailey(Orph.)	Oglethorpe	Moores	274/9	Wilkinson
Sparks, John	Jackson	Cockrans	245/12	Wilkinson
Sparks, John	Washington	Collins	270/9	Wilkinson
Sparks, Mary	Washington	Blackshears	6/18	Wilkinson
Sparks, Mathew	Jackson	Cockrans	39/8	Baldwin
Sparks, Thomas Sr.	Franklin	Hoopers	100/9	Baldwin
Sparks, Thomas	Greene	Stewarts	173/17	Wilkinson
Spear, John(S.of Ellis)	Wilkes	Roreys	327/13	Wilkinson
Spears, John	Jackson	Wrights	127/7	Wilkinson
Speer, David	Greene	Reas	125/26	Wilkinson
Speer, Moses	Greene	Carltons	44/16	Wilkinson
Speers, Wm.	Greene	Loves	154/12	Baldwin
Speight, John	Washington	Kendricks	140/16	Wilkinson
Speights, Unity(Wid.)	Montgomery	59	249/16	Wilkinson
Spell, George	Screven		17/13	Wilkinson
Spell, Howell	Screven	Hutchinsons	150/13	Wilkinson
Spence, Harris	Burke	Spains	242/13	Wilkinson
Spence, Isaac	Burke	Hilliards	115/19	Wilkinson
Spence, Zachariah	Burke	Hilliards	41/19	Baldwin
Spencer, Griffith	Elbert	Thompsons	235/10	Wilkinson
Spencer, Samuel	Chatham	Whites	44/14	Wilkinson
Spencer, Silas	Warren	Carters	77/7	Baldwin
Spencer, Thomas	Elbert	Mobleys	233/16	Wilkinson
Spencer, Thomas	Washington	Howards'	184/24	Wilkinson
Spencer, Thomas	Washington	Howards	162/10	Baldwin
Spencer, Wm.H.	Chatham	Pettybones	100/7	Wilkinson
Spicer, Claborn	Franklin	Cleghorns	289/14	Baldwin
Spicer, Hardy	Oglethorpe	Hitchcocks	107/9	Baldwin
Spight, Levi	Hancock	Shivers'	315/22	Wilkinson
Spight, Polly	Hancock	Shivers	87/13	Baldwin
Spight, Wm.Sr.	Hancock	Shivers	13/20	Baldwin
Spikes, Jonas	Jackson	Cockrans	34/6	Baldwin
Spinks, Garrett	Clarke	Robinsons	11/17	Wilkinson
Spires, Hezekiah	Lincoln	Busseys	64/8	Wilkinson
Spivey, Joab	Columbia	9	189/14	Wilkinson
Spivy, Joab	Columbia	9	143/16	Baldwin
Spivy, Moses	Columbia	2	32/7	Baldwin
Spradling, James	Baldwin	2	2/18	Baldwin

NAME	COUNTY	MIL.DIST.	LOT/DIST	DREW LAND
Spratlin, Elizabeth	Wilkes	M.Hendersons	108/13	Wilkinson
Spratlin, James Jr.	Wilkes	M.Hendersons	41/15	Wilkinson
Springer, Job Sr.	Baldwin	1	158/13	Wilkinson
Springer, Nancy	Baldwin	1	128/20	Baldwin
Springer, Thomas	Warren	Neals	138/6	Baldwin
Spruce, Wm.	Jackson	Cockrans	34/20	Wilkinson
Spurlin, Jeremiah	Warren	Devereux's	55/7	Wilkinson
Spurlin, John	Wilkinson		193/8	Wilkinson
Spurlock, James	Oglethorpe	Hatchetts	114/22	Wilkinson
Spurlock, Mary(Wid.)	Washington	Garretts	44/6	Baldwin
Spurlock, Samuel	Montgomery	50	47/18	Wilkinson
Stackhouse, Sam'l.H.	Chatham	Whites	160/15	Wilkinson
Stacks, Samuel	Jackson	Wrights	126/15	Wilkinson
Stacy, Stephen	Clarke	Martins	214/8	Wilkinson
Stallings, James(Cole)	Columbia	1	156/18	Baldwin
Stallings, John Jr.	Burke	Ballards	238/7	Wilkinson
Stallings, John Sr.	Burke	Ballards	83/9	Baldwin
Stallings, Moses	Oglethorpe	Bells	92/10	Baldwin
Stamps, James	Oglethorpe	Moores	167/16	Baldwin
Stanaland, Boaz	Bulloch	Denmarks	229/25	Wilkinson
Standford, Benjamin	Warren	Willsons	70/27	Wilkinson
Standford, Jesse	Warren	Willsons	74/11	Wilkinson
Standford, Joseph	Warren	Willsons	178/20	Wilkinson
Standford, Leveon	Warren	Willsons	69/15	Wilkinson
Standford, Leveon	Warren	Willsons	96/23	Wilkinson
Standford, Thomas	Warren	Willsons	314/21	Wilkinson
Standifer, Anderson	Elbert	McGuires	95/6	Wilkinson
Standiford, Benjamin	Elbert	McGuires	197/13	Wilkinson
Standley, Shadrack	Tattnall	Staffords	148/8	Wilkinson
Standridge, Alexr.	Franklin	Wems'	141/13	Baldwin
Stanford's, Stephen(Orphs.)	Columbia	9	11/25	Wilkinson
Stanford, John	Bulloch	Williams	9/10	Baldwin
Stanford, Nancy	Columbia	9	52/20	Wilkinson
Stanford, Thomas	Columbia	5	176/15	Baldwin
Stanley, Melissant	Greene	Butlers	17/19	Baldwin
Stanley, Sherwood	Greene	Butlers	132/6	Wilkinson
Stanston, Rebecca	Hancock	Winsletts	234/24	Wilkinson
Stanton's, Wm.(Orphs.)	Lincoln	Kennons	23/15	Wilkinson
Stanton, Ann	Wilkes	Parks'	49/28	Wilkinson
Stanton, Drusilla	Jefferson	Hardwichs	68/8	Wilkinson
Stanton, John	Wilkes	Heards	247/25	Wilkinson
Stapler's, John(Orphs.)	Columbia	4	292/20	Baldwin
Stapler, Robert	Jackson	Johnsons	149/13	Wilkinson
Stapler, Thomas	Jackson	Johnsons	8/15	Wilkinson
Stapler, Wm.	Columbia	8	254/15	Wilkinson
Staples, David	Elbert	Keelings	213/20	Baldwin
Staples, John	Elbert	Olivers	101/14	Baldwin
Stapleton, Job	Jefferson	Bosticks	16/10	Wilkinson
Stark, Ebenezer	Chatham	Herbs	53/24	Wilkinson
Starkey, Nancy	Oglethorpe	Stewarts	239/19	Baldwin
Starks, William	Columbia	10	120/25	Wilkinson
Starnes, Elizabeth	Richmond		24/6	Baldwin
Starns, Charles	Warren	Neals	67/10	Baldwin
Statem, Wm.	Washington	Andersons	185/9	Baldwin
Stathum, William	Greene	Jinkins'	55/20	Baldwin
Stead, Philip	Columbia	3	209/17	Baldwin
Stead, Philip	Columbia	3	55/21	Wilkinson
Steel, Alexander	Clarke	Mitchells	176/9	Wilkinson
Steel, Alexander	Clarke	Mitchells	26/26	Wilkinson
Steel, William	Wilkes	Wellborns	183/14	Wilkinson
Steen, James	Baldwin	3	279/11	Wilkinson
Step, John	Oglethorpe	Stewarts	299/24	Wilkinson
Step, John	Oglethorpe	Stewarts	62/8	Baldwin
Step, Stephen	Oglethorpe	Stewarts	9/6	Baldwin
Stephens', Nathaniel(Orphs.)	Greene	Stewarts	193/9	Baldwin
Stephens, Alex.W.(Orph.)	Bryan	Austins	59/16	Baldwin
Stephens, Alexander	Wilkes	Youngs	255/19	Baldwin

NAME	COUNTY	MIL.DIST.	LOT/DIST	DREW LAND
Stephens, Balaam	Warren	Newsoms	119/10	Baldwin
Stephens, Beverly	Burke	Mulkeys	124/19	Wilkinson
Stephens, Caleb	Warren	Newsoms	165/13	Baldwin
Stephens, George W.	Greene	Jenkins	144/8	Wilkinson
Stephens, George W.	Greene	Jinkins	250/7	Wilkinson
Stephens, John	Liberty		60/22	Wilkinson
Stephens, John	Wilkes	M.Hendersons	30/14	Baldwin
Stephens, Jonas	Jefferson	Hardwichs	270/24	Wilkinson
Stephens, Jonas	Jefferson	Hardwicks	67/28	Wilkinson
Stephens, Martha	Chatham	Abrahams	196/9	Wilkinson
Stephens, Moab	Montgomery	51	196/9	Baldwin
Stephens, Moab	Montgomery	51	60/10	Baldwin
Stephens, Nathaniel(Orph.)	Glynn		284/20	2
Stephens, Soloman	Franklin	Wems'	202/26	Wilkinson
Stephens, Stephen	Elbert	Willifords	49/8	Wilkinson
Stephens, Stephen	Washington	Paces	155/20	Wilkinson
Stephens, Stephen	Washington	Paces	220/6	Wilkinson
Stephens, Thomas(Capt.)	Baldwin	2	222/28	Wilkinson
Stephens, William	Chatham	Whites	8/17	Baldwin
Stephens, William	Elbert	Groves	134/28	Wilkinson
Steptoe, Eliz.(Orph.)	Burke	Sandifords	71/24	Wilkinson
Steptoe, Thomas	Burke	Forths	188/17	Wilkinson
Sterrett, Josiah M.	Jefferson	Wrights	231/20	Wilkinson
Steward, Reubin	Jackson	Cockrans	199/18	Wilkinson
Stewart's, Allen(Orphs.)	Greene	Carltons	8/20	Baldwin
Stewart's, Charles(Orphs.)	Liberty		96/8	Wilkinson
Stewart's, Jacob(Orphs.)	Columbia	7	29/23	Wilkinson
Stewart's, Josiah(Orphs.)	Liberty		39/8	Wilkinson
Stewart's, Wm.(Orphs.)	Columbia	7	40/14	Wilkinson
Stewart, Absalom	Jackson	Cockrans	86/16	Baldwin
Stewart, Alexander Sr.	Bulloch	Williams	6/7	Wilkinson
Stewart, Alfred	Clarke	Hitchcocks	254/8	Wilkinson
Stewart, Archibald	Burke	Thompsons	246/12	Wilkinson
Stewart, Archibald	Burke	Thompsons	48/7	Baldwin
Stewart, Bethia	Warren	Newsoms	301/20	Baldwin
Stewart, Delilah	Lincoln	Busseys	315/13	Wilkinson
Stewart, Eliz.(Wid.)	Clarke	Browns	77/15	Baldwin
Stewart, George	Clarke	Stewarts	189/11	Wilkinson
Stewart, Gravener	Wilkes	Youngs	58/17	Wilkinson
Stewart, Henry	Greene	Stewarts	126/16	Wilkinson
Stewart, Henry	Washington	Wiggins'	52/6	Baldwin
Stewart, Isaac	Clarke	Hopkins	75/6	Baldwin
Stewart, James Sr.	Clarke	Stewarts	254/19	Wilkinson
Stewart, James(Capt.)	Jackson	Hendersons	153/7	Wilkinson
Stewart, James	Clarke	Mitchells	166/25	Wilkinson
Stewart, Jemima(Orph.)	Bryan	Birds	218/10	Wilkinson
Stewart, John M.	Oglethorpe	Beasleys	280/20	Wilkinson
Stewart, John	Greene	Carltons	207/20	Baldwin
Stewart, John	Greene	Carltons	96/13	Wilkinson
Stewart, John	Jackson	Cockrans	271/13	Wilkinson
Stewart, Mary(Single)	Clarke	Stewarts	53/13	Baldwin
Stewart, Mathew W.(Orph.)	Chatham	Whites	278/19	Baldwin
Stewart, Nancy	Burke	Forths	45/17	Baldwin
Stewart, Nancy	Columbia	7	316/13	Wilkinson
Stewart, Reubin	Jackson	Cockrans	381/8	Wilkinson
Stewart, Sarah	Columbia	7	85/8	Wilkinson
Stewart, Susannah	Columbia	9	125/20	Wilkinson
Stewart, Thomas Sr.	Greene	Stewarts	200/12	Wilkinson
Stewart, Thomas	Burke	Forths	314/9	Wilkinson
Stewart, William	Greene	Watsons	106/7	Baldwin
Stibbs, John	Chatham	Pettybones	211/6	Wilkinson
Stigall, John	Washington	Kendricks	166/19	Wilkinson
Stiles, Joseph	Bryan	Austins	325/8	Wilkinson
Still, Susannah(S)	Hancock	Pinkstons	282/10	Wilkinson
Stillwell, Asa	Greene	Alfords	13/19	Wilkinson
Stillwell, Jacob	Greene	Loves	131/17	Wilkinson
Stillwell, Jacob	Greene	Loves	60/11	Baldwin

NAME	COUNTY	MIL.DIST.	LOT/DIST	DREW LAND
Stinson, Burrell	Oglethorpe	Smiths	180/13	Wilkinson
Stinson, Mary	Jackson	Johnsons	37/14	Baldwin
Stinson, Wm.	Baldwin	2	98/24	Wilkinson
Stokes', George(Orphs.)	Clarke	Butlers	128/12	Wilkinson
Stokes, Henry	Washington	Andersons	303/20	Wilkinson
Stokes, Mark	Burke	Spains	240/15	Wilkinson
Stokes, Samuel	Baldwin	2	76/18	Baldwin
Stokes, William	Wilkinson		5/19	Wilkinson
Stokes, Wm.Jr.	Lincoln	Normans	96/12	Baldwin
Stokes, Wm.Jr.	Lincoln	Normons	149/11	Baldwin
Stone, Eliz.(Wid.)	Glynn		34/22	Wilkinson
Stone, Hardeman	Chatham	Pettybones	91/12	Baldwin
Stone, Henry D.	Greene	Carltons	214/20	Baldwin
Stone, John	Elbert	Faulkners	362/21	Wilkinson
Stone, Osborn	Wilkes	Roreys	61/6	Wilkinson
Stone, Warren	Greene	Butlers	6/21	Wilkinson
Stone, William	Lincoln	Gartrells	211/10	Baldwin
Stone, William	Wilkes	Edges	25/13	Wilkinson
Stonum, Bryan	Hancock	Weeks	2/11	Wilkinson
Stonum, James	Hancock	Weeks'	127/21	Wilkinson
Storey, Ann	Montgomery	54	23/16	Baldwin
Storey, Asa	Montgomery	54	222/8	Wilkinson
Storey, Benjamin	Warren	Newsoms	195/19	Wilkinson
Storey, Thomas	Franklin	Henrys	79/8	Wilkinson
Storrs, Hiram	Jefferson	Wrights	71/6	Baldwin
Story, Anthony	Elbert	Willifords	78/25	Wilkinson
Story, Elizabeth	Chatham	McLeans	34/12	Baldwin
Stouf, Isidore	Chatham	Abrahams	179/11	Baldwin
Stovall, Benjamin	Oglethorpe	Smiths	19/20	Wilkinson
Stovall, Charles	Lincoln	Mays	315/24	Wilkinson
Stovall, David	Lincoln	Mays	322/12	Wilkinson
Stovall, Drury	Lincoln	Mays	90/25	Wilkinson
Stovall, George Sr.	Elbert	Keelings	112/12	Wilkinson
Stovall, George	Greene	Butlers	29/6	Wilkinson
Stovall, Peter	Wilkes	Stovalls	148/11	Wilkinson
Stovall, Tabitha(Single)	Oglethorpe	Smiths	201/22	Wilkinson
Stow, Warren	Franklin	Dixons	33/6	Baldwin
Stowers, John	Franklin	Cleghorns	165/14	Wilkinson
Stowers, Lewis	Elbert	McGuires	146/11	Wilkinson
Stowers, Lewis	Elbert	McGuires	235/11	Wilkinson
Stowers, Thomas	Jackson	Johnsons	69/13	Baldwin
Strain, Wm.W.	Greene	Carltons	382/21	Wilkinson
Strakey, John	Oglethorpe	Stewarts	29/10	Wilkinson
Strange, Littleberry	Jefferson	Bosticks	165/19	Baldwin
Strange, Sterling	Franklin	Griffiths	108/7	Wilkinson
Stranger, John	Oglethorpe	Hudsons	42/23	Wilkinson
Straughn, Edmund	Elbert	Keelings	105/19	Baldwin
Strawn, Daniel	Jackson	Cockrans	70/20	Wilkinson
Strawn, James	Jackson	Cockrans	73/15	Baldwin
Street, George	McIntosh		171/14	Wilkinson
Streetman, Wm.	Jackson	Johnsons	198/28	Wilkinson
Strength's, John(Orphs.)	Baldwin	2	131/6	Wilkinson
Strength, Margaret	Baldwin	2	25/23	Wilkinson
Stribling, Anthony	Lincoln	Kings	97/8	Wilkinson
Strickland, Henry	Franklin	Cleghorns	170/6	Wilkinson
Strickland, Robert	Baldwin	2	175/25	Wilkinson
Strickland, Simon	Jackson	Cockrans	178/7	Wilkinson
Strickland, Solomon	Elbert	Willifords	96/7	Baldwin
Strickland, Solomon	Jackson	Cockrans	288/8	Wilkinson
Stringer, Celia(Wid.)	Burke	Martins	23/27	Wilkinson
Stringer, James	Burke	Gordons	239/11	Wilkinson
Stringer, Reddin	Montgomery	50	232/24	Wilkinson
Stringer, Smith	Burke	Martins	83/7	Baldwin
Stringer, Susannah(Wid.)	Screven		185/13	Wilkinson
Stringfellow, Benjamin	Greene	Davenports	176/14	Wilkinson
Stringfellow, Enoch Sr.	Greene	Watts'	166/9	Baldwin
Stringfellow, George	Baldwin	4	25/16	Baldwin

NAME	COUNTY	MIL.DIST.	LOT/DIST	DREW LAND
Strobhart, Abraham	Chatham	Pettybones	109/23	Wilkinson
Stroder, John	Wilkes	Youngs	34/17	Wilkinson
Strong, Christopher B.	Oglethorpe	Smiths	29/19	Baldwin
Strong, John Sr.	Clarke	Dukes	202/13	Baldwin
Strong, Samuel	Oglethorpe	Smiths	18/26	Wilkinson
Strong, Sherwood	Clarke	Dukes	219/16	Wilkinson
Strosier, Mary	Washington	Holts	140/14	Baldwin
Strother, Francis	Lincoln	Gartrells	228/6	Wilkinson
Strother, French	Oglethorpe	Hatchetts	38/25	Wilkinson
Strother, Richard	Hancock	Shivers	121/22	Wilkinson
Stroud's, Mark(Orphs.)	Clarke	Browns	153/11	Baldwin
Stroud, Clary	Wilkes	Sheets	215/19	Wilkinson
Stroud, John	Clarke	Robinsons	185/28	Wilkinson
Strozer, Peter Jr.	Wilkes	J.Hendersons	227/28	Wilkinson
Strozer, Peter Sr.	Wilkes	J.Hendersons	327/24	Wilkinson
Strozer, Wm.	Wilkes	J.Hendersons	96/11	Baldwin
Stubblefield's, John(Orphs.)	Jackson	Cockrans	248/23	Wilkinson
Stubblefield's, John(Orphs.)	Oglethorpe	Watkins	36/12	Baldwin
Stubblefield, John	Wilkes	Heards	306/21	Wilkinson
Stubbs, James	Jefferson	Fultons	135/10	Baldwin
Stubbs, James	Jefferson	Fultons	98/16	Wilkinson
Stubbs, Peter	Elbert	Blackwells	22/11	Wilkinson
Stuckey, John	Burke	Forths	174/10	Wilkinson
Studdard, James	Baldwin	5	19/27	Wilkinson
Studstill, Thomas	Burke	Browns	195/25	Wilkinson
Studstill, Thomas	Burke	Browns	86/20	Baldwin
Studstill, William	Tattnall	McDonalds	210/19	Wilkinson
Sturdivant's, Mathew(Orphs.)	Lincoln	Flemings	3/16	Baldwin
Sturdivant's, Mathew(Orphs.)	Lincoln	Flemings	67/13	Baldwin
Sturdivant, Joel	Hancock	Shivers	329/13	Wilkinson
Sturdivant, Polly	Baldwin	2	76/27	Wilkinson
Subtil, William	Richmond		5/14	Wilkinson
Suddoth, Agatha	Lincoln	Normans	30/12	Baldwin
Suddoth, Elijah	Lincoln	Flemings	281/16	Wilkinson
Suddoth, Lewis	Oglethorpe	Hatchetts	165/19	Wilkinson
Suddoth, Litis	Lincoln	Kings	144/20	Wilkinson
Sudor, Joseph	McIntosh		48/10	Baldwin
Sudor, Peter	Chatham	Whites	227/25	Wilkinson
Suit, Nelly(Orph.)	Elbert	Dyes	203/22	Wilkinson
Sulfridge, Robert	Elbert	McGuires	145/10	Wilkinson
Sullagree, John	Liberty		57/6	Baldwin
Sullivan, Daniel	Glynn		256/22	2
Summerall, David	Bulloch	Williams	79/15	Baldwin
Summerlin, Fanny(D./Elisha)	Montgomery	58	231/11	Wilkinson
Summers, John	Clarke	Harpers	175/11	Baldwin
Summerville, George	Washington	Howards	55/18	Wilkinson
Summon, Eliz.(Wid.)	Clarke	Hopkins	41/28	Wilkinson
Sumner's, Lewis(Orphs.)	Burke	Gordons	46/16	Wilkinson
Sumner, Benjamin	Burke	Mulkeys	126/6	Wilkinson
Sumner, Benjamin	Burke	Mulkeys	97/9	Baldwin
Sumner, John	Burke	Mulkeys	132/6	Baldwin
Sumners, Wm.	Chatham	McLeans	58/12	Wilkinson
Suttle, Isaac	Clarke	Butlers	131/9	Wilkinson
Suttle, Jesse	Elbert	Mobleys	163/19	Wilkinson
Sutton, Benjamin	Wayne	1	163/15	Wilkinson
Sutton, Edward	Baldwin	4	46/23	Wilkinson
Sutton, James Sr.	Franklin	Yowells	171/22	Wilkinson
Sutton, Jesse	Greene	Moores	45/16	Baldwin
Sutton, Jesse	Greene	Moores	61/9	Baldwin
Swain, William	Glynn		271/24	2
Swan, James	Lincoln	Kennons	79/9	Wilkinson
Swan, Mary	Greene	Baxters	331/17	Wilkinson
Swanson, James	Oglethorpe	Beasleys	103/9	Baldwin
Swanson, John	Greene	Greers	117/15	Baldwin
Swanson, William	Oglethorpe	Stewarts	36/7	Baldwin
Swayne, Job	Warren	Carters	254/21	Wilkinson
Sweat, Nathan	Bulloch	Williams	174/14	Wilkinson

NAME	COUNTY	MIL.DIST.	LOT/DIST	DREW LAND
Sweat, William	Bulloch	Williams	114/10	Wilkinson
Swicord, Mary(Orph.)	Burke	Hardees	136/6	Wilkinson
Swift, Tyra	Franklin	Hoopers	121/26	Wilkinson
Swift, William	Baldwin	5	229/20	Wilkinson
Swinny, Joachim D.	Hancock	Huffs	232/25	Wilkinson
Swinny, Ransom	Hancock	Weeks'	270/13	Wilkinson
Swinny, Ransom	Hancock	Weeks'	8/15	Baldwin
Swint, Eliza.(Wid.)	Hancock	Pinkstons	10/10	Wilkinson
Sykes, Arthur(Orp/Danl.)	Montgomery	58	450/7	Wilkinson
Sykes, James	Burke	Ballards	256/10	Wilkinson
Sylvester, Augustin	Liberty		314/7	Wilkinson
Sylvester, John	Screven		71/27	Wilkinson
Tabb, Jean	Burke	Ballards	18/6	Wilkinson
Tabb, Thomas	Burke	Ballards	69/9	Wilkinson
Tabb, Thomas	Burke	Ballards	75/11	Wilkinson
Taber, John Sr.	Elbert	Keelings	98/15	Baldwin
Tabot, Edmund	Washington	Chivers	45/14	Wilkinson
Tait, John	Elbert	Thompsons	62/16	Wilkinson
Talbard, Samuel	Franklin	Cornelius'	178/13	Wilkinson
Talbert, Thomas	Hancock	Candlers	229/13	Wilkinson
Talbot, Joseph	Wilkes	Hendersons	55/26	Wilkinson
Talbot, Mathew	Wilkes	Sheets	219/7	Wilkinson
Taliaferro, Benjamin	Hancock	Candlers	268/22	Wilkinson
Tallant, Lott	Bulloch	Williams'	167/15	Wilkinson
Tally, Page	Jackson	Tarvers	26/25	Wilkinson
Tamplin, Edmund	Baldwin	1	24/7	Baldwin
Tamplin, George	Hancock	Gumms	65/7	Baldwin
Tanbrink, Manny	Screven	Williamsons	153/22	Wilkinson
Tankersley, George G.	Columbia	1	144/15	Baldwin
Tankersly, Fountain	Clarke	Robinsons	147/19	Baldwin
Tankersly, Wm.Brook	Hancock	Smiths	67/17	Wilkinson
Tanner's, Seth(Orphs.)	Hancock	Hudsons	125/9	Baldwin
Tanner, Abraham	Wilkes	Coopers	70/13	Baldwin
Tanner, Archibald	Jackson	Cockrans	182/27	Wilkinson
Tanner, Eliz.(Wid.)	Washington	Chivers	56/9	Wilkinson
Tanner, John	Oglethorpe	Hudsons	206/10	Wilkinson
Tanner, Joseph	Bulloch	Williams'	100/12	Baldwin
Tanner, Thomas	Washington	Chivers	295/22	Wilkinson
Tanner, Vincent	Washington	Chivers'	332/10	Wilkinson
Tapley, Ephraim	Montgomery	58	269/15	Wilkinson
Tapley, New	Montgomery	57	396/8	Wilkinson
Tapley, Sally	Montgomery	57	228/20	Wilkinson
Tarver, Celia	Burke	Carswells	45/8	Baldwin
Tarver, Frederick	Baldwin	2	265/10	Wilkinson
Tarver, Jacob Sr.	Wilkes	Edges	42/14	Wilkinson
Tarver, Jacob Sr.	Wilkes	Edges	98/8	Wilkinson
Tarver, Jacob	Hancock	Holts	99/12	Baldwin
Tarver, Robert	Burke	Carswells	163/15	Baldwin
Tarver, William	Warren	Bakers	276/22	Wilkinson
Tarvin, George	Montgomery	52	128/6	Wilkinson
Tarvin, Ulisses	Burke	Montgomerys	12/7	Wilkinson
Tate, Charity(Orph.)	Elbert	Thompsons	186/14	Wilkinson
Tate, Enos Jr.	Elbert	Hillyers	261/12	Wilkinson
Tate, James M.(Orph.)	Elbert	Thompsons	186/14	Wilkinson
Tate, James(Orph.)	Elbert	Thompsons	157/27	Wilkinson
Tate, James	Franklin	Allens	235/8	Wilkinson
Tate, Mary(Orph.)	Camden	Smiths	58/17	Baldwin
Tate, Robert L.	Elbert	Thompsons	157/15	Baldwin
Tate, Sarah(Orph.)	Camden	Smiths	58/17	Baldwin
Tate, William	Greene	Jenkins	59/6	Wilkinson
Tatem, Epps	Greene	Flournoys	30/16	Baldwin
Tatom, Abner	Lincoln	Normans	209/6	Baldwin
Tatom, Jane(Wid.)	Lincoln	Mays	22/8	Baldwin
Tatom, John	Lincoln	Normans	106/11	Baldwin
Tatom, John	Lincoln	Normans	24/26	Wilkinson
Tatom, Peter	Hancock	Huffs	143/20	Wilkinson
Tatom, Seth	Hancock	Hudsons	79/11	Wilkinson

NAME	COUNTY	MIL.DIST.	LOT/DIST	DREW LAND
Tatom, William	Hancock	Hudsons	308/20	Baldwin
Tattnall, Harriet	Chatham	Herbs	243/14	Baldwin
Tattnall, Josiah	Chatham	Herbs	243/14	Baldwin
Tattnall, Thos.	Chatham	Herbs	243/14	Baldwin
Tawneyhill, Andrew	Franklin	Yowells	179/20	Baldwin
Tawnihill, Andrew	Franklin	Yowells	82/13	Wilkinson
Taylor's, Armistead(Orphs.)	Franklin	Wems'	206/17	Baldwin
Taylor's, Richard	Franklin	Yowells	260/20	Baldwin
Taylor's, Thomas(Orphs.)	Washington	Kendricks	207/10	Baldwin
Taylor, Ann(Wid.)	Wilkes	Malones	287/12	Wilkinson
Taylor, Benjamin	Elbert	Balckwells	41/21	Wilkinson
Taylor, Benjamin	Elbert	Blackwells	124/9	Baldwin
Taylor, Benjamin	Screven		181/1	Wilkinson
Taylor, Charles	Franklin	Cornelius'	213/28	Wilkinson
Taylor, David Jr.	Chatham	Pembertons	142/9	Baldwin
Taylor, Dempsey	Wilkinson		306/24	Wilkinson
Taylor, Edmond	Screven	Hutchinsons	11/28	Wilkinson
Taylor, Edwd.W.	Clarke	Silmans	227/10	Baldwin
Taylor, George Sr.	Lincoln	Normans	354/13	Wilkinson
Taylor, George	Wilkinson		41/18	Wilkinson
Taylor, Henry	Clarke	Silmans	208/26	Wilkinson
Taylor, Henry	Clarke	Silmans	261/24	Wilkinson
Taylor, Jacob	Wilkinson		177/17	Baldwin
Taylor, James	Burke	Burks	114/9	Wilkinson
Taylor, James	Greene	Davenports	207/16	Baldwin
Taylor, James	Wilkinson	3	127/13	Wilkinson
Taylor, James	Wilkinson	3	202/19	Baldwin
Taylor, Jeremiah	Franklin	Hollingsworths	383/21	Wilkinson
Taylor, John(259)	Baldwin	2	295/11	Wilkinson
Taylor, John(S.of Thos.)	Oglethorpe	Bells	259/19	Wilkinson
Taylor, Joseph(Orph.)	Effingham		90/20	Wilkinson
Taylor, Josiah	Washington	Burneys	191/16	Baldwin
Taylor, Josiah	Washington	Burneys	96/14	Wilkinson
Taylor, Kinchin	Washington	Paces	135/20	Baldwin
Taylor, Margaret	Burke	Ballards	349/10	Wilkinson
Taylor, Nimrod	Clarke		204/1	Baldwin
Taylor, Rachel	Bulloch	Godfreys	87/23	Wilkinson
Taylor, Robert	Hancock	Thomas'	41/13	Wilkinson
Taylor, Robt.Sr.	Elbert	Faulkners	66/23	Wilkinson
Taylor, Sally(Orph.)	Burke	Mulkeys	95/19	Wilkinson
Taylor, Sarah(Wid.)	Montgomery	54	61/23	Wilkinson
Taylor, Sarah	Burke	Mulkeys	45/15	Baldwin
Taylor, Sarah	Washington	Burneys	304/21	Wilkinson
Taylor, Semility(S.W.)	Screven		185/15	Baldwin
Taylor, Thomas	Baldwin	1	77/15	Wilkinson
Taylor, William	Chatham	Pettybones	21/20	Baldwin
Taylor, William	Chatham	Pettybones	81/27	Wilkinson
Taylor, William	Montgomery	55	253/20	Baldwin
Taylor, Willis	Greene	Jinkins	142/20	Wilkinson
Taylor, Willis	Greene	Jinkins	37/9	Wilkinson
Taylor, Winnifred	Montgomery	59	349/22	Wilkinson
Taylor, Wm.	Wilkinson		168/26	Wilkinson
Taylors, Charles	Hancock	Shivers	284/9	Wilkinson
Teedwell, Jeremiah	Clarke	Stewarts	169/23	Wilkinson
Temple, Benjamin	Hancock	Pinkstons	202/23	Wilkinson
Temple, Sally	Hancock	Barnes	27/16	Wilkinson
Temples, Andrew	Montgomery	55	85/11	Baldwin
Temples, Frederick Sr.	Montgomery	55	174/16	Baldwin
Templeton, Alexander	Burke	Carswells	194/16	Wilkinson
Tenfield, Josiah	Chatham		71/22	Wilkinson
Tennison, Mathew	Burke	Blounts	30/9	Baldwin
Terrell, Jeremiah	Elbert	Roebucks	179/8	Baldwin
Terrell, Jeremiah	Elbert	Roebucks	27/26	Wilkinson
Terrell, John	Greene	Owsleys	392/21	Wilkinson
Terrell, Joseph	Franklin	McDowells	58/21	Wilkinson
Terrell, Richmond	Wilkes	Roreys	147/12	Wilkinson
Terrell, Richmond	Wilkes	Roreys	175/8	Baldwin

NAME	COUNTY	MIL.DIST.	LOT/DIST	DREW LAND
Terry, Thomas	Baldwin	5	3/22	Wilkinson
Tever, Jacob	Wilkes	Parks'	93/20	Baldwin
Tharp, Vincent A.	Warren	Neals	39/10	Wilkinson
Theiss, Henry	Lincoln	Busseys	330/8	Wilkinson
Theiss, Jacob Sr.	Chatham	McLeans	84/21	Wilkinson
Theiss, Jacob Y.	Chatham	Hardens	58/20	Wilkinson
Theiss, Jacob	Chatham	McLeans	59/13	Wilkinson
Thigpen, Nathan	Wilkes	Youngs	60/16	Wilkinson
Thigpin, Travis	Montgomery	53	110/24	Wilkinson
Thom, Allen D.	Wilkes	Heards	176/8	Baldwin
Thomas', Evan(Orphs.)	Jackson	Johnsons	91/11	Baldwin
Thomas, Allen	Camden	Crews	95/14	Baldwin
Thomas, Berry	Burke	Sandifords	108/10	Wilkinson
Thomas, Bradley	Jackson	Johnsons	229/19	Wilkinson
Thomas, Daniel	Jackson	Fultons	146/14	Wilkinson
Thomas, David	Jackson	Thomas	63/21	Wilkinson
Thomas, David	Jackson	Wrights	34/16	Baldwin
Thomas, Elisha	Wilkes	Malones	43/11	Wilkinson
Thomas, Etheldred	Warren	Jones	110/11	Wilkinson
Thomas, Evans	Washington	Kendricks	122/22	Wilkinson
Thomas, James T.	Baldwin	1	134/17	Wilkinson
Thomas, Jesse	Screven		134/18	Baldwin
Thomas, John	Baldwin	3	120/18	Wilkinson
Thomas, Jonathan	Baldwin	2	217/26	Wilkinson
Thomas, Joseph	Camden	Crews	323/14	Wilkinson
Thomas, Merrell	Clarke	Silmans	101/26	Wilkinson
Thomas, Merrell	Clarke	Silmans	353/21	Wilkinson
Thomas, Samuel	Hancock	Thomas'	255/9	Wilkinson
Thomas, Susannah	Burke	Gordons	209/15	Wilkinson
Thomas, William	Franklin	Everetts	351/22	Wilkinson
Thomas, William	Warren	Heaths	232/6	Wilkinson
Thomas, Zachariah	Franklin	Dixons	74/13	Baldwin
Thomason, George	Elbert	Blackwells	207/19	Wilkinson
Thomason, William	Franklin	Cleghorns	3/11	Wilkinson
Thomason, William	Jackson	Hendersons	14/17	Wilkinson
Thompson's, John(Orphs.)	Clarke	Cooks	231/15	Baldwin
Thompson, Alexander	Elbert	Groves'	233/9	Baldwin
Thompson, Alexr.Sr.	Washington	Renfroes	9/8	Baldwin
Thompson, Andrew	Jackson	Hardwicks	162/17	2
Thompson, Anna	Baldwin	4	5/18	Baldwin
Thompson, Archibald	Montgomery	51	157/20	Baldwin
Thompson, Beatrix	Hancock	Crowders	80/17	Baldwin
Thompson, Benjamin	Jackson	Hardwicks	324/10	Wilkinson
Thompson, Charles	Washington	Howards	151/6	Wilkinson
Thompson, Duncan	Montgomery	51	58/6	Baldwin
Thompson, Elijah	Clarke	Silmans	321/17	Wilkinson
Thompson, Gains(Orph.)	Elbert	Dyes	181/8	Wilkinson
Thompson, George	Wilkes	Hendersons	137/18	Baldwin
Thompson, George	Wilkes	Hendersons	218/9	Baldwin
Thompson, Henry	Greene	Moores	199/9	Baldwin
Thompson, Henry	Lincoln	Busseys	228/19	Wilkinson
Thompson, Henry	Lincoln	Busseys	23/25	Wilkinson
Thompson, Isham(Orph.)	Elbert	Dyes	181/8	Wilkinson
Thompson, James	Bulloch	Godfreys	341/20	Baldwin
Thompson, James	Columbia	3	38/16	Baldwin
Thompson, James	Lincoln	Mays	73/14	Baldwin
Thompson, John P.	Oglethorpe	Howells	307/22	Wilkinson
Thompson, John	Baldwin	4	19/14	Wilkinson
Thompson, John	Bulloch	Denmarks	10/14	Baldwin
Thompson, John	Hancock	Weeks'	81/21	Wilkinson
Thompson, Joseph(S.of Benj.)	Jackson	Cockrans	15/26	Wilkinson
Thompson, Mary	Warren	Newsoms	81/20	Baldwin
Thompson, Moses	Warren	Newsoms	161/11	Baldwin
Thompson, Nathaniel	Warren	Willsons	232/10	Wilkinson
Thompson, Nathaniel	Warren	Willsons	62/17	Wilkinson
Thompson, Patsy(Orph.)	Elbert	Dyes	181/8	Wilkinson
Thompson, Reubin	Burke	Thompsons	48/17	Wilkinson

NAME	COUNTY	MIL.DIST.	LOT/DIST	DREW LAND
Thompson, Robert	Elbert	Hillyers	146/27	Wilkinson
Thompson, Robert	Elbert	Hillyers	259/14	Wilkinson
Thompson, Robert	Greene	Davenports	67/25	Wilkinson
Thompson, Robert	Oglethorpe	Hitchcocks	179/14	Baldwin
Thompson, Robert	Warren	Newsoms	111/19	Baldwin
Thompson, Sarah	Washington	Howards	197/12	Baldwin
Thompson, Susannah(Wid.)	Baldwin	3	219/9	Baldwin
Thompson, Thomas Sr.	Bryan	Birds	135/26	Wilkinson
Thompson, William(Capt)	Elbert	Thompsons	65/15	Baldwin
Thompson, William	Elbert	Groves	260/10	Wilkinson
Thompson, William	Jackson	Hendersons	160/24	Wilkinson
Thompson, Wm.(Dr.)	Wilkes	Edges	94/16	Baldwin
Thompson, Wm.(Taylor)	Columbia	2	397/7	Wilkinson
Thompson, Wm.L.	Clarke	Trammells	131/18	Baldwin
Thompson, Wodday	Franklin	Griffiths	198/8	Wilkinson
Thorn, David	Screven		25/20	Wilkinson
Thorn, David	Screven		387/8	Wilkinson
Thornhill, Mary(Orph.)	Burke	Forths	211/24	Wilkinson
Thornhill, Wm.(Orph.)	Burke	Forths	211/24	Wilkinson
Thornton, Daniel	Elbert	Clarks	134/20	Wilkinson
Thornton, Dozier Jr.	Elbert	Dyes	283/20	Wilkinson
Thornton, Dread	Oglethorpe	Smiths	148/23	Wilkinson
Thornton, Henry	Hancock	Winsletts	231/17	Wilkinson
Thornton, John(S.of Solomon)	Wilkes	Coopers	117/20	Baldwin
Thornton, Mark Jr.	Elbert	Thompsons	177/17	Wilkinson
Thornton, Rachel(Single)	Hancock	Candlers	215/16	Wilkinson
Thornton, Samuel	Chatham	Hardens	310/12	Wilkinson
Thornton, Samuel	Hancock	Smiths	150/28	Wilkinson
Thornton, Sarah(Wid.)	Wilkes	Wellborns	69/11	Wilkinson
Thornton, Thomas	Franklin	Wems'	121/11	Wilkinson
Thorp, Joseph	Hancock	Weeks'	352/12	Wilkinson
Thrash, George	Oglethorpe	Watkins	124/13	Wilkinson
Thrash, Valentine	Wilkes	Hendersons	299/14	Wilkinson
Thrasher, Isaac	Greene	Butlers	272/15	Baldwin
Thrasher, Joseph C.	Greene	Butlers	19/23	Wilkinson
Thrasher, Nancy W.(Wid.)	Greene	Butlers	170/16	Wilkinson
Thrasher, Sarah(Orph.)	Franklin	Hoopers	14/21	Wilkinson
Thrawer's, Levi(Orphs.)	Warren	Heaths	146/10	Baldwin
Thrawer, Thomas	Chatham	Hardens	171/17	Baldwin
Threewitts, James	Jackson	Colemans	7/8	Baldwin
Threlkield, Obadiah	Chatham	Abrahams	183/11	Wilkinson
Thriebner, C.F.	Chatham	Whites	227/23	Wilkinson
Thrower's, Wm.(Orphs.)	Screven		110/9	Baldwin
Thrower, Jeremiah	Baldwin	3	30/27	Wilkinson
Thrweatt, Eliz.(Single)	Hancock	Weeks'	182/13	Wilkinson
Thurmon's, Absalom(Orphs.)	Greene	Butlers	200/21	Wilkinson
Thurmon's, Absalom(Orphs.)	Greene	Butlers	34/13	Wilkinson
Thurmon, Charles	Greene	Butlers	78/21	Wilkinson
Thurmon, Daniel	Greene	Butlers	102/6	Baldwin
Thurmon, David	Oglethorpe	Howells	20/18	Baldwin
Thurmon, Fielding L.	Wilkes	Sheets	51/12	Baldwin
Thurmon, Frances(S.W.)	Wilkes	Sheets	282/22	Wilkinson
Thurmon, Haskey(Female)	Greene	Butlers	92/23	Wilkinson
Thurmon, Stephen(S.of Wm.)	Wilkes	Stovalls	188/17	Baldwin
Tidd, Benjamin	Chatham		138/26	Wilkinson
Tidwell, Rode	Clarke	Mitchells	32/16	Wilkinson
Tidwell, Rode	Clarke	Mitchells	85/12	Wilkinson
Tidwell, Sally	Elbert	Hillyers	128/15	Baldwin
Tidwell, William	Clarke	Mitchells	78/14	Baldwin
Tignor, Philip	Clarke	Trammells	251/20	Wilkinson
Tillery, Henry	Baldwin	2	56/14	Baldwin
Tillery, Sally	Oglethorpe	Beasleys	137/20	Wilkinson
Tillery, Thomas	Baldwin	4	86/8	Baldwin
Tillett's, Geo.(Orphs.)	Baldwin	1	9/16	Baldwin
Tillman, Jesse	Burke	Hilliards	156/21	Wilkinson
Tillman, Mary	Chatham	McLeans	396/7	Wilkinson
Tillman, Richard	Chatham	McLeans	273/14	Wilkinson

NAME	COUNTY	MIL.DIST.	LOT/DIST	DREW LAND
Tilly, David	Burke	Sandifords	236/24	Wilkinson
Tilly, Eliz.(D.of Thos.)	Columbia	11	137/21	Wilkinson
Tilly, William	Burke	Gordons	319/20	Baldwin
Tilman, Gideon	Tattnall	McDonalds	102/8	Wilkinson
Tilman, Isaac	Bulloch	Godfreys	156/7	Wilkinson
Tilman, James	Tattnall	McDonalds	158/20	Baldwin
Tilman, Jeremiah	Montgomery	58	160/28	Wilkinson
Tilman, Jesse	Burke	Hilliards	3/16	Wilkinson
Tilman, John	Burke	Spains	427/7	Wilkinson
Tilman, Littleberry	Burke	Martins	132/14	Baldwin
Tilman, Littleberry	Burke	Martins	44/10	Wilkinson
Timmons, Stephen	Liberty		5/28	Wilkinson
Tindall, Bird B.	Richmond		70/16	Baldwin
Tindall, John	Greene	Alfords	184/17	Baldwin
Tindall, Pleasant	Columbia	6	245/22	Wilkinson
Tiner's, Lewis(Orphs.)	Washington	Renfroes	126/11	Wilkinson
Tiner, Elijah	Effingham		59/6	Baldwin
Tinley, Jacob	Greene	Dawsons	99/18	Wilkinson
Tinley, William	Richmond		80/20	Baldwin
Tinsley, Mary	Jackson		181/6	Baldwin
Tinsley, Samuel	Wilkinson		129/7	Wilkinson
Tippin, Joseph B.(Orph.)	Chatham	Whites	126/17	Wilkinson
Tison, Camel	Effingham		154/26	Wilkinson
Tison, Delitha(Wid.)	Hancock	Barnes'	16/12	Wilkinson
Tison, Edmond	Effingham		64/6	Baldwin
Tison, Eliakim	Effingham		45/7	Wilkinson
Tobler, Ulric	Chatham	Pembertons	214/16	Baldwin
Todd's, Wm.(Orphs.)	Warren	Devereux's	159/6	Wilkinson
Todd, Elizabeth	Wilkes	Coopers	277/10	Wilkinson
Todd, Hardy	Washington	Willis'	46/18	Baldwin
Todd, James(Orph.)	Chatham	Abrahams	285/15	Wilkinson
Todd, Jemima	McIntosh		70/8	Wilkinson
Todd, John	Montgomery	57	276/12	Wilkinson
Todd, Mary(Wid.)	Hancock	Pinkstons	33/10	Wilkinson
Todd, William	Chatham	Herbs	111/7	Wilkinson
Todd, William	Wilkes	Coopers	59/23	Wilkinson
Toler, David	Warren	Willsons	183/9	Wilkinson
Tomkins, Betsy(Single)	Oglethorpe	Smiths	264/9	Wilkinson
Tomlin, John Harris	Burke	Ballards	133/6	Wilkinson
Tomlin, John Harris	Burke	Ballards	189/16	Baldwin
Tomlinson, John	Baldwin	2	123/15	Wilkinson
Tomlinson, John	Baldwin	2	65/15	Wilkinson
Tomlinson, John	Wilkes	Coopers	285/13	Wilkinson
Tommey, Henry	Greene	Jinkins	288/20	Baldwin
Tomms, Sally	Hancock	Coffees	251/9	Wilkinson
Tompkins, Burwell	Washington	Howards	151/16	Baldwin
Tompkins, John	Camden	Ashleys	98/25	Wilkinson
Tompkins, Eliz(Orph.)	Washington	Kendricks	226/18	Wilkinson
Tompkins, Nancy	Washington	Howards	86/20	Wilkinson
Tondee, Charles	Effingham		189/21	Wilkinson
Toney, Charles	Franklin	Wems'	67/19	Wilkinson
Toney, Eliz.(Wid.)	Jackson	Wrights	43/10	Baldwin
Toney, Sherwood	Elbert	Thompsons	6/22	Wilkinson
Tooke, Harlow Herod	Washington	Kendricks	170/11	Baldwin
Toole, Eli	Baldwin	1	42/9	Baldwin
Toomer, Daniel	Effingham		201/19	Baldwin
Torrence, Ebenezer	Hancock	Crowders	199/15	Wilkinson
Touchstone, Christopher	Glynn		148/8	Baldwin
Towns, Drury	Elbert	Thompsons	75/26	Wilkinson
Towns, John	Greene	Carletons	135/12	Baldwin
Towns, Marlin	Greene	Carltons	219/22	Wilkinson
Townsen, Andrew	Baldwin	5	241/25	Wilkinson
Townsen, Samuel Sr.	Greene	Butlers	151/19	Wilkinson
Townsend, Henry	Baldwin	2	157/19	Baldwin
Townsend, John	Oglethorpe	Hudsons	166/28	Wilkinson
Townsend, William	Effingham		306/20	Wilkinson
Townsin, James	Bulloch	Williams'	63/19	Baldwin

NAME	COUNTY	MIL.DIST.	LOT/DIST	DREW LAND
Townsin, Thomas	Bulloch	Williams'	2/9	Baldwin
Townsin, Wm.Jr.	Bulloch	Williams'	138/16	Baldwin
Townsin, Wm.Sr.	Bulloch	Williams'	168/9	Wilkinson
Trailer, Lucy(Wid.)	Baldwin	4	70/14	Baldwin
Trammel, Peter	Baldwin	4	227/17	Wilkinson
Trammell, Daniel	Clarke	Trammells	179/16	Wilkinson
Travis, Asa	Tattnall	Halls	50/6	Wilkinson
Travis, David	Jackson	Hendersons	63/24	Wilkinson
Travis, Thomas	Montgomery	51	54/12	Baldwin
Traylor's, John(Orph.)	Baldwin	4	309/7	Wilkinson
Traylor's, Pascal(Orphs.)	Oglethorpe	Smiths	106/23	Wilkinson
Traylor, Edward	Baldwin	4	86/10	Baldwin
Traylor, Randolph	Clarke	Martins	37/25	Wilkinson
Traylor, Susannah(Wid.)	Hancock	Weeks'	263/19	Wilkinson
Traylor, Thomas	Oglethorpe	Smiths	177/15	Wilkinson
Traylor, William	Oglethorpe	Smiths	190/8	Wilkinson
Traywich, Moses	Washington	Holts	178/9	Wilkinson
Traywick, Francis	Hancock	Pinkstons	255/7	Wilkinson
Traywick, George	Hancock	Pinkstons	311/15	Baldwin
Traywick, Lunsford	Clarke	Mitchells	131/13	Baldwin
Traywick, Robert	Hancock	Pinkstons	127/11	Wilkinson
Treble, Benjamin	Oglethorpe	Hartsfields	52/22	Wilkinson
Treble, Dicy(S.W.)	Oglethorpe	Hartsfields	117/10	Baldwin
Tredwell, Isaac	Clarke	Hopkins	190/24	Wilkinson
Tredwell, John	Franklin	Cornelius'	73/6	Wilkinson
Tredwell, Stephen	Clarke	Hopkins	256/23	Wilkinson
Tredwell, Stephen	Clarke	Hopkins	328/24	Wilkinson
Tremble, John	Greene	Butlers	172/26	Wilkinson
Trent, Nathaniel	Jackson	Johnsons	161/27	Wilkinson
Trentham, Absalom	Franklin	McDowells	142/27	Wilkinson
Trewett, Riley	Greene	Loves	1/21	Wilkinson
Trewett, Riley	Greene	Loves	83/17	Wilkinson
Trice, Benjamin	Baldwin	1	239/14	Baldwin
Trice, John	Hancock	Holts	320/13	Wilkinson
Trimble, John	Franklin	Allens	148/18	Wilkinson
Tripp, John Jr.	Hancock	Barnes'	31/10	Wilkinson
Tripp, Robert	Hancock	Barnes'	119/24	Wilkinson
Trotman's, Thomas(Orphs)	Washington	Kendricks	257/9	Wilkinson
Troup, Geo.M.	Bryan	Austins	32/8	Baldwin
Troup, James	Chatham	Herbs	21/14	Wilkinson
Trout, Nathaniel(Heirs)	Jackson	Johnsons	161/27	Wilkinson
Trowell, James	Jackson	Thomas'	65/13	Wilkinson
Trueluck, John	Jackson		22/23	Wilkinson
Trueluck, Joseph	Jackson		146/21	Wilkinson
Trueluck, Sutton	Washington	Willis	329/7	Wilkinson
Trueman, Alexander M.	Wilkes	Stovells	290/8	Wilkinson
Trushet, Eliz.(Wid.)	Chatham	Pettybones	90/21	Wilkinson
Tucker, Bartlett	Elbert	Clarks	242/19	Wilkinson
Tucker, Danl.	Baldwin	1	100/17	Wilkinson
Tucker, Danl.	Baldwin	1	180/13	Baldwin
Tucker, Gabriel	Effingham		151/20	Wilkinson
Tucker, Reubin	Washington	Burneys	259/9	Wilkinson
Tucker, William	Baldwin	4	388/7	Wilkinson
Tufts, Gardner	Chatham	Abrahams	18/15	Wilkinson
Tuggle, Charles	Elbert	Groves	243/24	Wilkinson
Tuggle, Nancy	Greene	Watsons	50/10	Wilkinson
Tuggle, Robert	Greene	Moores	310/10	Wilkinson
Tuggle, Sally	Greene	Watsons	111/10	Wilkinson
Tullis, Aaron	Lincoln	Mays	4/8	Wilkinson
Tullos, John	Effingham		194/16	Baldwin
Tullos, Joshua	Richmond		204/6	Baldwin
Tullos, Temple(S.of John)	Effingham		28/20	Baldwin
Tumblin, Thomas	Screven		390/22	Wilkinson
Tunnell, John	Oglethorpe	Watkins	106/14	Wilkinson
Turk, John	Franklin	Dixons	277/20	Wilkinson
Turk, Theodocius	Hancock	Gumms	74/15	Wilkinson
Turk, Velinda	Hancock	Gumms	69/14	Wilkinson

NAME	COUNTY	MIL.DIST.	LOT/DIST	DREW LAND
Turkonett, Jacob	Baldwin	3	77/7	Wilkinson
Turmon, Eliz.(Wid.)	Elbert	Hillyers	97/11	Baldwin
Turmon, Thomas Sr.	Elbert	Hillyers	223/20	Wilkinson
Turner, Abner	Greene	Armors	202/27	Wilkinson
Turner, Benjamin	Camden	Hardees	94/22	Wilkinson
Turner, Betsy	Baldwin	3	53/16	Baldwin
Turner, Charles	Burke	Martins	157/21	Wilkinson
Turner, Edward	Jackson	Wrights	62/20	Wilkinson
Turner, George	Wilkes	Sheets	204/17	Baldwin
Turner, Henry Jr.	Burke	Blounts	31/12	Baldwin
Turner, Henry Sr.	Burke	Blounts	326/8	Wilkinson
Turner, Henry	Hancock	Barnes'	5/12	Baldwin
Turner, James	Clarke	Martindales	116/15	Baldwin
Turner, James	Jackson	Hendersons	139/14	Baldwin
Turner, John Sr.	Warren	Jones	162/13	Baldwin
Turner, John	Jackson	Cockrans	349/21	Wilkinson
Turner, John	Jackson	Thomas'	114/26	Wilkinson
Turner, John	Oglethorpe	Smiths	116/6	Baldwin
Turner, Leven Jr.	Hancock	Gumms	14/20	Wilkinson
Turner, Leven Sr.	Hancock	Wallers	114/11	Wilkinson
Turner, Levin Jr.	Hancock	Gumms	223/10	Wilkinson
Turner, Lucretia	Wayne	3	47/12	Wilkinson
Turner, Martha	Wayne	3	78/18	Baldwin
Turner, Meshack	Wilkes	Malones	235/9	Wilkinson
Turner, Milly	Lincoln	Kings	334/10	Wilkinson
Turner, Nancy	Lincoln	Mays	105/19	Wilkinson
Turner, Nathan	Franklin	Christians	30/10	Wilkinson
Turner, Pleasant	Wilkes	Wellborns	109/25	Wilkinson
Turner, Pleasant	Wilkes	Wellborns	47/13	Baldwin
Turner, Reubin	Liberty		191/28	Wilkinson
Turner, Samuel Sr.	Hancock	Barnes'	179/9	Baldwin
Turner, Sarah(Orph.)	Washington	Garretts	96/24	Wilkinson
Turner, Thomas	Jackson	Tarvers	10/16	Baldwin
Tutchstone, Ann	Baldwin	2	17/15	Baldwin
Tutchstone, Caleb	Baldwin	4	29/10	Baldwin
Tutle, Edward	Burke	Ballards	120/11	Baldwin
Tuttle, Solomon	Jackson	Johnsons	162/14	Baldwin
Tweedle, James	Elbert	Barretts	251/19	Baldwin
Twiggs, Abraham	Jackson	Thomas'	183/12	Wilkinson
Twiggs, Abraham	Jackson	Thomas'	386/8	Wilkinson
Twining, Nat.	McIntosh		84/7	Wilkinson
Twitty, George Sr.	Lincoln	Normans	167/19	Baldwin
Tyler, Thomas	Hancock	Barnes'	19/15	Baldwin
Tyson's, Isaac(Orphs.)	Wilkes	Youngs	339/21	Wilkinson
Ulmer, Anna	Chatham	Hardens	80/17	Wilkinson
Ulmer, Charles	Effingham		128/27	Wilkinson
Underwood's, Geo.(Orphs.)	Washington	Paces	208/20	Wilkinson
Underwood's, Joshua(Orphs.)	Elbert	Blackwells	337/12	Wilkinson
Underwood's, Reubin	Washington	Paces	166/27	Wilkinson
Underwood, Ezekiel	Elbert	Blackwells	76/23	Wilkinson
Underwood, John G.	Liberty		130/25	Wilkinson
Underwood, John G.	Liberty		26/17	Wilkinson
Underwood, Sarah(Wid.)	Liberty		94/14	Wilkinson
Underwood, William	Columbia	1	19/17	Wilkinson
Upshaw, Catharine	Elbert	Olivers	137/12	Wilkinson
Upshaw, John Sr.	Elbert	Olivers	12/16	Baldwin
Upshaw, LeRoy	Elbert	Olivers	298/17	Wilkinson
Upshaw, Sarah	Elbert	Olivers	202/20	Baldwin
Upton, John	Columbia		31/23	Wilkinson
Upton, William	Columbia	11	101/28	Wilkinson
Urquhart, John	Washington	Willis'	142/13	Baldwin
Usher, Daniel	Richmond		17/14	Wilkinson
Ussery, David	Tattnall	Staffords	19/11	Wilkinson
Ussery, Middleton	Warren	Newsoms	276/6	Wilkinson
Ussry, Milly	Burke	Sandifords	104/13	Wilkinson
Ussry, Thomas	Baldwin	5	163/6	Baldwin
Valey, John(Orph.)	Chatham	Pettybones	285/9	Wilkinson

NAME	COUNTY	MIL.DIST.	LOT/DIST	DREW LAND
VanAlen, Cecelia(Wid.)	Wilkes	Coopers	207/23	Wilkinson
Vandenna, Eliza	McIntosh		105/20	Baldwin
Vann, Benjn.	Screven		70/6	Wilkinson
Vann, Henry	Washington	Willis'	378/8	Wilkinson
Vann, Sanders	Hancock	Wallers	192/9	Wilkinson
Varner, George	Jefferson	Hardwichs	20/9	Wilkinson
Varner, James	Elbert	Olivers	110/16	Wilkinson
Vasons, Mary	Wilkes	Malones	13/6	Wilkinson
Vaughan's, James(Orphs.)	Elbert	Moons	198/9	Wilkinson
Vaughan, Daniel	Columbia	10	23/23	Wilkinson
Vaughan, Daniel	Columbia	10	342/10	Wilkinson
Vaughan, Reubin	Columbia	1	270/14	Baldwin
Vaughn, Benjamin	Jackson	Johnsons	99/12	Wilkinson
Vaughn, Wm.	Oglethorpe	Howells	305/10	Wilkinson
Vayden, Wm.H.	Wilkes	Normans	46/13	Baldwin
Veale, Nathan	Washington	Renfroes	151/14	Baldwin
Veasey, Elizabeth(S.)	Hancock	Barnes'	17/15	Wilkinson
Veasey, Ezekiel	Greene	Stewarts	4/21	Wilkinson
Veasey, James Sr.	Hancock	Coffees	129/11	Wilkinson
Veasey, Jesse	Hancock	Barnes'	4/11	Baldwin
Veasey, John Jr.	Hancock	Coffees	273/17	Wilkinson
Venable, Charles	Jackson	Wrights	55/6	Wilkinson
Venable, John Sr.	Jackson	Wrights	24/8	Baldwin
Venable, Nathaniel	Jackson	Wrights	249/25	Wilkinson
Venable, Robert	Jackson	Cockrans	244/20	Wilkinson
Vendrick, Lydia	Tattnall	Halls	20/8	Wilkinson
Vickers, Abraham	Washington	Paces	74/6	Wilkinson
Vickers, Bryan	Washington	Delks	203/15	Baldwin
Vickers, Elijah	Washington	Delks	178/11	Baldwin
Vickers, Elizabeth	Washington	Chivers'	17/14	Baldwin
Vickers, James	Burke	Spains	237/14	Baldwin
Vickers, John	Burke	Spains	163/9	Baldwin
Vickers, John	Burke	Spains	36/27	Wilkinson
Vickers, John	Clarke	Silmans	190/25	Wilkinson
Vickers, Nancy(Wid.)	Washington	Chivers	86/7	Baldwin
Vickers, Willey	Wilkinson		219/6	Wilkinson
Vickers, William	Clarke	Hitchcocks	63/22	Wilkinson
Vickory, Hezekiah	Screven		102/11	Baldwin
Vincent's, James(Orphs.)	Camden	Johnsons	27/14	Baldwin
Vincent, Elisha	Hancock	Wallers	212/9	Wilkinson
Vincent, James	Camden	Smiths	219/14	Baldwin
Vincent, Moses	Franklin	Christians	172/11	Wilkinson
Vincent, Selby	Hancock	Birdsongs	236/22	Wilkinson
Vincent, West	Hancock	Thomas'	95/23	Wilkinson
Vinen, Phoebe(Wid.)	Baldwin	3	180/16	Baldwin
Vining, Benjamin	Jefferson	Wrights	77/21	Wilkinson
Vining, William	Jefferson	Colemans	122/20	Wilkinson
Vinson, George	Washington	Balckshears	74/18	Wilkinson
Vinson, George	Washington	Blackshears	79/13	Wilkinson
Vivion, Eliza	Jefferson		152/26	Wilkinson
Vollaton, Eliz.(Wid.)	Chatham	Pettybones	185/23	Wilkinson
Waddle, John	Chatham	Trammells	100/25	Wilkinson
Wade, Anna(Wid.)	Elbert	Roebucks	196/11	Wilkinson
Wade, Asa	Chatham	Robinsons	51/21	Wilkinson
Wade, Isaac	Washington	Burneys	168/6	Baldwin
Wade, Isaac	Washington	Burneys	325/10	Wilkinson
Wade, James Jr.	Wilkes	Sheets	156/23	Wilkinson
Wade, James Sr.	Wilkes	Sheets	208/25	Wilkinson
Wade, John	Elbert	Groves	69/17	Baldwin
Wade, William	Warren	Flournoys	292/20	Wilkinson
Wadsworth, James	Lincoln	Flemings	121/13	Baldwin
Wadsworth, John	Washington	Holts	82/22	Wilkinson
Wafford, William	Jackson	Hendersons	141/15	Baldwin
Waggoner, Geo.Jr.	Warren	Hills	130/28	Wilkinson
Waggoner, Mary(Wid.)	Warren	Hills	226/28	Wilkinson
Waggoner, John	Bulloch	1	166/19	Baldwin
Wagnon, Daniel	Hancock	Huffs	139/15	Baldwin

NAME	COUNTY	MIL.DIST.	LOT/DIST	DREW LAND
Wailes, Leven	Richmond		163/13	Wilkinson
Walburger, George(Orph.)	Chatham	Pembertons	9/22	Wilkinson
Walburger, Jacob(Orph.)	Chatham	Pembertons	9/22	Wilkinson
Walden, James	Chatham	Trammells	295/20	Wilkinson
Walden, John	Jefferson	Colemans	129/14	Baldwin
Walden, John	Jefferson	Colemans	82/21	Wilkinson
Walden, Richard	Chatham	Martindales	131/8	Baldwin
Walden, Samuel	Jefferson	Colemans	134/16	Wilkinson
Walden, Samuel	Jefferson	Colemans	143/12	Baldwin
Waley, James	Montgomery	57	122/15	Wilkinson
Walker's, Charley(Orphs.)	Wilkes	Coopers	169/15	Baldwin
Walker's, David(Orphs.)	Warren	Newsoms	225/9	Wilkinson
Walker's, Elisha(Orphs.)	Washington	Andersons	48/8	Wilkinson
Walker, Andrew	Columbia	10	244/9	Wilkinson
Walker, Andrew	Greene	Carltons	65/11	Wilkinson
Walker, Benjamin	Warren	Neals	69/26	Wilkinson
Walker, Charity	Bulloch	4	59/24	Wilkinson
Walker, David Sr.	Columbia	6	313/24	Wilkinson
Walker, David	Burke	Bynes	83/9	Wilkinson
Walker, David	Jackson	Johnsons	18/14	Baldwin
Walker, Edward	Columbia	7	369/22	Wilkinson
Walker, Eliza T.(Orph.)	Richmond		313/7	Wilkinson
Walker, Freeman	Richmond		182/11	Wilkinson
Walker, Geo.(Orph.)	Richmond		313/7	Wilkinson
Walker, George	Bulloch	1	33/22	Wilkinson
Walker, Hackey	Bulloch	4	14/13	Wilkinson
Walker, Hannah	Jackson	Wrights	263/25	Wilkinson
Walker, Hartford(Orph.)	Richmond		313/7	Wilkinson
Walker, Isham Sr.	Wayne	2	76/12	Wilkinson
Walker, James	Richmond		295/6	Wilkinson
Walker, Jane	Hancock	Thomas'	129/23	Wilkinson
Walker, Jas.(Son/Sam'l)	Wilkes	Coopers	7/8	Wilkinson
Walker, Jno.(Orph.)	Richmond		313/7	Wilkinson
Walker, John H.	Lincoln	Gartrells	235/16	Wilkinson
Walker, Margaret	Richmond		331/10	Wilkinson
Walker, Mary T.(Orph.)	Richmond		313/7	Wilkinson
Walker, Mary(Wid.)	Warren	Newsoms	5/10	Baldwin
Walker, Minge(Orph.)	Richmond		313/7	Wilkinson
Walker, Needom	Tattnall	Halls	268/15	Baldwin
Walker, Purnal	Jackson	Cockrans	208/9	Wilkinson
Walker, Rebecca(Wid.)	Warren	Hills	310/13	Wilkinson
Walker, Robert	Greene	Reas	74/26	Wilkinson
Walker, Robert	Richmond		24/20	Wilkinson
Walker, Sarah(Orph.)	Richmond		313/7	Wilkinson
Walker, Silvanus	Bulloch	4	173/6	Baldwin
Walker, Simeon	Wilkes	Milners	145/19	Baldwin
Walker, Thomas	Lincoln	Busseys	171/21	Wilkinson
Walker, William	Jackson	Cockrans	108/20	Baldwin
Walker, William	Wilkes	Heards	178/21	Wilkinson
Walker, William	Wilkes	Hendricks	191/12	Baldwin
Walker, William	Wilkes	Hendricks	91/7	Wilkinson
Walker, Wm.B.C.(Orph)	Richmond		313/7	Wilkinson
Wall, Clayborn	Hancock	Barksdales	263/20	Baldwin
Wall, Henry	Jefferson	Hardwichs	40/28	Wilkinson
Wall, John	Chatham	Harpers	190/27	Wilkinson
Wall, John	Warren	Hills	332/14	Wilkinson
Wall, John	Warren	Hills	61/8	Baldwin
Wall, Joseph	Bulloch	1	431/7	Wilkinson
Wall, Willis	Elbert	Clarks	334/24	Wilkinson
Wall, Willis	Elbert	Clarks	7/14	Baldwin
Wallace, Benjamin	Hancock	Weeks	151/17	Baldwin
Wallace, Elizabeth	Greene	Reas	68/15	Wilkinson
Wallace, James	Chatham	Stewarts	54/21	Wilkinson
Wallace, James	Glynn		324/8	Wilkinson
Wallace, Nancy(Wid.)	Greene	Reas	164/28	Baldwin
Wallace, Samuel	Lincoln	Normans	352/13	Wilkinson
Wallace, Wm.	Chatham		156/15	Baldwin

NAME	COUNTY	MIL.DIST.	LOT/DIST	DREW LAND
Waller, Cretia(Orph.)	Chatham	McLeans'	15/20	Wilkinson
Waller, James Jr.	Hancock	Wallers	299/21	Wilkinson
Waller, John(168)	Bulloch	2	115/16	Baldwin
Waller, John(168)	Bulloch	2	8/23	Wilkinson
Waller, Mima	Chatham	Pettybones	21/6	Wilkinson
Waller, Nimrod	Wilkes	Sheets	332/8	Wilkinson
Waller, Priscilla Jr.	Washington	Howards	226/10	Wilkinson
Waller, Rebecca	Wilkes	Hendricks	119/6	Wilkinson
Waller, Samuel	Chatham	Pettybones	322/7	Wilkinson
Waller, Samuel	Chatham	Pettybones	94/13	Baldwin
Waller, Smith	Hancock	Candlers	124/7	Baldwin
Waller, Wm.H.	Bulloch	2	109/28	Wilkinson
Wallice, John	Burke	Martins	211/8	Wilkinson
Wallice, Sterling	Burke	Martins	287/14	Baldwin
Walraven, John Jr.	Franklin	Everetts	179/7	Wilkinson
Walraven, John Jr.	Franklin	Everetts	278/24	Wilkinson
Walraven, Wm.	Franklin	Everetts	29/9	Wilkinson
Walsingham, John Geo.	Effingham		104/19	Baldwin
Walstone, William	Wilkes	Roreys	82/19	Wilkinson
Walten, Clement	Franklin	Hollingsworths	472/7	Wilkinson
Walten, Robert Sr.	Franklin	Conners	201/6	Wilkinson
Walters, David	Screven	Williamsons	137/7	Baldwin
Walters, David	Screven	Williamsons	270/19	Baldwin
Walters, Elizabeth	Franklin	Conners	161/24	Wilkinson
Walters, George	Screven	Williamsons	258/10	Wilkinson
Walters, Samuel	Oglethorpe	Popes	187/26	Wilkinson
Walton's, Ro.(Orphs.)	Wilkes	Stovalls	210/10	Baldwin
Walton, James Sr.	Burke	Blounts	159/10	Baldwin
Walton, John H.	Lincoln	Normans	97/15	Baldwin
Walton, Killis	Franklin	Yowells	370/22	Wilkinson
Walton, Polly	Lincoln	Busseys	490/7	Wilkinson
Walton, Robert Sr.	Lincoln	Busseys	227/20	Wilkinson
Walton, Robert	Burke	Ballards	46/12	Wilkinson
Walton, Robt. Sr.	Lincoln	Busseys	348/21	Wilkinson
Walton, Thomas	Burke	Blounts	502/7	Wilkinson
Walton, Timothy	Lincoln	Kings	105/12	Baldwin
Walton, William	Burke	Gordons	51/24	Wilkinson
Walton, Wm.Walker	Franklin	Hoopers	185/12	Baldwin
Wamack, Rebecca	Oglethorpe	Popes	154/18	Wilkinson
Wammack's, Abn.(Orphs.)	Hancock	Coffees	174/13	Baldwin
Wanderwedle, Henry	Hancock	Candlers	237/23	Wilkinson
Wansley, John Jr.	Elbert	Clarks	92/14	Wilkinson
Wanslow, Patsy	Elbert	Clarks	166/18	Baldwin
Ward, Amos	Greene	Owsleys	171/14	Baldwin
Ward, Charity(Single)	Oglethorpe	Hitchcocks	284/15	Baldwin
Ward, James	Burke	Sandifords	239/7	Wilkinson
Ward, James	Oglethorpe	Stewarts	81/6	Baldwin
Ward, Jesse	Warren	Newsoms	17/20	Wilkinson
Ward, John	Greene	Alfords	212/7	Wilkinson
Ward, Jonathan	Greene	Reas	217/9	Wilkinson
Ward, Mary(Wid.)	Montgmery	56	43/8	Wilkinson
Ward, Mathias	Elbert	Barretts	343/7	Wilkinson
Ward, Newit	Warren	Newsoms	53/8	Baldwin
Ward, Wylie	Greene	Armors	195/15	Baldwin
Ware, Clary(Orph.)	Richmond		165/24	Wilkinson
Ware, Elizabeth(Orph.)	Richmond		165/24	Wilkinson
Ware, Frances(Wid.of Wm.)	Columbia	6	122/10	Wilkinson
Ware, James Jr.	Lincoln	Jones'	275/15	Wilkinson
Ware, James Jr.	Lincoln	Jones	48/9	Wilkinson
Ware, Jenny(Orph.)	Richmond		165/24	Wilkinson
Ware, John Jr.	Chatham	Mitchells	123/22	Wilkinson
Ware, John(Orph.)	Richmond		165/24	Wilkinson
Ware, Joseph	Richmond		292/21	Wilkinson
Ware, Mary(Orph.)	Richmond		165/24	Wilkinson
Warmack, John	Montgomery	54	325/12	Wilkinson
Warmack, John	Montgomery	54	64/7	Baldwin
Warmack, William	Montgomery	54	171/27	Wilkinson

NAME	COUNTY	MIL.DIST.	LOT/DIST	DREW LAND
Warnal, Jacob	Liberty		242/6	Wilkinson
Warnal, William	Liberty		143/18	Wilkinson
Warner, Thomas	Jefferson	Colemans	244/23	Wilkinson
Warner, Thomas	Jefferson	Colemans	71/13	Baldwin
Warnoch, Catharine	Burke	Martins	357/8	Wilkinson
Warnoch, Lotty	Burke	Martins	195/11	Wilkinson
Warnoch, Susannah	Burke	Martins	75/10	Wilkinson
Warren, Abraham	Jackson	Wrights	8/13	Baldwin
Warren, Amos	Montgomery	58	186/16	Baldwin
Warren, Archibald	Burke	Sharps	182/26	Wilkinson
Warren, Bray	Warren	Newsoms	118/14	Baldwin
Warren, Bray	Warren	Newsoms	273/25	Wilkinson
Warren, Edmund	Chatham	Pettybones	77/24	Wilkinson
Warren, Edward	Warren	Willsons	307/20	Wilkinson
Warren, Elijah	Washington	Garretts	388/8	Wilkinson
Warren, George	Montgomery	56	98/13	Wilkinson
Warren, Hackley	Greene	Housleys	239/9	Wilkinson
Warren, Hackley	Liberty		214/14	Wilkinson
Warren, James	Montgomery	58	113/11	Wilkinson
Warren, Jesse	Liberty		103/19	Baldwin
Warren, Polly(S)	Hancock	Weeks	207/22	Wilkinson
Warren, Rachel	Montgomery	50	285/19	Wilkinson
Warren, Sally(Single)	Hancock	Weeks	181/13	Baldwin
Wasden, Eliz.(Single)	Jefferson	Colemans	169/9	Wilkinson
Wasden, Thomas	Jefferson	Colemans	28/11	Wilkinson
Washbourn's, John(Orphs.)	Columbia	2	202/18	Wilkinson
Washbourn's, John(Orphs.)	Columbia	9	45/6	Wilkinson
Waterman, Asaph	Richmond		37/15	Baldwin
Waters, Abraham	McIntosh		129/19	Wilkinson
Waters, Abraham	McIntosh		224/23	Wilkinson
Waters, Isaac	Screven		273/12	Wilkinson
Waters, John	Chatham	Pettybones	127/12	Wilkinson
Waters, John	Chatham	Pettybones	91/6	Wilkinson
Waters, Philip	Lincoln	Busseys	98/27	Wilkinson
Waters, Thomas	Glynn		66/13	Wilkinson
Waters, William	Chatham	Pettybones	113/16	Baldwin
Wates, Jonathan	Jackson	Hendersons	309/14	Wilkinson
Wates, Joseph	Jackson	Hendersons	29/17	Baldwin
Watkins, Catharine	Burke	Bynes	65/20	Wilkinson
Watkins, Isham	Wilkes	Sheets	98/10	Wilkinson
Watkins, James	Elbert	Thompsons	186/12	Baldwin
Watkins, James	Elbert	Thompsons	36/9	Wilkinson
Watkins, John	Elbert	Hillyers	227/7	Wilkinson
Watkins, John	Hancock	Gumms	277/20	Baldwin
Watkins, John	Oglethorpe	Stewarts	116/28	Wilkinson
Watkins, Reese	Oglethorpe	Smiths	338/21	Wilkinson
Watkins, William Sr.	Elbert	Thompsons	204/7	Wilkinson
Watkins, William	Oglethorpe	Hewells	208/12	Wilkinson
Watkins, Wm.Jr.	Elbert	Hillyers	207/17	Wilkinson
Watson, Amy	Oglethorpe	Moores	147/13	Wilkinson
Watson, Douglass	Greene	Watts	58/19	Wilkinson
Watson, Isaac	Warren	Willsons	53/19	Baldwin
Watson, Jacob	Warren	Willson	105/6	Wilkinson
Watson, James	Bulloch	5	8/26	Wilkinson
Watson, Jesse	Columbia	9	293/21	Wilkinson
Watson, Jesse	Wilkinson		73/13	Wilkinson
Watson, John Jr.	Columbia	9	259/21	Wilkinson
Watson, John Sr.	Columbia	9	58/10	Baldwin
Watson, John	Richmond		210/6	Wilkinson
Watson, Laban	Wilkinson		169/8	Baldwin
Watson, Reddick	Wilkinson		209/24	Wilkinson
Watson, Sarah(Wid.)	Franklin	Thompsons	27/17	Wilkinson
Watson, Solomon	Wilkes	Youngs	309/8	Wilkinson
Watson, Thomas	Jackson	Cockrans	157/18	Wilkinson
Watson, William	Greene	Watts	120/27	Wilkinson
Watterson, John	Jackson	Hendersons	199/6	Wilkinson
Watts', Thomas(Orphs.)	Greene	Watts'	53/7	Wilkinson

NAME	COUNTY	MIL.DIST.	LOT/DIST	DREW LAND
Watts, Archibald	Greene	Flournoys	107/14	Wilkinson
Watts, Benjamin	Jackson	Cockrans	312/22	Wilkinson
Watts, Harrison	Greene	Carltons	143/10	Wilkinson
Watts, Jacobus	Greene	Carltons	25/8	Baldwin
Watts, Jeremiah	Greene	Watts'	11/10	Wilkinson
Watts, Jeremiah	Greene	Watts	260/12	Wilkinson
Watts, John	Greene	Carltons	112/14	Baldwin
Watts, John	Greene	Carltons	76/28	Wilkinson
Watts, John	Tattnall	McDonalds	83/16	Baldwin
Watts, Reubin	Tattnall	McDonalds	115/16	Wilkinson
Watts, Tabitha	Washington	Kendricks	77/8	Wilkinson
Watts, Wm.H.	Wilkes	Malones	57/15	Baldwin
Waumick, Lucy(Wid.)	Chatham	Pettybones	171/23	Wilkinson
Waumick, Wylie	Chatham	Pettybones	183/18	Baldwin
Way's, John(Orphs.)	Liberty		275/8	Wilkinson
Way, John	Liberty		13/15	Wilkinson
Way, William	Richmond		94/25	Wilkinson
Way, Wm.N.	Liberty		148/26	Wilkinson
Way, Wm.Sr.	Liberty		220/17	Wilkinson
Wayne, Rich.Sr.	Chatham	Pettybones	263/12	Wilkinson
Wayne, Richard Jr.	Screven		258/13	Wilkinson
Wayne, Thomas	Hancock	Weeks'	141/7	Wilkinson
Wayne, William	Hancock	Weeks	25/19	Baldwin
Weatherford, Charles	Jackson	Cockrans	323/21	Wilkinson
Weatherford, Charles	Jackson	Cockrans	64/17	Wilkinson
Weathers, Jesse Sr.	Greene	Armors	308/24	Wilkinson
Weaver's, John(Orphs.)	Wilkes	J.Hendersons	25/11	Baldwin
Weaver, Cordy	Warren	Heaths	73/7	Wilkinson
Weaver, Edward	Wilkes	Jos.Hendersons	149/11	Wilkinson
Weaver, Eliz.(Wid.)	Wilkes	J.Hendersons	53/11	Baldwin
Weaver, Elizabeth	Burke	Carswells	182/22	Wilkinson
Weaver, Jethro	Wilkinson		125/8	Baldwin
Weaver, Penelope(S)	Warren	Bakers	235/20	Wilkinson
Web, Sarah(Wid.)	Lincoln	Cartrells	261/8	Wilkinson
Webb, Austin	Elbert	Faulkners	152/17	Wilkinson
Webb, Charles(Orph.)	Chatham	Abrahams	68/25	Wilkinson
Webb, Clabourn	Elbert	Faulkners	310/15	Wilkinson
Webb, Edmund	Oglethorpe	Hudsons	154/8	Baldwin
Webb, Giles	Washington	Blackshears	256/20	Wilkinson
Webb, John	Washington	Blackshears	285/7	Wilkinson
Webb, Kinchen	Washington	Andersons	99/9	Wilkinson
Webb, Rice	Jefferson		112/20	Baldwin
Webb, Rice	Jefferson		28/27	Wilkinson
Webb, William	Elbert	Faulkners	30/17	Baldwin
Webb, William	McIntosh		192/13	Baldwin
Webster's, Abner(Orphs.)	Wilkes	Parks	158/22	Wilkinson
Webster, Jonathan	Wilkes	Heards	88/9	Wilkinson
Webster, Peter	Elbert	Clarks	130/20	Baldwin
Weeks, Carey	Wilkes	Heards	200/22	Wilkinson
Weeks, Francis	Washington	Jones Kendricks	57/12	Baldwin
Weeks, Hannah	Jackson	Johnsons	64/28	Wilkinson
Weeks, James	Jefferson		277/14	Wilkinson
Weeks, Michael	Warren	Neals	25/12	Wilkinson
Weeks, Michael	Warren	Neals	79/20	Wilkinson
Weeks, Nancy(Wid.)	Bulloch	4	316/17	Wilkinson
Weeks, William	Burke	Carswells	234/21	Wilkinson
Welch, Benjamin Sr.	Elbert	Moons	195/12	Wilkinson
Welch, Delia	Jackson	Hendersons	274/11	Wilkinson
Welch, James	Burke	Bynes	151/17	Wilkinson
Welch, Judith	Jackson	Hendersons	29/18	Wilkinson
Welch, Warren	Burke	Bynes	221/12	Wilkinson
Weldon, Andrew	Columbia	4	102/27	Wilkinson
Weldon, Caty	Columbia	4	204/10	Baldwin
Weldon, Dangerfield	Hancock	Barksdales	164/10	Baldwin
Weldon, Isaac Jr.	Columbia	4	56/16	Baldwin
Weldon, Isaac Sr.	Columbia	4	165/22	Wilkinson
Weldon, Jacob	Columbia	4	2/12	Baldwin

NAME	COUNTY	MIL.DIST.	LOT/DIST	DREW LAND
Weldon, Moses	Columbia	4	22/19	Wilkinson
Weldon, Moses	Columbia	4	250/14	Wilkinson
Wellborn, Amos	Greene	Butlers	9/15	Wilkinson
Wellborn, Jonathan	Wilkes	Malones	36/6	Baldwin
Wellborn, Samuel	Wilkes	Heards	148/14	Wilkinson
Wellman, Francis H.	Chatham	Whites	127/19	Baldwin
Wells', Isaac(Orphs.)	Bryan	Austins	130/18	Baldwin
Wells, Caty(Orph.)	Jefferson	Thomas'	105/13	Wilkinson
Wells, Ezekiel	Elbert	Moons	46/8	Wilkinson
Wells, Hetty	Wilkes	Roreys	185/20	Baldwin
Wells, Martha	Jefferson	Thomas'	70/18	Wilkinson
Wells, Sally(Orph.)	Jefferson	Thomas'	105/13	Wilkinson
Wells, Thos.(Orph.)	Jefferson	Thomas'	105/13	Wilkinson
West, James	Tattnall	Armstrongs	132/14	Wilkinson
West, Rachel	Tattnall	Armstrongs	10/11	Baldwin
Westberry, Moses	Tattnall	Staffords	160/23	Wilkinson
Westberry, Moses	Tattnall	Staffords	287/11	Wilkinson
Westbrook, John Jr.	Franklin	Allens	345/21	Wilkinson
Westbrook, John Sr.	Franklin	Allens	224/7	Wilkinson
Wester, Edward	Bulloch	4	101/17	Wilkinson
Westler, John W.	Greene	Greers	262/14	Baldwin
Westmoreland's, John(Orphs.)	Hancock	Weeks'	101/19	Wilkinson
Weymouth, Jonathan(Orph.)	Chatham	McLeans	67/22	Wilkinson
Weymouth, Mary(Orph.)	Chatham	McLeans	67/22	Wilkinson
Whaley, Charles	Chatham	Cooks	99/19	Wilkinson
Whaley, John	Greene	Stewarts	180/26	Wilkinson
Whaley, John	Greene	Stewarts	42/19	Wilkinson
Whatley, Betsy(Orph.)	Greene	Baxters	194/10	Wilkinson
Whatley, John H.Jr.	Bulloch	4	95/14	Wilkinson
Whatley, Liza(Wid.)	Oglethorpe	Hatchetts	107/6	Baldwin
Whatley, Richard	Lincoln	Normans	177/19	Baldwin
Whatley, Wm.R.	Greene	Butlers	217/12	Wilkinson
Whatley, Wm.R.	Greene	Butlers	8/16	Baldwin
Wheeler, Amos	Warren	Carters	253/14	Baldwin
Wheeler, Betsy	Warren	Newsoms	1/28	Wilkinson
Wheeler, Charles	Columbia	6	196/25	Wilkinson
Wheeler, George	Elbert	Roebucks	22/26	Wilkinson
Wheeler, Isham	Warren	Newsoms	233/19	Baldwin
Wheeler, Joseph	Chatham	Martindales	381/7	Wilkinson
Wheeler, Joseph	Chatham	Martindales	90/15	Baldwin
Wheeler, Mark	Wilkinson		181/22	Wilkinson
Wheeler, Merideth	Warren	Heaths	271/10	Wilkinson
Wheeler, Raphael	Wilkes	Harris	218/15	Wilkinson
Wheeler, Raphael	Wilkes	Harris	59/22	Wilkinson
Wheeler, Richard	Wilkinson		177/28	Wilkinson
Wheeler, Sally	Warren	Newsoms	293/9	Wilkinson
Wheeler, Stephen	Burke	Martins	37/22	Wilkinson
Wheeler, Thomas	Chatham	Martindales	180/6	Wilkinson
Wheeler, Vinson	Warren	Heaths	176/19	Wilkinson
Wheeler, William	Franklin	Hollingsworths	31/7	Baldwin
Wheeler, Winnifred	Warren	Newsoms	116/12	Wilkinson
Wheely, Wm.	Jackson	Wrights	44/19	Baldwin
Wheless, Abner	Hancock	Huffs	107/27	Wilkinson
Whelis, Elisha	Greene	Butlers	126/20	Wilkinson
Whelis, Joab	Greene	Alfords	170/21	Wilkinson
Whiddon, Elias	Tattnall	Staffords	241/6	Wilkinson
Whigham, William	Jefferson	Fultons	58/27	Wilkinson
Whigham, Wm.	Jefferson	Fultons	31/25	Wilkinson
Whinning, Francis	Warren	Heaths	143/14	Wilkinson
Whitaker's, Isaac(Orphs.)	Franklin	Allens	26/14	Baldwin
Whitaker, John	Washington	Howards	1/20	Wilkinson
Whitaker, Joshua Sr.	Richmond		139/21	Wilkinson
Whitaker, Samuel	Richmond		204/25	Wilkinson
Whitaker, Thomas	Burke	Spains	123/14	Baldwin
White's, Moses(Orphs.)	Elbert	Moons	185/20	Wilkinson
White's, Wm.(Orphs.)	Franklin	Hollingsworths	26/6	Baldwin
White, Andrew	Chatham	Robinsons	190/26	Wilkinson

NAME	COUNTY	MIL.DIST.	LOT/DIST	DREW LAND
White, Biddy(Wid.)	Oglethorpe	Bells	218/6	Baldwin
White, Daniel	Burke	Fields	130/10	Wilkinson
White, David	Wilkes	Sidwells	151/13	Baldwin
White, David	Wilkes	Sidwells	225/21	Wilkinson
White, Elender	Hancock	Holts	35/12	Wilkinson
White, Eliz.(Wid.)	Warren	Bakers	334/11	Wilkinson
White, George	McIntosh		39/6	Wilkinson
White, Jacob Sr.	Franklin	Griffiths	193/21	Wilkinson
White, James	Greene	Loves	280/14	Baldwin
White, Jane(S)	Hancock	Barnes'	183/16	Wilkinson
White, Joab	Bulloch	4	109/21	Wilkinson
White, John Jr.	Elbert	Mobleys	170/6	Baldwin
White, John M.Sr.	Elbert	Clarks	121/9	Wilkinson
White, John	Jackson	Cockrans	149/17	Baldwin
White, John	Screven		289/15	Baldwin
White, John	Warren	Newsoms	295/9	Wilkinson
White, Joseph	Bulloch	4	281/17	Wilkinson
White, Joseph	Elbert	Clarks	126/9	Baldwin
White, Joshua	Elbert	Olivers	131/8	Wilkinson
White, Lenny	Hancock	Coffees	108/16	Wilkinson
White, Luke	Elbert	Kneelings	120/20	Wilkinson
White, Sally(Wid.)	Franklin	Thompsons	157/8	Baldwin
White, Sally	Bulloch	3	134/10	Wilkinson
White, Samuel	Hancock	Barness	231/12	Wilkinson
White, Simeon	Wilkes	Roreys	82/20	Wilkinson
White, Thomas	Columbia	9	384/9	Wilkinson
White, Thomas	Elbert	Blackwells	170/12	Baldwin
White, William	Burke	Fields	158/28	Wilkinson
White, William	Warren	Bakers	314/14	Wilkinson
White, Wm.Baxter	Burke	Sharps	258/23	Wilkinson
White, Wm.Baxter	Burke	Sharps	322/14	Wilkinson
White, Zachariah	Effingham		291/7	Wilkinson
Whiteall, George	Oglethorpe	Moores	136/11	Baldwin
Whiteall, George	Oglethorpe	Moores	70/9	Wilkinson
Whitefield, George(Orph.)	Richmond		254/20	Wilkinson
Whitefield, John	Franklin	Cleghorns	205/6	Wilkinson
Whitefield, Rachel	Richmond		277/19	Wilkinson
Whitefield, Richard	Chatham	Neyles	137/24	Wilkinson
Whitefield, Tucker	Elbert	Willifords	56/8	Baldwin
Whitehead, David	Greene	Moores	16/12	Baldwin
Whitehead, Eliz.(Single)	Chatham	Stewarts	242/11	Wilkinson
Whitehead, Eliz.	Jackson	Cockrans	63/25	Wilkinson
Whitehead, James	Jackson	Wrights	283/12	Wilkinson
Whitehead, John	Bulloch	2	151/13	Wilkinson
Whitehead, John	Bulloch	2	50/7	Baldwin
Whitehead, Joseph	Franklin	Yowells	30/11	Baldwin
Whitehead, Richard	Jackson	Johnsons	184/16	Baldwin
Whitfield, Richard	Chatham	Neals	101/10	Baldwin
Whitley, Micajah	Chatham	Hopkins'	198/10	Baldwin
Whitley, Micajah	Chatham	Hopkins'	324/14	Wilkinson
Whitlock's, Joseph(Orphs.)	Greene	Baxters	215/23	Wilkinson
Whitlock, John	Greene	Baxters	126/20	Wilkinson
Whitman, William	Elbert	Morrisons	377/8	Wilkinson
Whitney, Nathan W.	Elbert	Thompsons	155/14	Wilkinson
Whitsell, George	Oglethorpe	Moores	136/11	Baldwin
Whittenton, Colven	Bulloch	4	123/17	Baldwin
Whittick, Earnest C.	Greene	Carletons	191/13	Baldwin
Whitton, Dempsy	Montgomery	50	199/12	Baldwin
Whitton, James	Camden	Ashleys	180/19	Baldwin
Whitton, Lott	Wayne	3	28/22	Wilkinson
Whitton, Lott	Wayne	3	46/13	Wilkinson
Wholebrooks, Jacob	Franklin	Cornelius'	365/9	Wilkinson
Wicker, Benjamin	Washington	Wm.Renfroes	190/17	Baldwin
Wicker, John Jr.	Washington	Renfroes	84/6	Wilkinson
Wicker, Nathaniel	Washington	Collins	24/22	Wilkinson
Wicker, Nathaniel	Washington	Collins	329/8	Wilkinson
Wicker, Robert	Bulloch	1	54/24	Wilkinson

NAME	COUNTY	MIL.DIST.	LOT/DIST	DREW LAND
Wickerly, John	Chatham	Hardens	238/17	Wilkinson
Wigfall, Samuel	Richmond		119/21	Wilkinson
Wiggins', George(Orphs.)	Washington	Collins	236/20	Wilkinson
Wiggins, Elizabeth	Washington	Willis	350/11	Wilkinson
Wiggins, Jesse	Burke	Carswells	122/12	Wilkinson
Wiggins, John	Bulloch	Hendleys	331/8	Wilkinson
Wiggins, Martha	Montgomery	53	86/19	Baldwin
Wiggins, Sally	Burke	Carswells	72/25	Wilkinson
Wilborn, Thomas	Franklin	Christians	280/11	Wilkinson
Wilcher, Mary(Wid.)	Jefferson	Colemans	219/16	Baldwin
Wilcox, Moses	Franklin	Hoopers	100/6	Baldwin
Wilcox, Moses	Franklin	Hoopers	282/19	Wilkinson
Wilcox, Thomas	Montgomery	51	225/11	Wilkinson
Wild, Ann(Orph.)	Richmond		115/13	Wilkinson
Wild, Catharine(Orph.)	Richmond		115/13	Wilkinson
Wild, Jas.(Orph.)	Richmond		115/13	Wilkinson
Wild, Jno.(Orph.)	Richmond		115/13	Wilkinson
Wild, Richard(Orph.)	Richmond		115/13	Wilkinson
Wilder, Simeon	Wilkes	Stovalls	202/13	Wilkinson
Wilder, William	Effingham		201/26	Wilkinson
Wilder, Winifred(S)	Warren	Hills	41/14	Wilkinson
Wildman, William	Franklin	Wims'	187/11	Wilkinson
Wilds, Abraham	Washington	Wm.Renfroes	244/11	Wilkinson
Wilds, Jesse	Burke	Gordons	23/7	Wilkinson
Wilds, Mary	Richmond		72/14	Baldwin
Wiley's, Peter(Orphs.)	Oglethorpe	Popes	224/10	Baldwin
Wiley, James	Jackson	Johnsons	153/17	Baldwin
Wiley, William	Columbia	8	1/24	Wilkinson
Wiley, Wm.	Franklin	Christians	20/13	Baldwin
Wilhite, Philip	Elbert	Faulkners	390/8	Wilkinson
Wilkerson, Bailey	Columbia	10	266/17	Wilkinson
Wilkerson, Bailey	Columbia	10	274/15	Wilkinson
Wilkerson, Dempsey	Greene	Butlers	322/22	Wilkinson
Wilkerson, John	Hancock	Barksdales	102/19	Wilkinson
Wilkerson, Nancy	Hancock	Hudsons	382/9	Wilkinson
Wilkes, Amos	Oglethorpe	Hatchetts	260/8	Wilkinson
Wilkes, Amos	Oglethorpe	Hatchetts	367/7	Wilkinson
Wilkes, John Sr.	Oglethorpe	Hatchetts	200/13	Baldwin
Wilkes, Moses	Oglethorpe	Hatchetts	363/21	Baldwin
Wilkes, Rachel	Oglethorpe	Hatchetts	133/20	Baldwin
Wilkes, Ruth(Wid.)	Franklin	Wims'	105/15	Wilkinson
Wilkie, William	Chatham	Pettybones	226/19	Baldwin
Wilkins, Elizabeth	Chatham	Hardens	155/14	Baldwin
Wilkins, Jabez	Hancock	Pinkstons	42/7	Baldwin
Wilkins, Jonathan	Columbia	4	140/8	Baldwin
Wilkins, Paul H.	Liberty		162/26	Wilkinson
Wilkins, Samuel	Oglethorpe	Bells	33/9	Baldwin
Wilkins, William	Chatham	Robinsons	12/9	Baldwin
Wilkins, William	Chatham	Robinsons	18/19	Wilkinson
Wilkins, William	Columbia	6	255/8	Wilkinson
Wilkins, William	Elbert	Mobleys	174/15	Baldwin
Wilkinson's, James(Orph.)	Liberty		172/10	Baldwin
Wilkinson's, Reubin(Orphs.)	Bulloch	1	123/6	Wilkinson
Wilkinson, Benj.	Wilkes	Heards	185/25	Wilkinson
Wilkinson, Duncan	Washington	Collins	94/16	Wilkinson
Wilkinson, Frances(Wid.)	Liberty		64/23	Wilkinson
Wilkinson, Hugh	Jefferson	Bosticks	122/19	Wilkinson
Wilkinson, Pleasant	Wilkes	Malones	125/15	Wilkinson
Wilkinson, Reubin	Screven	Hutchinsons	209/9	Baldwin
Wilkinson, Robert	Greene	Loves	253/7	Wilkinson
Wilkinson, Sherwood	Greene	Baxters	130/16	Wilkinson
Willburn, Patty(Wid.of Wm.)	Columbia	3	110/20	Baldwin
Williams', Bowrey(Orphs.)	Oglethorpe	Hudsons	229/14	Baldwin
Williams', Frederick(Orphs.)	Greene	Baxters	84/10	Wilkinson
Williams', Isaac(Orphs.)	Bulloch	1	150/11	Baldwin
Williams', Isaac(Orphs.)	Montgomery	58	235/22	Wilkinson
Williams', Joseph(Orphs.)	Hancock	Holts	326/12	Wilkinson

NAME	COUNTY	MIL.DIST.	LOT/DIST	DREW LAND
Williams', Noah(Orphs.)	Burke	Sandifords	164/14	Baldwin
Williams', Willson(Orphs.)	Camden	Smiths	337/7	Wilkinson
Williams, Anderson Sr.	Screven		390/21	Wilkinson
Williams, Anson	Bulloch	Godfreys	112/19	Wilkinson
Williams, Arthur	Burke	Gordons	48/10	Wilkinson
Williams, Augustin(Orphs.)	Greene	Davenports	73/6	Baldwin
Williams, Barbary	Elbert	Morrisons	3/12	Baldwin
Williams, Benjamin M.	Hancock	Wallers	179/27	Wilkinson
Williams, Benjamin	Burke	Montgomerys	141/17	Wilkinson
Williams, Burwell	Jackson	Johnsons	121/27	Wilkinson
Williams, Clarissa	Washington	Holts	216/15	Baldwin
Williams, Cornelius	Liberty		151/22	Wilkinson
Williams, David Sr.	Bulloch	Williams	268/21	Wilkinson
Williams, Easter(Wid.)	Burke	Martins	237/9	Wilkinson
Williams, Edward	Jackson	Hendersons	143/7	Wilkinson
Williams, Edward	Jackson	Hendersons	22/6	Baldwin
Williams, Elijah	Warren	Neals	157/18	Baldwin
Williams, Elijah	Warren	Neals	18/26	Wilkinson
Williams, Francis	Oglethorpe	Beasleys	181/16	Baldwin
Williams, Frederick K.	Washington	Delks	243/20	Wilkinson
Williams, George	Bulloch	2	247/23	Wilkinson
Williams, George	Bulloch	2	34/12	Wilkinson
Williams, Henry	Chatham	Pettybones	458/7	Wilkinson
Williams, Isaac	Greene	Carltons	25/14	Baldwin
Williams, Isaac	Oglethorpe	Moores	70/17	Wilkinson
Williams, James	Warren	Heath	410/7	Wilkinson
Williams, James	Warren	Heaths	3/14	Baldwin
Williams, Jesse	Wilkes	Heards	164/9	Wilkinson
Williams, John A.	Burke	Spains	24/11	Baldwin
Williams, John W.	Warren	Flournoys	139/20	Baldwin
Williams, John	Camden	Browns	139/22	Wilkinson
Williams, John	Chatham	Whites	18/28	Wilkinson
Williams, John	Greene	Baxters	320/10	Wilkinson
Williams, John	Screven	Hutchinsons	287/20	Baldwin
Williams, John	Warren	Hills	134/20	Baldwin
Williams, John	Washington	Andersons	14/6	Wilkinson
Williams, Joseph J.	Greene	Butlers	119/20	Wilkinson
Williams, Joseph J.	Greene	Butlers	9/7	Wilkinson
Williams, Joseph	Elbert	Morrisons	153/10	Baldwin
Williams, Judy(Wid.)	Jackson	Johnsons	143/9	Baldwin
Williams, Keziah(Wid.)	Warren	Flournoys	39/17	Wilkinson
Williams, Lavina	Bulloch	3	159/20	Wilkinson
Williams, Lucy	Oglethorpe	Stewart	191/7	Wilkinson
Williams, Mathew J.	Elbert	Morrisons	100/15	Baldwin
Williams, Matthew J.	Elbert	Morrisons	80/11	Baldwin
Williams, Miles	Jefferson	Hardwicks	190/15	Baldwin
Williams, Moses(Orph.)	Chatham	Pettybones	179/12	Wilkinson
Williams, Moses	Greene	Greers	358/7	Wilkinson
Williams, Moses	Warren	Devereux	230/18	Wilkinson
Williams, Parmenius	Jackson	Johnsons	42/6	Baldwin
Williams, Paul	Washington	Kendricks	146/8	Wilkinson
Williams, Peter	Elbert	Keelings	63/8	Wilkinson
Williams, Robert	Hancock	Pinkstons	388/22	Wilkinson
Williams, Rowland Jr.	Wilkes	J.Hendersons	54/25	Wilkinson
Williams, Rowland	Bryan	Birds	79/18	Wilkinson
Williams, Sally(S)	Hancock	Weeks'	106/14	Baldwin
Williams, Sam'l.(Orp/Thos.)	Montgomery	57	36/13	Wilkinson
Williams, Sam'l.	Bulloch	Hendleys	389/21	Wilkinson
Williams, Samuel	Chatham	Abrahams	129/9	Wilkinson
Williams, Samuel	Chatham	Abrahams	222/22	Wilkinson
Williams, Samuel	Richmond		157/25	Wilkinson
Williams, Sarah N.(D./Jas.)	Columbia	6	98/28	Wilkinson
Williams, Sarah	Jefferson	Hardwicks	108/15	Wilkinson
Williams, Sheppard	Bulloch	Williams	78/9	Baldwin
Williams, Sugar	Greene	Flournoys	64/12	Baldwin
Williams, Tabitha	Wilkes	Heards	256/16	Wilkinson
Williams, Theophilus	Burke	Spains	108/11	Wilkinson

NAME	COUNTY	MIL.DIST.	LOT/DIST	DREW LAND
Williams, Theophilus	Burke	Spains	139/8	Baldwin
Williams, Thomas F.	Chatham	McLeans'	298/13	Wilkinson
Williams, Thos.F.	Chatham	McLeans	132/7	Baldwin
Williams, William	Burke	Gordons	213/15	Wilkinson
Williams, William	Columbia	7	110/10	Baldwin
Williams, Willis	Bulloch	5	342/12	Wilkinson
Williams, Wiston	Oglethorpe	Moores	221/6	Wilkinson
Williams, Wm.(B)	Hancock	Barness	173/13	Wilkinson
Williams, Wm.Sr.	Bulloch	Hendleys	111/19	Wilkinson
Williamson's, Wm.(Orphs.)	Franklin	McDowells	151/27	Wilkinson
Williamson, Barbara(Wid.)	Jackson	Johnsons	134/21	Wilkinson
Williamson, Charles(Orph.)	Richmond		274/12	Wilkinson
Williamson, Christian Jr.	Washington	Paces	181/25	Wilkinson
Williamson, Francis(S.W.)	Wilkes	Edges	188/8	Wilkinson
Williamson, George	Oglethorpe	Hudsons	15/6	Baldwin
Williamson, Green	Hancock	Smiths	8/28	Wilkinson
Williamson, Henry	Bulloch	3	35/13	Baldwin
Williamson, Jonathan	Wilkes	Edges	211/17	Wilkinson
Williamson, Jonathan	Wilkes	Edges	311/12	Wilkinson
Williamson, Joseph	Franklin	Griffiths	32/13	Wilkinson
Williamson, Mary(S)	Wilkes	J.Hendersons	66/19	Wilkinson
Williamson, Robert M.Sr.	Screven	Williamsons	142/7	Baldwin
Williamson, Robt. Jr.	Screven	Williamsons	284/19	Wilkinson
Williamson, Thomas	Chatham	Whites	57/19	Wilkinson
Williamson, Wiley	Washington	Paces	47/19	Wilkinson
Williamson, William	Hancock	Smiths	206/19	Baldwin
Williamson, William	Hancock	Smiths	275/10	Wilkinson
Williamson, Wm.Wash.	Wilkes	Edges	7/20	Wilkinson
Williford, Hartwell	Warren	Devereux	221/17	Wilkinson
Williford, Stephen	Elbert	Willifords	140/28	Wilkinson
Willifrod, John Sr.	Elbert	Groves	83/15	Baldwin
Willingham's, Wm.(Orphs.)	Columbia	3	366/8	Wilkinson
Willingham, Joseph	Columbia	11	247/7	Wilkinson
Willingham, Molly(D./Thos.)	Columbia	11	41/8	Baldwin
Willis, Ephraim	Montgomery	53	176/15	Wilkinson
Willis, Etheldred	Bulloch	2	257/17	Wilkinson
Willis, Etheldred	Bulloch	2	297/12	Wilkinson
Willis, Francis	Wilkes	Roreys	171/15	Baldwin
Willis, George Sr.	Wilkes	Milners	208/16	Baldwin
Willis, George	Liberty		214/20	Wilkinson
Willis, Jacob	Warren	Devereux	203/10	Wilkinson
Willis, James Sr.	Warren	Devereux	75/12	Baldwin
Willis, James Sr.	Wilkes	Sidwells	147/20	Baldwin
Willis, James	Warren	Devereux	179/26	Wilkinson
Willis, Joel (Rev.)	Columbia	6	4/17	Wilkinson
Willis, Patty	Washington	Willis	139/24	Wilkinson
Willis, William	Washington	Willis	192/14	Wilkinson
Willis, Wm.	Wilkes	Stovalls	79/12	Baldwin
Willmutt, John	Columbia	11	124/10	Baldwin
Willson's, Allick(Orphs.)	Warren	Devereux	175/14	Wilkinson
Willson's, James(Orphs.)	Columbia	9	116/15	Wilkinson
Willson, Achillis	Greene	Watsons	2/16	Baldwin
Willson, Ann	Bulloch	1	34/24	Wilkinson
Willson, Charlotte	Greene	Moores	132/21	Wilkinson
Willson, Eliz.(Orph.)	Chatham	Pettybones	184/9	Wilkinson
Willson, Fennell	Jackson	Johnsons	79/17	Baldwin
Willson, Jacob	Jefferson	Thomas'	204/14	Wilkinson
Willson, James W.	Hancock	Birdsongs	75/18	Wilkinson
Willson, James	Chatham	McLeans	107/23	Wilkinson
Willson, John	Bulloch	1	162/7	Wilkinson
Willson, John	Bulloch	3	20/15	Baldwin
Willson, John	Hancock	Coffees	200/19	Baldwin
Willson, John	Jackson	Johnsons	102/19	Baldwin
Willson, John	Warren	Carters	243/10	Wilkinson
Willson, John	Warren	Carters	323/13	Wilkinson
Willson, Joshua	Greene	Dawsons	269/7	Wilkinson
Willson, Patsy	Wilkes	J.Hendersons	84/17	Wilkinson

NAME	COUNTY	MIL.DIST.	LOT/DIST	DREW LAND
Willson, Samuel Jr.	Bulloch	2	75/23	Wilkinson
Willson, Solomon	Burke	Martins	105/25	Wilkinson
Willson, Stephen	Bulloch	3	175/9	Wilkinson
Willson, Wm.(77)	Bulloch	2	19/20	Baldwin
Willson, Wm.Jr.	Jackson	Hendersons	35/20	Baldwin
Willson, Wm.Sr.	Jackson	Hendersons	101/15	Baldwin
Wilson's, John(Orphs.)	Franklin	McDowells	157/16	Baldwin
Wilson, Catharine	McIntosh		207/8	Wilkinson
Wilson, Eliz.(Wid.)	Effingham		191/22	Wilkinson
Wilson, Jesse	Effingham		102/21	Wilkinson
Wilson, Jesse	Effingham		17/6	Wilkinson
Wilson, Leighton	Glynn		57/9	Baldwin
Wilson, Luke	Effingham		99/27	Wilkinson
Wilson, Michael	Franklin	Wems'	36/17	Wilkinson
Wilson, Samuel	Jackson	Wrights	281/21	Wilkinson
Wilson, Susannah M.	Oglethorpe	Stewarts	25/8	Wilkinson
Wilson, William Jr.	Effingham		151/15	Wilkinson
Wilson, Wm.	Franklin	McDowells	171/24	Wilkinson
Wiltshire, John	Jackson	Wrights	269/10	Wilkinson
Wimberly, Ezekiel Sr.	Washington	Renfroes	149/23	Wilkinson
Wimmey, William	Burke	Ballards	205/19	Wilkinson
Wimpey, John	Burke	Ballards	326/22	Wilkinson
Wims, Washington	Franklin	Bryants	176/24	Wilkinson
Windham's, Jesse(Orphs.)	Jackson	Cockrans	2/6	Wilkinson
Winfrey, Isaac	Columbia	10	219/9	Wilkinson
Wingate, Thos.(Orph.)	Richmond		113/11	Baldwin
Wingate, Gatsey(Orph.)	Richmond		113/11	Baldwin
Wingate, Mary(Orph.)	Richmond		113/11	Baldwin
Wingate, Nelly	Warren	Devereux	220/26	Wilkinson
Wingate, Pamelia(Orph.)	Richmond		113/11	Baldwin
Wingate, Scinthia(Orph.)	Richmond		113/11	Baldwin
Wingfield's, Thos.(Orps.)	Wilkes	Hendricks	86/12	Wilkinson
Wingfield, Garland	Wilkes	Roreys	133/7	Baldwin
Wingfield, Jno.Sr.	Wilkes	Parks	81/19	Wilkinson
Wingfield, John Sr.	Wilkes	Parks	312/15	Baldwin
Wingfield, John	Oglethorpe	Hatchetts	316/24	Wilkinson
Wingfield, Thomas	Greene	Reas	373/9	Wilkinson
Wingfield, Thomas	Wilkes	Hendricks	182/12	Wilkinson
Winkler, Richard(Orph.)	Chatham	Pettybones	15/15	Wilkinson
Winkles, Mary	Burke	Hilliards	245/7	Wilkinson
Winn, Benjamin B.	Liberty		8/14	Wilkinson
Winn, John	Liberty		107/20	Wilkinson
Winslett, James	Greene	Alfords	190/20	Baldwin
Winslow, Eliz.(Orph.)	Jefferson	Wrights	111/13	Wilkinson
Wirridge, Mary Ann(Wid.)	Chatham	Abrams	13/9	Wilkinson
Wise, Henry	Bulloch	Williams'	233/15	Baldwin
Wise, Henry	Bulloch	Williams'	46/11	Baldwin
Wise, Jacob	Oglethorpe	Smiths	63/8	Baldwin
Wise, Patern	Oglethorpe	Smiths	57/23	Wilkinson
Wise, Patterson	Chatham	Browns	97/14	Wilkinson
Wise, Sherwood	Wilkes	M.Hendersons	138/20	Baldwin
Witmire, Stephen	Jackson	Hendersons	146/28	Wilkinson
Witts, Thomas(Orph.)	Greene	Armors	44/17	Wilkinson
Wolf, John	Chatham	McLeans	226/19	Wilkinson
Womack, Abraham	Franklin	Cleghorns	318/12	Wilkinson
Womack, Jacob	Franklin	Cleghorns	220/15	Wilkinson
Womack, John H.	Franklin	Cleghorns	18/16	Wilkinson
Womack, Mansel	Hancock	Weeks'	298/10	Wilkinson
Womack, Richard	Franklin	Cleghorns	163/6	Wilkinson
Womack, Robert	Jefferson	Colemans	132/15	Baldwin
Wood's, Allen(Orphs.)	Franklin	Griffiths	321/15	Baldwin
Wood's, Isaac(Orphs.)	Liberty		148/13	Baldwin
Wood's, Isaac(Orphs.)	Liberty		179/22	Wilkinson
Wood, Aaron	Jackson		149/27	Wilkinson
Wood, Aaron	Jackson		25/26	Wilkinson
Wood, Abraham	Washington	Paces	341/22	Wilkinson
Wood, Alexander	Chatham	Whites	252/9	Wilkinson

NAME	COUNTY	MIL.DIST.	LOT/DIST	DREW LAND
Wood, Anna	Hancock	Shivers	172/7	Wilkinson
Wood, Aristarchus	Bulloch	4	13/14	Wilkinson
Wood, Ashley	Jefferson	Tarvers	272/17	Wilkinson
Wood, Bennett	Elbert	Groves	292/22	Wilkinson
Wood, David	Bulloch	5	125/18	Baldwin
Wood, Dempsey	Tattnall	Sherrards	279/24	Wilkinson
Wood, Green	Greene	Alfords	35/18	Baldwin
Wood, John	Richmond		54/15	Baldwin
Wood, Jonathan	Columbia	1	143/15	Baldwin
Wood, Mary(Wid.)	Chatham	Trammells	34/15	Wilkinson
Wood, Pennel	Elbert	Groves	232/20	Wilkinson
Wood, Polly	Chatham	Robinsons	112/21	Wilkinson
Wood, Rebecca(Wid.)	Franklin	Griffiths	112/16	Baldwin
Wood, William Sr.	Jefferson	Colemans	206/12	Wilkinson
Wood, William Sr.	Jefferson	Colemans	92/12	Baldwin
Wood, William	Chatham	Trammells	407/7	Wilkinson
Wood, William	Jackson	Wrights	253/10	Wilkinson
Woodall, James	Greene	Moores	112/7	Baldwin
Woodall, Jonathan	Greene	Loves	233/22	Wilkinson
Woodall, Jonathan	Greene	Loves	67/13	Wilkinson
Woodall, Joseph	Elbert	Blackwells	183/19	Wilkinson
Woodall, Joseph	Elbert	Blackwells	220/28	Wilkinson
Woodard, Robert	Wilkes	Sheets	158/10	Wilkinson
Woodgard's, John(Orphs.)	Warren	Hills	184/19	Wilkinson
Woodruff's, Jos.(Orphs.)	Wilkes	Roreys	316/12	Wilkinson
Woodruff, George	Chatham	Pembertons	114/25	Wilkinson
Woodruff, Israel	Chatham	Whites	88/20	Baldwin
Woodrum, John	Jefferson		34/18	Wilkinson
Woods', John(Orphs.)	Bulloch	1	291/20	Baldwin
Woods', Thomas(Orphs.)	Bulloch	2	164/25	Wilkinson
Woods, Abel	Bulloch	1	139/16	Baldwin
Woods, James	Elbert	Moons	220/12	Wilkinson
Woods, James	Greene	Jinkins	24/11	Wilkinson
Woods, James	Wilkes	Wellborns	142/20	Baldwin
Woods, Martha	Burke	Montgomerys	13/25	Wilkinson
Woods, Sam'l.Sr.	Elbert	Moons	63/16	Wilkinson
Woods, William	Elbert	Dyes	129/11	Baldwin
Woodson, Wm.	Franklin	Griffiths	128/18	Baldwin
Woodward, Aaron	Jackson	Cockrans	36/10	Wilkinson
Woodward, Lewellen	Warren	Jones	132/16	Baldwin
Woolbright, Daniel	Wilkes	J.Hendersons	338/8	Wilkinson
Wooldridge, Thomas	Elbert	Thompsons	293/20	Wilkinson
Woolhopter, Philip D.	Chatham	Whites	258/25	Wilkinson
Wooten, Bartlett Sr.	Chatham	Tramells	90/28	Wilkinson
Wooten, Collen	Greene	Moores	65/16	Baldwin
Wooten, Elizabeth	Wilkes	Milners	58/7	Baldwin
Wooten, Gilly	Bulloch	5	4/10	Wilkinson
Wooten, Hardy	Burke	Hilliards	112/17	Wilkinson
Wooten, James	Wilkes	Heards	173/16	Baldwin
Wooten, Jeremiah	Bulloch	5	296/15	Wilkinson
Wooten, Mary	Chatham	Abrahams	15/10	Baldwin
Wooten, Nancy(Single)	Chatham	Trammells	278/16	Wilkinson
Wooten, Redden	Montgomery	54	55/6	Baldwin
Wooten, Thomas	Bulloch	4	102/17	Baldwin
Wooten, William	Bulloch	4	91/17	Baldwin
Worsham's, John(Orphs.)	Hancock	Wallers	158/10	Baldwin
Worsham, Mary	Hancock	Wallers	37/16	Wilkinson
Worsham, Richard	Wilkes	Roreys	33/15	Baldwin
Worsham, Richard	Wilkes	Roreys	346/10	Wilkinson
Wortham, Eliz.T.	Wilkes	Sheets	11/11	Baldwin
Wortham, Thomas O.	Wilkes	Sheets	334/22	Wilkinson
Wortham, Thos.Sr.	Wilkes	Sheets	326/22	Wilkinson
Worthy, Thos.(S.of Thos.)	Columbia	11	34/16	Wilkinson
Wrae, Thomas Jr.	Columbia	1	14/18	Baldwin
Wray, Rachel	Lincoln	Flemings	190/10	Wilkinson
Wray, Sarah	Lincoln	Flemings	287/10	Wilkinson
Wrenn, Francis	Jefferson	Bosticks	165/20	Baldwin

NAME	COUNTY	MIL.DIST.	LOT/DIST	DREW LAND
Wright's, Arthur(Orph.)	Wilkes	Heards	146/18	Baldwin
Wright's, James(Orphs.)	Columbia	7	387/22	Wilkinson
Wright's, Nabakuk(Orphs.)	Columbia	9	274/17	Wilkinson
Wright's, Richard(Orph.)	Warren	Bakers	72/10	Baldwin
Wright, Absalom S.	Greene	Loves	125/12	Baldwin
Wright, Amos	Warren	Hills	46/25	Wilkinson
Wright, Arthur	Wilkes	Heards	21/24	Wilkinson
Wright, Asa	Warren	Newsoms	208/20	Baldwin
Wright, Drusilla(S)	Warren	Hills	27/15	Baldwin
Wright, Eliza G.(Orph.)	Jefferson	Wrights	116/16	Baldwin
Wright, Elizabeth	Lincoln	Jones'	106/13	Wilkinson
Wright, Jack	Lincoln	Jones'	16/28	Wilkinson
Wright, James	Columbia	4	36/11	Baldwin
Wright, James	Columbia	4	55/19	Wilkinson
Wright, Jerret	Greene	Flournoys	12/15	Baldwin
Wright, John	Warren	Hills	272/14	Wilkinson
Wright, John	Wilkes	J.Hendersons	270/8	Wilkinson
Wright, John	Wilkes	Milners	47/14	Baldwin
Wright, Joseph	Tattnall	McDonalds	53/10	Wilkinson
Wright, Joseph	Tattnall	McDonalds	84/13	Baldwin
Wright, Josias	Warren	Jones	194/8	Wilkinson
Wright, Laban	Chatham	Pembertons	68/12	Wilkinson
Wright, Lewis	Warren	Bakers	107/7	Baldwin
Wright, Michael	Greene	Watsons	78/18	Wilkinson
Wright, Obadiah	Franklin	Conners	241/8	Wilkinson
Wright, Rebecca(Wid.)	Glynn		331/21	Wilkinson
Wright, Rebecca(Wid/Isaiah)	Columbia	5	168/11	Wilkinson
Wright, Richard	Warren	Bakers	23/20	Wilkinson
Wright, Robert Sr.	Greene	Watts	114/14	Wilkinson
Wright, Stephen J.	Hancock	Smiths	244/15	Wilkinson
Wright, Thomas	Franklin	Conners	358/8	Wilkinson
Wright, William	Chatham	Browns	190/6	Baldwin
Wright, William	Columbia	4	269/21	Wilkinson
Wright, William	Effingham		184/23	Wilkinson
Wright, William	Effingham		48/20	Baldwin
Wright, William	Richmond		150/17	Wilkinson
Wright, William	Warren	Jones	448/7	Wilkinson
Wright, Wm.Dionysius	Hancock	Smiths	90/10	Baldwin
Wyatt's, Payton(Orphs.)	Lincoln	Kings	144/18	Wilkinson
Wyatt, Hardy	Wilkinson		339/11	Wilkinson
Wyatt, James	Bulloch	5	127/14	Wilkinson
Wyatt, James	Warren	Carters	66/6	Baldwin
Wyatt, John Sr.	Bulloch	5	361/24	Wilkinson
Wyatt, Lewis	Burke	Blounts	158/9	Baldwin
Wyatt, William	Jefferson	Colemans	16/15	Baldwin
Wyche, Peter	Elbert	Morrisons	199/21	Wilkinson
Wyche, Peter	Elbert	Morrisons	91/10	Baldwin
Wylie, Eliz.(Orph)	Greene	Armors	42/8	Baldwin
Wylie, Elizabeth	Jackson	Wrights	172/19	Baldwin
Wylie, Fanny(Orph.)	Greene	Armors	42/8	Baldwin
Wylie, Washington(Orph.)	Greene	Armors	42/8	Baldwin
Wylly, Wm.C.	Effingham		164/27	Wilkinson
Wyly's, E.(Orphs.)	Screven	Olivers	57/26	Wilkinson
Wynn, Abner	Jackson	Cockrans	40/6	Baldwin
Wynn, Thomas Sr.	Hancock	Weeks'	38/28	Wilkinson
Wynn, Thomas	Bulloch	2	324/7	Wilkinson
Wynne, Anna	Warren	Carters	165/7	Wilkinson
Wynne, Benjamin	Warren	Carters	161/15	Baldwin
Wynne, Clement	Warren	Carters	21/27	Wilkinson
Wynne, Eliz.(Wid.)	Burke	Forths	275/24	Wilkinson
Wynne, Francis	Warren	Carters	293/10	Wilkinson
Wynne, Geo.(Son/Jno.)	Wilkes	Stovalls	114/11	Baldwin
Wynne, Hamilton	Burke	Sandifords	193/9	Wilkinson
Wynne, John Sr.	Warren	Carters	55/17	Baldwin
Wynne, John	Wilkes	Stovalls	315/9	Wilkinson
Wynne, Richard	Burke	Martins	75/13	Baldwin
Wynne, Robert	Warren	Carters	112/10	Baldwin

NAME	COUNTY	MIL.DIST.	LOT/DIST	DREW LAND
Wynne, William	Burke	Forths	306/16	Wilkinson
Yarborough, Jas.(S.of L.)	Columbia	6	118/12	Baldwin
Yarborough, Jas.Jr.	Hancock	Weeks	185/13	Baldwin
Yarborough, John	Baldwin	1	118/6	Wilkinson
Yarborough, John	Bulloch	Williams	73/25	Wilkinson
Yarborough, Joseph	Wilkinson		244/17	Wilkinson
Yarborough, Polly(Miss)	Warren	Heiths	192/25	Wilkinson
Yarborough, Sarah(Miss)	Warren	Heiths	134/16	Baldwin
Yarborough, Thomas	Clarke	Hitchcocks	258/15	Wilkinson
Yarborough, Thomas	Clarke	Hitchcocks	301/17	Wilkinson
Yarborough, Wm.(S.of L.)	Columbia	6	237/19	Wilkinson
Yarborough, Wm.	Clarke	Hitchcocks	154/25	Wilkinson
Yarbro, Nanny(S.W.)	Screven		363/7	Wilkinson
Yarnell, Aaron	Hancock	Hudsons	10/7	Baldwin
Yarnell, Daniel Sr.	Hancock	Hudsons	360/24	Wilkinson
Yates, Eli	Lincoln	55	39/6	Baldwin
Yates, James	Lincoln	55	420/8	Wilkinson
Yates, Wm.Sr.	Lincoln	55	179/8	Wilkinson
Yeager, Reubin	Franklin	Wems'	191/9	Baldwin
Yearby, Burwell	Clarke	Stewarts	196/8	Wilkinson
Yearby, Burwell	Clarke	Stewarts	60/15	Baldwin
Yearty, Abraham	Jefferson	Colemans	90/22	Wilkinson
Yearwood, Robert	Franklin	Yowells	70/19	Wilkinson
York, Archibal	Jackson	Hendersons	229/9	Wilkinson
York, John	Lincoln	Jones	37/20	Baldwin
York, William	Columbia	10	135/14	Wilkinson
York, Wm.	Franklin	Everetts	257/24	Wilkinson
Young's, Mathew(Orph.)	Baldwin	4	214/13	Baldwin
Young's, Peter(Orphs.)	Columbia	4	117/12	Baldwin
Young's, Thomas(Orphs.)	Washington	Garretts	18/21	Wilkinson
Young's, Whitson(Orphs.)	Burke	Montgomerys	64/24	Wilkinson
Young's, Wm.(Orphs.)	Washington	Kendricks	97/23	Wilkinson
Young, Alexander	Greene	Jinkins	22/15	Wilkinson
Young, Anna	Chatham	McLeans	128/11	Wilkinson
Young, Anna	Chatham	McLeans	255/13	Wilkinson
Young, Christina(Wid.)	Chatham	Pettybones	185/18	Baldwin
Young, Edward Sr.	Burke	Mulkeys	65/23	Wilkinson
Young, Elizabeth(Wid.)	Washington	Kendricks	234/11	Wilkinson
Young, George	Oglethope	Beasleys	169/6	Baldwin
Young, Isaac	Chatham	McLeans	128/11	Wilkinson
Young, Isaac	Chatham	McLeans	255/13	Wilkinson
Young, Isabella	McIntosh		203/16	Baldwin
Young, Jacob	Jefferson	Bosticks	346/21	Wilkinson
Young, Jacob	Washington	Anderson	122/11	Wilkinson
Young, James B.	Chatham	McLeans	255/13	Wilkinson
Young, James	Chatham	McLeans	128/11	Wilkinson
Young, James	Franklin	Wems'	162/12	Baldwin
Young, John	Tattnall	Halls	91/21	Wilkinson
Young, John	Screven		196/28	Wilkinson
Young, John	Wilkes	Youngs	153/18	Baldwin
Young, Joseph	Greene	Loves	105/26	Wilkinson
Young, Lucy	Baldwin	4	160/10	Baldwin
Young, Perigune	Warren	Bakers	225/10	Baldwin
Young, Thomas	Greene	Butlers	80/12	Baldwin
Young, Thomas	Jefferson	Bosticks	21/19	Baldwin
Young, Wootson	Oglethope	Beasleys	364/8	Wilkinson
Youngblood, Arthur	Hancock	Holts	133/23	Wilkinson
Youngblood, Arthur	Hancock	Holts	273/10	Wilkinson
Youngblood, Benjamin	Columbia	6	251/15	Baldwin
Youngblood, Jacob	Washington	Chivers	210/10	Wilkinson
Youngblood, Joshua	Columbia	7	187/9	Wilkinson
Yowell, Joel	Franklin	Yowells	125/19	Wilkinson
Zacchary, James	Warren	Heiths	94/12	Wilkinson
Zachary, Abner	Baldwin	4	109/8	Wilkinson
Zeigler, George	Screven	Williamsons	100/20	Wilkinson
Zeigler, Lucas	Screven	Williamsons	264/10	Wilkinson
Zettler, Mary(Orph.)	Chatham	Pettybones	143/7	Baldwin

NAME	COUNTY	MIL.DIST.	LOT/DIST	DREW LAND
Zipperer, Ann Mary(Wid.)	Effingham		252/19	Wilkinson
Zipperer, Christian J.	Effingham		252/19	Wilkinson
Zipperer, Christian(Orph.)	Effingham		215/20	Wilkinson
Zipperer, Christiana(Wid.)	Effingham		178/10	Wilkinson
Zipperer, Hann(Orph.)	Effingham		215/20	Wilkinson
Zipperer, Jonathan(Orph.)	Effingham		215/20	Wilkinson
Zipperer, Samuel(Orph.)	Effingham		215/20	Wilkinson
Zipperer, Samuel	Effingham		106/21	Wilkinson
Zitterauer, John Geo.	Effingham		164/19	Baldwin
Zitterauer, Solomon	Effingham		1/13	Wilkinson
Zitterauer, Solomon	Effingham		93/15	Baldwin
Zuber's, Abram Sr.(Orphs.)	Oglethorpe	Beasleys	267/20	Wilkinson
Zuber, Daniel	Oglethorpe	Hudsons	122/14	Wilkinson

www.ingramcontent.com/pod-product-compliance
Lightning Source LLC
Chambersburg PA
CBHW020652300426
44112CB00007B/351